# The Politics of Equity Finance in Emerging Markets

# The Politics of Equity Finance in Emerging Markets

Kathryn C. Lavelle

**OXFORD**
UNIVERSITY PRESS

2004

# OXFORD
UNIVERSITY PRESS

Oxford   New York
Auckland   Bangkok   Buenos Aires   Cape Town   Chennai
Dar es Salaam   Delhi   Hong Kong   Istanbul   Karachi   Kolkata
Kuala Lumpur   Madrid   Melbourne   Mexico City   Mumbai   Nairobi
São Paulo   Shanghai   Taipei   Tokyo   Toronto

Copyright © 2004 by Oxford University Press, Inc.

Published by Oxford University Press, Inc.
198 Madison Avenue, New York, New York 10016

www.oup.com

Oxford is a registered trademark of Oxford University Press

Lavelle, Kathryn C.
    The politics of equity finance in emerging markets / Kathryn C. Lavelle.
        p.   cm.
    Includes bibliographical references and index.
    ISBN 0-19-517409-7; 0-19-517410-0 (pbk.).
    1. Securities—Developing countries. 2. Stock exchanges—Developing countries. 3.
Developing countries—Economic policy.   I. Title.
    HG5993.L38 2004
    332.63'22'091724—dc22      2004004042

9 8 7 6 5 4 3 2 1

Printed in the United States of America
on acid-free paper

*To Christine, who has taught me to have so much respect for her work, and without whom this work would not have been possible.*

INGO WALTER

NEW YORK UNIVERSITY AND INSEAD

# Foreword

There is a growing body of evidence suggesting that few factors are more important in explaining economic growth than the development of efficient, stable, and equitable capital markets. And within that financial market infrastructure, the creation of viable equity markets seems to be of particular importance. The evidence that supports these findings is both compelling and sensible. Application of market discipline in the allocation of capital helps maximize the level of output and income, and in a broader context helps ensure that productive resources are aligned to global comparative advantage. Perhaps even more important, viable capital markets tend to provide finance to industries on the leading edge of the economic spectrum, exploiting new opportunities created by technology, trade liberalization, regulatory change, and other factors in the economic environment. No less important, they help deny capital on the lagging edge of the economic spectrum, ensuring that they beat an orderly retreat and release resources to nascent and expanding sectors of the economy. This "creative destruction" in which the capital markets play a key catalytic role is the core of a system against which all other approaches to economic organization have, one by one, fallen by the wayside.

In addition to their efficiency and growth dimensions, capital markets carry out a central and complementary governance function in the linkages between owners and managers. Governance in part focuses on the internal organization of firms—managerial incentives, organizational strategy and structure, internal resource allocation, and the role of boards of directors as representatives of the shareholders. Externally to the firm, governance involves the monitoring, reporting, and accountability linkages between boards and shareholders, and involves a variety of intermediaries—auditors, law firms, rating agencies, asset managers, banks, and broker-dealers. They, in turn, together with the framework within which firms operate, are governed by sets of rules anchored in self-regulatory organizations, stock exchanges, and securities regulation, corporate chartering, judicial decisions, and regulatory structures that are themselves the product of democratic processes. In this way, democracy and capitalism become two sides of a coin, and help ensure not only efficiency and growth in the real economy, but also outcomes that are broadly regarded as fair and politically tolerable.

Developing countries have varied widely in terms of their ability and willingness to apply these lessons. Their comparative performance in terms of a range of socioeconomic criteria can often be mapped accordingly, separating the winners from the losers in terms of sustained progress. So it is hardly surprising that organizations charged with promoting economic development have emphasized much more strongly the role of banking and finance in recent years than in former times, generally characterized by project and program lending as well as balance of payments finance and macroeconomic stability.

In this volume, Kathryn Lavelle explains in clear, succinct terms how national political processes lead to equity market growth, and how that growth affects the process of corporate governance — and why it sometimes fails to do so as governments maintain a continuing grip on firms (especially those that were formerly state owned). She links this discussion — through case studies focusing on eastern Europe, Asia, Latin America, and Africa — to cross-border equity flows and global capital markets, and to the role of international development organizations. The discussion covers the appearance of new financial products and new kinds of financial intermediaries in emerging markets, notably viable equity markets. Much of the discussion provides good news, although there are plenty of shadows involving missed opportunities and the potential for economic contamination through volatile cross-border capital flows.

Based as it is on careful research, including fieldwork, Professor Lavelle has provided in this volume a most welcome addition to the economic development literature — one that adds a fresh perspective to what we think we know about the role of financial institutions, products, and markets.

# Preface

This book originated in extensive discussions about the mechanics of finance with my sister Christine Lavelle during the years when she completed an MBA in finance at Columbia University and began a job at one of Wall Street's preeminent "equity houses." It developed in additional discussions about U.S. corporate securities law with my sister Polly Moorman, and then with both sisters' countless friends in the investment banking and legal communities of New York and Cleveland. It crystallized as a topic through additional conversations with my friend, Atsi Sheth, after she graduated from Northwestern University, took a position at Moody's, and convinced me of the importance of reconnecting theoretical international political economy to the reality of financial practice. The book was strengthened in discussions with my sister-in-law, Simmi Singh, who would not let me back down on my arguments.

I began the actual research for the project with a series of interviews with individuals in the Capital Markets Department at the International Finance Corporation (IFC). As a result of these interviews, I realized that it was necessary to extend them outside the formal confines of the organization to individuals in the financial services community who had worked with the corporation on the early funds. The assistance of David Gill at the IFC, Nicholas Bratt at Scudder Kemper Investments, and John Niepold at Emerging Markets Management was invaluable in getting this early work off the ground. The project began to take a more definitive shape when I traveled to Abidjan, Cote d'Ivoire, as a West Africa Research Association Fellow. The time in Abidjan allowed me the opportunity to interview additional sets of market participants, banks, diplomats, donors, and representatives of international organizations that worked to promote the regional bourse. Upon my return, I had a clear understanding of the type of financial information that would be needed to investigate the ownership structure of large enterprises in differing national settings, how reporting on that information varies by country, and most importantly how it could, and could not, be compared. The remaining task was to uncover that information from a variety of industry and public sources, and situate it within the development strategies of the state in question.

Specific thanks go to those individuals who read early drafts and offered useful suggestions to advance the book. Andy Hira, Kelly McMann, Bill Munro, Mary Murray, and Matthew Rudolph contributed greatly to this volume both by extending their regional expertise and by reading chapters at such an early stage that their comments influenced the final product in ways far beyond what they could imagine. John Echeverri-Gent, Leslie Elliott Armijo, Art Cyr, and Laura Ymayo Tartakoff provided valuable specific comments on draft chapters. Antoine Van Agtmael and Sue Ellen Wells not only commented on the International Finance Corporation section, but also extended their assistance by sharing useful primary source materials on the early emerging market funds industry in addition to the material I had obtained for previous studies. Peter Gourevitch and David Lake, as well as several anonymous reviewers at *International Organization*, stand out as having supported the case study of the Abidjan bourse from its earliest draft through final publication. In addition, Paul Donnelly stands out for his support at Oxford University Press.

No project could be completed without the necessary material resources. The West Africa Research Association granted me a much-needed fellowship that allowed me to travel to Abidjan to initiate this work. I am also fortunate to have an unusually supportive family that assisted this research in unconventional ways beyond those mentioned previously. Patrick Lavelle provided emergency housing when I needed a week away from Cleveland to work uninterrupted. My nieces, Emily Moorman and Roshni Lavelle, provided their unfailing good humor. And as they always do, my parents provided their unconditional love and emotional support that made it possible for me to complete the task.

# Contents

Foreword, by Ingo Walter   vii

Introduction   xiii

1. Politics and the Extension of Equity Finance to Emerging Markets   3

I. EQUITY FINANCE IN HISTORICAL PERSPECTIVE

2. Financing Joint-Stock Companies in the Colonial Era   27

3. New States, New State Involvement   45

4. Globalization without Integration: International Considerations   59

5. Privatization and Share Supply in Emerging Markets   75

II. CASE STUDIES OF STOCK EXCHANGES IN REGIONAL PERSPECTIVE

6. Latin America and the Caribbean   93

7. Asia and the Pacific   113

8. Russia and Eastern Europe   142

9. Africa and the Middle East   164

III. CONCLUSION

10. Stock Markets in the Global Political Economy   189

Appendix: IFC Involvement in Financial Sector and Privatization
        Projects, by EM Country Examples  199

Notes  221

Bibliography  251

Index  267

# Introduction

Although few investors buy stock intending to control a firm, ownership of stock is consequential within a state's financial institutional structure because the characteristics the shares contain, and the manner in which blocs of shares are grouped, determine who will ultimately make decisions for large enterprises, and what these individuals' nationality will be. The characteristics of stocks, and their groupings, take on special significance in developing areas of the world where economic authority appears to lie disproportionately outside the state in question. Nonetheless, a profound transformation in equity finance took place at the end of the twentieth century both in terms of what equity products from developing countries were sold in the world's financial centers, as well as what financial market institutions were created in individual developing states.

In international financial centers, the category "developing states" itself grew to encompass the former Soviet bloc in a newly constituted group of "emerging markets." Whereas only 7 people worked in the Latin American debt department at J. P. Morgan & Company in 1988, more than 200 people worked in the emerging markets department at the same firm in 1994, underwriting, trading, and selling a variety of securities across the world, in addition to making loans.[1] By the fourth quarter of 1993, research, sales, and trading positions in emerging markets accounted for 80%–90% of hiring by New York firms.[2] The results of this transformation were such that by 1993 it appeared to some as if the world's economic balance was shifting away from wealthy, yet smaller economies like Canada, toward poorer, yet potentially larger economies like Mexico. In 1995 Merrill Lynch continued the trend by embarking on a rapid and extensive global plan to offer complete investment banking services in all of the major markets in Asia, Latin America, Europe, and Africa.[3] Bankers described this revolution as comparable to the second industrial revolution, taking place at the speed of the industrialization of Japan in the postwar period. The foundations of new industrial empires could be laid in this period, and world leadership could potentially pass from one city, country, or region to another.[4]

A conscious shift in authority for intermediating capital accompanied the new attitudes and higher level of resources invested in the developing world. With the rise in equity finance in particular, emphasis shifted from public lending authorities to private ones, from analyses based on macro-level political and economic variables to those based on the company itself. Leading bankers who were involved in the transformation, such as Nicolas Rohatyn at J. P. Morgan, saw themselves as responsible for building departments that would represent the "biggest and best group in the world to intermediate capital between the developing and developed markets, . . . (contributing to a) fundamental good for the world."[5]

The most apparent institutional change on the state side of the transformation was the formation and growth of formal securities markets within an extraordinarily diverse group of states. Former socialist states created stock exchanges or reopened pre-World War II era exchanges; 10 of the 18 exchanges in Africa alone appeared since 1988. The capitalization of all low- and middle-income markets from 1990 to 1998 grew over 269%, whereas the corresponding capitalization of all high-income countries during the same period grew 144%.[6] Although these developments at first glance appeared to emanate from strictly structural causes and appeared to generate similar financial products transferred across borders, remarkable growth occurred on exchanges that remained stubbornly local in terms of disclosure laws, liquidity function, closing requirements, and custody arrangements.

To understand why so many states created equity markets in the 1980s and 1990s, and why control remains local, this book examines stock as both a financial product and a political product. In conceptualizing emerging market stocks as an important nexus of states, markets, and firms, the book argues that equity products have mediated the relationship among these three constructs over time by allocating ownership and control rights in a variety of international political settings. The state-firm connection is particularly salient on emerging markets because so many large issues are former state enterprises, and state enterprises that remain partially owned. As emerging stock markets grew in the 1980s and 1990s, however, none developed a wide-ranging institutional function for the price mechanism in corporate governance along the lines of the U.S. and British markets.

The evidence uncovered here thus begins a significant departure from analyses of financial systems derived from Western industrial experience. Within literature in the fields of law, business, and political science, stock markets are commonly understood to exert external pressure on a firm's management in the U.S. and British models. Although shareholders cannot monitor all aspects of a firm's behavior, they do monitor its performance in terms of the profit it generates. If the shareholders are not satisfied with this performance, they sell their shares and the price drops. In theory then, a rival group could buy the lower-priced shares and run the company themselves. Thus management has a strong performance incentive to operate the firm for the shareholders' profit. Through the price mechanism, stock performs the external monitoring role.

To understand the divergence in equity market function that takes place in emerging markets with respect to the price mechanism, it is necessary to look at the financial product itself, and how it fits into the ownership and governing structure of the firm. Aggregate economic analyses of emerging markets miss the dimension of institutional development because they fail to consider the share-holder arrangements of large issues of listed firms. Based on an investigation of shareholder arrangements, this book challenges the notion that many emerging markets perform even one, common, institutional function for all firms listed.

Therefore, as a study in the field of international relations, this book asks the question, what explains the international convergence in state behavior in creating and promoting stock markets in emerging economies since the 1980s, when local markets remain so restrictive? To answer this question, it initially looks to the distribution of power emanating from the world's financial centers and how that distribution produced similar outcomes. However, while the structural view explains the appearance of the markets, and the standardization of procedures on many of them with respect to transparency, settlement times, and custody arrangements, it does not explain the proliferation of functions equity markets perform in individual domestic political economies as they grow.

The requisite domestic-level explanation offered here for the variation in market function at the subnational level hinges on variations in the state's historical experience with equity finance. States that have experienced the most variation in development strategies, for example, export-oriented imperial, statist developmental, and neo-liberal strategies, have the most ownership and control structures with respect to the stock market. States with the least variation experienced a near-total break with past historical experience in the form of a Communist revolution, such as Communist China, where all vestiges of the extraterritorial British stock exchange disappeared, and the interim revolutionary strategy did not include equity participation. Nonetheless, even states with little variation have not configured the ownership structures of their firms along Anglo-American or German-Japanese lines.

To synthesize the international and domestic political processes that resulted in equity market creation, the initial chapters of the book look at the structural factors in the international political economy that led to the convergence in practice on existing exchanges and the move to create exchanges where none had existed before; in short, they look at the factors that make the markets appear similar. The later chapters of the book examine the formation of specific ownership and control structures with respect to large issues of equity products on emerging markets at the end of the twentieth century; in short, they look at the factors that make the markets different. A combined inquiry into both the domestic political and international political processes that led to equity market creation leads to two important conclusions about these financial instruments as political products.

First of all, an inquiry into the domestic political processes leading to equity market growth reveals that models of corporate governance with respect to stock markets fail to aggregate at the national level in most of these cases. Thus the lack of a wide-ranging share price mechanism makes it unlikely that shareholders will be able to control, or even influence, the management of large enterprises in emerging markets. Yet even as national financial institutions disintegrate in the globalization era, the state retains an ability to exert its authority through the shareholding pattern of divested firms. Therefore, for the state to facilitate economic development in the private sector, one model of firm monitoring, be it through the price mechanism of the stock market, through bank or stakeholder representation on the governing boards of firms, or regulations on the operations of transnational corporations, will not fit all firms. Monitoring through the legal system, access to international markets, or through the parent company will have to be tailored to accommodate the varied types of ownership structures. Although this promises to be a complex project, the ownership structure of these firms renders their control less vulnerable to international forces than some of the more sensationalistic globalization literature would imply.

Second, an inquiry into the international political processes leading to equity market creation reveals the continuing importance of the distribution of political and economic power in the world system of states. The United States in particular exercised its power through international financial organizations, such as the International Monetary Fund (IMF) and the World Bank, that advanced a specific economic ideology, promoted specific liberalization policies, forged equity markets through design and finance, and to a degree standardized markets with respect to operational practices. The role of these organizations in the process of globalization has been criticized from multiple directions. However, an inaccurate understanding of exactly what the organizations did during the years in question results in inaccurate proposals for their reform.

For some observers, the role of these institutions in "saving" Mexico in the 1995 peso crisis created an ongoing problem of international "moral hazard." That is, international lenders had become careless in their activities because they could count on the IMF to bail them out should a crisis occur. For other observers, the problem with the public-sector international financial institutions was with the drastic and (in their view) inappropriate changes required as part of the rescue packages that undermined investor confidence and actually worsened the situation. Given different understandings of the role of the organizations in the crises, suggestions for altering their role also varied from disbanding them and allowing private actors to take over their work, to altering their lending policies, to making them more transparent, to forming new organizations completely, depending on the commentary.[7]

What is often overlooked, however, is the role public-sector international financial institutions have played in creating private markets where none existed before. Much of this activity occurs over long periods of time and is not connected to market booms and busts that make international headlines. Therefore discussions of economics associated with international financial crises, as well as discussions of the politics of financial liberalization in developing countries, lack a deeper understanding of the political origins and spread of equity market institutions. A deeper understanding, in turn, contributes to a more accurate understanding of the nature of the participation of poorer countries in the globalization process.

## The Plan of the Book

This book is formally divided into three parts. The first explores equity finance in historical perspective. Chapter 1 opens with a theoretical premise for explaining international convergence in state behavior in creating and promoting stock markets, despite the lack of resulting national governance structures associated with them. Focusing on the commanding heights of privatized industry, it uses the metaphor of a two-level game to argue that when political leaders privatize large enterprise, they must negotiate with individuals outside the state to seek outcomes that are acceptable to structural international necessity, and they must negotiate with domestic constituencies to seek outcomes that are politically acceptable at home. Using this metaphor, leaders create and reinvigorate preexisting exchanges to satisfy level I requirements such as the structure and operations of transnational equity markets, as well as to satisfy the demands of international organizations. However, leaders need to satisfy domestic political constituencies on level II simultaneously.

This book argues that to do so, policymakers created the specific financial instruments, with specific ownership and control characteristics, offered for sale during the 1990s period. Most offerings sought to maximize control of the firm in a distinct group of shareholders. Since the new offerings joined whatever shares may or may not have already been listed on a given exchange, the resulting financial institutional structures fail to converge on one "model" of corporate governance, or another, as Western financial institutions have converged over time. This theoretical premise would thus predict a large number of new exchanges appearing, at least in name, yet having vastly different volumes and types of listings relative to the size of the local economy. The number of owners grows, but the owners will not be able to control the firm in question through these additional shares listed.

Chapter 2 explores the origins of global equity markets in order to situate the new offerings in the context of whatever shares may or may not have been previously listed. Contemporary emerging markets have deep historical roots. Stocks were created to finance trade and expansion overseas as part of the European imperial project, yet prior to the imposition of direct rule. Later, equity finance in the industrial era brought together large amounts of capital to finance industrial projects overseas such as railroads, electric projects, and water projects. The structure of global equity markets mirrored the structure of the markets within the colonial metropole. Just as British industries exclusive of rail, electric, and water were largely internally financed, or financed on a local British stock exchange, industries overseas were either internally financed or financed on a local stock exchange. French investors did not favor the joint stock company form of business organization, and relied on the central Paris bourse when it was necessary. Likewise, early firms operating in francophone African territories either listed their shares in Paris or were not organized as joint stocks.

Chapter 3 continues the historical investigation. It argues that stock exchanges organized in the postcolonial era were created to indigenize a degree of foreign direct investment. Transnational corporations listing shares on exchanges in the developing world sought a quotation for the benefit of local employees and recognition as a truly transnational firm. Generally these listings were expensive, illiquid, and managerial control remained foreign. However, states found them attractive in an era of "anti" foreign investment since they dampened criticism of foreign investment, and the capital raised usually remained in the country in question.

Moving to the contemporary era, chapter 4 examines level I (i.e., international) considerations in creating contemporary equity markets. The chapter explores both the role of international organizations in promoting equity market finance and the circumstances of the international market for equities, which make a local market necessary. These circumstances are such that the market for transnational equities is really only available to large, multinational firms and sophisticated institutional investors. Hence national or local markets become necessary for the creation of certain securities, particularly those associated with privatization programs. Yet the structure of equity markets does not explain why certain firms are listed on an exchange when a privatization takes place and others are not. Nor does it explain the specifics of the securities offered. To understand the local market in this sense, an analyst must look to the domestic political economy and its corresponding financial institutions.

Chapter 5 completes the picture presented in the fourth chapter. It considers the issue of share supply on peripheral stock exchanges (i.e., level II considerations). It argues that since the 1980s, states have created new exchanges not as vehicles to raise capital, but to reserve a role for local capital as it disengages from active management of the firm. Thus the state and the market do not act in opposition to each other; rather, the state creates a local market to allow its citizens access to ownership of local firms despite the fact that the ultimate control of many of these firms may be overseas. The operative goal of the sale is thus participation in control, combined with revenue, and not just revenue alone.

Part II considers the historical trajectory of the domestic political economies and financial institutions in a given region. Since growth on emerging market exchanges is not exclusively from privatized firms, this section expands the discussion to a wider range of large issues and situates the discussion within the individual institutional circumstances where the issues have appeared. To determine the linkages among state, shares offered, and corporate governance, the country studies explore the overall development program and the politics of a specific, representative deal offered on an exchange in question. Each then situates the deal within the broader market picture. As the historical chapters show, the functions of local stock markets have varied as state-firm relations have varied over time. Since the book's *explanandum* is stock exchange growth viewed through the prism of the markets' function with respect to control, the regional chapters consider what potential equity products possess for influencing corporate governance either through the price mechanism or another type of stakeholder mechanism.

Chapter 6 examines Latin America, where the earliest and largest volume of divestitures occurred on a case-by-case basis. These listings resulted from complex negotiations where organized labor was able to extract a percentage of shares in most major issues. It considers cases from Brazil, Argentina, Chile, and Mexico.

Chapter 7 examines Asia, where the greatest diversity of state experiences occurred. The Indian exchanges have the longest continuous history and the greatest variation in shareholder patterns. The Chinese exchanges have the least variation. Firms do not make autonomous decisions to list on the Chinese exchanges, nor do they use economic criteria for listing. Rather, the government directs the firms and amount of minority shares to be listed, and utilizes an extensive stock classification system to prevent foreign takeovers. The Korean exchange developed from an ongoing collaborative effort between the government, the World Bank, and its affiliate, the International Finance Corporation. Initial growth on this market occurred when the government forced the *chaebol* to list shares. Foreign firms did not control Korean subsidiaries prior to the financial crisis, and the Korean state prohibited foreign investment on its exchange until the 1980s. Currently the shareholder arrangements of the *chaebol* prevent a hostile takeover. The Thai case is one where firms offered minority blocs on a state-created exchange. Privatization issues have been complicated by the workers' demands.

Chapter 8 considers former Soviet bloc examples, three of which overtly modeled their securities market institutions on Anglo-American practice. The Hungarian exchange opened to great fanfare after the collapse of communism. However, as sales of large firms have progressed on a case-by-case basis, most have been conducted off the exchange. The Russian case is notable for the low degree of publicly listed shares and the concentration of governing power in the hands of former managers who have bought workers shares. They have thus consolidated their hold on the firms' assets. A high degree of corruption has prevented some transnational corporations from exercising their controlling rights over Russian shares, and this situation has contributed to the lack of foreign interest in investment in Russia. Although the Czech voucher distribution scheme attempted to form an Anglo-American-style corporate governance system, a network of investment funds appeared as the scheme progressed that has shifted economic power back toward state-controlled banks. Finally, the Polish system emulated the German-Japanese example. However, as large firms have sought to forge *keiretsu*-style conglomerates and failed, the state has reentered their management.

The examples in chapter 9 chosen from the African region diverge among countries as the Asian examples did. Two exchanges, Johannesburg and Cairo, are among the oldest, most established in the world. Firms on the Johannesburg stock exchange have responded to the opportunities presented by the international system to switch their listings to London. However, given the shareholding patterns of these firms, what little external pressure on management has occurred has developed from the listing requirements of the London, not the Johannesburg exchange. The Cairo exchange boomed in the 1990s along with other emerging markets, yet it boomed by selling minority shares of family-controlled firms. Privatized firms similarly list minority shares. When a controlling bloc of government firms has been sold, the government has placed strict managerial restrictions on the buyer. Finally, the two west African exchanges are examples of extremely small, thin markets dominated by issues of one or two privatized firms. In the case of Ghana, the firm was originally an international, British firm. In the case of Sonatel, the government continues to play a direct role in its management.

The third and final part contains a concluding tenth chapter. It considers contending views on stock exchanges as the *explanans* in investigations of economic growth, financial contagion, and democracy in the semiperiphery and periphery of the world system. Along with investigating implications of the study for the future, the final chapter reevaluates stock markets within the current globalization literature. While the configurations of ownership structure detailed here are far from exclusive to emerging markets, the quantity and variety of these controlling-minority firms on the exchanges in question foretells a minimal aggregate institutional role for the markets in influencing management through the price mechanism.

# The Politics of Equity Finance in Emerging Markets

# Politics and the Extension of Equity Finance to Emerging Markets

This book focuses on one aspect of the globalization phenomenon: the spread of equity finance in what are currently termed emerging markets.[1] The issue is one of growing importance because by the end of the twentieth century, stock issuance relative to gross domestic product (GDP) in emerging markets rose to a level that roughly matched issuance in German, Japanese, U.K., and U.S. markets.[2] The issue is also paradoxical. The growing ease of portfolio equity investment across borders contributes to the commonly held notion that globalization forges seamless, integrated financial markets, wherein financial instruments are traded interchangeably across state borders. As opportunities for raising capital internationally grow, and deep capital markets overseas offer so many advantages, it would appear that local stock exchanges are not even necessary. Shares can be traded outside of a formal exchange, and many emerging market exchanges possess many economic disadvantages.[3] Yet as globalization has progressed, not only have existing emerging equity markets grown, states that did not have exchanges have created new ones.

Emerging market exchanges have always had a distinctly political quality, both because they are instruments of a state's current development strategy with respect to financial market institutions, and because the large issues that dominate trading on them are generally shares that have been sold by state enterprises. Even when the state does not act directly as the vendor of shares, it asserts its influence through securities laws that can influence a firm's decision to list shares and foreigners' ability to exert control through the shares they own. Therefore the markets follow a political logic associated with seeking authority and control, in addition to the economic logic associated with the maximization of profit. Moreover, the political logic is national, as well as international, meaning that share issues are structured with an eye on the state's ability to influence the domestic economy, as well as to function alongside other states in the global system. The upshot of this political dimension to equity finance is that the management of these firms does not operate strictly as an agent of shareholders' interests, but also as an agent of the state's interest in capitalist development.

Most analyses of emerging stock markets originate in the economics literature, and thus contribute to a debate over whether or not a local stock market is good or bad for development. According to this literature, the market's value lies in its ability to allocate capital efficiently and reward risk appropriately.[4] Political science literature subsumes discussions of stock markets within broader discussions of capital market liberalization. As states lose the ability to control the allocation of credit associated with liberalization, they also lose their ability to pursue a strategic course of adjustment in response to global economic change.[5] Globalization literature links the transformation of global capital markets, stock exchanges included, into a new supranational order where nationally based financial operations shrink and international, city-based operations take their place.[6]

In examining stock as both a political and an economic instrument, this study begins from a completely different premise. It situates the financial product within the ownership and control structure of the firm, and investigates not only what makes these financial products similar across states and time, but also what makes them different. Stocks represent the proprietorship element of a corporation, which has been divided into shares and is sold as transferable certificates. An examination of large issues of stock on emerging markets in the late twentieth century reveals that most shares resulted from a broader process of states reconfiguring their relationship with economic enterprise, and many of these firms predate the state in question. When states sell shares, they seek wealth, but they seek control as well. While they may not be able to own (and thus control) economic enterprise outright, they can use the ownership and control structure of a firm to configure a variety of outcomes that enhance their capacity to either control economic activity in the new circumstances, or to ensure that control remains with the private sector within their own territory.

Among the variety of outcomes that benefit the state in restructurings are those where the state retains a controlling bloc of shares, a bloc of shares with board representation, or a golden share that is necessary for a takeover to occur. In other circumstances, ownership can be configured such that a citizen of the state in question retains control with a minority of shares. When transnational corporations purchase state enterprises, stock can be issued in such a way that a broad group of citizens owns the firm as well, or a concentrated group participates in management with the transnational. Stipulations placed on the transfer can influence the firm's ability to make decisions after the sale. Firms can be sold to family business groups that are not themselves vulnerable to the market for managerial control.

To demonstrate the use of stock to configure control in any of these instances, however, it is necessary to examine specific cases of stock issuance on emerging markets, and the politics associated with the issue. When cases are examined, it becomes apparent that there is not one systematic measure of beneficiaries, since participants seek a variety of political and economic benefits from stock sales. For example, if an individual sought control of the firm and the share price dropped, those individuals seeking control may have realized their goal, while those investors seeking profit may have lost theirs. If a particular interest group, such as a labor union, sought to retain a percentage of ownership, it may realize its goal with a given issue. Yet depending on how the shares are distributed among the membership, individual union members may nonetheless lose their jobs.

The issue of aggregating benefits is further complicated when analysts seek to fit emerging markets into one or another model of corporate governance derived from Western industrial experience, that is, one where shares are dispersed and shareholders influence firm management through the price mechanism, or one where shares are held in blocs and banks play a role.[7] This study rejects these models in emerging markets, since none have developed the sort of price mechanism that influences firm governance as in the United States and United Kingdom. Moreover, while the shares of some firms are held in blocs, and some banks do influence some firms' behavior, these patterns are not systematic as they are in Germany and Japan. When the cases are situated within the broader history of state-firm relations, the diversity of many of these relations over time becomes apparent. That is, one firm may have been structured in one way under the colonial state, restructured in the nationalist era, and restructured again in the privatized era. Firm structures from other eras still function alongside newer structures, resulting in a myriad of shareholder arrangements.

Therefore this study conceptualizes stock as a political instrument that is used to negotiate the transitions associated with building and dismantling the state sector in emerging markets. Private-sector corporations in developing countries are increasingly expected to act as agents of industrial development in lieu of states. Therefore the ownership structure of large firms in these countries matters because it determines who will ultimately be responsible for making the firm's decisions. In advanced industrial economies, the primary contradiction with respect to corporate governance occurs between the owners, or principals, and the managers, or agents. In emerging markets, the contradictions multiply. The primary contradiction occurs between majority and minority owners of shares.[8] Yet when a firm is headquartered overseas, an additional contradiction occurs between foreign and domestic shareholders. When a small minority of shareholders controls the firm, another occurs between the controlling minority and the majority.

These multiple contradictions point to dynamics in share issuance that do not arise in Western economic restructurings because policymakers in advanced industrial economies do not need to comply with the requirements of external actors. For example, the Thatcher privatizations in the United Kingdom were internally driven. They were not negotiated with outside actors, such as the International Monetary Fund (IMF) and World Bank. The British could offer shares of privatized firms on a deep, liquid, domestic capital market. Policymakers in emerging markets must satisfy both internal and external demands simultaneously. These competing demands result in equity-holding patterns that prohibit universal types of broad-based corporate governance models from forming and restrain the ability of shareholders to influence management. Political interests retain a degree of ability to control a course of action in some firms through ownership of a bloc of shares. Some firms maximize profits on behalf of the shareholders of the parent company in another state, whereas other firms promote the interests of domestic shareholders and act as agents of economic development. Some firms prioritize a family's interests within a broader business group. Others retain the state as an active participant in management of the firm and continue to promote the broader developmental goals of society.

## Ownership of Stock and Control of the Firm

This book investigates the ownership and control features of emerging market stock at the international, national, and firm levels. Thus it questions the potential for shareholders to control large enterprise and influence management in emerging market countries, depending on the specific features attached to individual financial instruments, as well as the features of a particular financial institutional setting. In order to begin this investigation, it is therefore necessary to examine how certain features of this financial instrument allow for control of a firm's management in different financial institutional settings, and how shareholders can, or cannot, influence management when stock is sold across national borders.

At the most basic level, ownership of any asset generally includes the ability to control that asset.[9] Yet the modern corporate form separates the two functions of ownership and control, wherein ownership of the corporate assets is parceled out in fractions to stockholders, and control of the assets rests with professional managers. Stocks, therefore, are securities representing a fraction of the ownership element of the corporation. As the number of individuals or banks that own stock in a given corporation grows, the fraction they possess declines, and ownership is even more distant from control because any voting rights attached to the stock become negligible.

Without having any real, effective control over his or her asset, the investor owning stock of a corporation nonetheless realizes two significant benefits: the expectation of dividends, and the liquidity of stock as an asset. As Berle and Means pointed out in their seminal study of the corporate form, stock generates a stream of income and can be sold for ready cash within days or even hours. By bringing together potential buyers and sellers, stock exchanges in developed industrial democracies ensure the liquidity of previously issued shares and allow investors of dramatically different time frames to participate in owning the same assets, since an individual can own a share of stock for a week, a month, a year, or longer. Nonetheless, the liquidity of the asset further separates the functions of ownership and control because any generic interest of shareholders ceases to exist when management must choose, for example, between the interests of short-term and long-term investors, or between the interests of local versus distant shareholders.[10]

Therefore the corporate form itself is not a method of sharing *control*, because the form separates the functions of ownership and control. Nor do stock markets themselves necessarily mobilize capital for industrial development. Rather they allow for broad, anonymous ownership, liquid assets, and provide stores of wealth and streams of income.[11] If a company prospers, its common stockholders can expect to share in the expanding profits through a combination of dividend increases and a higher stock price. Although few investors actually buy stocks to try to manage a firm, the fact that the *possibility* of control exists means that different financial instruments assign different voting rights, and the manner in which investors hold different blocs of instruments creates different potentialities for firm control.

In contrast, bonds represent indebtedness of the corporation to the holder. As such, a bond is an IOU, sometimes reinforced by collateral. Bondholders receive interest rates at a fixed percentage rate during the years they own the bonds, as compensation for the use of their money. If a company prospers, its bondholders can expect to receive only the stream of income and the return of principal that was specified by contract when the bond was issued.[12] Therefore, while it is relatively easy to analyze bonds (i.e., loans) similarly across firms and states, an analysis of stocks must connect the financial instrument to the firm. What voting rights are attached? What proportion of shares with voting rights was offered to the public?

As capital markets have become increasingly international, the reasons for the spread and integration of debt markets differ fundamentally from the reasons for the spread and (modest) integration of equity markets, particularly in emerging markets. In brief, firms issue offshore debt to evade state activity, that is, to escape banking regulations, credit allocations, and taxes. Yet when firms issue international equity shares, they generally seek to issue shares in locations with deep markets, characterized by high degrees of liquidity, high standards of trading, and high standards of corporate governance and disclosure. Hence firms seek high levels of state activity, and even the so-called international equity markets of issue, predominantly New York and London, are essentially national markets with strict regulations.[13] Nonetheless, local markets persist, and are similarly connected to high levels of state activity.

### Stock and the Price Mechanism in Advanced, Industrial Economies

Although individual investors do not usually buy stock with the intention of controlling a firm, stock markets in the aggregate have the potential to exert pressure on management to act on behalf of shareholders. Institutions are understood here to be arrangements among economic units that define and specify the ways actors can cooperate or compete.[14] As institutions, stock markets pool capital and lower information costs. Depending on the circumstances, they can allow for managerial takeover, or discourage it. Stock markets perform different institutional functions in the national and international economies. In the international realm, they allow for a degree of ownership of the firm to remain with nationals, even as managerial control of the firm may be transferred to foreigners, or vice versa. In the national realm, they function within the broader financial institutional structure of the state.

Considerations of national financial institutional structures in political science, business, and law roughly group them into two models: a market-oriented model and a bank-oriented model.[15] The United States and the United Kingdom are the universal examples of the former, wherein security issues (i.e., stocks and bonds) are the predominant source of long-term industrial funds. British capital markets evolved in the context of gradual British industrialization, wherein the private sector had accumulated a considerable amount of capital from earnings in trade and modernized agriculture. Hence banks were sources of short-term capital in a state that did not need banks for long-term investment purposes. The London Stock Exchange of the nineteenth century was not a market of new issues, but was a market for transferable securities as liquidity improved and first-time investors knew their money would not be tied up permanently.[16] In the United States, interest groups attached to industrialization consciously restricted the dominant financial institutions from the end of the nineteenth century.[17]

As a result of such historical experiences, Zysman, Visentini, and Cunningham each point out that ownership of shares in the market-oriented model is fragmented and freely transferable; thus shareholders can exit the corporation at will, often called the "Wall Street Rule" or "Wall Street Walk."[18] If owners are unhappy with management's performance, they sell their shares, the price of the stock drops, and management becomes vulnerable to a takeover wherein new managers will attempt to improve on the performance. Even though individual stockholders do not exercise much control over management, the stock market thus disciplines managers through the Wall Street Rule. Banks do not act as owner-managers and do not hold substantial shares of the stock of any particular firms; contracts set employee, supplier, creditor, and customer rights.

The state played a more interventionist role in countries that industrialized after the United Kingdom and the United States. Gerschenkron posits that the banking system solved the problems of late industrial development because it allowed greater leeway for the state to mobilize capital for development and influence resource allocation among competing sectors. Therefore, in combining capital market functions, universal banks allowed the state to eliminate fratricidal struggles among competing elements and to mobilize scarce capital for specific industrial purposes.[19] For Hirschman, Latin American "late-late" developers tend toward foreign direct investment or foreign lending to solve the problem of their industrial development.[20]

Given these historical experiences with industrialization, banks do play a significant role in channeling capital from households to companies with the bank-oriented model as it exists in Germany, continental Europe, and Japan. With the bank-oriented model, corporations collect capital from banks, and banks in turn own stock in the corporations. Hence these firms have a much higher percentage of bank debt on their balance sheets and have major shareholders in their ownership structure.[21] Together with the small and powerful body of shareholders and debt holders, labor operates as a third key participant in the leadership of most European firms. German corporations, for example, operate with worker councils which management must consult on a variety of matters concerning policy.[22] Therefore different stakeholders control corporate activity and the Wall Street Rule does not operate as it does in the market-oriented model.

*Stock and the Price Mechanism in Emerging*
*Market Economies*

This book argues that the problem with using the market- and bank-oriented models to analyze the connections among equity finance, firms, and states in emerging markets is that the firms that are the largest issuers of shares on these markets did not result from the same historical experiences with industrialization, or the state, as those in the West. Emerging market equity products result from several forms of state engagement and disengagement with the financial sector, and engagement and disengagement from active management of economic enterprise. To use Gerschenkron's and Hirschman's terminology, these exchanges develop *post* late-late industrialization in cases such as Brazil and Argentina, and appear as instruments of *late* late-late development in cases such as Cote d'Ivoire and Ghana.[23]

This study argues that emerging market states attempt industrialization more than once, and in more than one structural era of the world economy. Thus it challenges Gerschenkron's and Hirschman's understanding of the process wherein the political outcomes within a state are affected by the character of the world economy at the time when the state attempts industrialization because there is not just *one* time when these states attempt it.[24] It challenges the overtly firm-centered varieties of capitalism approach of Hall and Soskice on the grounds that external finance and corporate governance structures for emerging market firms are not uniform by design, because the states have changed the designs over time.[25]

According to the argument offered here, different firms, originating in different eras, are differently subjected to the market for managerial control. Their varying forms result in a variety of manners in which economic actors can cooperate or compete. Hence financial institutions fail to aggregate at the national level. To understand this process it is necessary to examine the ownership of individual firms. Management's vulnerability to the price mechanism depends on how, and to whom, the shares were issued. However, an investigation of how, and to whom, the shares were issued requires an investigation into the ownership and control structure of specific firms.

One of the most apparent features of the corporate world outside the industrial core of the world economy is that controlling minority shareholders and states, both of whom are shielded from the market for corporate control, control most large firms.[26] Moreover, firms are arranged in varieties of business groups bound together through both formal and informal mechanisms. Some have legal links, others own each other's shares. Economists consider these groups to be functional substitutes for capital markets because they usually have, or acquire, a bank as part of the group. Generally the state is enmeshed in these business groups as well, because key actors within the state form their own firms.[27]

When states participate in the market for equities, they do so for vastly different reasons than firms do, and when large numbers of formerly state-owned firms offer shares on a given exchange, they magnify these differences in emerging markets. Whereas both governments and firms issue *bonds* to raise capital for a particular project, firms issue equity to take themselves public for the first time, to finance a particular project, or to raise capital when debt financing is not available either in the bond market or through a bank.[28] Firms generally do not issue equity with the intention of transferring control, albeit management can lose control in a takeover. Conversely, governments do not issue equity to finance particular projects, and they can figuratively "take themselves public" many times by participating in ongoing privatization programs wherein they sell off various parastatals in sequence. Most importantly, when a government privatizes a state-owned entity, it generally intends to transfer at least a degree of managerial authority from the government to the private sector.

Privatization issues accounted for a considerable increase in the market capitalization of European exchanges, as well as exchanges in emerging markets in the 1980s and 1990s.[29] The same control mechanisms, such as golden shares or the right of the government to restrict the building of a significant stake in a company, have also been used both in developed and developing countries. What makes emerging market privatizations different, however, is the high concentration of trading in these issues, and the state's historical experience with industrialization and corporate governance. In its broadest sense, corporate governance could include every force involved in a firm's decision making, such as insolvency powers of debt holders, commitments to employees, regulations of government agencies, and government statutes. In considering governance with respect to stock markets, however, this book considers the role external equity finance plays in determining which individuals will ultimately be responsible for making the firm's decisions.[30]

Therefore, wherein previous understandings of stock and the price mechanism held that the financial institutional structure evolved as part and parcel of industrialization, and the price mechanism disciplined or did not discipline corporations, corporate governance of many of the newest listed equities of the 1980s and 1990s can be traced to the politics of how an individual privatization deal was structured. A stock market provides the necessary infrastructure for the privatization to occur. Nonetheless, the market does not necessarily perform the same function *after* the privatization occurs, when the newly listed firms join existing firms. In some cases the exchange can indeed be an anonymous international platform for selling shares, and many of the western European stock markets are increasingly integrated through the shares of privatized enterprises offered internationally. Yet as the number of privatized firms increases on an exchange, and in the absence of liquidity, the connection between state and stock market can also tighten.

### Control of the Firm and Specific Features of Transnational Equity Securities

To understand the political implications of the structure of a given privatization deal in emerging markets since the 1980s, it is necessary to understand how ownership and control rights of a firm shift when stocks are traded across national borders. Control rights to transnational equity securities vary according to the myriad possibilities for how transnational sales can occur. Thus the *specific features* of the equities matter, because policymakers can maneuver them to raise capital in a variety of locations and comply with multiple political expediencies.

Transnational investors generally tap international stock offerings in four main ways, each of which confers differing control rights. First, an individual in one country can purchase stock on a stock exchange in another country in what is termed a "cross-border" transaction. In 1990, approximately 11.8% of all equity trading was in purchases on the firm's local stock exchange by foreigners, that is, cross-border transactions. Although Japan and the United States were close to the world average, other centers such as the United Kingdom and France had much higher ratios—at least 25%. At times, a country may prohibit foreigners from purchasing shares, or from purchasing enough shares of a firm as to assert control.

Second, an individual can purchase shares of a foreign company listed on the exchange of the country where he or she lives in what is termed a "cross-exchange" transaction. The most important site for cross-exchange trading is the Stock Exchange Automated Quotations (SEAQ) international exchange in London. The SEAQ accounts for approximately 65% of overall cross-exchange trading.[31] Voting rights attached to these shares vary by issue, and the regulations of the individual exchange. The New York and London Stock Exchanges, for example, discourage listings that do not have voting rights attached.

The third way in which investors purchase transnational stocks is by purchasing depository receipts. Although firms can list shares on exchanges such as the SEAQ or New York Stock Exchange (NYSE) outside the territory where they are headquartered, they do not usually list the shares themselves. Rather, they list a tradable receipt for the stock called an International Depository Receipt (IDR), Global Depository Receipt (GDR), or American Depository Receipt (ADR), depending on the circumstance.[32] Each IDR/GDR/ADR has a ratio of ordinary (i.e., underlying) shares of the foreign corporation to the depository receipt itself. Ownership rights attached to each of these securities vary, generally depending on whether or not the program is sponsored by the firm in question or not. Most active IDRs are sponsored, meaning the company provides financial information and other assistance to the depository, subsidizes the administration of the IDRs, and may permit voting rights to the underlying shares; however, this is not always the case.

Other distinctions among shares are important because they determine the manner in which firms can participate in the United States and other markets. Of the main classifications of ADRs traded in the U.S. market, level I or "pink sheet" ADRs trade in over-the-counter public markets. The reporting requirements for these securities are not generally rigorous. Level II and III ADRs are listed and trade on the NYSE, National Association of Securities Dealers Automated Quotation (NASDAQ), or American Stock Exchange (AMEX), and are subsequently subjected to stringent reporting and registration requirements similar to U.S. companies. "Private placement" ADRs are exempt from registration requirements under Rule 144A, and may be purchased and traded in the United States only by qualified institutional buyers.[33]

Investors seeking to purchase companies outside the United States desire ADRs because they are quoted in U.S. dollars; they trade, clear, and settle in the same way as U.S. stocks. They allow prompt dividend payment (in U.S. dollars) and corporate action notification. Moreover, they can be compared with the share prices of similar U.S. companies; they are exempt from foreign turnover taxes, and do not involve global custodial charges. Finally, they offer the same advantages as equities in general: they are liquid assets whose liquidity is the sum of both its U.S. and local market liquidities. Nevertheless, investors who wish to buy and sell shares of overseas companies without trading in markets overseas do not necessarily gain the same control rights with their shares, depending on the terms of the GDR/IDR/ADR.

The fourth way in which investors can purchase a firm's shares across borders is through the purchase of an investment fund — or collective investment vehicle — which is sold overseas. All transnational stock dealings involve some transfer of ownership, but with a fund, ownership of a variety of equities is pooled and controlled by the fund's managers subject to regulations set forth in the fund's prospectus. Funds can be structured into "open" and "closed" types. With a closed-end fund, a sum is raised and the shareholder group is closed. Shares are then traded (on an exchange or not) at a price, which may reflect a premium or discount to its underlying net asset value (NAV). With an open-end fund, the manager agrees to sell or to buy back any shares at the published daily NAV. Therefore open-end funds grow or shrink as investors buy or sell their shares.[34]

Investment in a fund differs from many other investment schemes because funds *by their nature* do not seek to control the firm whose equities the fund holds. In fact, funds are generally restricted from investing too high a percentage of their total assets in any one firm, let alone from buying enough of the firm's outstanding shares to exert control. This feature made them very popular with the governments of many emerging markets in the 1980s, when country funds were the only way outside investors could purchase the equities of some national markets.[35]

The exact manner in which the fund is structured determines the extent of control an individual firm is allowed. Therefore, just as the advent of joint-stock companies divided the position formerly occupied by one capitalist owner-manager into two physical entities — stockholder (or owner) and executive (or manager),[36] funds facilitate a three-way split into direct stockholder (or owner of shares), indirect stockholder (or owner of fund shares), and executive (or manager). Depending on the firm's home state, the legitimate basis of managerial authority can change as well, from one based solely on property rights, to one delegated by shareholders acting as a group, to one delegated by certain eligible shareholders. "Eligibility" in the final case could be determined by the nationality of the shareholder or the nature of the fund.

Therefore, in sum, the four ways in which equities can be purchased internationally are through cross-border transactions, cross-exchange transactions, the purchase of depository receipts, and the purchase of an equity investment fund. While the expansion of transnational investment opportunities for stocks grew significantly in the globalization era of the late twentieth century, growth had the effect of increasing the liquidity and dividend opportunities of equity investment. However, given the numerous specifics attached to individual issues, the expansion did not forge uniform financial institutions that allow for pressure on management through the price mechanism.

## Economic Explanations for Local Stock Market Growth

Although a comparison of the price of equity securities offered in different markets would be difficult to effect because accounting and valuation standards vary so widely, evidence does exist that transaction costs for equity issues in developing markets are significantly higher.[37] Therefore, if emerging market firms can offer shares overseas with so many different specific features, and deep transnational markets offer cost and liquidity advantages over thin, local markets, why have local stock markets grown? A variety of economic theories have surfaced attempting to account for this phenomenon, from those centered on costs, to those centered on the benefits to the economy, to those centered around the functional necessity of a local market, to those emphasizing market behaviors. However, as this section will show, none of the macro-level economic literature considers how the existence of a local market for equity securities can have an effect on how control of an individual firm is configured. Therefore, while these studies implicitly or explicitly acknowledge the importance of the state in explaining the persistence of local markets, they do not explicitly examine the domestic and international political implications of how individual shares come to be offered where, and how, they do. Thus studies that aggregate market growth, as does much of the economic and political science literature, overlook the deeply political aspects of assigning control nationally and internationally.

The initial set of economic explanations for the persistence of local exchanges compare the cost of local deals to the cost of alternative transnational deals. Some theorists argue that market participants choose to deal in national markets to compensate for the high failure rate of international trades. Disparities in clearance systems and procedures (i.e., systems and procedures to ensure participants in the transaction that they have a deal) result in failure to settle by the designated settlement date (i.e., the money is not exchanged as planned) in more than 40% of all international trades. This failure rate far exceeds the rate for domestic trades, albeit the great majority of international trades do end up settling at a later point in time.[38] Other theorists hypothesize that controlling shareholders of corporations in emerging markets trade off the benefits of cheaper access to deep transnational financial markets against the value of fewer constraints on the exercise of control when listings remain local.[39] The fact that participants generally choose to deal in their own markets cuts arbitrage pressure to ensure that similar assets bear the same price. Hence international equity markets fail what Van Zandt terms the "test of one price," wherein a borrower or its underwriters could approach all potential investors regardless of their residence, and a truly *integrated* market for equity securities would exist.[40]

Other explanations for local exchanges based on costs point out how state intervention, generally through the corporate tax structure, can compensate for the higher cost of capital on developing exchanges, particularly when the state practices preferential credit allocation to begin with. For example, the Korean government altered the relative cost of capital in different markets as early as 1972 when it selected certain firms and forced them to go public by threatening a 40% corporate tax rate hike and denied itemized deductions should they refuse. The Korean government further increased listings when a presidential decree tightened the audit and supervision of bank credit for all nonlisted firms. Other such measures followed throughout the 1970s.[41]

Combining cost explanations with explanations based on the functional necessity for a local exchange to exist, business finance literature treats exchanges as a functional requirement for public equity trades. According to this literature, a firm has three main sources of capital: internally generated funds, bank loans, or capital markets (i.e., issues of stocks and bonds). The choice of financial instrument and the firm's resulting capital structure depends on the cost of capital in these different forms (e.g., bank loans, bonds, stocks), the company management's preference for debt or equity, and an evaluation of the advisability of additional debt or equity which affects the cost of capital in different forms.[42]

According to the pecking-order theory of capital structure, cost matters first. Risk matters second because management should not overburden the firm with debt, owing to the possibility of bankruptcy. For some firms (and particularly where the tradition of family ownership is strong), control matters as well, because whoever controls the equity receives the firm's perquisites. Finally, privacy may matter because not disclosing financial information may have economic benefits for the company.[43] In light of these considerations, firms generally issue shares when they sell equity on the market for the first time, that is, an IPO, or when they seek to finance expansion without taking on additional debt. While cost remains a key consideration, how firms actually determine their capital structures remains debated among financial economists.[44] The persistence and creation of new emerging market stock exchanges poses a problem for microeconomic explanations of firm behavior because the costs to the firm and individual investor are higher in developing countries than they are in developed countries.

Other more strictly functional explanations for the persistence of local equity markets argue that the evolution of the financial system is an essential aspect of the economic growth process. Although equity markets may not be necessary at the early stages of economic development, as an economy grows, equity markets increase the efficiency of all financial markets.[45] Popular literature explaining the appearance and growth of stock exchanges in developing countries echoes the functionalist emphasis on the development of equity markets as an essential aspect of the growth process. Popular literature suggests that states encourage the growth of stock exchanges because these countries have overcome their postcolonial distrust of capitalism and see equity markets as legitimate vehicles for attracting domestic and foreign capital. One day, "junior" exchanges will become electronically linked to London, New York, and Tokyo and will thus become part of an international equity market, which could one day rival the bond and money markets in size and importance.[46] States that create them are positioning themselves to take advantage of broader integration when it eventually arrives.

However, the problem with relating stock exchanges to the postcolonial distrust of capitalism and development is the same as the problem of functionalist explanations in general: that is, why have the institutions been necessary in some cases and not in others? Some colonies did develop stock exchanges, while others did not. For example, in Africa, the Alexandria Stock Exchange opened in 1888,

Cairo in 1903, South Africa in 1887, and southern Rhodesia (now Zimbabwe) in 1946. Tanzania did not open a stock exchange until the most recent wave in 1998, and it initially had only one firm's shares listed. In the contemporary era, as large transnational markets grow, listing stock on a larger, more efficient market provides capital at a lower cost and could fulfill the functionalist requirement. Nonetheless, states continue to create exchanges, and existing local exchanges continue to function.

In part to account for the question of why stock markets form, or fail to form, a certain amount of economic literature debates whether or not they bestow benefits on the states that have them, particularly states in the developing world. The implication of this debate is that markets develop because they are an advantage, and they do not develop because they are not an advantage. An example of the former type, Cho argues that equity markets bestow benefits because they increase the allocative efficiency of credit by making financing available to risky groups who would otherwise not be able to get it. They benefit the state because they complete the process of financial sector liberalization; thus if a state does not have a viable equity market it should develop one to complete the liberalization process, according to this argument.[47]

Examples of the latter type of argument vary according to the rationale for how stock markets can potentially harm an economy. Some empirical studies criticize all stock markets for their speculative nature, and emerging markets in particular, insofar as they leave domestic economies vulnerable to destabilizing international investment flows. Schiller points out that speculative equity booms around the world are generally followed by periods of declining share price.[48] Other empirical studies points out that developing countries have few institutional investors, effective organizations for channeling savings into the securities market, or independent sources of information about the market. Such limited market access severely curtails whatever mass benefits may be generated by these markets. Even economic writing from quarters that view liberal capital markets favorably acknowledges that their benefits are not evenly distributed, and the uneven distribution impedes market growth for political reasons. Notable work by Rajan and Zingales in this regard points out that certain potential interest groups inhibit the development of competitive financial markets because financial incumbents lose an economic advantage when markets are liberalized.[49]

Additional empirical studies have implied that markets fail to develop (or should fail to develop) based on specific characteristics of individuals who have access, or lack access, to them. Calamanti's study of securities markets in developing countries pointed out that access to the market is extremely limited for small and medium investors, or any potential investor who does not live in the immediate vicinity of the financial centers where the stock exchange, banks, and brokers work. Stocks tend to be very heavily concentrated in the hands of a small number of individuals in the wealthiest classes.[50] Most enterprises have major difficulties in gaining access to the securities markets, thus negating their fund-raising role, and reinforcing the all-around preference for bank credit. In the years after Calamanti's criticisms were published, Ajit Singh echoed many of his concerns and questioned the wisdom of applying the U.S. capital market model to the developing world. He concluded that if developing countries have a choice, they should foster bank-based financial systems rather than stock markets.[51] Nagaishi's study of stock market development and economic growth in India concludes that the Indian markets failed to meet the macroeconomic goals of their formation, that is, domestic savings mobilization, foreign portfolio investment, and a higher macro-growth scenario.[52]

A final set of economic explanations for the persistence and growth of local exchanges in emerging markets does not debate their advantages or disadvantages, but argues that these markets provide investors with the option of alternative market *behaviors*. For Flowers, markets such as Jamaica, Taiwan, and the United States contrast statistically with one another beyond price and risk measures. These markets process information differently, form expectations differently, and have different volatility responses to good and bad news. Hence larger markets will not supplant them even if the larger markets continue to merge on a basis of price and risk.[53] Domowitz, Glen, and Madhavan highlight the importance of intermarket informational linkages in understanding the efficiency (or lack thereof) of cross-listings.[54] Dickie's study of the Jakarta Stock Exchange points to the role of the state in share supply for both local and foreign firms.[55] Dickie points out that in the 1970s, many developing country governments attempted to develop stock markets not just to mobilize capital for industrialization, but for the political goal of diversifying ownership of foreign companies.

Yet to allow for state intervention or varying market behaviors, the economic literature requires a theory of state behavior as an explanatory variable for offerings on emerging market exchanges. While an emerging market exchange may be a functional requirement for the state to offer competitive capital markets in the future (i.e., promoting the exchange will lead to lower *future* cost of capital), the literature fails to address why some states pursued this activity in the nineteenth century and others have only begun to pursue it now. Moreover, economic literature examines market growth in the aggregate and does not consider the specific control features attached to individual offerings. The specific control features, and political implications of each, can only be considered by examining what large issues have appeared on emerging markets across time and regions.

## The Argument of the Book

The central contention of this book is that certain characteristics of equity shares, as well as certain holding patterns of blocs of shares, leave anonymous shareholders bereft of any significant influence over the management of most large firms in emerging markets. The price mechanism fails to operate for historical reasons associated with state strategies of engagement and disengagement from economic management, while advancing developmental goals. As a result of these strategies, past and present, the state remains a stakeholder, and it retains control over several key functions and operations of some firms, even in cases where it has divested shares. Since the characteristics of equity shares and holding patterns from previous eras remain in firms structured in previous eras, the pattern of state involvement is not consistent within an exchange, or across emerging market exchanges.

Thus one pattern of corporate governance associated with the price mechanism fails to aggregate at the national level as it did in the advanced industrial economies of the United States, Europe, and Japan, where state involvement (or lack thereof) was more consistent over time.

The greatest diversity in governance structures can be seen in cases where the state attempted a variety of developmental strategies. For example, the Indian exchanges' history extends to the late nineteenth century and had local participation at an early stage. Shares listed on the Indian exchanges include minority shares of the subsidiaries of transnational corporations, noncontrolling blocs of family business houses, blocs of state enterprises, and new firms' listings. The price mechanism operates with respect to some of these firms, yet not others, depending on how the shares are offered.

There is the least diversity in shareholding patterns where there was a complete break with the developmental past in the form of a Communist revolution. For example, private large-scale economic enterprise did not survive the Communist revolution in China. The new stock exchanges in China have converged on a similar governance structure because the state has designed these structures from their inception. Nonetheless, large retained state shareholdings prevent the price mechanism from functioning. The corporate governance models also converge at the national level more closely in the former Soviet bloc. For example, the Czech economy was privatized within a short time frame through a massive voucher scheme, and large firms' governance models have converged somewhat in relation to the banking system.

Therefore, the argument of this book is historical. Yet it is also political. In order to understand the vast expansion of equity shares issued on emerging markets in the late twentieth century, it is necessary to understand that political actors divest shares in a particular historical epoch, and under particular structural political circumstances. These actors must operate simultaneously on two levels: the international and the national. International relations theory has proposed the metaphor of the two-level game as a way of integrating domestic and international political imperatives with respect to diplomatic negotiations, and accounting for reciprocal causation.

As the metaphor has been formulated by Robert Putnam, national political leaders negotiate with foreign leaders to arrive at outcomes that will be acceptable to domestic political coalitions.[56] Thus Putnam does not consider whether a given set of negotiations is wise economically, but how it comes to be politically possible. Governments adopt policies that are different from those that they would have adopted in the absence of international negotiations. However, an international agreement is possible only because part of each government's constituency favored the agreement on domestic grounds. Therefore neither a purely domestic or international understanding could account for the result of these negotiations. According to the metaphor, each side of an international transaction has a negotiator who negotiates to reach a tentative agreement at "level I." He or she sits at a table with his or her foreign counterparts for these negotiations. At "level II" a separate set of discussions takes place within each group of constituents, seated at a table behind the negotiator, about whether to endorse or implement the level I agreement. A negotiator cannot ignore either table, and a rational economic move at one table (or level) may not be politically feasible at the other.

In transferring the metaphor to contemporary stock issues in emerging markets, level I would represent international arrangements involving privatization of large industry, such as those associated with the conditionally based lending programs of international financial institutions. Yet even in cases where large issues are not privatized shares, level I agreements are understood to be completed within the confines of the transnational market for equity shares and the listing requirements of the major exchanges, for example, the SEAQ and the NYSE.[57] Each exchange sets its own listing requirements. For example, the NYSE requires a certain amount of pretax earnings, a certain number of shares publicly held, a certain amount of net assets, and a certain number of holders of 100-share units for listing. The NYSE and SEAQ exchanges discourage listings without voting rights attached. Policymakers and business leaders must account for these requirements when deciding where, and how, to list shares.

Level II represents the domestic political necessities of privatization in a given state. Economic policymakers must gain the endorsement of key political constituencies to sell off state shares, and the divestment pattern of shares generally accommodates these key constituencies. Domestic political constituencies generally seek stock offerings that keep control of the firm's management within the territorial confines of the state or reserve a role for labor or local participation in management to the greatest extent possible. Thus, while these offerings are issued in multiple manners, they are similar in that control cannot generally be transferred internationally, regardless of how many shares are issued in transnational markets.

Therefore, in creating local stock markets, and in issuing shares on them, states (and economic policymakers) advance a broader range of goals than merely seeking revenue from the sale of a firm. Chiefly, states have the goal of seeking to retain a degree of control over the operations of economic enterprise within their territories and to preserve employment. Whereas level I (i.e., international) imperatives have compelled states to disengage from active economic management of firms within their economies and constrained the type of offerings that can be made across borders, level II (i.e., domestic) considerations have caused the market capitalization and number of firms listed on local exchanges to grow as a result of this disengagement, and these constraints.

### The Historical Context

The initial set of historical arrangements governing international (i.e., level I) equity transactions emerged from British and Dutch imperialism, in a liberal financial era that peaked prior to the outbreak of World War I (see table 1.1). In the colonial era, and the era of what some historians have termed the "informal" British empire in Latin America, shares of large industrial concerns were held and traded both in London and locally.[58] Of the indigenous firms that developed, most grew from formal or informal family groupings where a bank operated within the group as a source of finance. These shares were not traded publicly because the

TABLE 1.1 Appearance of Organized Equities Markets

| Territory | Year established | Major exchange |
|---|---|---|
| *Pre-World War I Era (1842–1912)* | | |
| Venezuela | 1847 | Caracas Stock Exchange |
| Argentina | 1854 | Stock Exchange of Buenos Aires |
| Peru | 1860 | Lima Stock Exchange |
| New Zealand | 1870 | Auckland Stock Exchange |
| New Zealand | 1874 | Dunedin Stock Exchange |
| India | 1875 | Bombay Stock Exchange |
| Greece | 1876 | Athens Stock Exchange |
| Brazil | 1877 | Bolsa de Valores do Rio de Janeiro |
| South Africa | 1887 | Johannesburg Stock Exchange |
| Egypt | 1888 | Alexandria Stock Exchange |
| Brazil | 1890 | Sao Paulo Bolsa de Valores |
| Hong Kong, China[a] | 1891 | Hong Kong Stockbrokers Association |
| Shanghai, China | 1891 | Shanghai Sharebrokers Association |
| Chile | 1893 | Bolsa de Comercio de Santiago |
| Mexico | 1894 | Bolsa Mexicana de Valores |
| Sri Lanka | 1896 | Colombo Stock Exchange |
| Portugal[b] | 1901 | Lisbon Stock Exchange |
| Egypt | 1903 | Cairo Stock Exchange |
| Indonesia | 1912 | Jakarta Stock Exchange |
| *Indigenization Era (1927–1978)* | | |
| Philippines | 1927 | Manila Stock Exchange |
| Colombia[c] | 1928 | Bolsa de Bogota |
| Morocco | 1929 | Casablanca Stock Exchange |
| Palestine/Israel[d] | 1935 | Tel Aviv Stock Exchange |
| Zimbabwe | 1946 | Zimbabwe Stock Exchange |
| Pakistan | 1947 | Karachi Stock Exchange |
| India | 1948 | New Delhi Stock Exchange |
| Kenya | 1954 | Nairobi Stock Exchange |
| Republic of Korea[e] | 1956 | Korean Stock Exchange |
| Bangladesh | 1956 | Dhaka Stock Exchange |
| Malaysia[f] | 1960 | Malayan Stock Exchange |
| Nigeria | 1960 | Nigerian Stock Exchange |
| Colombia | 1961 | Bolsa de Medellin |
| Taiwan | 1962 | Taiwan Stock Exchange |
| India | 1963 | Bangalore Stock Exchange |
| Iran | 1968 | Tehran Stock Exchange |
| Jamaica | 1968 | Jamaica Stock Exchange |
| Tunisia | 1969 | Tunis Stock Exchange |
| Ecuador | 1969 | Quito Stock Exchange |
| Thailand | 1975 | Securities Exchange of Thailand |
| Costa Rica | 1976 | Costa Rica Stock Exchange[g] |
| Cote d'Ivoire | 1976 | Bourse d'Abidjan |
| Jordan | 1978 | Amman Financial Market |
| *Privatization Era (1981–1999)* | | |
| Trinidad & Tobago | 1981 | Trinidad & Tobago Stock Exchange |
| India | 1983 | Ludhiana Stock Exchange |

(*continued*)

TABLE 1.1 *(continued)*

| Territory | Year established | Major exchange |
| --- | --- | --- |
| Kuwait | 1984 | Kuwait Stock Exchange |
| Turkey | 1986 | Istanbul Stock Exchange |
| Barbados | 1987 | Barbados Securities Exchange |
| Mauritius | 1988 | Stock Exchange of Mauritius |
| Botswana | 1989 | Stockbrokers Botswana Ltd. |
| United Arab Emirates | 1989 | Bahrain Stock Exchange |
| Singapore[h] | 1990 | Stock Exchange of Singapore, Ltd. |
| Ghana | 1990 | Ghana Stock Exchange |
| Hungary[i] | 1990 | Budapest Stock Exchange |
| Yugoslavia[j] | 1990 | Yugoslav Stock Exchange |
| Swaziland | 1990 | Swaziland Stock Market |
| Panama | 1990 | Bolsa de Valores de Panama |
| China | 1990 | Shanghai Securities Exchange |
| China | 1991 | Shenzhen Securities Exchange |
| Croatia | 1991 | Zagreb Stock Exchange |
| Mongolia | 1991 | Mongolian Stock Exchange |
| Slovak Republic | 1991 | Bratislava Stock Exchange |
| Poland[k] | 1991 | Warsaw Stock Exchange |
| Czechoslovakia | 1992 | Prague Stock Exchange |
| El Salvador | 1992 | Stock Exchange of El Salvador |
| Namibia | 1992 | Namibian Stock Exchange |
| Lithuania[l] | 1993 | National Stock Exchange of Lithuania |
| Zambia | 1994 | Lusaka Stock Exchange |
| Nicaragua | 1994 | Stock Exchange of Nicaragua |
| Cyprus | 1996 | Cyprus Stock Exchange |
| Malawi | 1996 | Malawi Stock Exchange |
| Uganda | 1997 | Kampala Stock Exchange |
| Bulgaria | 1997 | Bulgarian Stock Exchange—Sofia |
| Cayman Islands | 1997 | Cayman Islands Stock Exchange |
| Tanzania | 1998 | Dar es Salaam Stock Exchange |
| Mozambique | 1999 | Maputo Stock Exchange |

[a]Securities trades in Hong Kong date to 1866. In 1986 the four exchanges in Hong Kong were unified and the Hong Kong Stock Exchange began trading.
[b]The first regulations for the Lisbon Stock Exchange were written in 1901.
[c]Securities transactions in Medellin date to 1901.
[d]The Tel Aviv Stock Exchange was reorganized in 1953 under the state of Israel, however, trades date to the British era.
[e]Securities transactions in Korea date to as early as 1911 in the period of Japanese colonialism.
[f]Equities of British corporations were traded in peninsular Malaysia in the late 1800s. The Malayan exchange (Malaysia and Singapore) was established in 1960 where firms were traded until the two split. The Kuala Lumpur Stock Exchange was formally established in 1973. The Stock Exchange of Singapore, Ltd. was established in 1990.
[g]The Costa Rica Stock Exchange mostly handles debt instruments.
[h]See Malaysia above (note f).
[i]Securities were traded in Hungary from 1867 to 1948.
[j]Equities were traded on the Belgrade Stock Exchange from 1894 to 1941.
[k]The Warsaw Stock Exchange dates to 1817. It was closed during the Communist period.
[l]The stock exchange of Lithuania first opened in 1775 as a place for export goods. In 1923 the exchange traded foreign currencies. The Vilnius Stock Exchange operated from 1926 to 1936.

family feared loss of control, or because exchange requirements excluded indigenous participation. Since the deepest integration was within the British empire, interstate political concerns were nonexistent.

The liberal era ended with the World War I, and planners attempted to restore a degree of openness in the international economy with respect to trade at the Bretton Woods conference following World War II. However, planners were far more comfortable with state intervention in the postwar years than they had been previously, and they did not attempt to restore open financial flows.[59] The new states viewed stock exchanges in highly symbolic terms, ranging from symbols of colonial oppression to symbols of new national financial sophistication. With this symbolism, stock exchanges grew highly politicized. Many transnational corporations were encouraged, or forced, to list on local exchanges. The shareholder pattern that developed in these instances was either one with a large controlling bloc held by the transnational and the rest held by atomized local shareholders, or it was a joint venture with the controlling bloc split and the rest atomized. Subsidiaries of a large state enterprise could also be held with a family group or a transnational corporation.

By the 1970s, when almost all of these states had acquired sovereign independence, a new era of international financial openness dawned as the fixed exchange rate regime designed by the Bretton Woods planners collapsed, policymakers failed to implement effective capital controls, and transnational firms increasingly turned away from bank institutions to disintermediated forms of capital. Moreover, the global system of credit grew unevenly across the world's three principal financial centers, that is, New York, London, and Tokyo.[60]

The equity component of this "reborn" or "resurrected" global finance did not progress as rapidly as the debt component did, particularly in lower-income areas of the world. Many developing countries' equity markets had not grown significantly in the interventionist era because many governments exercised preferential credit allocation, making the cost of capital for preferential debt lower than that for equity. In addition, firms sought to avoid disclosure requirements or (potential) loss of managerial control associated with public listings. Integration of these small markets with deeper ones was complicated by the fact that most developed and developing equity markets have different disclosure, custody, liquidity, and closing requirements, making it difficult to buy and sell securities interchangeably across state lines.[61]

When integration did begin to develop across equity markets, the Bretton Woods international organizations initiated and fostered it in three main respects. First, they mobilized private capital for investment on the exchanges. Second, international organizations could engage in direct technical assistance missions to establish securities market infrastructure, unlike private firms. With direct contact between international organizations and government, advisors could work *around* governments by devising diverse financial products that avoided or circumvented certain regulations. For example, investment funds were devised as "private" offerings in the United States to circumvent disclosure requirements associated with "public" offerings, or funds were domiciled in one particular state while the investors were in another. Third, international organizations directly contributed to the extension of stock exchange globalization because they created and fostered networks between public and private sectors. Just as a private investment bank's main resource is in knowing its clients, the International Finance Corporation (IFC) in particular has private- and public-sector contacts that allow it to facilitate outcomes among coalitions of interests who might not otherwise be acquainted with each other.

### Reconciling the National and International Levels

Equity markets' growth and integration has been one aspect of a much larger process of growth and integration in the entire world economy. This larger process deepened in much of the developing world following the Mexican debt crisis of 1982. After 1982, the IMF and World Bank engaged developing economies in a new and more assertive manner through conditional lending programs. These programs promote a vision of state distance from direct economic management and global economic interdependence. At times directly, and at times indirectly, states have privatized certain components of industry in compliance with these conditional lending programs. Nonetheless, privatization attracts and alienates different domestic political constituencies.

Therefore, when policymakers issue shares of large firms on emerging market exchanges, they must do so while considering national and international political necessities simultaneously. At the international level (i.e., level I), they must consider what type (if any) of compliance the international lender requires, what degree of managerial distance they must accomplish from a given enterprise (e.g., complete, partial, etc.), and what shares can be offered on the large transnational markets at a given price. At the domestic level (i.e., level II), policymakers cannot ignore domestic political circumstances. A certain type of offering may be economically rational, but not politically feasible. To accommodate the national level in the current neoliberal era, shares can be divided into classes reserved for citizens of the state and foreign nationals, or they can be divided into voting and nonvoting shares. The state can sell an enterprise completely to a family group or a local subsidiary of a transnational corporation from the former era. The state can also retain a golden share.

Each of these arrangements subjects the management of the firm to a different type of institutional monitoring. Whereas transnational corporations are monitored according to the dictates of their home country, and whatever shareholder or stakeholder pressure is possible there, local capitalists can be shielded from monitoring in many emerging markets simply because they are the only national group with the resources to buy the controlling bloc of shares, when a national group must hold the controlling bloc. In this case, the government can either protect minority shareholders through the law, or it must change the stipulation that a national group must hold the controlling bloc (i.e., allow the opportunity for a foreign takeover). In the absence of either of these mechanisms, the only monitoring device is the firm's desire to issue more minority shares for a high price on the market. If management loots the firm, further share issues will not be possible. Given the unique historical trajectory of these exchanges, a governance function fails to converge at the national level. Rather, as integration has progressed and been facilitated by international organizations, multiple governance models operate with respect to heavily traded stock. These monitoring mechanisms result in a vastly diminished likelihood that minority shareholders will have a significant influence over the management of most large firms.

In sum, the book does not analyze emerging stock markets solely according to economic criteria associated with the maximization of wealth, but adds to the analysis political criteria associated with the maximization of control, particularly in circumstances where a state does not have enough wealth to maintain total ownership of a firm or to preferentially allocate credit. When historical and political criteria are overlooked, and data is aggregated, analyses fail to uncover key aspects of the logic associated with the management of firms judged to be too sensitive to be governed for the benefit of shareholders alone (via the indirect control of the price mechanism) or even stakeholders (along the lines of the German and Japanese governance models). The state retains a role in the governance of most large issues on emerging exchanges through either direct or indirect means.

The dependent variable in this book is the growth and development of emerging market exchanges. Despite the focus on an individual financial product that appears to be easily quantifiable, the book does not measure growth merely in terms of the number of shares listed or market capitalization. It questions the functions the equity market performs within the domestic political economy of the state and the international political economy. Specifically, it questions the functions of the price mechanism of stock with respect to the market for managerial control of the firm. To explore this question, it looks at large emerging market firms individually, or from the "bottom up," to see how ownership and control are structured. In most cases, the price mechanism will fail to exert any real pressure on the firm's management to act strictly in the interest of shareholders.

# PART I

# EQUITY FINANCE IN HISTORICAL PERSPECTIVE

# Financing Joint-Stock Companies in the Colonial Era

The political connection between stock markets and states extends to the origins of each institution. The first joint-stock companies themselves were a part of imperial state formation in Europe and were created to solve the problem of financing long-distance trade. They were fostered by the extension of European limited liability laws. Share trading occurred in many parts of European colonies overseas, and thus many "emerging markets" in fact have long historical roots. They expanded along with their counterparts in the industrial core of the world economy, during the period of European growth from 1843 to 1873, accompanying the building of railroads and the opening of new territories. Among these older exchanges, the Stock Exchange of Buenos Aires (Argentina) was formally established in 1854, the Bombay Stock Exchange (India) was established in 1875, the Alexandria (Egypt) Stock Exchange was established in 1883, and the Johannesburg (South Africa) Stock Exchange was established in 1887.

The early period is significant because the shares of the successors to some of these firms continue to be listed in emerging markets. Moreover, the international shareholding pattern (e.g., all domestic shares, all privately held shares, or shares split between the local and the London market) was established then. Local stock markets did not emerge during this period so much as a means of exerting local control, but as an extension of the colonial project. Just as the colonial project transplanted the modern nation-state to most non-European areas, it transplanted financial systems as well. What are now considered to be "emerging" stock markets were in many cases stock exchanges created to manage investment in an integrated capacity with the colonial metropole. Therefore many equity markets that are now closely identified with national economies were in fact created to facilitate international investment in the manner in which it was conducted in the metropole.

In the decades prior to World War I, Great Britain, France, and Germany were the major exporters of capital. The United States, Canada, Australia, Sweden, Italy, South Africa, Argentina, and India were the main importers.[1] Even in cases where colonies had gained independence in the 1800s and thus were considered sovereign units, the financial institutions of the foreign power providing financial capital generally determined the institutions in the newly independent state. For example, the newly independent Latin American states in the 1800s developed stock exchanges and shareholding patterns that resembled those of Great Britain in the same era.

Despite the heavy involvement of British finance during this period, the British certainly did not establish stock exchanges in each locale, nor even in each locale where they asserted territorial control and created institutions of rule. The Nairobi (Kenya) Stock Exchange did not open until 1954; the Kampala (Uganda) Stock Exchange did not open until 1997. The explanation offered here for why exchanges were necessary in some pre–World War I areas and not in others treats colonial stock exchanges as functional requirements of private investment, reflecting the financial institutional structure of the foreign power. Thus investors created exchanges to channel international investment from the colonial metropole and other European centers to colonial (and in the case of Latin America, postcolonial) territories, and these investments reflected the British preference for infrastructure projects such as railroads.

The key difference between the colonial and later eras is that individuals responsible for making financial decisions did not have to satisfy two sovereign states in the earlier era. While there was tension in many cases between the government of the metropole and the government of the colony, transnational firms operated as an integral aspect of the imperial state, both at home and abroad. At times, the firm functioned as the governing institution in the colony.

Therefore this chapter explores the origins of emerging markets to demonstrate the symbiotic connection between corporations, stock markets, states, and colonies throughout their respective histories. To demonstrate this connection, the chapter begins with an examination of the origins of stock as a financial instrument. It then considers the connected rise of exchanges in the European centers of the Netherlands, Great Britain, France, and Russia. Taking as a point of departure Schwartz's contention that an international economy, defined as a complex division of labor linking economic areas located in different political units, existed long before transportation improvements forged microeconomies into national political units, this chapter argues that stock exchanges, and equity finance in general, were no exceptions to this historical rule.[2] Hence the modern state system emerged in Europe at a time when the international economy was the only real market economy, and international equity markets were forged before national markets were.

Numerical estimates of the amount of capital transfer across borders, and within imperial systems, are subject to a considerable degree of error, particularly when the estimates are made to conform to today's investment classifications. Nonetheless, historical evidence points to the fact that investment in emerging markets was considerable by the nineteenth century. Moreover, nonresidents controlled a large portion of investment originally classified as portfolio (or noncontrolling) investment at the time. The degree of nonresident holding is significant because it alludes to the highly international nature of equity holdings of the period. It is also confusing because in some cases a firm had two boards of directors: one in London, concerned mainly with investment management, and the other in the host country, concerned mainly with organizational and operational matters.[3]

This chapter will show that the early stock exchanges in emerging markets functioned similarly to those in the core of the world economy. That is, they provided liquidity for investors and served as a point of entrée for foreign capital for colonial projects. Following the early pattern of exchanges in Europe, they were not engines of self-generating industrial growth. Unlike the later eras, the vendors of shares of joint-stock companies were the owners of the private firms themselves, and not the state selling its shares of a joint-stock company. Indeed, the state sold bonds on most of the same exchanges, and many of the firms were highly political. However, the vast majority of the exchanges themselves were private associations among individuals brokering stocks and bonds.

## Equity Securities Appear in European History

The history of equity securities is irretrievably linked to the history of joint-stock companies in Europe, and the rise of the modern nation-state system, because equity securities by their nature facilitated the separation of ownership and control that is required to pool volumes of anonymous capital in the joint-stock company. Yet little market activity occurred prior to the industrial revolution. The early history of equity markets is thus more a story of states and firms' sorting out authority relationships between each other than it is a story of markets.

Most business forms in the Middle Ages were partnerships, varying in form from simple service contracts to genuine partnerships where each party participated in the company's operations. Medieval law impeded the free circulation of most financial instruments by necessitating formalities and limitations that were not determined by legal or diplomatic principle. Moreover, the limits were not hard-and-fast rules, meaning each security was limited by the circumstances of its particular case.[4]

The joint-stock company's eventual innovation over these partnerships would be in separating the function of management from ownership. The Italians created an elementary form of the joint-stock company and exported it to England in the middle of the sixteenth century. Yet when long-distance trade opened up in Elizabeth I's reign, the prevailing business arrangement was the regulated company. Regulated companies operated like guilds in that they admitted participants into their monopoly of trade in some commodity or country and supervised commerce without engaging in it. Although the regulated company had a complete constitution, perpetual succession, and a permanent body of officials, it was subject to the rules of the governor and his assistants. Each member could use his own capital as he thought best, meaning that the company offered protection to its members, but not large-scale success.

When nascent joint-stock companies were formed, members subscribed to individual operations. For example, the early English organization of the East India Company had different distinct ventures, each of which had a separate capital. On the termination of one voyage, the entire assets of the venture were divided among the participants. The sum of the divisions did not simply represent dividends, but profit and the return of the capital subscribed, which varied in amount for different expeditions. To add to the confusion, stocks overlapped insofar as a fresh voyage would be subscribed before the capital of a previous one had been repaid. Therefore long-distance shipping to distant countries could not be adequately financed with this type of operation, and true "stock markets" did not exist. Even when the capital available for investment increased in the later sixteenth century, merchants were reluctant to commit to anything requiring a long-term overhead expenditure. Rather than establishing a permanent joint-stock company, the British East India Company continued to create separate and terminable stocks for each voyage until 1613.[5]

As the joint-stock company evolved, it brought together larger funds, for longer periods of time. These expanded resources made ventures such as ongoing trade with India or Russia possible because investors' capital could purchase an entire fleet of ships that investors did not need to monitor individually. Hence an investor merely needed capital, and not specific skills, to invest and realize profits. The newer form of organization made it possible to draw in nonmerchant wealth to these long-distance ventures on an unprecedented scale. The first joint-stock company of this type is considered to be the Russia Company, established in 1553. Between 1575 and 1630, 6300 people participated in various ventures in Great Britain alone.[6]

Lacking the resources of the Dutch in the same years, British merchants perceived their business to be trade. Should force be necessary, British merchants were prepared to use it. Yet they made no attempt to capture forts or otherwise acquire bases or colonies—particularly in Asia in the late sixteenth century. By the early seventeenth century, British investors used joint-stock companies to finance business enterprises other than long-distance trade, for example, mines, fisheries, glass works, and water supply ventures. Companies formed in London had the advantages of a scope of operations throughout the entire empire, exclusive of Scotland. Nevertheless, for much of the period from 1600 to 1750, the Dutch, and not the British, were the greatest commercial power in Europe. Hence the Dutch enterprises had the greater scale of operations and the more sophisticated financial instruments.

During the period from 1600 to 1750, there were two important issuers of corporate shares in the United Provinces at the Peace of Munster: the Dutch East India and Dutch West India companies. Although prosperous Dutch citizens retained most of their wealth in houses, land, and bonds, the equities of these companies are important for their role in European imperialism, and for their role in facilitating the separation of ownership from control in the joint-stock company. The rise of these two firms created a permanent and anonymous capital that could be traded on exchanges, and it connected the firms closely to imperial growth and control of overseas territories.

Dutch merchants and other interests engaged in trade with the Spice Islands established the first company, the East India Company, in 1602; the company subsequently held a monopoly in trade with these territories.[7] The precompanies joined by the company's charter had not wanted to create a centralized monopoly company, but the Netherlands were at war, and a united company would pose a more formidable threat against Spain and Portugal. The firm's charter incorporated the company for 21 years. Following the pattern of other long-distance shipping joint-stock enterprises of the era, its authors did not consider investments made by the subscribers as permanent, anonymous capital.

The charter directed the company to make a public account of its financial state at the end of the first 10 years. When it failed to do so, public protests seemed imminent in 1610, and again in 1612. At these times, the States of Holland defended the company against accusations that it had used resources of the company for costly fortifications instead of sound business investments. By 1623 the directors refused to make the financial state of the company public on the grounds that the company was no longer an ordinary business association. The directors argued that its affairs were also the affairs of the state and had to be kept secret.[8]

In the years that followed, the Dutch East India Company reached its definitive organizational form as the largest corporation of the age, becoming the largest commercial enterprise in the country, and had by military means acquired substantial territories in Indonesia, Ceylon, and the Cape. By the middle of the seventeenth century, the directors' refusal to share information or to distribute capital as prescribed in its charter meant that the company had an autocratic management style, leaving shareholders practically no say in its affairs and with no access to information concerning its finances. When armed conflict occurred between the English and Dutch East India companies, traders who were too weak to defend themselves ran the risk of being deprived of their goods. Therefore the companies sent armed ships and later fortified stations in the territories where goods could be stored until they were conveyed to Europe.[9]

In this way, the Dutch East India Company integrated the functions of a sovereign power with the powers of a business partnership. The same hierarchy of company managers and officials made political decisions and business decisions. Nonetheless, failure or success was always measured in terms of profit.[10] Profit in the spice trade was complicated by the fact that spices were not necessities in the seventeenth century. This complication meant that profits were high and competition fierce; yet the market was also small, and oversupply was a serious possibility. Therefore the company primarily sought stable prices and the preservation of overall capital. It distributed dividends as a secondary concern.

As the Dutch East India Company evolved into a stronger, more autocratic organization, investors in the firm could withdraw by selling their shares with increasing ease. Apparently not anticipated when the company was founded, these shares became objects of negotiation and speculation, and had not traded below par since the first shares changed hands after the closing of the subscription in 1602. For investors, this presented an advantage in terms of liquidity of their investment. For the enterprise as a whole, it meant another step on the way from the trading partnership to permanent, anonymous capital.[11]

When the British financial revolution took place in the last decade of the seventeenth century, the British clearly imitated Dutch financial techniques. The Dutch themselves had already set a standard for indifference in business. Accordingly, neither religion, nor politics, should interfere with the pursuit of profit.[12]

The Bank of England, the national debt, and the laws regulating the activities of brokers of stocks and shares were created in the British financial revolution. These new British means of long-term public finance emulated Dutch bond markets. A 1697 British parliamentary act "To Restrain the number and ill Practice of Brokers and Stock jobbers" prevented an individual from acting as a broker either in commodities or transactions concerning joint-stock companies unless he was licensed. A register of brokers would be kept at the Royal Exchange and at Guild Hall, and the 100 brokers were to carry a silver medal as a token that they had been properly admitted.[13] Again, the London stock market copied the Amsterdam bourse.

The British financial revolution was accompanied by the rise of specialized merchant banks in the City, a de facto gold standard, a rise in the market for mortgages, increasing use of bills of exchange to settle domestic and international obligations, increasing use of maritime and fire insurance, and the appearance of a financial press.[14] These developments meant that the sheer volume of tradable securities in existence by this time grew dramatically and allowed for a division of labor among participants. Brokers who were active on a daily basis could buy or sell directly or could arrange a deal for other parties. Joint-stock companies were required to record the transfer of shares, and they kept transfer books solely to record such transfers.[15] Moreover, the physical organization of the British stock market was highly centralized in the coffeehouses of Exchange Alley in central London. Few visible barriers existed to separate anyone interested in buying and selling.[16]

Therefore the joint-stock business form and its accompanying market for shares grew exponentially in the seventeenth century in Great Britain as well as the Netherlands. Yet few joint-stock companies were created in the next (eighteenth) century. A major scandal associated with the South Sea Company (one of two companies whose shares constituted a significant portion of the London market) led to parliamentary regulations discouraging the business form. More important, the joint-stock company did not grow due to the type of commercial and economic development that was taking place in England. Industrial processes were simple and the amount of fixed capital involved was generally small. In many trades, an employer delivered materials to workers for processing in their own homes. Thus the employer's capital consisted of raw materials, work in progress, and finished goods awaiting sale.[17] This mostly internal financing for industry did not require the greater amounts of capital that the joint-stock company form provided. The rapid expansion of international equity markets would accompany later phases of the industrial revolution in Great Britain.

## Stock Exchanges and the Industrial Revolution in Europe

The industrial revolution in Europe would propel the growth of markets for shares of joint-stock companies. The markets would develop locally to allow for a transfer of managerial control without losing ownership. Yet they would also develop across European borders to allow for broader participation in industrial development. The emerging European network of equity transactions was strongest in Great Britain, where the industrial revolution occurred first, yet it grew to include

France, Russia, and other European markets. States participated in financial market development by using markets to raise funds, yet they also participated directly in the growth of the joint-stock company by granting charters and setting listing requirements for national stock exchanges.

During the first wave of the industrial revolution in Britain from 1780 to 1840 involving cotton and textiles, British industry continued its pattern of internal finance. This pattern was possible because business units remained on a small scale and their needs were usually met by capital privately obtained within families, or by reinvested profits. Given these relatively modest financial requirements, calls on the London capital market were rare and the growth of the public debt dominated stock exchange transactions.[18]

It was not until the second phase of British industrialization, associated with the building of the railroads, that the nature of British capital markets was transformed. Between 1830 and 1850 some 6000 miles of railroads opened in Britain, mostly as the result of two extraordinary bursts of concentrated investment followed by construction: the little "railway mania" of 1835–1837, and the larger one of 1845–1847. By 1850 the basic English rail network was more or less in place.[19] When the British spurts ended, world railroad construction continued on an increasingly massive scale. Mostly British capital, British materials and equipment, and British contractors built the later railroads. Parliamentary legislation in 1856 helped this expansion because it allowed companies to form on the principle of limited liability. Limited liability encouraged more adventurous investment since a shareholder only lost his investment and not his entire fortune in the event of bankruptcy.[20]

The structure of British capital markets until the mid-nineteenth century was decentralized, yet connected, with London at its hub. Only London-based joint-stock companies' issues traded on the London Stock Exchange. The London Stock Exchange itself was mostly a market for government securities; it listed both stocks and bonds. Non-London issuers' securities were traded in the area where the firm operated, and where the majority of their shareholders lived. The markets were interconnected in that individual brokers in each area maintained direct personal contact by regular correspondence with other areas. Nonetheless, this arrangement was not so much a national market, but brokers trying to effect a deal elsewhere on behalf of a client if the local market was inadequate. Hence local markets in Manchester, Liverpool, and Glasgow were products of the railroad boom of 1845 and the accompanying "stock mania" of the 1840s.

In subsequent years the public joint-stock company that hardly existed outside of the banking and transport industry before 1880 multiplied in other industries, such as electricity. As the business form grew, so too did a new social class of individuals who lived on the profits and savings of the previous generations' accumulations. The separation of ownership and control meant that stocks and shares could provide for relatives unable to be associated with the management of property and enterprise.[21] Therefore the industrial and commercial joint-stock companies which were established in the late nineteenth and early twentieth centuries, and which did obtain a stock exchange quotation, were almost entirely established businesses already possessing capital, as opposed to new concerns seeking to raise finance. Generally these companies listed because their leadership sought to release ownership and control to a publicly quoted company.[22]

Hence the London Stock Exchange of the nineteenth century was not a market of new issues, but a market for transferable securities. As liquidity improved, first-time investors were more easily persuaded to participate since they knew their money would not be tied up permanently. Moreover, the London Stock Exchange was also a market for holders of the national debt who resided far from London. Even when an alternative and more convenient stock exchange existed, London provided a market that was large enough, and sufficiently well organized, to cope quickly with substantial purchases and sales without extreme fluctuations in price in this sector. Later, activity on the London Stock Exchange came to involve securities on behalf of non-British brokers and dealers.

After the Battle of Waterloo in 1815, foreigners held decreasing numbers of British securities and British investors held increasing numbers of foreign securities, especially the securities of governments in continental Europe, the United States, and South America.[23] By 1830 the London firm of Marjoribanks, Capel & Co. handled business of which 88% was British government stock, 7% foreign government stock (mainly France, Denmark, and the United States), 4% East India Company, and 4% other British and colonial securities.[24] By 1840 a total of 32.8% of known securities in London were foreign.[25]

Therefore, before 1909, a segmented, yet integrated securities market existed in Britain for both domestic and international stocks. On the lower level, provincial stock exchanges or direct broker-to-broker trading in London handled transactions for the securities of small firms. Though this market was not active or sophisticated, it provided a means by which purchases and sales could be made without difficulty. At the same time, links among exchange members meant that investors could purchase securities of any nonlocal concerns that attracted them.

On a higher level, larger joint-stock concerns, such as railroads and later many industrial commercial and mining ventures, issued stocks and shares that were increasingly traded throughout the country. These securities were not exclusive to any one exchange, although each exchange had its specialties. For example, the Liverpool Stock Exchange specialized in insurance. Despite the fact that the London Stock Exchange was not the best market for the securities of many types of joint-stock enterprises, it was willing to quote these securities once they reached a size that could generate sufficient business. Prices on the London exchange and in other markets were brought together through the telegraph, which made arbitrage possible.[26]

The international outlook of the London capital market was reflected in the firms conducting the merchant banking business for much of the nineteenth century. Two of the largest firms, Barings and Rothschild's, were essentially family firms that kept in close contact with events on the continent. For example, the five Rothschild brothers and their successors maintained a daily correspondence until 1914. Most of the other London merchant banks were groupings of Huguenots, Jews, Scots, Quakers, Greeks, and Lutherans. Although ethnic loyalties proved weak or ineffective once the alien group acclimatized itself to London,

Chapman suggests that the foreign nature of the immediate environment for these groups contributed to their international outlook and investment preferences.[27]

The Paris Bourse prior to World War I was similar to the London Stock Exchange in that both had a large amount of government securities and foreign securities listed. A key difference between London and Paris, however, was that joint-stock companies did not develop as rapidly in France as they did in Britain. At the time of the French Revolution, a discount company and a waterworks company were nearly the only instances of this form. Very few formed under the empire as well. The joint-stock principle did not really spread until the 1830s.[28] Another often noted difference between the British and French experiences was the high degree of government involvement in the securities listed. French government control of the bourse has been traced back as far as 1785 and was active by the 1830s. A firm could only list with the consent of the Ministers of Finance and Foreign Affairs, and the government refused quotations as a weapon somewhat frequently.

Mostly foreign governments listed in Paris, although some foreign railways, public utilities, mines, and industrials did so as well. In this manner the government was able to influence the nature and direction of French overseas investments, often along purely political lines.[29] Up to the outbreak of the war, more than half the stocks and bonds listed on the Paris Bourse were of foreign origin.[30] In 1914 Paris was the leading market for Russian bonds and for a large part of the public debt of Spain, Portugal, Turkey, Greece, Egypt, Algiers, Tunis, Romania, and Serbia and other Balkan states.[31]

Unlike Great Britain and France, the Russian state fostered the industrial revolution in Russia by taxing the population, distributing the funds to industrial entrepreneurs, and encouraging the import of foreign expertise.[32] However, similar to states elsewhere, the railroad industry was an important component of industrialization both because the industry served as a source of demand, and as a means of integrating the national market. The Russian rails were built with heavy state involvement, either by the state's directly contributing through the budget or by guaranteeing the interest on railroad bonds issued overseas. From 1900 to 1913 the country's industrial output increased 75%, or 46% per capita.[33] Nonetheless, the rapid Russian industrialization was similar to industrialization in other emerging markets of the current era in that its volume catapulted Russia to the top group of producers for its day, but it did not generate a broad social impact. Most turn-of-the-century Russians were agricultural producers, and the country as a whole was an agricultural exporter. In addition, industrialization was concentrated regionally.

Among European states, a particularly strong connection developed between the Paris Bourse and the St. Petersburg Bourse in the late nineteenth century. Originally established by Peter the Great in 1703, the St. Petersburg stock exchange had been a place for merchants to gather, exchange information, and make deals. In the nineteenth century, brokers traded government securities, and by the 1830s, shares of joint-stock companies as well.[34] Yet given Russia's dependence on foreign capital imports, large industrial shares were difficult to place in St. Petersburg. The banks could earn greater profits if the shares were sold in Paris. Thus Russian banks introduced Russian shares on foreign markets, even when Russians bought them overseas. In this manner, the Paris and Brussels bourses became more prominent for Russian shares than the St. Petersburg market was.[35]

French citizens sought shares in Russian companies to evade French taxes, but also to avoid the cumbersome necessity of obtaining imperial authorization to form a company. In addition, by buying shares in Russian companies, they were not as often perceived as being "foreign" when operating in Russia.[36] For whatever the reason, on the eve of World War I the French held one-third of the Russian shares issued overseas and one-seventh of the total Russian shares issued. These holdings were concentrated in the mining, metallurgy, and banking industries.[37]

## Stock Exchanges in the Colonial Territories

The industrial revolution in Europe progressed concurrently with the expansion of European empires overseas.[38] As European states established more formal governing institutions in colonial territories in the mid-nineteenth century, they established financial market institutions that complemented their own. As the joint-stock company and Paris Bourse had not played the same role in French industrialization as the company and market had in British industrialization, they were not replicated in the French colonies. Since the company and local exchange connected to London had eventually played a role in British industrialization, they came to play a role in British colonies, as well as territories where ongoing British intervention could be said to constitute an "informal" empire. Today's "emerging markets" are a disproportionate set of these markets established in connection with British rule or involvement, and the pre–World War I outline of local stock exchange connections to London developed to the extent that its outlines closely resemble the outlines of the contemporary market for equity shares.

The British began to consolidate their rule over India following the Sepoy Mutiny of 1857, and over much of the interior of Africa following the Berlin Congo Conference of 1884–1885. Approximately 30 banking corporations with head offices in London operated in the "self-governing" colonies by 1905. Most of these, outside of India, were banks of note issue and not well developed in granting agricultural credit. As was the case in Britain, most economic power rested on urban, not rural, bases, and in the hands of commercial and financial groups centered in foreign trade, as opposed to manufacturers or agriculturalists. Colonial finance differed from the finance of the metropole because a colony was a subordinate, yet distinct part of the national organism. Its financial system always adapted to this political relationship. A colony was not simply a local unit of the national government because such great diversity of conditions existed across parts of a given colonial empire.[39]

Analysts at the turn of the century argued that a large colonial corporation, known in the financial centers through direct personal contact with the leaders of finance, had far greater opportunities for obtaining funds than a purely local institution did. While all parts of the business of banking were transported to the colonies, the operations of discounting, exchange, or issue assumed a different character under the new conditions. Men and enterprises were judged far more according to subjective standards in the colony than they were in the metropole. Moreover, the business of exchange assumed a more important role in the colonial bank, given the unsettled condition of colonial currencies.[40]

The national and international equity markets followed the shareholding pattern of local and transnational listings in Great Britain. Stock exchanges in colonies or areas of heavy British investment specialized in local shares, yet shares of larger firms were also quoted in the metropole, London. At least 10 separately organized markets in London existed: the Consols market, the Colonial stock market, the Indian railroads market, the Canadian and American railroad markets, foreign government stock markets, South African mining group (itself subdivided into several sections), British Columbian, Australian, and West African mines market, foreign rail market, and smaller markets in Mexican and Uruguayan bonds.[41]

A vast system of arbitrage connected these London specialty markets with markets overseas. Arbitrage in this context refers to the traffic of the purchase and sale of a given amount of stock on one stock exchange, with the simultaneous resale or repurchase of the same amount of stock on another exchange. Communication among exchanges and active trading of the same securities in different markets created opportunities for members of each to profit from any price differentials. Active arbitrage contacts existed between members of the London Stock Exchange and numerous centers overseas, many of them far from Britain. For example, gold-mining shares were traded in Johannesburg and other major centers like Paris, Amsterdam, Berlin, and New York, as well as minor ones like Havana, Colombo, and Alexandria.[42]

Of the web of emerging markets that exists today, in 1997 the IFC classified (in descending order) Brazil, South Africa, China, Mexico, India, the Russian Federation, Malaysia, Chile, Turkey, and Saudi Arabia as the "top 10" emerging stock markets.[43] Of the eight non-European "top" emerging markets, six had been established by World War I. In the case of the remaining two—China and Malaysia—circumstances point to a similarly long tradition of local equity exchange. The Shanghai Sharebrokers Association, established in 1891, was the largest securities market of its time in the Far East. Although the current markets in China are by no means attempts to resurrect this market, they do point to a pattern predating the present. In the case of Malaysia, the Kuala Lumpur Stock Exchange split with Singapore in 1990. However, British corporations traded shares in peninsular Malaysia in the late 1800s. With the rubber boom in 1910, share brokering was a major activity in Singapore and Malaysia. The growth of the tin mining industry also resulted in the flotation of many tin companies at that time.[44]

Moreover, these markets are not just top markets in terms of capitalization, liquidity, or number of firms listed. They also lead the world in announced international equity issues from emerging markets, or "tier one" transactions. Table 2.1 lists announced international equity issues by the nationality of the issuer from 1995 to 1997.

Of the 15 emerging market issuers listed, 11 were issues from a nationality wherein an exchange has existed since the turn of the twentieth century and whose

TABLE 2.1 Announced International Equity Issues by
Nationality of Issuer (in US$ billions)

| Countries | 1995 | 1996 | 1997 |
|---|---|---|---|
| All countries | 54.3 | 82.3 | 117.5 |
| Developed countries | 43.0 | 59.6 | 85.4 |
| Developing countries | 8.2 | 13.9 | 23.2 |
| Latin America | 0.5 | 3.6 | 5.9 |
| Argentina | — | 0.2 | 2.0 |
| Brazil | 0.2 | 0.4 | 2.4 |
| Chile | 0.2 | 0.3 | 0.6 |
| Mexico | 0.1 | 0.7 | 0.8 |
| Peru | — | 1.1 | — |
| Venezuela | — | 0.9 | 0.1 |
| Middle East | 0.3 | 0.8 | 1.8 |
| Israel | 0.3 | 0.8 | 0.7 |
| Kuwait | — | — | 1.1 |
| Africa | 0.4 | 0.6 | 1.1 |
| South Africa | 0.4 | 0.6 | 1.1 |
| Asia | 6.6 | 8.2 | 13.9 |
| China | 0.9 | 2.1 | 9.0 |
| India | 0.3 | 1.3 | 1.0 |
| Indonesia | 1.5 | 1.3 | 1.0 |
| South Korea | 1.3 | 1.2 | 0.6 |
| Malaysia | 0.6 | 0.6 | 0.4 |
| Philippines | 0.7 | 1.0 | 0.3 |
| Taiwan | 0.7 | 0.6 | 1.6 |
| Thailand | 0.5 | 0.2 | — |

Source: Bank for International Settlements, *Bank for International Settlements
68th Annual Report*, 1998.

shares had been traded internationally since that time. For three of the remaining
four (Malaysia, the Philippines, and Israel), trades extend to this era under different
political circumstances.

Table 2.2 is a summary of stock exchanges established in the pre–World War
I era. An exact comparison of the value of British overseas investments with these
exchanges is difficult because foreigners could and did subscribe to issues made
in London, and British residents could and did subscribe to issues made overseas
(what are referred to as cross-border transactions in the contemporary era). Sometimes an issue was made in two or more centers and the exact amount subscribed
in each is not known. Furthermore, the secondary market contained the same
types of transactions. Foreigners could buy existing securities from British citizens
and vice versa. Moreover, the volume of such transactions was probably larger in
relation to the volume of securities on the market than it is today because of the
high volume of the arbitrage business. Hence the amount and composition of
overseas assets was constantly changing. Yet by one estimate, a little less than half
of the sum of publicly issued overseas securities, investment in private companies,
and property abroad was held in the dominions and colonies, about 20% in the

United States, 20% in Latin America, 15% in Europe, and the remainder scattered in relatively small amounts. More than 40% was in railroads, 30% in loans to foreign governments and municipalities, 10% in mines and plantations, 8% in banks and financial institutions, and 5% in other utilities.[45] The pattern of stock exchanges in the imperial era reflects this distribution and shows stock exchanges to be a functional requirement for certain kinds of British investment overseas (see table 2.2).

The railroad category of investment predominated, and within it, business and the state acted closely together. Some railroads were undertaken as joint-stock enterprises and some were financed by the state in question. Yet even when a company was formed as a joint-stock, the state usually participated in some way, for example, by guaranteeing interest on loans or granting land.[46]

## Structure and the Need for Exchanges

If stock exchanges were a functional necessity of imperial investment and empire, why were there areas—particularly under British colonial domination in Africa—without stock exchanges? After the partition of Africa in the late 1800s, very little political activity actually occurred outside the capital cities.[47] Few roads and hardly any railways were built. The lives of most Africans barely changed. The reasons for this stagnation were financial. Private European investors were uninterested in Africa (unless infrastructure was related to mines), metropolitan legislatures opposed major public expenditures on colonies, and even the Western commercial firms didn't want to move inland before governments inland were "pacified."[48] Some colonial regimes tried to provide basic infrastructure through concession companies; that is, companies would take on the major costs of initial modernization in return for exclusive rights to exploit areas under their control. However, these companies were not financially successful in most areas.

Faced with a lack of private investment, colonial administrators in Europe and Africa either undertook construction on their own, with borrowed funds from public and private sources, or subsidized private entrepreneurs by offering various combinations of land concessions and public guarantees on returns of their capital. As a result of overwhelming state planning, the purpose of a given railway project might be either military control or competition with another colonial power, and the financing methods left colonial governments with a heavy debt burden to the metropole. The Kenya-Uganda line is a case of a railway built from public funds for essentially strategic purposes, despite the fact that it tapped an inland region with real commercial potential. The British hoped to protect the Suez Canal from the threat of a dam built across the Upper Nile that would cut off water supplies to Egypt.[49] In a sense, the first African "debt crisis" occurred as governments borrowed to build such railroads and then diverted money from the private disposable incomes of Africans, or from other government projects, to meet payment obligations. Since repayment was in foreign exchange, debt obligations added another incentive for promoting export production at the expense of alternative types of economic enterprise.[50]

The lack of joint-stock investment in French colonies is less remarkable than

TABLE 2.2 Summary of Stock Exchanges Established in the Imperial Era

| Stock exchange | Year established | Territory | Colonial power or primary source of foreign capital when established | Historical circumstances |
|---|---|---|---|---|
| **Africa** | | | | |
| Alexandria Stock Exchange | 1888 | Egypt | British occupation and protectorate period, Belgian and French investment | The Alexandria Stock Exchange was established in 1888. European economic power prior to World War I was pervasive in Egypt, and deeply resented. European capitalism was in a position to dominate Egyptian economic behavior through institutions such as the stock exchange. In 1923 legislation required that one-quarter of shares in new companies be offered for purchase in Egypt. |
| Cairo Stock Exchange | 1903 | Egypt | British occupation and protectorate period, Belgian and French investment | The Cairo Stock Exchange was established after the Alexandria Stock Exchange, in 1903. They were among the most active in the world in the 1940s. |
| Johannesburg Stock Exchange | 1887 | South Africa | Britain | The Johannesburg Stock Exchange was established in 1887 to provide a location for trading shares in mining ventures in the Rand. |
| **Americas** | | | | |
| Bolsa de Comercio de Santiago | 1893 | Chile | British investment | The first attempt was in 1873 when 160 corporations (mostly mines) and 6 foreign corporations organized. Later, an organized market operated in Valparaiso. As Santiago grew, the President of Chile and Minister of Finance decreed an incorporated stock exchange in Santiago in 1893. |
| Bolsa de Valores do Rio de Janeiro | 1877 | Brazil | British investment | As early as 1790, independent brokers called corretores worked in the Plaza of Rio de Janeiro and other provincial centers of the Portuguese colony. They occasionally traded shares of stock. In 1876 twenty-five brokers belonged to the Rio Stock Exchange when it organized. They traded national and foreign bonds, letters of exchange, commercial loans, precious metals, and shares of stock the next year. |

| | | | | |
|---|---|---|---|---|
| Bolsa Mexicana de Valores | 1894 | Mexico | British investment | In 1880, a group of Mexican and foreign investors began regular meetings at the offices of the Compania Mexicana de Gas to trade shares of mining companies. Another exchange developed at a place called "the home of the widow of Genin." As activities grew, individuals began to specialize in the securities business. In 1894 they formed the Bolsa de Valores. Competition from a later Bolsa de Mexico meant liquidation in 1896. The Bolsa de Mexico eventually also liquidated. By 1897 only three public and private issues were listed. In 1907 members of the two defunct bolsas formed "la Bolsa Privada de Mexico." A later name change made it the Bolsa de Valores de Mexico. |
| Caracas Stock Exchange | 1805–1821 | Venezuela | Spain, five years later, British investment | Local merchants incorporated the first bolsa in 1805. In 1873 stocks were traded without a formal organization at the Esquina de San Francisco and Esquina de la Bolsa. Laws passed in 1873 and 1919 regulated securities operations. |
| Lima Stock Exchange | 1860 | Peru | British investment | Financiers established the exchange at a time when banks sought to expand their limited activities. Schemes between domestic investors and merchant bankers in London, Paris, and New York secured capital necessary to control strategic monopolistic and oligopolistic concerns. From 1902 to 1915 the Lima stock market attracted attracted capital for bank and insurance company securities, as well as agricultural, livestock, service, public, and semipublic firms. |
| Sao Paulo Bolsa de Valores | 1890/1895 | Brazil | British investment | The Bolsa Oficial de Valores de Sao Paulo was founded in 1895, yet as in the Brazilian case above, individuals conducted trades previously. |
| Stock Exchange of Buenos Aires | 1854 | Argentina | British investment | When Spanish rule ended in 1810, English merchants created trading organizations, but excluded Argentine nationals. In 1822 the government established a mercantile exchange. In 1829 the Buenos Aires Commercial Room was established for both national and foreign traders. In 1854 national and foreign businessmen formed the Bolsa, which is the oldest continuous Latin American exchange. The Argentine government did not participate. |

*Asia and Pacific*

| | | | | |
|---|---|---|---|---|
| Bombay Stock Exchange | 1875 | India | Britain | The Stock Exchange, Mumbai, India, was established in 1875 as "The Native Share and Stockbrokers Association" with the objective of promoting industrial development in the country through efficient resource mobilization by way of investment in corporate securities. It is the oldest in Asia. |

(continued)

TABLE 2.2 (continued)

| Stock exchange | Year established | Territory | Colonial power or primary source of foreign capital when established | Historical circumstances |
| --- | --- | --- | --- | --- |
| Calcutta Stock Exchange | 1903 | India | British | The first attempts to organize an exchange in Calcutta extend to 1858, but these attempts did not succeed until 1908. |
| Colombo Stock Exchange | 1896 | Ceylon (Sri Lanka) | British | In 1896 the Colombo Brokers Association began trading shares in limited liability companies. This equity capital was channeled into plantation companies (tea, rubber, and agricultural products) sponsored by the association. It also created an active secondary market. |
| Hong Kong, China, Stock Exchange | 1891 | Hong Kong | British | Equities trades in Hong Kong date to 1866. An Association of Stockbrokers in Hong Kong was established in 1891. It was renamed the Hong Kong Stock Exchange in 1914. |
| Jakarta Stock Exchange | 1912 | Dutch East Indies (Indonesia) | Dutch | The Dutch established the first securities market in 1912. Most active shares were mostly Dutch East Indies government agencies and other Dutch companies, particularly plantations. |
| Korea Stock Exchange | 1911 | Korea | Japan | The first securities trades in Korea are believed to have taken place around 1906 and the first organized securities market came into being in 1911 under the Japanese occupation. |
| Shanghai Sharebrokers Association | 1891 | China | British extraterritorial zone | Foreign brokers formed the Stock and Sharebrokers Association with registration in Hong Kong under the provisions of the Companies Ordinance. Indigenous Chinese supplied a significant portion of capital. |
| Shanghai Stock Exchange | 1904 | China | British extraterritorial zone | The Sharebrokers Association was renamed the Shanghai Stock Exchange and membership formalized. It became the largest securities market in the Far East for its time. |

Sources: Mexico, Argentina, Brazil, Venezuela, and Chile: David K. Eiteman, Stock Exchanges in Latin America, Michigan International Business Studies, no. 7. Ann Arbor, MI: University of Michigan, 1966. Jakarta Stock Exchange: John Niepold, "Indonesia," in Keith K. Park and Antoine W. Van Agtmael, eds. The World's Emerging Stock Markets, Chicago: Probus Publishing, 1993, pp. 161–180. Korea: J. Park, "Internationalization of the Korean Securities Market," International Tax and Business Lawyer, 7(1): 3–56. Bombay and Calcutta: Radhe Shyam Rungta, The Rise of Business Corporations in India, 1851–1900, London: Cambridge University Press, 1970. Egypt: Robert L. Tignor, State, Private Enterprise and Economic Change in Egypt, 1918–1952, Princeton, NJ: Princeton University Press, 1984.

its absence in some British colonies, since the French did not utilize the form as much themselves, relying more heavily on bank lending. As was the case in the metropole, the colonial banks were closely connected to the government. The first French colonial banks appeared in the sugar-growing colonies immediately after slavery was abolished. In the absence of slavery, local farmers needed more money to manage their plantations, and credit institutions appeared in each of the sugar colonies to protect their economic existence. That is, by the law of July 11, 1851, colonial banks organized in Martinique, Guadeloupe, and Reunion. Guiana and Senegal established such banks a few years later.

French colonial banks organized as semipublic institutions. The treasurer of the colony was ex officio a member of the council of administration, and the director (president) of the bank was appointed by the president of the republic upon nomination by the Minister of Finance. No dividends could be declared without the approval of the Minister of Finance, represented by the governor of the colony. The banks mostly granted agricultural loans and almost entirely serviced the sugar industry, so any failure in a sugar crop dealt a serious blow to the credit institutions. Colonial governments were often called upon to lend assistance to maintain the credit of these institutions.[51]

In Africa specifically, the French pursued a crude form of colonial economic development by buying African commodities cheaply and selling French manufactured goods at high prices in return. They constituted the Federation of French West Africa in 1905 and operated it as an integrated unit with a common tariff structure applied uniformly. Hence the federation was a single trading zone administered from Dakar.[52] Administrators spent revenues on government operating costs, and they invested in infrastructure to promote colonial trade: roads, the port of Dakar, and the railroad. French investment was kept to a minimum to sustain the colonial trading system. After 1928 West Africa was virtually a closed market that bought French goods, especially textiles. By 1935 France had invested less in the combined federation than the British had invested in the Gold Coast (now Ghana), a territory less than one-tenth of the size. French colonial administration relied on forced labor until 1946 to carry out public works projects, and almost no manufacturing activity existed in the federation prior to World War II.[53]

French trading houses controlled all levels and aspects of the West African export-import trade. When French commercial banks were established in French West Africa, they joined forces with the colonial administration and the trading houses to block independent traders' access to credit. The Senegalese had no access to bank credit until 1956, in spite of Senegalese businessmen's persistent demands that the colonial administration take a stand against the unfair and discriminatory lending policies of the French banks.[54]

Incidentally, the British in West Africa did not extend credit to Africans either. Advances could only be obtained against produce that was ready for shipment and had a ready market in Europe and North America. Thus almost all advances were short term and to European businesses. The volatility of West African trade, together with the lack of a developed local money market, forced the banks to keep their assets as liquid as possible. Low-yielding portfolios made it impossible to offer attractive returns on deposits and to mobilize African savings, which was left to the Post Office Savings Bank.[55]

Taken together, a large number of stock exchanges functioned around the globe by the eve of World War I. Concentrated in areas of British foreign investment, these exchanges managed joint-stock investment with London and functioned similarly to the web of exchanges in the United Kingdom in terms of providing liquidity for investors and serving as a point of entrée for some foreign capital. Nonetheless, just as the colonial powers did not invest uniformly across colonial territories, an exchange did not appear in each British colony, nor did they appear in French colonies.

## Analysis and Conclusion

The process of separating ownership and control in the joint-stock company was thus intertwined with the European need to finance long-distance, ongoing trade, and later, transportation networks in parts of the world that came to constitute formal and informal empires. Hence the market for shares of transnational firms developed prior to unified national markets. Early financing patterns of British imperialism in particular were outside the state's direct control, and exchanges in British colonial territories followed the pattern of local exchanges in Manchester, Liverpool, and Glasgow in that they traded shares of local firms. The shares of large firms, such as railroads, were traded in London. As a group, markets provided liquidity to the assets and allowed for increasingly distant (physically and in terms of involvement) owners to receive a stream of income from those assets. By the end of the nineteenth century, the map of what are now considered to be emerging markets was reasonably well defined. The absence of share trading was greatest in the French and British African colonial territories, where miniscule foreign investment occurred, with the notable exception of South Africa.

Therefore, in an international system characterized by imperialism, the transmission of British capital determined much of the pattern of stock exchange activity. The French did not industrialize with the same pattern of joint-stock companies, and thus did not transplant the form to their colonies. When the French bought and sold Russian shares, they conducted the operations in Paris. Likewise, German industrialization occurred along different lines, with different financial structures, and without the same overseas territorial conquest. World War I disrupted the era of liberal foreign investment in the colonial world and several factors, such as the worldwide recession and collapse of international capital markets in the late 1920s, stunted investment growth in the period between the wars (1918–1939). In fact, postwar political upheaval and boundary changes slowed international investment in Europe as well. The financial connection between Russia and the continent was broken with the Bolshevik revolution. On an immediate level, the revolution dispossessed the small group of luxury-goods consumers in Russia that accounted for 10% of its imports. On a longer-term level, the revolution eliminated the possibility of foreign borrowing with the nationalization of private property and abrogation of Tsarist debt.[56]

# New States, New State Involvement

Ownership and control of large enterprise evolved as part of European state formation in the modern era. As European states industrialized and asserted their political control over empires, the manner in which large enterprise was financed in Great Britain was copied in the British empire overseas. Nonetheless, many features of the international system, including colonial empires, were again transformed by the hegemonic struggles of World War I and World War II. Gilpin terms these struggles "hegemonic" in terms of the number of participants in the conflicts, the nature of the issue at stake (i.e., the governance of the system), and the unlimited scope of the warfare.[1] The conclusion of these two cataclysmic wars of the twentieth century ultimately led to the replacement of the Pax Britannica with the Pax Americana.

Beginning with the independence of India in 1947 and continuing through the independence of African states in the 1960s, colonialism ceased to exist as a form of political organization. Some features of the international system, such as foreign direct investment, grew characteristic of the international economy with the American ascendance. Foreign direct investment changed the economic structure because with it the home firm asserts managerial control over its subsidiary in another country. The international landscape also changed with the rise of multilateral institutions as mechanisms of control and coordination. Postwar multilateral organizations ranged from the United Nations and its attendant bodies to the Bretton Woods international financial organizations: The World Bank, IMF, and General Agreement on Tariffs and Trade (GATT).

Coordinating behavior among states on the basis of generalized principles of conduct, multilateral organizations sought to end discriminatory trade barriers, currency arrangements, and even colonization by reflecting a particularly American agenda. As such, they did not seek a return to the laissez-faire economic policies of the nineteenth century. The organizations opted instead to pursue American "open door" policies that would accommodate the domestic interventionism of the New Deal.[2] A desire for a degree of economic interventionism resonated with European states in the postwar era as they sought to rebuild their domestic economies. Interventionist states exhibited a clear preference for bank lending, as opposed to equity finance, because states could more systematically allocate scarce capital through banking financial intermediaries. Equity finance in the former colonial territories did not grow until the new states themselves assumed an interventionist role.

Therefore three structural changes in the international political economy resulted in the transformation of equity finance in what was then referred to as the "third world": the formation of a constellation of multilateral organizations accommodating interventionism, the increased use of foreign direct investment as a method of overseas finance, and the eventual rise of economic nationalism in the postcolonial states. As new states entered the international economy, their leaders had to confront both an international as well as a domestic political reality. Thus the changed international structure of juridical sovereignty, combined with domestic political calls for leaders to assert direct control over economic enterprise, explain what products were offered for sale, or more commonly removed from sale, in these years.

This chapter argues that with the new level of state involvement, the political purposes of these exchanges were dramatically different from those of the earlier era. The nineteenth century exchanges fostered investment from the colonial metropole, or from London to the British informal empire in Latin America. The mid-twentieth century ones attempted to indigenize international investment and disperse ownership. In this regard, states assumed a more direct role in *creating* equity finance. International organizations would later help to connect this mode of finance. While a number of new exchanges appeared in the developing world in the postwar era, a number of older exchanges slowed or ceased functioning. In states experiencing a Communist revolution, such as Russia or China, the state takeover of large industrial enterprise meant that the corporate form of private business organization was no longer viable.

## The Bretton Woods System and the Postcolonial Core

The creation of the Bretton Woods financial institutions transformed the nature of the international financial system because the institutions are, by their nature, organizations having states as members. As colonies became states, the growth in number of the new members changed the work mandates of the organizations and created the need for even more development organizations. For example, the International Finance Corporation (IFC), which became part of the World Bank Group, was formed to address the developmental and financial needs of the postcolonial states. To understand these developments, however, it is necessary first to consider the evolution of European financial markets in the interwar period, and corporate ownership and control patterns in the United States. Governments determined the direction of many of these developments to cope with the effects of World War I and the Great Depression of the 1930s. The actions of European powers prior to the war began the transformation of financial systems in colonial states and Central and Latin American markets.

## The Interwar Years

The interwar period set the stage for important changes in London, and later American, domestic equity markets that would have international implications in the years to follow. Prior to World War I, industrial capitalism and the major financial institutions in Great Britain operated in somewhat different spheres of activity. Most British industry up to 1914 was either self-financed or relied on local stock exchanges, and most of the major financial institutions were global in outlook. Between 1865 and 1914, only two-fifths of all London Stock Exchange issues were for domestic firms, and immediately before the war, only three-tenths were. War and international competition in the 1920s brought domestic industrial capitalists and the major financial institutions closer together.

As the number of oligopolies in Britain grew in response to international competition and the need to supply the military after 1919, stock exchange finance accomplished many of the mergers. Hence domestic issues of capital on the London Stock Exchange grew after 1919, particularly domestic industrial and commercial issues. Between the wars, domestic issues were twice the value of overseas issues. In the 1930s, the process continued as the Bank of England overtly sought to bring the City and provincial industry together, as well as to create more efficient big business.[3] Traditional merchant bankers facilitated a certain amount of the finance. For example, Barings acted as advisors to Armstrongs (the armaments firm) and underwrote flotations for underground railroads, breweries, and tire firms. Kleinworts promoted issues for cotton firms and shipbuilders.

The changes in London were not, however, definitive. By 1939 even large firms that had merged with the help of stock exchange finance still mostly raised new capital internally. Smaller firms still found London to be too expensive a listing. The number of industrial companies listed did indeed rise from 569 in 1907 to 1712 in 1939, meaning the combined market value was five times greater in 1939 than it was before World War I.[4] Yet when placed in the context of the growth of the exchange overall, it is apparent that the market was still cosmopolitan in nature, and still more organized to provide capital to foreign countries than to British industry. Partly due to the massive increase in public debt associated with World War I, industrial securities still made up only 10% of the value of all quoted securities in the 1930s, up from 8% in 1913.[5]

During the same interwar years, New Deal legislation in the United States likewise set the stage for important changes in American business and financial institutional structures that would have a profound influence after the war. The main provisions of the New Deal legislation confirmed the fragmented banking structure of the United States by keeping bank branching restrictions (McFadden Act), severing commercial from investment banking (Glass-Steagall Act), and adopting deposit insurance, which propped up small banks. Of these provisions, Glass-Steagall had the further effect of creating two deep, but distinct, financing channels at a time when many European banks were universal.[6] The modern corporation that emerged from the New Deal was similar to its European counterparts in the separation of ownership and control, yet different in its distant shareholders and centralized managers.

These pieces of legislation resulted from the American public's anti-Wall Street sentiment that bankers, and Wall Street bankers in particular, had caused the Depression and needed to be punished. While the desire to fragment power meant that the financial structure was fragmented, the power in the hands of the management of large U.S. firms was far *more* concentrated.[7] Immediately after the war, U.S. bank trust departments' last direct link to equity was severed by fiduciary rules limiting a bank's trust funds to no more than 10% investment in the stock of any single corporation. This gesture served to hyperfragment portfolios even further.[8]

The growing interventionist ideology of countries in the core of the world economy spread throughout colonial empires and Latin America. The years leading up to World War II proved to be an important turning point for Latin American financial development due to the competition for influence between Allied and Axis powers in the region. Axis influence was particularly strong in Argentina and Bolivia; nonetheless, German networks of communications and airlines throughout Latin America constituted strategic threats to the Allies.[9] Fascist economic and financial ideology promoted self-sufficient economic activities, as opposed to the previously liberal policies. Since the Latin American states lost export markets in Europe, there was a real threat that they would adopt fascist development strategies to cope with economic collapse.

To meet the threat, U.S. policymakers such as Nelson Rockefeller devised strategies toward Latin America that would preserve a degree of liberalism in their orientation. Heavily influenced by Keynesian economic ideology, Rockefeller sought to reconcile state goals with those of private corporations, and in so doing, aid the economic and financial role of the state in the 1930s and 1940s. Overall, Latin American countries would be transformed into a semiperiphery that would absorb U.S. products, especially used and new industrial equipment.[10] And similar to the manner of the United States and Great Britain, these states would intervene.

While fascist development ideologies did not have the same influence in African colonies as they did in Latin America, events in wartime France contributed to securities market development in the francophone African colonies. As of February 1941, bearer stocks were abolished in France and the owners and purchasers of securities were required to register them and deposit them with an authorized agent, that is, a bank or a stockbroker. In June 1941, the *Caisse Centrale des Depots et Virement de Titres* was created to centralize French security deposits. Because it seemed advisable to introduce a similar system in colonial territories, officials established similar agencies in the colonies to serve the interests of French settlers. Whatever the goal, the effect of the action was to help organize and centralize secondary markets in securities in the territories where none had existed before.[11]

### Multilateral Organizations and Decolonization

At the conclusion of the war, the Bretton Woods agreement of 1944 proposed a new set of rules and institutions to govern international monetary and trade relations. American perceptions of the causes of the 1930s economic catastrophe, and beliefs about the role the U.S. dollar and economy should play in the postwar world, framed the agreement. Hence the end of World War II signaled the decisive shift in financial leadership from Great Britain to the United States, or from London to New York. Moreover, the system obstructed a return to the open financial system of pre-1931, since the original Bretton Woods agreement permits governments to restrict capital movements without review (e.g., for balance-of-payments purposes). The agreement takes a strong stand against current account restrictions. Thus free capital movements took second place in the Bretton Woods system to the free movements of goods across borders, and states were able to undertake interventionist financial policies within certain parameters.[12]

At the same time as the new set of multilateral organizations entered across the international financial community, the era of decolonization began when the British Parliament passed the Indian Independence Act in 1947. Although the causes and circumstances of decolonization varied according to the colonial power and circumstances, the process was rapid and nearly universal. From 1955 to 1960, 40 new states (many African) joined the United Nations (UN); by the 1970s, UN membership had reached 150 states. The new states were juridically sovereign, yet they retained important formal and informal financial ties to the former colonial power. These ties carried over into their membership in the Bretton Woods financial institutions as well. At decolonization the new countries all joined the UN, most joined the IMF/International Bank for Reconstruction and Development (IBRD), but few became contracting parties to the GATT. It was possible to sidestep formal GATT membership because if the General Agreement had been applied in a colonial territory, the postindependence state could continue to apply the GATT on a de facto basis and postpone formalizing its status.[13] Therefore, of the three Bretton Woods financial institutions (i.e., the IMF, GATT, and World Bank), the World Bank became the focal point for many of the new states.

As membership in the World Bank grew, and the institution increasingly oriented itself away from postwar reconstruction and toward basic economic development in what came to be referred to as the "third world," individuals at the World Bank began to envision an IFC that would provide venture capital to private businesses and thus foster private-sector development through equity investment. The idea for an IFC was well received by the U.S. International Development Advisory Board under Nelson Rockefeller. Rockefeller sought to emphasize development, as opposed to defense, in competition with the Soviets. Nonetheless, many opponents to the plan disagreed and took issue with the idea of equity investment and multilateral institutions in particular.[14]

Chief among the opponents to the IFC plan were the Treasury Department, Board of Governors of the Federal Reserve, and the Export-Import Bank. These agencies, together with many investment banks and the National Foreign Trade Council, reasoned that the IFC would run contrary to the free enterprise system. As a matter of principle, the government does not own the equity of private firms in the American system. They reasoned that public governmental institutions should also not own equity through an IFC. If certain projects required public international support, the opponents to the IFC argued that the projects were most likely not economically justifiable. In addition, the opponents feared a "proliferation of international institutions" was occurring.[15]

A coalition of support for the proposal eventually did emerge. Samuel Anderson became the Assistant Secretary of Commerce and this department, together with the Securities and Exchange Commission (SEC), commercial banks, and the qualified support of the State Department, brought the plan to fruition. Yet the World Bank had offered the U.S. Treasury two concessions to get its support: restrictions on equity holdings and small size of initial capital. The original IFC charter stated that as a development agency, lending would not be determined solely on the basis of economic priority, but would be determined on the basis of productive projects. The corporation was not to compete with private capital.[16]

Despite two subsequent amendments to the articles making equity holding possible and making borrowing from the World Bank possible, the IFC's record from 1956 to 1961 was unimpressive. Large U.S. firms operated on a scale exceeding the IFC's capacity and small U.S. firms had little incentive to operate overseas when domestic opportunities were great. The IFC was located in Washington, DC, and lacked local contacts and knowledge. Thus it found it difficult to attract domestic private partners. Furthermore, its loans were denominated in U.S. dollars, whereas typical equity investments were not.[17]

After 1962 the situation improved with the appointment of Eugene Black as president. In the mid-1960s the corporation became a more experienced venture capital investor and a more successful partner, with additional investors and projects. The expansion of its gross investments (as opposed to the net investments financed from its own funds) demonstrates that underwritings and syndications became an important part of its activities. Nonetheless, the emphasis on foreign investment meant that the IFC was going against a trend in its member countries where restrictions and regulations grew. In many of these countries the investment climate worsened. Apart from promoting and financing development banks in the 1960s, the IFC invested in capital and intermediate goods industries like iron and steel, nonferrous metals, timber pulp and paper, fertilizer, etc.[18]

When Robert McNamara took over the bank, poverty alleviation became a priority of the bank's activities and many of the IFC's initiatives in industrial action shifted to the bank itself. New leadership at the IFC (e.g., Executive Vice President William Gaud, appointed by McNamara) leaned away from equity. More important though, as inflation outstripped interest rates in the 1970s, borrowing became a more attractive way to finance commercial activities than equity. Oil money propelled commercial banks to expand lending to developing countries, and opportunities opened for the IFC to support and participate in that lending. Hence the IFC's mode of operations shifted dramatically from equity investment to straight loans. The venture investor was gone and the commercial banker took over. The image of the IFC at the time was not of development, but of assistance to multinational corporations for penetration of the developing world.[19]

As the decolonization project continued to unfold, and the IFC was finding its niche in the constellation of multilateral arrangements dedicated to development, states formed a series of regional development banks to extend credit to industrial enterprises that could not easily raise funds in the domestic or foreign capital market. Nineteen Latin American and Caribbean countries together with the United States formed the oldest and largest of these, the Inter-American Development Bank, in 1959. Later, eight other Western nations joined the bank. The African Development Bank was established in 1964 and the Asian Development Bank in 1966. As was the case with the Inter-American Development Bank, the latter two had regional developing members as well as the United States and other Western nations as members.

Taken together, the Bretton Woods structure that emerged after the war was a system that embodied the concept of embedded liberalism as it had evolved in the West, meaning an essentially liberal capitalist world order with provisions for state policy. Postwar planners were influenced not only by John Maynard Keynes, but also by Karl Polanyi, who warned of the dangers of orthodox liberalism's "self-regulating market" with little concern about its effects on society. Hence postwar planners designed the international economic order on the basis of an interventionist or embedded liberal compromise. That is, postwar efforts to maintain an open liberal international economy were embedded in societal efforts to provide domestic security and stability for the populace.[20] The structure differed from the colonial system because it was a system of sovereign states. But it was nonetheless a system that promoted "development." Some argued this concept was merely a cosmetic substitution for imperialism.[21]

International financial organizations were to cushion domestic economies from external disruptions and promote domestic stability. As such, they embarked on an ambivalent relationship with both the states and the New York financial community. On the one hand, the organizations threatened certain lucrative businesses of the private investment banks and competed with them for business. On the other hand, they were clients of major investment banks such as First Boston and Morgan Stanley.[22] Government guarantees required for bank involvement facilitated a variety of business activities that would not have otherwise been possible.

## Foreign Direct Investment and Overseas Finance

In addition to the proliferation of multilateral institutions after World War II, multinational corporations arose as a second structural feature that changed the postwar landscape of the international political economy. As was discussed in chapter 2, the corporate form had certainly existed and operated in many countries since its origins in the sixteenth century. However, postwar American aid to Europe (much of it channeled through the multilateral institutions) set the stage for large amounts of U.S. private investment there. Moreover, the multinational that arose after the war utilized global systems of production and was, at least for a time, regarded as an American business form.[23]

While most American foreign direct investment was directed at other advanced industrial economies, the rise of the American corporation is significant because with the American form, financial power was fragmented after the Glass-Steagall reforms, and managerial power was much more heavily concentrated than in the American firms' European counterparts. Multinational investment made New York City somewhat less important as a financial power immediately after the war, because multinational corporations could raise capital through financial intermediaries in all of the United States's regional centers.[24] Therefore American corporations sought direct managerial control over their subsidiaries in the former European colonies where they invested, and were not dependent on local sources of finance.

Since the economic power of the postwar multinationals rivaled that of many of the newer, smaller states, theorists argued that they held the potential to eclipse the state as the defining characteristic of the international system.[25] While the state has endured, multinationals did nonetheless reconfigure some important firm-state relations, particularly with respect to the international structures of particular industries and the strength of individual firms seeking market access.[26]

As Europe recovered from the war, the World Bank changed its focus and the pattern of foreign direct investment changed as well. Table 3.1 shows the escalating growth rates of flows of foreign direct investment from Western countries to developing countries in current dollars. The United States supplied approximately two-thirds of global foreign investment from 1965 to 1969. From 1975 to 1979, however, foreign direct investment from the original six European Economic Community (EEC) countries, Canada, and Japan grew, as did the number of the world's 50 largest industrial firms headquartered outside the United States. Hence, when the multinational was decreasingly identifiable as an American business form, the United States only accounted for 48% of foreign direct investment from 1975 to 1979, and 28% from 1980 to 1981.[27]

Nonetheless, regardless of the source, the recipient pattern of private direct investment had not shifted dramatically from the colonial era. Figure 3.1 depicts a breakdown of Western countries' investment by region in 1978, showing Central and South American countries continued to receive the lion's share, and African countries continued to account for little foreign investment.

TABLE 3.1 Average Annual Growth Rates of Flows of Direct Foreign Investment from Developed[a] Countries to Developing Countries, 1960–1978 (in Current Dollars)

| Years | Average annual growth rates |
|---|---|
| 1960–1968 | 7.0% |
| 1968–1973 | 9.2% |
| 1973–1978 | 19.4% |

Source: Derived from OECD *Development Co-Operation*, various years, and unpublished data provided by the Development Assistance Committee. As printed in *International Investment and Multinational Enterprises, Recent International Direct Investment Trends*, Paris: OECD, 1981, p. 43.

[a]The developed countries include Australia, Austria, Belgium, Canada, Denmark, Finland, France, Germany, Italy, Japan, Netherlands, New Zealand, Norway, Switzerland, United Kingdom, and the United States.

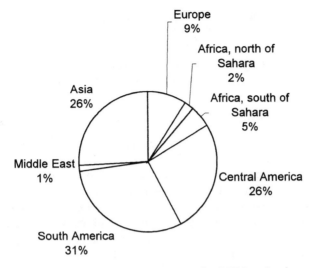

FIGURE 3.1. Developed countries' stock of FDI in developing countries by host region, end 1978. *Source:* OECD, *International Investment and Multinational Enterprises,* Paris: OECD, 1981, p. 46.

Capital outflows only finance a proportion of all international direct investment, at least for older, established investing countries. In the late 1960s and early 1970s the U.S. firms' share of reinvested earnings (compared with other forms of financing like capital flows) increased from an average of 41% in 1966–1971, peaked at 86% in 1974, and remained stable at about 60% after that year. These figures hint that borrowing locally was an important source of financing for U.S. firms during these years, although the amount appears to fluctuate much more as a residual of asset changes.[28]

A multinational corporation setting up or continuing operations in a developing country had a variety of financing options available to it; in some ways similar to and in other ways different from the British global firms of the nineteenth century. In a similar fashion to British global firms, the postwar multinational corporation could raise money at home either through debt or equity, or it could raise money overseas. Unlike the situation with nineteenth century British global firms, twentieth century transnational corporations now conducted their overseas operations in juridically sovereign territories. Thus equity capital acquired a political dimension connected to "development" strategies.

The key difference that emerged in the developing world between the earlier era and the postcolonial era was in the political purpose of raising equity capital in a particular locale. Whereas equity markets in the United States, Europe, and nineteenth-century empires evolved in response to the need for capital generated by the industrial revolution, the postcolonial exchanges reflected the increasing acceptance of economic intervention for political purposes. That is, it mattered to the new state in question that the equity market was located where it was. Some state goals were developmental: where they encouraged markets, states sought financial deepening and more advanced market institutions to finance other goals. Other state goals were strictly political: local securities markets forced foreign firms to diversify ownership and in turn democratize their economic systems.[29]

## Economic Nationalism in Postcolonial States

The third structural change in the international political economy of the postwar era that transformed the nature of equity finance was the rise of economic nationalism in the postcolonial states. Depending on the nature of the revolution that ousted foreign influences, stock markets were closed, large firms nationalized, or multinationals' local shares listed in an attempt to diversify ownership. In most cases, new states saw stock markets in strongly symbolic terms. Moreover, states sought to achieve a degree of direct control over economic enterprise by active engagement in economic development. Yet the various strategies meant that some emerging market stock exchanges shrank in this era, while others grew.

### Retrenchment of Equity Shares

The most dramatic retrenchment of equity finance occurred in states that experienced Communist revolutions. Thus the Shanghai Stock Exchange stands out as a prominent turn-of-the-century exchange that disappeared completely, since Communist ideology prohibited the private ownership of the means of production and finance was handled through state-owned banks that implemented the directives of a planned economy. Although not colonial exchanges, a similar transformation occurred in eastern Europe under Soviet domination. Of the states that had functioning stock exchanges, many ceased trading in the economic turmoil of the Great Depression of the 1930s. They were then completely disbanded in Communist takeovers.

A less dramatic break occurred in states experimenting with socialism. In many of these cases, the colonial stock exchange became irrelevant as states bought shares of firms when they nationalized industries, and thus trading slowed to a miniscule amount or ceased altogether. Indonesia is an example of this type. The market closed in 1958 when the Sukarno regime nationalized Dutch assets. Egypt is another example during the Nasser regime in the 1960s. Nasser's military government nationalized almost all large-scale Egyptian commercial firms.

Of the colonial exchanges that continued to function, much of the activity centered on trades of transnational corporations that governments had encouraged (or forced) to list shares. The Indian government was the first such state to insist that wholly owned subsidiaries of transnational firms list shares locally and to establish ownership requirements for Indian nationals. The Suharto regime likewise instituted national ownership requirements on shares of foreign firms when it resurrected the Jakarta Stock Exchange in 1977. Suharto announced that foreign-owned companies must transfer a majority of their shares to Indonesian nationals, specifically ethnic Pribumi, because critics of his regime had argued that economic development benefited foreign firms, corrupt government officials, and ethnic Chinese. Therefore, when Suharto reopened the exchange, it was a response to political pressure and against the advice of many Western advisers counseling in favor of developing banks and a stronger long-term debt market first.[30] In time, however, the Jakarta exchange became an importance source for these transnationals to raise capital.[31]

Latin American states with longstanding equities markets progressed somewhat less dramatically through these years, since the era of decolonization had occurred earlier. The exchanges did not embody the same postcolonial symbolism, although trading slowed on most of them as developmental states preferred directed bank lending to equity finance. In addition, wealthy individuals in these states preferred to hold real assets, or to remove their capital from the country completely, than to hold equity shares. Hyperinflation and tax policies reinforced the trend.[32] Some early notable examples did prove to be exceptions. Brazil, for example, incorporated capital market development into its developmental strategy in the 1960s with a plan to create fiscal investment funds. Although the plan was an initial success, the government did not continue the program following a market crash in 1971.

### New Exchanges in New States

In the examples of new states that did not have colonial exchanges, many moved to establish a national stock exchange regardless of its institutional compatibility with broader developmental goals. In this sense, the exchanges were promoted as symbols of nationhood and were connected to the state's economic prestige in the same way airlines symbolized global reach and battleships symbolized military might. For some states, the efforts to establish an exchange at this time ended with the construction of a stock exchange building. Others echoed the themes of the Indian and Indonesian strategies to broaden the ownership base of enterprises, improve the distribution of income, raise the level of domestic savings, and provide more reliable, risk-related long-term finance for industry.[33]

The initial group of new exchanges appeared in many new states that had been created from colonial territories that had had an exchange. For example, several stock exchanges formed and disbanded in the city of Lahore in northern Pakistan between 1934 and 1947. During the war years, three stock exchanges operated. They closed in 1947 when most of the city's prominent business families were displaced. When Pakistan became a separate juridical unit from India, Karachi became the center of business activity. Without access to the Bombay Stock Exchange, a group of entrepreneurs assembled to trade shares. Thus the Karachi Stock Exchange came into being on September 18, 1947, and other exchanges followed in Dacca and Lahore.[34]

Likewise, securities trading in Malaysia dates to the era of British rule. The British colonized the Malay peninsula and used Singapore as their commercial center. Thus both colonies used the same currency. When a formal stock exchange was established in May 1960, companies registered in Singapore and the Malay peninsula traded shares in Singapore. A formal political union between the two territories occurred in 1963, however, the Federation of Malaysia expelled Singapore in 1965. Nonetheless, the two countries retained a common currency until 1973, the same year Malaysia adopted its own Securities Act and established the Kuala Lumpur Stock Exchange. Despite the split, many Malaysian-registered companies remain listed on the stock exchange of Singapore, and vice versa. The two exchanges split conclusively in 1990.[35]

Of the new states that established stock exchanges where no colonial exchange had existed, Kenya was the first in sub-Saharan Africa in 1958. The exchange came about through the initiative of stockbrokers who had been dealing securities sporadically, and at times regionally. The Nairobi exchange financed a degree of productive investment, and the Kenyan public spending deficit, but it operated mostly as a means of noncoercive indigenization of the country's economy. Although it is one of the largest on the continent, it is not a major source of capital for the private sector, and the public at large holds only a limited number of shares.[36]

In 1967 Morocco was the first francophone African country to set up a stock exchange. As far back as 1929, Moroccan companies had issued, placed, and traded shares on the French market. The leading banks of Casablanca set up a rudimentary secondary market in the *Office de Compensation de Valeurs Mobilieres* that dealt with any issues of Moroccan companies not quoted abroad. Yet this market had been a small one, and really more of an appendix to a foreign one. Stockholders fixed prices arbitrarily and dealings only cleared once a week. When the French left in 1956, the market crashed. The 1967 exchange did not expressly state "Moroccanization" as a goal, however, when new companies list, they normally reserve a share subscription for persons of Moroccan nationality.[37] Similarly, the Tunisian exchange set up in Tunis in 1967 did not make an overt indigenization effort.[38]

Later exchanges created in Africa and elsewhere increasingly did express indigenization of shares as a goal. For example, the government of Nigeria established the Lagos exchange in 1961 and used it as the principle means of coercing business indigenization. Firms went along with much of the "Nigerianization" project as a way of reducing their own investment of risk capital. Most were typical of the time: joint ventures with foreign firms, and colonial firms offering a degree of participation. The first offering was made prior to the opening of the formal exchange. The Federal Government of Nigeria, the Eastern Region Government, the Colonial Development Corporation, and the Tunnel Portland Cement Company Ltd. (the project manager) sponsored the company, the Nigerian Cement Company Ltd. The second offering was a portion of the wholly owned subsidiary of British American Tobacco Company Ltd., a firm operating in Nigeria since 1951. The prospectus for the offering stated that it was offering a share in equity capital of the company to strengthen the bond of common interest between the company and the Nigerian public. In the third public issue, John Holt & Company Ltd. attempted to dispel the negative feeling toward itself. It had controlled a large amount of foreign trade since the nineteenth century, and was thus associated with the colonial period.[39] In 1972 and 1977, the government required the largest companies to transfer portions of their equity to local shareholders. In addition, the government set limits on individual holdings and at times even set the offering price to the public at below-market levels.[40]

Seeking almost total indigenization of equity capital, the South Korean stock exchange, reestablished in the 1960s, heavily restricted foreign investment. The previous exchange had ended with the period of Japanese colonialism, and Korean government officials sought to avoid a resurgence of foreign control of the state's economy. Thus the exchange was situated within a broader developmental state that allocated credit mainly through the banking system.

## Analysis and Conclusion

The postwar era for equity finance in emerging markets changed dramatically along with the entire structure of the international system, which had been transformed by the war. Great Britain was no longer the financial center, the United States was. Colonialism ceased to exist as a viable form of political organization and newly sovereign states were connected to the international financial system through a series of multilateral organizations. As the number of new states grew, the purposes and number of these organizations grew to manage problems associated with economic development. The developmental aspirations of the new states and new organizations implicitly accorded a high degree of state involvement in economic activity. Therefore economic intervention resulted in a retrenchment of equity finance in many emerging markets and a nationalist, symbolic start in others.

None of these exchanges were created to act as autonomous institutions for monitoring corporate performance through the price mechanism, along the lines of the American or British model. Many, such as the Seoul Stock Exchange, prohibited foreign investment outright. Thus the equity finance that appeared (and disappeared) in the postcolonial world of the 1960s and 1970s was a vehicle of state engagement and management of economies. Corporations and international organizations did not seek equity market development in these years, but states did. However, corporations used foreign listings to a certain degree of advantage in terms of political capital and foreign exchange.

Equity markets underwent some significant changes of their own in the United States and Britain of the 1970s. The NYSE abolished fixed commission rates on "Mayday"—May 1, 1975. The idea behind the abolition of the commissions was that a stock exchange could not operate as a private club with rules that prevented market access by nonmembers; the new rule required a fixed, minimum, nonnegotiable per-share commission rate.[41] Also in the early 1970s, the over-the-counter automated quotation system, or NASDAQ, opened in the United States. The computerized system meant that market makers on over-the-counter stocks could quote prices on a computer screen that could be accessed by brokers nationwide. This development made trading in many of the smaller stocks easier. But more important, NASDAQ commissions were flexible.[42] Despite these changes, money did not flow into the U.S. stock market. Interest rates rose, and the money flowed instead into money market funds introduced by brokerage houses and investment companies that could pay higher interest than banks. (During those years banks were still subject to U.S. Federal Reserve limitations on the amount of interest they could pay to depositors.)

October 27, 1986, is generally accepted as the "Big Bang" on the London Stock Exchange. At that time, the London Stock Exchange merged with the International Security Regulatory Organization, abolished fixed commission rates, eliminated the "single capacity" system, which prevented stock exchange members from acting both as brokers (agents) for customers and dealers (principals) for their own accounts, established a new system for trading securities, and lifted membership restrictions so British firms and financial institutions could participate. The new trading system, called the Stock Exchange Automated Quotation (SEAQ), was modeled on the NASDAQ and replaced the traditional exchange-floor arrangements that had existed from the nineteenth century. The automated system lends itself to 24-hour operation, and more members. By 1987 the London Stock Exchange sought to become the world's leading market for internationally traded shares.[43]

However, in the immediate postwar years until the debt crisis of the 1980s, equity finance in the developing world was primarily a function of governments' attempts to control large-scale enterprises, and not private owners' attempts. Multilateral lending agencies created after the war reflected states' preferences for bank lending and a degree of government intervention in the development process. Therefore, while the exchanges served a business purpose in some cases, their value was mostly nationalistic.

# Globalization without Integration: International Considerations

The experiments with equity finance in the 1960s and 1970s left a patchwork of local stock exchanges in the developing world, where few shares were listed and little trading occurred. These markets held few advantages for either states or firms over markets in more developed countries, particularly when most of the controlling blocs of shares were held by citizens outside the state in question, when costs were higher in the peripheral markets, and when shares were difficult to issue. Moreover, the exchanges were not deeply embedded within the overall financial institutional structure. Bank finance predominated this structure, and state allocation of commercial credit conditioned it. Governments exerted direct control over management of state-owned firms.

Nonetheless, a dramatic change began to unfold in the 1980s. Whereas in the early 1980s most Latin American countries had stock market capitalizations of 5% to 10% of GDP, by 1994 most Latin American market capitalizations rose to between 50% and 100% of GDP. East Asian market capitalizations relative to the size of the individual economies grew similarly during the same years. At the speculative peak in 1994, many East Asian countries had stock markets with values approaching 100% of GDP.[1] This and the following chapter begin to consider how the growth in equity finance has occurred and the manner in which markets have connected to each other. Taken together, the two chapters propose that political explanations provide a more complete picture of the changes than a focus on financial considerations alone, because political considerations allow for an introduction of analyses of control of the firm.

This book advances the metaphor of a two-level game to understand how control results from the symbiotic interaction of national and international political imperatives. That is, economic policymakers must operate on two negotiating levels simultaneously to arrive at economic solutions that are politically practical. The international level (level I) imperatives explored in this chapter explain the widespread appearance of new listings and exchanges, similarities in their operations, and the overall increase in the use of equity finance around the world.

Domestic politics (level II), introduced in the next chapter, explain the rapid advance in the nature and size of share supply even when control of the firm becomes an issue for states supplying shares.[2]

The international (level I) considerations explored here arise from the particular historical circumstances associated with sovereign debt in the 1980s and 1990s. A new era of multilateral influence over the day-to-day operations of governments in developing countries began with Mexico's declaration of a moratorium on its international debt payments in 1982. Difficulties in rescheduling massive debts concentrated in a few states facilitated the entry of public institutions into the rescheduling process.[3] When the World Bank became involved in broader-ranging conditionally based lending programs, termed structural adjustment loans, its policies were closely linked to the IMF's arrangements.[4] The conditionality requirements of the structural adjustment loans accelerated the process of globalization by tying the physical resources of developing countries more firmly into the global economy. Simultaneously, structural adjustment facilitated the financial machinery (such as stock markets) necessary to transport wealth into and out of states.

The IFC (a part of the World Bank Group) actively promoted equity finance in the 1980s; thus many similarities resulting from these international efforts with respect to equity finance are apparent. The IFC, like other international organizations, has states as members (or more appropriately shareholders). Thus it is acutely aware of the political realities associated with equity finance. Much of the IFC's early work was done in the funds industry, where control of the firms whose shares were included was an ongoing consideration of IFC advisors. Later, IFC advisors worked with government officials in Africa and the former Communist bloc to write securities regulations and set up functioning stock exchanges. In these cases, policymakers retained their concern for influencing who would control large enterprise in a given state.

Local stock exchanges are a necessity for certain kinds of equity finance attempted in this period because of the listing requirements of the large transnational exchanges. Local investors own roughly 90% of the market capitalization of emerging markets. Nevertheless, the impact of the 10% market capitalization sourced abroad is disproportionate to its volume.[5] Therefore the result of the efforts of international financial institutions and international investors is an increasingly *globalized* system of equity transactions in terms of market regulations, custody arrangements, software operations, etc. However, shares are not *integrated*, in the sense that they do not move around the globe interchangeably.

This chapter therefore focuses on international imperatives for equity market development in the 1980s and 1990s, and their connection to each other. It first considers the set of policies emanating from the debt crisis of the 1980s, and how the crisis reconfigured certain international organizations. This investigation underscores the issue of equity within the international financial organizations, chiefly within the World Bank and its affiliate, the IFC. The chapter then explores the structural changes associated with the collapse of Communism, and the role the IMF and World Bank played in promoting equity products there. Finally, the chapter considers the set of issues associated with the listing requirements of the markets for international equities. These issues are significant for states that privatized firms and also for states that use equity markets to attract foreign capital flows. The following chapter completes the picture of the markets beyond their seeming similarities, with an investigation of what equity products states offer for sale and how those products fit into the ownership structure of the firm.

## The Debt Crisis of the 1980s

A set of international developments in the 1980s culminated in pressure on individual governments for action with respect to debt. That pressure eventually resulted in a turn to equity finance. The financing schemes of states in the 1970s created a dramatic buildup of sovereign debt to private banks in a system where lending was connected across states, but equity finance was not. New lending procedures such as credit syndication and floating-rate loans had broadened lender participation, and the lenders targeted certain developing states as clients.[6] Of this private debt, Brazil alone accounted for 30% of all non-oil developing countries, and a limited number of additional states in Latin America and East Asia comprised most of the rest. All of the non-oil, less-developed African states owed less than 9%.[7] When the general commodity price boom ended in the late 1970s it was accompanied by the second oil shock.

This combination of factors continued the need for high levels of borrowing, yet diminished the resources to service the debt. Eventually the interest rates on these loans rose, since they were not fixed, and an overall squeeze in international liquidity made the debt service unmanageable. At the same time, a paradigmatic shift in thinking concerning development had taken place in the West, roughly corresponding to the rise of Margaret Thatcher in the United Kingdom and Ronald Reagan in the United States. Specific neoclassical ideas informed the "new" paradigm, summed up as the four "ations," that is, stabilization, liberalization, deregulation, and privatization. Policy changes associated with these ideas aimed to realign exchange rates, improve price incentives, lessen the role of the public sector, and expand the role of the private sector.

### International Financial Organizations and Equity

The debt crisis transformed the role of the IMF and World Bank. In its expanded role, the IMF focused on immediate stabilization agreements. It required that banks extend a certain level of commercial credit as a precondition for IMF participation in stabilization agreements. This precondition isolated regional banks reluctant to extend credit, but renewed the involvement of larger banks that approved of the collective action IMF involvement made possible. In the early years of the Latin American crisis, the IMF, along with the Federal Reserve and U.S. Treasury, were the more conspicuous actors. As the World Bank expanded its role through structural adjustment lending (SAL), it focused on longer-term issues associated with funding trade and institutional changes.[8]

As the pace of programs to deal with the crisis grew, the controversial nature of both the bank and the fund grew as well, since their lending programs incorporated expanded conditionality requirements. The degree of coercion involved in conditionally based loans (and its implications for the loan recipient's sovereignty) quickly became an important issue in associated literature. Whereas the donors tended to view conditionality as reinforcing a policy direction to which the recipient government was already committed, critics tended to view conditionality as the imposition of the donors' will on governments. Academic analysts have understood the requirements to be ones where donors "buy" reforms governments would otherwise hesitate to make.[9]

As explained in chapter 3, equity investment for development finance, as opposed to loans for development finance, had a rocky history within the constellation of international organizations established after World War II; the IFC was originally intended to be the locus within the World Bank Group for equity investment, yet was prohibited from holding stock in the enterprises it helped to finance until 1962. On one hand, the IFC was intended to help establish and expand sound private enterprises in the developing world by investing in profitable enterprises, sharing risks, and participating in gains. On the other hand, the IFC was viewed as a public institution that should not assume management responsibility for private enterprises lest the distinction between the two blur.[10] Therefore the corporation was supposed to pursue profitable projects without subsidizing their finance, yet it was also supposed to further economic development along the lines of the World Bank.

Some of this contradiction was resolved by the "catalytic" principle under which the IFC operated, that is, that the corporation should mobilize others' investment rather than simply investing for itself. After an initially slow start, the IFC had grown in the 1960s into an experienced venture capital investor. It worked more closely with foreign investors in joint ventures and expanded into new sectors. Its direction shifted away again, however, when Robert McNamara took over the World Bank Group in 1968. Nonetheless, many of the developments that occurred under Robert McNamara's leadership laid the groundwork for equity initiatives to come.

One of the most significant of these developments resulted from the Commission on International Development—headed by Lester Pearson and also called the "Pearson Commission." The commission prepared a series of recommendations for the bank and its management in 1969, and addressed the tension between the corporation's development and profitability goals. It concluded that the development goals should take priority and the standard of project profitability could be lowered.[11] At the same time, the IFC could take responsibility for developing a project from its conception through putting together a final plan. Thus the project to result from the Pearson Commission was the initiation of a Capital Markets Department in 1971 to assist developing member countries in improving their capital and money markets.[12]

The goal of capital market development had been included as a clause in the Articles of the International Bank for Reconstruction and Development at Bretton Woods. Yet few professional economists acknowledged differences in the "quality" of money prior to the debt crisis. Of the few who had in the late 1960s, Raymond Goldsmith of Yale University, Alvin Shaw of Harvard, and Ronald McKinnon of Stanford addressed the issue in such as way that it convinced policymakers at the

IFC, and later in individual governments, of the incentives of strong equity markets. David Gill, who directed the Capital Markets Department of the IFC, considered Goldsmith's work on financial structure and the relationship between real growth and financial intermediation to be particularly useful.[13]

Goldsmith elaborated the need for capital market institutions in the developing world by arguing that in the course of a country's development, its financial superstructure grows more rapidly than the infrastructure of national product and national wealth. This increase slows after a point. Therefore the ratio of all financial instruments to tangible net national wealth rises to a number between 1 and 1.5 and then levels off. Developing countries have lower ratios, ranging from 0.33 to 0.66. The main determinant of the size of a country's financial superstructure for Goldsmith is the separation of the functions of saving and investing among different economic units and groups. The higher the ratio of new issues of debt and equity securities to national product, the more pronounced the separation of the processes of saving and capital formation. Equity securities issues are stalled in developing countries because of the limitations imposed in many countries on equity ownership by financial institutions. Thus corporate stock is predominantly owned directly by individual shareholders.[14]

As a policy measure, enlarging the range of financial assets increases the efficiency of investment and raises the ratio of capital formation to national product. Broader markets enlarge the circle of potential buyers and sellers, and of potential transactions, eliminating the need for every buyer and seller to find a partner for the same object at the same place and at the same time. Hence a financial superstructure accelerates economic growth and improves economic performance to the extent that it facilitates the migration of funds to the best user, that is, to the place in the economic system where the funds will yield the highest social return. Influenced by Goldsmith's theories, IFC economists reasoned that a Capital Markets Department could promote economic performance by creating financial infrastructures. Although actual projects proceeded slowly at first, from 1971 through June 1988, 73 countries requested and received capital markets assistance in various forms from the IFC's Capital Markets Department. In 50 of these countries, the assistance was specifically for securities market development.

When the Latin American debt crisis first broke out in the early 1980s, the IFC was experiencing a series of changes in leadership.[15] Nonetheless, in the 1980s the groundwork laid by the Capital Markets Department allowed it to progress on several additional initiatives that promoted equity financing in the developing world. For example, in an individual government technical assistance project, the IFC worked on a multiyear project in Chile from 1980 to 1986 in a joint effort to write the Securities Law and Companies Law. Six years later the IFC helped to rewrite both laws to reflect market experience.[16] Other initiatives, however, would not just focus on one state. They would connect core markets with peripheral markets, and thus reconfigure the manner in which capital could pass from one to the other.

One of the earliest and most significant of these transnational initiatives was the creation of the Emerging Markets Data Base (EMDB) that began a major contribution to the knowledge of equity markets in developing countries necessary to expand investment there. This project, directed by Antoine Van Agtmael and assisted by Peter Wall and Vihang Errunza, documented price, dividend, and capitalization changes for more than 200 companies from 10 developing countries (representing 40% of market capitalization and the most actively traded stocks) beginning in 1975. It was later increased to 17 countries and more than 400 companies.

The EMDB was significant because it was the first time a comprehensive database had been compiled on developing countries. From this data, price indices could be developed, allowing the comparison of actual stock performance from developing countries with industrialized countries. Since then, other publications and electronic information services, including Morgan Stanley Capital International, Salomon Brothers, and Reuters, have slowly included more developing country markets as part of their global market coverage.[17] The increasing volume of research on the markets from the investment banks, and gradually from major financial publications, meant that international investors could obtain detailed reports and forecasts on emerging markets.[18]

In time, the IFC's board confirmed a set of redefined guidelines for cooperation with the World Bank. According to the 1991 guidelines, the bank would take primary responsibility for promoting private-sector development in the fields of macroeconomic and sectoral policies, and in shaping the institutional environment. It would work on the framework for privatization, and the financing of social and physical infrastructures. The IFC, for its part, would work on direct transactions with the private sector, on institution building for capital markets, and on advising foreign investment policies and privatization. Thus the IFC would participate in the bank's country strategy process in the area of private-sector development.[19]

### The IFC and Emerging Market Funds

Another key initiative in the 1980s of the Capital Markets Department was the corporation's sponsorship of foreign portfolio investment in emerging markets with country and regional closed-end funds. Funds pool a variety of equities subject to regulations set forth in its prospectus. Hence the extent of control of the firms whose shares are included can be clarified from the outset. Funds are then structured into "open" or "closed" types. With a closed-end fund, a sum is raised and the shareholder group is closed. Shares are then traded (on an exchange or privately) at whatever price the market will bear, either above or below the sum of the underlying assets' net value. With an open-end fund, the manager agrees to sell or to buy back any shares at the published daily net asset value (NAV). Open-end funds grow or shrink as investors buy or sell their shares. The concept of closed-end funds was far from new. King William I of the Netherlands is said to have formed the first one in 1822. More recently, the Japan Fund of 1962 was the first country-specific fund.

Closed-end investment funds appealed to developing states in the 1980s because they eased concerns about volatile money flows. By definition, when investors sell shares of the fund, the investment manager is not forced to sell the fund's portfolio. Therefore, if a number of investors choose to sell their shares of the fund simultaneously, the share price drops with respect to NAV, but the manager does not need to sell the underlying assets. The first country fund to be formed with IFC involvement was the Mexico Fund, created in 1981. Although the IFC advised on the fund's structure, it did not underwrite it in the end, due to concerns over the lack of separation between government and fund management. It was not a success. Mexico defaulted on its foreign debt in 1982 and the fund fell 75% from its offering price.[20]

However, the Korea Fund, launched in 1984, sparked a real expansion of this type of transnational investment between 1987 and 1992.[21] Unlike the Mexican Bolsa, the Korean Stock Exchange had been virtually closed to foreign investment. Nonetheless, international investors had been seeking shares there because they perceived that Korean firms would one day compete successfully with U.S. firms. These investors' inquiries at the Korean Ministry of Finance in the 1970s had revealed that the Koreans objected strongly to foreign ownership, particularly Japanese ownership.[22] Therefore a group of investors existed that were interested in the possibilities inherent in the Korean economy, and continued to search for ways to invest for purposes of return, exclusive of control.

The government's concerns about foreign investment meant that when the IFC began work on a fund, it used the Japan Fund as a model and attempted to address two key concerns with respect to control of the firms included in the fund: the issue of governance of the firms whose equities the fund holds, and the issue of governance of the fund itself. The structure of the Korea Fund as a closed-end investment vehicle addressed the first issue. It was structured so that it could only use up to 5% of its total assets for the securities of a single issuer. No more than 25% of the fund's total assets could be invested in a single industry. Furthermore, the fund could not purchase any security if it would then own more than 5% of any class of securities of an issuer or make investments for the purpose of exercising control or management. The goal of the fund at its inception was long-term capital appreciation through investment in Korean securities listed on the Korean Stock Exchange. Therefore the Korea Fund did not seek to enter into the management of any of the firms in which it invested or influence the industrial sectors of the Korean economy in which it invested.[23]

Unlike the Mexico Fund, the Korea Fund was a success. Once it launched, many similar closed-end investment products appeared in different settings. In the 10 years between FY1977 and FY1986, the IFC approved 18 country, regional, and venture capital funds, with IFC investment totaling US$51 million. In the six years between FY1987 and FY1992, it approved 62 funds totaling US$354 million.[24] Much of the language in the prospectus for the Korea Fund served as an overt model for later closed-end funds.

Regardless of the speed with which the industry grew, plans for other closed-end country funds had been in the making for several years at the IFC and in its host governments. The IFC had worked with the Brazilian government, for example, two and a half years prior to the Brazil Fund's launch to open its stock market to foreign portfolio investors. In that particular instance, the Brazilian government refused to approve the deal at the last minute, and the IFC did not play a "participant" role in the final deal as it had in Korea.[25] Nonetheless, having advised the government for a period of time, the corporation did influence the context within which the financial actors and Brazilian treasury concluded the deal. The Brazil and Argentina funds were nearly Korea Fund clones in that they were developed with governments, listed on the NYSE, and managed by the investment counsel firm of Scudder, Stevens, and Clark.

Following the successful country funds, the IFC initiated one of the early *global* emerging market funds in 1986. The genesis of the idea was a 1977 mandate to the corporation from the development committee of the World Bank to create a global fund. It would mobilize foreign capital and act as an incentive for domestic investors to invest in the stock markets of their own countries. When the IFC could not raise sufficient funds from other investors, it requested authorization to invest an additional US$2.2 million to reach the US$50 million minimum size, giving the IFC a 17.4% share along with 12 private institutional investors. The Reagan administration supported what came to be called the Emerging Market Growth Fund (EMGF), even while private actors in the investment community remained skeptical.[26]

The IFC selected Los Angeles-based Capital Research and Management Company to manage the EMGF because the firm was willing to devote substantial resources to the project without prospects for immediate profits. Ultimately the fund turned out to be one of Capital's most profitable projects. After the EMGF performed well, two private placements in 1988 and 1989, and other public offerings in 1992 raised a total of US$2.6 billion. Templeton (which had left talks with the IFC for managing the EMGF on issues of fund governance) listed a similar closed-end fund directed at emerging markets on the NYSE in 1987.[27]

The EMGF altered the structural context within which the emerging market funds industry operates in that its manager began intensive visits to emerging market companies to obtain detailed, reliable information on them. During the EMFG's first year, Capital visited more than 150 companies, and by 1994 it visited 500 per year.[28] The board of directors for the EMGF set the broad policy and country exposure limits based on the recommendations of Capital Research's managers. Therefore, since the initial investors elected the first board, the governance of the fund was structured to be independent from any government control.

The popularity of funds with investors propelled the emerging markets industry further. While the economic "fundamentals" of a country in question appear to drive foreign direct investment, investors who hope to benefit from undiscovered opportunities in fast-growing developing countries, diversify their risks in markets outside their own, and leave the management to others appear to drive portfolio investment. As was the case with the Korea Fund, a fund is attractive if it retains a monopoly on the shares it comprises, and is thus the only means of diversification into a given market. At first, retail investors (particularly high net worth individuals) bought the funds; later, institutional investors took over as the main buyers of these funds.

Eventually the closed-end investment fund industry declined in volume of capital flow. In terms of products, investors prefer open-end funds. Many of the funds exhibited mediocre performance and most trade below NAV. Many of the previously closed markets have opened to foreign investors. Some investors switched to a strategy of purchasing shares of multinational corporations with global holdings, reasoning that diversification was implicit in holding these shares. Furthermore, financial firms do not market closed-end funds as aggressively, probably because they are not as profitable as other financial products. By 1995, 50% of all emerging market funds were open-end.[29] In 1997 only 8 new closed-end funds appeared in the United States, and 25 closed-end funds merged, liquidated, or converted to open-end.[30] This development is not unexpected, however, because many of the early funds (such as the Korea Fund) were intended to open markets so that an array of investment products could follow.

Although the IFC's investment in the closed-end funds industry now appears to have been merely an episode in a broader process of market opening, the early funds were important because local investors grew more inclined to invest in a local stock market when foreign fund managers pushed for certain reforms such as faster settlement times, more reliable depository services, efficient clearing, and better enforcement of securities regulations. Therefore, as stated at the beginning of the chapter, whereas only 10% of holdings may be foreign, the influence of the foreign investment is disproportionate.

As the closed-end funds industry matured and private investment banks moved into the area, the IFC itself concentrated on special sector funds with unlisted investments, and individual corporations. The volume of these investments was considerable. In the three years between FY1993 and FY1995, the IFC approved 94 funds totaling US$671 million. However, these were index funds, bond funds, infrastructure-/industry-directed funds, and private funds. Later efforts were made to establish venture capital funds in Africa and transition countries, mutual and pension funds, and private equity funds.[31]

## The African Debt Crisis and the Collapse of Communism in the 1990s

As the Latin American debt crisis wore on, the financial crisis in Africa deepened in a different manner. A study by the Non-Aligned Movement concluded that, using 20% into arrears as a benchmark for "crisis" status in 1992, 38 African states could have been classified as having a "debt crisis," while only 13 Latin American and Caribbean states did, 6 Asian ones did, and 1 European one did (the former Yugoslavia). The average arrears of African, Latin American and Caribbean, Asian, and European states in 1992 were 84.5%, 71.6%, 63.8%, and 30.5% of scheduled debt service, respectively.[32] Significantly for Africans, though, the debt situation evolved not only in terms of who owed, but in terms of to whom it was owed, because African debt remained principally owed to official creditors.[33] Therefore the African accumulation never threatened the private banking system as the Latin American accumulation did. It did tie African states' economic management closer to international organizations than the Latin American crisis did.

African debtors treat multilateral institutions as "preferred creditors."[34] That is, when they are into arrears, the incidence of their arrears is greatest with respect to their debts to bilateral creditors and much less to their debts to multilateral institutions or private creditors. The total long-term debt of sub-Saharan African countries in 1992 was US$17.944 billion. Twenty-two percent of that amount was owed to multilateral financial institutions, 46% to governments and their agencies, and 32% to private creditors (or 78% to official creditors and 32% to private ones). Debt service payments, however, varied greatly—40% of total interest and amortization was paid to multilateral financial institutions, 14% to bilateral creditors, and 46% to private creditors. This means that multilateral creditors received 84% of the amount due, while private creditors received 69% and bilateral creditors only 14% of the total amount due.

African states' treatment of multilateral institutions as preferred creditors reinforced the relationship between the institution and the debtor state beyond what even the magnitude of the loans would imply. These sources are considered to be "lenders of last resort," and they have a certain difference in status. Therefore it is true that debt service payments to private creditors, which are all considered "nonconcessional," do accumulate faster than service payments to lenders of last resort.[35] However, at present, the significant difference in the patterns of debt outstanding and debt service payments—in particular between debt owed to multilateral creditors and debt owed to bilateral creditors—is not primarily due to different degrees of concessionality of debts. Rather, it is a logical consequence of the difference in status between multilateral and bilateral creditors.

Debt to "preferred creditors" is neither subject to rescheduling, nor to reduction, nor forgiveness. A country can only service multilateral creditors by incurring even larger arrears to bilateral and private creditors.[36] The increase in debt service payments (of the total 58 countries with arrears in excess of 20% in 1992) has been accompanied by a sharp decrease in loan disbursements. Therefore an increasingly larger portion of total debt service payments in Africa is directed to meet the stringent debt service requirements of multilateral creditors. African states are therefore more tightly connected to international organizations than their counterparts in Latin America, where private creditors played a role.

The connection between the African debt crisis and equity market development was both direct and indirect. For an example of indirect influence, when the IFC created its "investable index" of emerging market stocks in 1993, government authorities in Zimbabwe asked the corporation why Zimbabwe was not included. When the IFC responded with a list of requirements the Zimbabwean market did not meet, such as exchange controls on stock market purchases and prohibitions on foreigners owning stock, the government changed the regulations in a few months. By June 1993, foreign asset managers, analysts, and New York and London custodians traveled to Harare, and the market grew considerably.[37] Similar events transpired in Mauritius.

For an example of direct IFC influence on equity market development, the World Bank listed the creation of a stock exchange in Zambia as a condition of its 1993 Private Sector Development Loan. The government agreed that public listings would spread the ownership base of any widespread asset sale, and mutual funds could allow small savers to own shares. In March 1993, an IFC team visited Zambia, and by April a group of consultants (project manager, securities lawyer, stock exchange expert, trading specialist, and back-office/clearing specialist) were intensively working with a small Zambian team. They drafted laws, reviewed them, and put them into legislation by December. The systems were in place by January. However, the process halted for a year and a half after, when it became necessary to appoint a Securities Commissioner under the terms of the new legislation. The excruciatingly slow pace of the privatization program in Zambia further stalled market development. Only four companies listed for the first two years; Zambia Consolidated Copper Mines (a firm generating 43% of the country's GDP) listed its minority shares in Lusaka in early 1996.[38]

When the command economy model of economic management collapsed in eastern Europe in the 1990s, international organizations became involved in massive economic restructuring programs associated with privatizing government-owned firms. Privatizations of government-owned firms had been the most difficult of the Latin American restructurings because they contained the added issues of fair valuation and legitimate ownership change. Unlike the African cases, the eastern European restructurings had a much broader base of domestic political support and proceeded at a much more rapid pace. They drew on the expertise that the IFC had developed in the wake of the Latin American debt crisis of 1984, and the 1991 reforms that had clarified the relationship between the bank and the corporation with respect to privatization activity.

Therefore the IFC's capital markets work has extended across a range of activities that have promoted equity market growth and development since the 1980s. Some of these activities, such as the EMDB, created and disseminated information on emerging market firms that made cross-national comparisons possible. Other activities, such as the portfolio investment funds initiatives, made actual investments possible. Finally, corporate restructuring activities fostered privatized firms' actions in offering equity shares publicly. Since the IFC is often a partner with other agencies in its activities, the results are not completely uniform. Nonetheless, the public and private international consultants and investment bankers working on many deals around the globe did produce a certain degree of consistency. The appendix summarizes the IFC's activities in both financial sector and privatization activities for each of the emerging markets that will be examined in the next section of this book.

Incidentally, international organizations other than the IFC have also contributed to the seeming similarity of the markets. For example, the Inter-American Association of Securities Commissions (IOSCO) was founded in 1974 as the main multilateral vehicle for cooperation among securities regulators. The Basle Committee[39] has pressured this organization to negotiate capital standards for securities firms similar to those for banking. IOSCO has been working with the International Accounting Standards Committee to develop a core set of standards that might become a framework for financial reporting in cross-border securities offerings.

However, several problems exist with respect to IOSCO's work in this area. Chiefly, the broader membership in IOSCO than in the Basle Committee means that special problems related to the regulation of financial institutions in emerging markets arise. In addition, when IOSCO's working groups produce recommendations for its membership, they are advisory and nonbinding. Hence there is considerable disparity in terms of implementation of these recommendations.[40]

Finally, U.S. standards in accounting and disclosure differ from other countries. That is, the United States does not use a "merit" regulatory system (i.e., allowing only healthy companies to trade securities), but a "market" regulatory system (i.e., disclosure of full and fair risks to investors). To have international standards, the system would need auditors and regulators around the world to insist on rigorous interpretation and application of whatever set of standards were to be agreed upon. Otherwise the objectives of comparability and transparency will be eroded.[41]

The bulk of the actual project work of the international organizations with respect to equity therefore has been the work of the Capital Markets Department of the IFC, in concert with the IFC. This organization has been pulled throughout its history between the demands of being a profit-promoting entity and a public development agency. Therefore it exhibits a contradiction inherent in using private-sector firms to promote development when they have profit as a goal. The tension between profit goals and development goals is duplicated whenever private-sector firms are expected to act as development agents. The IFC's successes have been in expanding the types of financial products available to developing states as they disengage from active management of a firm.

## Listing Requirements of Transnational Exchanges

Many policymakers issue shares in accordance with the conditionality requirements of structural adjustment loans. Yet in some circumstances, domestic political initiatives compel politicians to privatize large firms, and thus issue shares. In other circumstances the state did not own shares outright. It may encourage the development of equity markets, however, in order to attract foreign, nondebt, capital inflows. When policymakers or business executives seek to initiate a public offering in the absence of international negotiations concerning sovereign debt, they need to consider the listing requirements of the international markets if they wish to tap deep international markets. These requirements can constitute a "second set" of level I imperatives that are not directly connected to those associated with structural adjustment lending. The upshot is that a given deal may be structured to comply with the requirements of transnational exchanges (e.g., disclosure may be more rigorous than for firms merely listing domestically), or it may be offered domestically simply because the transnational market is not available.

As discussed in chapter 1, the international market for equity securities is segmented into national markets with various listing requirements, and a relatively thin transnational market of large, well-known firms that issue equity shares across exchanges. Thus international investors may purchase shares of smaller, nationally listed firms by buying them through a broker in another country or by buying shares of a foreign firm (or its depository receipts) listed on their own national market.[42] However, shares of a foreign firm on their own national market are generally limited to large, transnational firms. In the example of foreign firms offering shares in the United States, most international market participants are sophisticated institutional investors because an individual must qualify (e.g., be willing to invest more than US$100,000) in order to purchase foreign securities in the United States that are privately placed. Thus many U.S. investors that own foreign equities own them indirectly through mutual funds.

International listing requirements pose a considerable barrier to relatively small firms being privatized from emerging markets as well as start-up firms from emerging markets. For example, the London Stock Exchange requires that securities admitted to the Official List comply with the disclosure obligations of the U.K. Listing Authority. To be admitted, a company seeking admission must attend a meeting at the exchange to discuss its application and identify a contact within the organization that will be responsible for communications with the exchange on an ongoing basis. Likewise, the NYSE requires that shares listed meet a minimum distribution criteria, as well as a market capitalization criteria. Both exchanges charge fees to listed companies.

Despite these requirements, some emerging market firms do list on transnational markets. However, these firms are generally located in larger developing countries, with deeper equity cultures and greater experience with sophisticated financial instruments. For comparative purposes, Figures 4.1 and 4.2 show the market capitalization of emerging market firms listed on two major international exchanges (London and New York) as of late 2001 and early 2002.

Of those listed in London, South African firms predominate overwhelmingly. Only South Korea, Greece, China, and Israel offer comparable numbers of shares. The sum total, however, of the entire South African market capitalization on the London Stock Exchange was £16,506; the market capitalization of Philip Morris, one individual U.S. firm cross-listed in London, was £72,671 million. The NYSE attracts a different geographical group: Latin American cross-listings predominate. In New York, Mexico cross-lists the most shares, followed by Brazil, Korea, Guernsey, Liberia, Argentina, Chile, and Panama.

In sum, when a firm decides to make a public offering of equity, it cannot necessarily offer shares on an international exchange, even if it would like to. The requirements of transnational exchanges constitute an additional set of level I considerations, which tend toward convergence in practice, and which need to be reconciled with the level II imperatives. Although many large western European privatizations have successfully offered international tranches, the parastatals of many low- to middle-income states divesting shares do not necessarily qualify for listings. Therefore, to broaden the menu of options available as a state divests and private firms in developing countries seek equity financing instruments, a local exchange is necessary. Many equity securities created from government privatizations, in particular, would not exist without local exchanges.

## Analysis and Conclusion

International actors such as international organizations and investors propelled equity market growth and linkages in significant ways during the 1980s and 1990s, although several projects had long gestation periods. The debt crises transformed the activities of the organizations and opened up a new role for private-sector development. As international investors saw new opportunities in these markets,

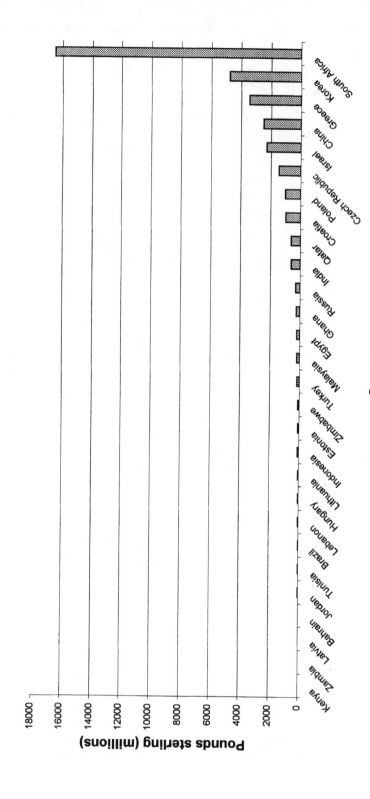

FIGURE 4.1. Market capitalization of emerging market firms listed in London. *Source:* London Stock Exchange, September 2001.

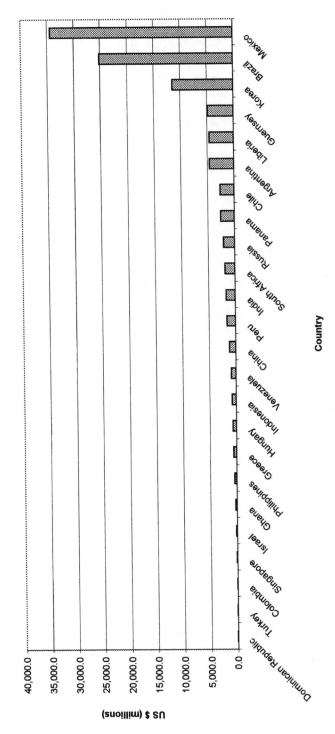

FIGURE 4.2. Market capitalization of emerging market firms listed in New York. *Source:* New York Stock Exchange, April 2002.

73

private actors such as investment bankers and consultants moved to operate across state lines. Thus international organizations negotiated with states on debt issues, created new investment vehicles, brought investors and projects together, and advised governments directly on securities market regulations and stock market procedures. As private-sector participation grew, these activities forged a growing similarity in financial market practice across state lines.

For example, emerging market units of investment banks worked on country funds with, or without, the IFC by using the structure of one successful financial product or set of securities regulations as a guide for a financial product or set of regulations elsewhere. With respect to the exchanges, Garside Miller, a British firm of consultants, gave the first course in how to run a stock exchange in Hungary to a group of Hungarian and Slovak officials. The French *Societe des bourses francaises*, together with the French state, gave assistance to Lithuania and Ukraine to help set up stock exchanges. The IFC helped the government of Romania find consultants from the *Commission des valeurs mobilieres du Quebec*. Canada-based Coopers & Lybrand worked on the Abidjan and Accra bourses. The Canadian International Development Agency worked on several African exchanges.

However, these extensive connections and strong influences on convergence in market practice do not complete the picture of equity market creation and growth because they do not reveal what shares were actually offered for sale. Nor do they reveal how the shares fit into the broader ownership structure of the firm offered. These images matter in the overall picture, because while privatization and international organization involvement has propelled the growth of the exchange, what shares are offered for sale determines how the institution of the equity market functions. Yet these structural images require an investigation of the politics of an individual large offering on the new, or reborn exchange.

Therefore the 1980s and 1990s were decades of great expansion for equity markets in the developing world in terms of new firm listings, rising prices for those already listed, and the creation of new stock exchanges where none had existed previously. Much of the outward similarity of this expansion can be attributed to strong international imperatives producing similar outcomes. International organizations such as the IMF and World Bank took on new roles during these years to address a debt crisis first concentrated in Latin America, and then Africa. The international organizations took on an even greater role in the aftermath of the collapse of Communism in the 1990s. As their role grew, markets connected to each other and standardized many procedures, yet individual equity securities remained characteristically local. The following chapter will explore how the process of creating shares from privatized firms results in dramatically different institutional functions, despite the outward similarity.

# Privatization and Share Supply in Emerging Markets

W hile privatization may at first glance appear to be a universal phenomenon extending from Thatcher's Great Britain, to Yeltsin's Russia, to Bedie's Cote d'Ivoire, this chapter will argue that the *manner* in which a government divests its shares results from level II political considerations. The manner of divestment creates new shares for sale on a given exchange with unique characteristics. These characteristics in turn create new domestic financial institutional structures, and thus new patterns of corporate governance with respect to the market for managerial control. Although the shares result from similar activities (i.e., government sell-offs), each deal is unique. Therefore, while state involvement (or lack of involvement) in industrialization determined the financial institutional structure in the prior era, the state continues to play a role in the present era through the politics of the privatization deals themselves.

Depending on the type of government divestment, share price may or may not exert the same type of external pressure on management as it does in traditional "capital market" financial institutional structures; large shareholders or stakeholders may or may not exert the same type of pressure on management as they do in traditional stakeholder models either. Hence financial institutional structures proliferate above and below the national level. These differences coexist notably in the developing world, where some partially divested and some fully divested government enterprises join firms controlled by the former mechanisms (such as foreign ownership of a controlling bloc of shares), or private conglomerates raising capital domestically.

As discussed in the last chapter, level I international imperatives weigh in on privatizations, since international financial organizations are actively engaged in the process of encouraging government disinvestments and creating markets where they did not previously exist. Nonetheless, the present chapter isolates state-level, or level II, activity because states and firms must still make the most basic decision to offer, or not to offer, shares. States and firms must decide whether to offer shares on an exchange or sell them privately, to list them domestically or to list them internationally. Moreover, states and firms must decide to whom to offer the shares, and what voting rights will be attached. These decisions ultimately determine what is for sale on an emerging stock exchange, how much of it is for sale, and whether or not the firm's shares are considered to be "strategic."

Therefore this chapter first considers evidence that government privatizations account for much of the growth in many regions. It then considers alternative paths to government divestment of shares, and the domestic political pressures for each of these paths. It concludes by considering the aggregate effects of shares having been divested in a particular manner on the domestic financial market institutions, and corporate governance overall. The second part of the book will build on this overview by examining cases of specific large offerings (private and otherwise) on emerging stock markets, and the role of politics in contributing to the market for managerial control of these firms.

## Government Privatizations as a Source of Shares

The term "privatization" is analogous to "globalization" insofar as both terms are used so widely and generally as to render them nearly meaningless. Any transfer of ownership or control from the public to the private sector could be considered privatization. For purposes of this chapter, however, privatization refers to transactions where the government (as vendor) transfers enough ownership or control of an enterprise that private operators or owners gain substantive independent power over it, although they will not always gain majority ownership.[1] The treasury of the state is the main beneficiary of the privatization rather than the enterprise itself, even when the privatization is accompanied by a financial restructuring.

As discussed in chapter 3, government ownership of enterprise had expanded both in the interwar period and in the period following World War II. The first indication of the shifting tide against government ownership was the British sell-off in the Margaret Thatcher era. That is, the British government initiated the first massive case-by-case privatization program in the 1980s by privatizing virtually all state-owned enterprises in competitive sectors, in many public utilities, and in government services. Later, the IMF and World Bank spread much of the Thatcher-Reagan liberal orthodoxy by urging, and in some cases requiring, developing countries to privatize their industries as part of broader stabilization, deregulation, and structural reform programs in the mid- to late 1980s.

After 1989, the post-Communist countries sought privatization on a massive scale as a critical step in their transformation into market economies.[2] Hence the different strategies, circumstances, times, and political pressures involved in different national instances make it difficult to generalize the privatization phenomena. Nonetheless, it is possible to generalize that the massive influx of new shares and sizable increases in market capitalizations of European exchanges resulted from privatizations because privatized firms are often the most valuable firms in their markets. Of the 135 largest common stock issues in history, 25 have been privatization issues.[3]

On the domestic side of shares traded, or local market shares, privatizations represented more than 55% of the number of equity issues in the 12 larger European economies; and they represented more than 70% of the total market capitalizations of Italy and Spain by 1999.[4] Yet probably more significantly, the OECD privatizations of the 1980s and 1990s have contributed to a sizable growth in the volume of shares traded transnationally. On average, privatizations accounted for approximately one-third of the total of international equity placements from 1996 to 1997, however, in some individual cases, more than 80% of the shares were sold to international investors (see figure 5.1). Concern about the prospect of extensive foreign control of industry appears to have diminished considerably in nearly all OECD countries.[5]

In the years between 1988 and 1993, Latin American countries divested 57% of the worldwide value for developing countries, whereas eastern Europe and central Asian countries divested only 19% of the value. Nonetheless, eastern European and central Asian countries accounted for 48% of worldwide transactions (1097 in all), whereas Latin American countries accounted for only 25% (561 in all). Therefore the Latin American states did not conduct as many transactions, but the ones they did conduct were for a greater value. The African transactions were similarly lower in value; only 3% of worldwide value, yet 11% (254) of worldwide transactions. Asian states divested 16% (367) of the total transactions and 21% of the value.[6]

Despite the fact that most emerging market governments do not undergo privatizations by way of IPOs on exchanges, and the fact that very few privatizations at all have taken place in sub-Saharan Africa and the Middle East and North Africa, privatized firms with a public component still assume disproportionate importance on these exchanges because they far outnumber any other types of offerings, and because the transnational market is not available to them. For example, privatizations in Europe taken together for 1993 and 1994 represent only 0.9% and 1.6% of market capitalization in Europe, respectively, when added to the volume of existing shares.[7] Ashanti Goldfields, taken together with the privatization of Nigeria's NNPC oil field, accounts for nearly 40% of total sub-Saharan African privatization; moreover, Ashanti Goldfields represents 55% of market cap-

FIGURE 5.1. International equities offered. *Source:* OECD, *Financial Market Trends,* February 1998, no. 69, p. 77.

italization on the current stock exchange in Accra (and incidentally, Ashanti Goldfields is one of the only sub-Saharan African firms listed internationally).[8] Similarly Sonatel (the Senegalese telecommunications parastatal) listed on the Abidjan bourse and market capitalization grew 26% in one day.

These figures are significant because they begin to speak to the difficulty in quantifying and comparing stock market growth and development in cross-national terms, as well as in accounting for growth attributable to various causes. Figure 5.2 shows the growth in equity issued as a percentage of GDP. From the graph one can see that the importance of equity as a component of a country's overall economy expanded during the late 1980s, particularly for the Asian tigers, despite the fact that when compared to volume in the core of the world economy, the value of shares listed on these exchanges remained low. In fact, by 1995 the equity issued as a percentage of GDP was higher for both the Asian tigers and emerging markets (using IFC classifications) than for the G4 industrial countries.

The two main ways of measuring market size makes determining the growth

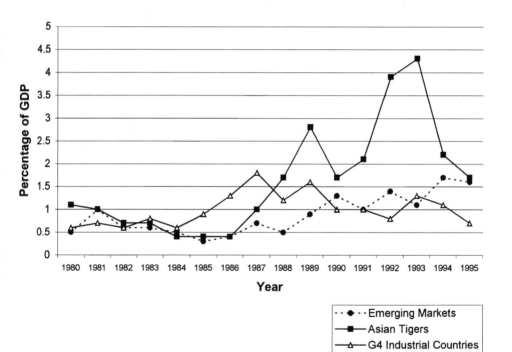

FIGURE 5.2. Domestic equity issuance activity. Emerging markets comprise Argentina, Brazil, Chile, China, Colombia, Greece, Hungary, India, Indonesia, Jamaica, Jordan, Kenya, Malaysia, Mauritius, Mexico, Pakistan, Peru, Philippines, Portugal, Sri Lanka, Thailand, Tunisia, Turkey, and Venezuela. The Asian Tigers comprise Hong Kong, Korea, Singapore, and Taiwan. The G4 comprises Germany, Japan, the United Kingdom, and the United States. *Source:* Anthony Aylward and Jack Glen, *Primary Securities Markets: Cross-Country Findings,* IFC Discussion Paper no. 39, Washington, DC: World Bank.

of an individual stock market within this group even more problematic, because each leads to different conclusions about cross-national relative growth. First of all, a market can be measured by market capitalization, that is, multiplying the number of shares listed by their price, and translating the result into U.S. dollars for comparative purposes. Market capitalization can therefore rise when share price rises, when firms offer additional shares on the exchange, or when the currency appreciates against the U.S. dollar. To compare actual firm profits (and their re-lationship to share price) across countries would require that these firms reconcile their financial statements to U.S. generally accepted accounting principles (GAAP), since a firm can show a profit using, for example, German standards, and a loss using GAAP. The cost of reconciliation is so great that many European firms do not seek U.S. exchange listings for this reason. Thus, the cost of recon-ciling all of the firms' statements on two exchanges to each other would be pro-hibitive, even if the firms were all willing to disclose this information to an outside investigator. There is no comprehensive database on the degree of new capital raised domestically, and less comprehensive data on the degree securities are listed and traded abroad.[9]

Nonetheless, growth in market capitalization (see figure 5.3) does give a crude measure of the increasing size of a state's stock market. Using this measure, from 1990 to 1997, the Latin American and Caribbean region grew in absolute volume the most among low- to middle-income countries (contributing 40% to the total growth of market capitalization for the group), followed distantly by the East Asian and Pacific, and European and central Asian regions (contributing 18% and 17% to the total, respectively). When the growth in market capitalization is adjusted for market size, however, sub-Saharan African markets grew the most in the period

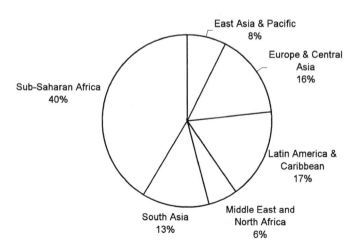

FIGURE 5.3. Growth in market capitalization as a percentage of GDP, all low and middle income countries, 1990–1998. *Source*: World Bank, *World Development Indicators*, Washington, DC: World Bank, 1999.

1990–1997, notwithstanding that these figures are skewed by the presence of one or two large markets that grew significantly.

Second, the number of listed companies also serves as a crude measure of stock market size (see figure 5.4). In looking at the growth in number of listed domestic companies on exchanges in the same group of low- to middle-income countries, a completely different picture emerges of where growth occurred. With this measure, listings on European and central Asian exchanges grew the most (44% of new listings), followed by listings in East Asia and the Pacific (36% of total new listings). The Latin American and Caribbean contribution shrinks to 8% of new listings.

Thus problems with these measures are immediately apparent without even attempting to distinguish among potential independent variables (e.g., government privatizations, companies raising capital, private companies issuing shares in IPOs, etc.) that contribute to the shares supplied in the 1990s. One government privatization, for example, could result in only one new listing, yet may represent a significant increase in market capitalization relative to GDP. Similarly many new companies could list and the market capitalization not grow proportionately. For example, 15 additional domestic companies listed in Venezuela between 1990 and 1997, yet the market capitalization actually decreased by US$774 million during roughly the same period. Companies can be privatized, and shares sold, yet not be reported by some countries if they are not listed publicly. Moreover, comparability of indicators among countries is even further limited by conceptual and

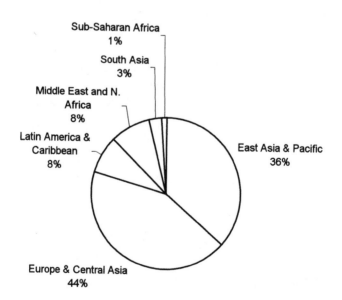

FIGURE 5.4. Growth in listed domestic companies, all low and middle income countries, 1990–1997. *Source*: World Bank, *World Development Indicators*, Washington, DC: World Bank, 1999.

statistical weaknesses such as inaccurate reporting.[10] The overwhelming role played by privatization offerings is apparent, however, when individual offerings are compared to the total size of the exchange. This method of comparison is used in the case studies in the following section.

## Manners of Transfer of Shares from States to Private Enterprise

When a government makes a decision to divest shares, how does it go about doing so? The British government employed four major methods of privatization in the 1980s: denationalization, conversion to a hybrid or mixed corporation, reduction or removal of previous monopoly powers, and introduction of private capital without altering control. Yet since the British wave, other instances have involved the complete transfer of ownership from the state to private entrepreneurs and the sale of controlling shares in the business to private investors. Moreover, some privatizations may not fit any of these categories, such as instances where the different departments of the government or quasi-government institutions hold the shares or interests in the entity that is supposedly privatized.[11]

If rudimentary classifications are possible given this caveat, privatizations fall into two main types: case-by-case privatizations and voucher based. With case-by-case privatization, including sales for cash or IPOs, the government gains efficiency. It generates revenues, gives shareholders control over managers, and provides access to capital and skills. But it is slow and does not promote widespread public participation. Voucher-based privatizations (more commonly associated with the Communist-transition countries) are designed to promote equality in the distribution of wealth through widespread participation. However, voucher-based privatizations do not ensure efficiency because they may not generate revenues, bring in new capital or skills, or give shareholders control over managers. Some combinations of the methods also exist, such as an "IPO-Plus" model wherein low-priced public shares are offered. Thus this method promotes equity through widespread participation in privatization, fosters capital market development, and creates independent financial institutions that press companies to improve their financial performance.[12]

Studies of aggregate privatizations conclude that most are partial, staggered sales. To enhance investors' confidence, a selling government may signal its commitment to a current policy by retaining a stake in the firm for some time, while transferring managerial control. In this manner, the government shows its willingness to bear some financial cost of the policy changes. In addition, governments may deliberately underprice privatization sales either in concert with domestic capitalists, or to convince the market to absorb larger sales. Perotti and Guney find larger underpricing and smaller initial sales in firms with policy-sensitive sectors. Likewise, they find more underpricing in privatization sales than in the IPOs of private firms. However, the mechanisms of privatization sales do not appear to differ across more- and less-developed markets.[13]

What are the mechanics of share transfer to the public with case-by-case privatizations? The main technique of transfer of shares in the OECD countries has been a public offering of shares, mainly to portfolio investors. With this method of transfer, a prospectus sets the terms of the offer, as well as details the offer's separation into tranches targeting various categories of investors (retail, institutional, "stable core," or international). At times, tranches are offered at different prices. In the British case, the government sold shares gradually, due to the limited capacity of the capital market to absorb the entire amount at one time. Some early partial sales were for 51% of stock, perhaps to transfer the majority of voting rights symbolically. By the end of the program, complete sales became common. The French and Spanish privatization programs similarly instituted partial sales programs.[14]

The French privatizations follow a system wherein a "stable core" (*noyau dur*) of equity holders agree to hold their shares for an extended period of time. Generally a group of five or six owners in this category pay a premium to hold 25%–40% of total equity and are thus in a position to exercise some collective managerial control over the company. Posing a defense against hostile takeovers, these investors are often selected from a relatively small number of domestic industrial or financial groups with significant cross-holdings.[15] Other OECD countries that pursued variations of the French strategy (and some would argue the French state itself), however, appear to be moving away from stable or core shareholder arrangements as large domestic institutional investors and asset management intermediaries develop significant shareholdings.[16]

Although a public offering (domestic or international) is the most transparent method of sale, it requires a degree of sophistication in financial markets and a well-developed legal infrastructure that many emerging markets lack. Smaller firms, privatized firms in emerging markets, and firms in need of major restructuring generally utilize a trade sale, or private offering of shares, to transfer ownership. A trade sale solves some of the problems of public offerings in emerging markets because with a trade sale, shares are offered to a strategic investor wishing to exercise managerial control over the company. The buyer is selected through a public tender offer or a private search conducted by an investment bank. Whereas trade sales represented less than one-fifth of the proceeds of privatizations for OECD countries in 1999, IPOs represented less than one-tenth of non-OECD privatizations.

As a group, the countries transitioning from Communism experimented with the widest variety of methods of transferring ownership, ranging from those similar to the OECD, to "spontaneous privatizations," a euphemism for individuals seizing the assets and operating them as if they were their own.

Table 5.1 shows the dramatically different methods of transferring ownership among transition economies. At first, states preferred the "sale to outside owners" method because it was the best-known model and had been successful in established market economies like the United Kingdom, and in middle-income developing countries like Chile. This method was also preferable because strategic, or core investors, would, in theory, bring in revenue. These "real" owners were thus thought to possess the knowledge and incentives to govern the company efficiently, and the capital to restructure it. Sales to outsiders (foreign or domestic) have largely fulfilled expectations about performance improvements. Nonetheless, they

TABLE 5.1 Methods of Privatization for Medium-Size and Large Enterprises in Seven Transition Economies (Percentages of Total)

| Country | Sale to outside owners | Management-employee buyout | Equal access voucher privatization | Restitution | Other[a] | Still in state hands |
|---|---|---|---|---|---|---|
| Czech Republic | | | | | | |
| By number[b] | 32 | 0 | 22[c] | 9 | 28 | 10 |
| By value[d] | 5 | 0 | 50 | 2 | 3 | 40 |
| Estonia[e] | | | | | | |
| By number | 64 | 30 | 0 | 0 | 2 | 4 |
| By value | 60 | 12 | 3 | 10 | 0 | 15 |
| Hungary | | | | | | |
| By number | 38 | 7 | 0 | 0 | 33 | 22 |
| By value | 40 | 2 | 0 | 4 | 12 | 42 |
| Lithuania | | | | | | |
| By number | <1 | 5 | 70 | 0 | 0 | 25 |
| By value | <1 | 5 | 60 | 0 | 0 | 35 |
| Mongolia | | | | | | |
| By number | 0 | 0 | 70 | 0 | 0 | 30 |
| By value | 0 | 0 | 55 | 0 | 0 | 45 |
| Poland | | | | | | |
| By number | 3 | 14 | 6 | 0 | 23 | 54 |
| Russia[e] | | | | | | |
| By number | 0 | 55 | 11 | 0 | 0 | 34 |

*Source*: World Bank, *World Development Report 1996: From Plan to Market*, New York: Oxford University Press, 1996, p. 53.

[a]Includes transfers to municipalities or social insurance organizations, debt-equity swaps, and sales through insolvency proceedings.
[b]Number of privatized firms as a share of all formerly state-owned firms. Includes parts of firms restructured prior to privatization.
[c]Includes assets sold for cash as part of the voucher privatization program through June 1994.
[d]Value of firms privatized as a share of the value of all formerly state-owned firms. Data for Poland and Russia are unavailable.
[e]Does not include some infrastructure firms. All management buyouts were part of competitive, open tenders. In 13 cases citizens could exchange vouchers for minority shares in firms sold to a core investor.

are expensive, difficult to implement, and slow. In addition, this mechanism of transfer became less and less popular because of the accompanying political tensions. Selling large numbers of firms to foreigners hurt nationalist sensibilities, and selling the firms to domestic owners did not please managers in some countries who were able to block the sales. However, in general, the mechanism was not satisfactory in the transition economies due to the sheer magnitude of the job of evaluating and negotiating deals one by one and then following up to be sure that the buyers fulfilled contract provisions.[17]

As an alternative to sales to outsiders, Croatia, Poland, Romania, and Slovenia used the "management-employee buyout" method. Many of the firms privatized through Lithuania's and Mongolia's voucher programs also became management-employee buyouts as employees and their families used vouchers and cash to buy major stakes in their own firms. Buyouts are fast and easy to implement; they may also provide more effective corporate governance than sales to outsiders, if insiders have better access to the information needed to monitor managers. Buyouts are problematic, however, for several reasons. The resulting benefits are unevenly distributed across the population because employees in well-functioning firms receive valuable assets, while those in poorly functioning firms receive little or nothing of value. Second, when governments charge low prices to insiders, the government realizes little revenue. Third, since insiders are generally unable to bring in *new* skills or capital, markets for the product itself, or for capital, fail to provide external discipline. In sum, buyouts can lead to an entrenchment of managers and workers that blocks further reform.

With the "equal-access voucher privatization" method, the government distributes vouchers across the population and attempts to allocate assets evenly among voucher holders. The Czech program has been the most successful of these to date; Mongolia and Lithuania were also among the first to attempt it. This method is very quick and equitable, but it does not realize revenue for the state. Moreover, it has unclear implications for corporate governance.

The choice of privatization method in the transition economies has significantly affected equity market development, as it has in the postcolonial states. In some countries, mass privatization via voucher schemes took place prior to the emergence of well-functioning secondary markets. Thus market infrastructure and regulation developed in response to demands from participants. Elsewhere, infrastructure and privatization through IPOs were realized simultaneously. In these cases, the regulations were drawn according to the standards of major OECD markets. Countries that used early mass privatization methods generally realized high capitalization levels, but low turnover ratios (liquidity); countries that used a more regulated approach with slower privatization realized higher turnover ratios (liquidity), but low availability of shares.[18]

## Share Supply as a Political Process: The Market for Managerial Control

Unlike the earlier examples where a financial institutional structure evolved as part and parcel of industrialization, and the financial structure disciplined or did not discipline corporations through the price mechanism (i.e., the Wall Street Rule), corporate governance of many of the newly listed equities of the 1980s and 1990s can be traced to the politics of how an individual privatization deal was structured. Hence, while corporate governance does not remain clearly linked to the state's ability to allocate finance, the state does retain an ability to use the financial system to influence firm decisions. When citizens in a variety of states own shares, the legal system of one state does not necessarily prevail. Nonetheless, the state that sold the shares usually prefers to keep the privatized entity under their own corporate legal jurisdiction. A domestic stock exchange serves this function.

Therefore a stock exchange provides the necessary infrastructure for the privatization to occur, but the stock markets do not necessarily perform the same function *after* the privatization occurs. In some cases the exchange can indeed be an anonymous international platform for selling shares, and many of the western European stock markets are increasingly integrated through the shares of privatized enterprises offered internationally. Nonetheless, as the number of privatized firms increases on an exchange, and in the absence of liquidity, the connection between state and stock market can also tighten.

Moreover, several key differences exist between a government's selling shares on a stock exchange to accomplish a privatization offer and a private firm's selling shares to raise capital. Governments involved in selling assets publicly seek four main objectives, the most obvious among them being to raise revenue.[19] The proceeds from privatization sales allow governments to reduce public borrowing, and in theory to tax less in the future. (Less taxation does not always result, however, since governments also lose a claim on the cash flow of privatized firms.) A second objective of privatization is wide share ownership that encourages participation in the stock market by individual investors. Third, governments seek more effective control of companies through privatization, which neoliberal economists argue arises when investors and analysts monitor management's performance, although this goal can be complicated when governments retain shares. Finally, a private firm can only issue an IPO once. Governments, however, can issue "initial" offerings on more than one occasion; and they generally do just that. Privatizations generally take place when a range of assets are sold sequentially. Hence the government, unlike a firm, has a goal of earning a good reputation (e.g., with pricing of the deal) in privatization IPOs to ensure future successes.

Since the goal of wide ownership is usually one of the more significant goals for governments, the allocation of shares generally reflects the political leverage of three main groups of political constituents. First among these are existing domestic entrepreneurs, second are management and workers of the enterprise in question, and third is the general public. In comparison, management, workers, and the general public were far more successful in acquiring ownership in eastern Europe and the former Soviet Union than in the Mexican privatizations, where shares were primarily allocated to strategic investors who bought the enterprise for the highest possible price.[20] Moreover, many of the Mexican firms are cross-listed in the United States, rendering these shares far more liquid than most eastern European firms' shares.[21]

The upshot of this political activity in transferring shares is that in many (but not all) instances the government wants to privatize, but also wants to retain a degree of control. The government can regulate share ownership or takeovers, it can extract promises that certain workers will not lose their jobs for a specified period of time, or it can retain shares itself to provide a conduit for participation in corporate governance. For example, government representatives can be appointed as members of the board of directors. They are then in an ambivalent position with respect to the interests of the government or the firm.[22] The tension between ceding corporate control and privatization is particularly pronounced with respect to enterprises listed on many emerging exchanges because they comprise such a large volume (as much as 100%) of market capitalization.

When aggregating the results of these various privatization deals, and when considering previously issued shares, one model of the market for corporate control fails to emerge in emerging markets. Hence most large firms will not be subject to the price mechanism of shareholders' indirect control. Yet most of the business, legal, and political economy literature on corporate governance continues to posit two (or three) main "models" of the market for corporate control. To review briefly, in the capital market model, equity shares are widely distributed and the possibility of influence through the price mechanism exists; with the "Wall Street walk," unhappy investors can sell their shares, the price drops, and the possibility of managerial takeover ensues. The ultimate economic authority thus rests with the shareholders through the price mechanism. Conversely, in the bank-model, ownership is concentrated in blocs of shares, banks play a role in corporate governance, and labor also participates as an active "stakeholder." Therefore the ultimate economic authority rests with owners of blocs of shares, lending authorities, and labor unions that are not subject to the market for managerial takeover.

These models are useful because they represent the bulk of equity market activity for advanced industrial economies. However, as governments continue to divest shares and contribute to the supply of equity shares in emerging markets, academic literature must confront the issue of dramatically different control structures, both inside and outside the industrial core of the world economy. Some shareholders amass superior voting rights that enable them to exercise control with very limited ownership of capital, and limited claims on cash flows. While such shareholders could be financial institutions, they could also be families or the government. In fact, most large enterprises in the world have a controlling group of shareholders—usually the state or families—and widely held firms, such as in the capital market model, are rare except in economies with very good shareholder protection.[23]

Hence corporate governance models do not fall neatly along the lines of "widely held" and "concentrated" ownership, particularly in emerging markets where a radical separation of control and cash flow rights is usually achieved through one of three mechanisms: dual classes of shares, stock pyramids, and cross-ownership ties. These structures have been termed "controlling-minority" structures, but have features of the other models. They resemble concentrated ownership insofar as the controllers are not threatened by managerial takeover, and they resemble dispersed ownership insofar as the controllers only own a small fraction of the firm's cash flow rights.[24]

Of the three mechanisms for separating control from cash flow rights, dual classes of shares are shares issued with varying voting rights. This is the most basic mechanism because a group of shareholders amasses superior voting rights simply by owning the shares with the rights. The most common mechanism for achieving a controlling-minority structure, however, is the stock pyramid. With stock pyramids, a controlling-minority shareholder holds a controlling stake in a holding company that, in turn, holds a controlling stake in an operating company.[25] The operating company may or may not, in turn, own a controlling stake in another firm. The third mechanism is cross-ownership. Here, horizontal holdings reinforce and entrench the central controllers' power. However, unlike a pyramid, voting rights used to control a group remain distributed over the entire group.[26]

At first glance it appears that there are no disciplining forces either inside or outside a firm that has any one of the three controlling-minority structures. However Bebchuk, Kraakman, and Triantis posit two constraints on the behavior of management that prevent it from looting the firm outright. The first constraint is the controllers' reputation should they seek further finance in the capital market. The second constraint is the legal system that may accord rights to minority shareholders that the controlling minority is powerless to ignore.[27] If states are the controlling minority, their reputation matters in future privatization deals. If a privatized firm is sold to a multinational controlling minority, the government may accord rights to minority shareholders along with the sale. Therefore a large increase in market capitalization or number of shares issued can signal an institutional change.

When the government privatizes shares in one of the variety of manners available to it, it engages these varying control structures and contributes to building a system of control that may or may not aggregate at the level of the state in question. Moreover, as states vary the market for corporate control, they confound the goals of the enterprise in question, that is, does it operate to maximize value and profit for shareholders, or does it operate as an agent of development and provider of employment? Evidence from emerging markets points to several main variations on the market for corporate control that the academic literature must confront: those where the state remains an active shareholder, those where transnational firms participate as majority or minority controllers, those where enterprises are monitored by foreign banks, and those where the firm operates to benefit insiders and enforcement of laws to prevent this behavior is irregularly enforced.

Variations in the market for corporate control are not limited to emerging markets. U.S. corporations, for example, demonstrate far more susceptibility to hostile takeovers deriving from multiple classes of shares and cross-holding ownership structures than much of the literature acknowledges. Yet U.S. corporations operate in a legal and financial institutional environment where, for example, shares of minority-controlled firms are more difficult to sell and property rights are more regularly enforced. This is dramatically different from Russia, where local governments have not consistently respected controlling foreign ownership rights, or Nigeria, where some foreign corporations have not been able to monitor their subsidiaries.[28]

## Analysis and Conclusion

While international necessity has compelled governments to divest shares of state-owned enterprises, and transnational actors have ensured a seeming degree of similarity in the equity securities resulting from such transactions, the privatization deal associated with a given enterprises can set the stage for who will assume the ultimate managerial control. Enterprises can be fully or partially sold to fulfill a variety of goals, among them that the management will remain within the state, that the state will receive a certain amount of revenue, or that workers and their unions will continue to play a role in management.

The political beneficiaries of the privatization are not easily classified, particularly when many variables—chiefly pricing—are so highly contentious in large deals. For example, staggered, or partial, sales could be a mechanism for the government to sell the enterprise and allow the market time to absorb shares. Or it could also be a stall tactic when the regime lacks a true commitment to wide-scale disinvestments and seeks to retain control. Many privatizations are works in progress, just as the industrial revolution is an ongoing process. Therefore the functions of primary and secondary markets associated with this process change over time across the world economy.

Nonetheless, the volume of government privatizations, and the prominence of their resulting shares on emerging stock markets does support the general contention that the manner in which they came onto the market determines who will manage the enterprise, and toward what purpose. Some deals preserve a role for the state, some preserve a role for nationals, and some preserve a role for unions. Some guarantee that the same managers will remain entrenched, some introduce the element of foreign control, and some can fan nationalist sentiments. Some can distort the balance of power within a state when no other domestic entrepreneur is large enough to operate in the market, except the domestic group, individual, or family who bought control when it was privatized.[29]

The next section of the book will therefore begin to fill in the picture of emerging market creation and growth with a qualitative examination of enterprises offered publicly on markets and how individual privatization deals fit within a given controlling ownership structure operating in the state in question.

# PART II

# CASE STUDIES OF STOCK EXCHANGES IN REGIONAL PERSPECTIVE

This book argues that equity products are political as well as economic instruments because they determine who will ultimately make decisions for large firms. The first part of the book examined the broad sweep of equity markets and how emerging markets have fit into varying structures of the overall international political economy since the inception of equity finance. This part uses cases to elaborate on the multiple permutations of ownership possible in the current era, as policymakers and private issuers of stock have conducted their activities on two levels of a metaphoric game.

On the international level (level I), policymakers needed to address circumstances associated with the debt crisis of the 1980s and the response of the international financial institutions to that crisis. Many states addressed these circumstances by disengaging from ownership of the government firms of the nationalist era and selling shares. Other states addressed similar international circumstances by promoting equity markets and equity finance itself as a way for private firms to attract foreign capital. If the state actively sold shares or not, the international level played a role in setting "best practices" for shares listed as depository receipts on major exchanges. Listing on these exchanges lowers the cost of capital, yet it also decreases shareholders' ability to extract resources from the firm. Moreover, it obligates the firm to comply with burdensome disclosure requirements.

Political issues associated with the loss of control of economic activity in a given territory must be addressed on the state level (level II). When privatizing shares, the politics of organized union opposition to a sale, and the interests of elites connected to it, have produced dramatically different shareholding patterns and voting mechanisms. The newly listed shares are sold alongside shares listed from previous eras of state development. Thus the combination of historical legacy and contemporary politics have produced dramatically different interstate, and intrastate, corporate governance models apart from both the capital market-oriented and bank-oriented models.

The interaction between levels is significant. Level I considerations force governments to embark on courses of action they might otherwise not take. The necessity of level II ratification, however, means that outcomes are neither dictated by international concerns, nor homogeneous. Although there is a degree of convergence in practice on world equity markets in the current era, the role that emerging market shares play in governance of the firm does not converge. Thus any analysis of emerging equity products must take nationalist concerns, and the developmental goals of the state, into account. An examination of the ownership structure of voting capital of the former state-owned enterprises reveals that the state retains influence on the management of most large firms as a result of the manner in which large privatization deals were conducted. For example, the state can act as a "stakeholder" along with unions and institutional investors by either retaining a bloc of shares, retaining the ability to appoint individuals to key management positions, or otherwise stipulating managerial directives at the time of transfer.

The regional chapters that follow flesh out these myriad dimensions to the growth in market capitalization and firms listed, and they situate the growth within each market's historical legacy. The book argues that the historical legacy matters because various strategies of state engagement and disengagement with industrial development determined many of the initial, and ongoing, listings. Therefore the plan is to introduce each country study with an overview of the origins and history of the state's financial market, and to explore each country's industrial development strategies, culminating with the international (level I) imperatives that propelled new listings in the 1980s.

Next, each country study considers a case of the domestic (level II) politics associated with a large equity issue on the market. The cases were mostly selected for size. Seven are among the 50 largest emerging market firms in the world. Six have the largest market capitalization on their national exchange. However, some cases were not selected for size, but because the prominence of the issue, or its timing, render it representative of a significant portion of overall activity. While most cases are privatizations that were ultimately listed on national exchanges, three cases were not privatizations, three were not listed publicly, and one was listed and then delisted. Each of the cases has a history that links them to the political economy of earlier eras. Taken together, they are meant to serve as windows into equity product creation that contribute to stock market institutional growth and development in these states, and in this era. They are not meant to be exhaustive.

Finally, each country study considers the "dependent variable" of the book, taken to be the growth and development of emerging stock markets. However, this study does not measure growth and development strictly in quantitative terms of market capitalization and the number of shares listed, because stock markets are both political and economic institutions. As arrangements among units that define and specify the ways actors can cooperate or compete, stock market institutions pool capital, lower information costs, allow for managerial takeover, or discourage it. Therefore the "dependent variable" section attempts to situate the case study within the broader institutional setting of the national financial market.

A focus on the equity products "for sale" thus shows that growth in market capitalization, or number of shares issued, does not always result in convergence on the U.S. or U.K. model, or the European continental bank-oriented model. Convergence can fail to occur even when a common set of commercial laws, disclosure laws, or exchange listing requirements exist. The book posits that while national financial markets will increasingly function alongside international markets, emerging market governments will continue to play a role in corporate governance. Thus models of corporate governance will proliferate at the national and international levels.

Ownership of large firms will increase along with increases in the number of firms listed and market capitalization; nonetheless, the potential to exert control through the price mechanism will diminish. While the fragmentation in models for managerial control is greatest in the postcolonial world where liberal colonial, state interventionist, and neoliberal development strategies have left their imprints, it will likely also occur in the developed, industrial markets as international listing opportunities proliferate.

# 6

# Latin America and
# the Caribbean

Latin American emerging markets are significant not only because they have
such long-standing financial institutional structures, but because they received
large proportions of what are currently termed "emerging market" investments
when such investments boomed. Brazil, Mexico, and Chile were three of the top
five "emerging market" recipients of annual net private capital inflows from 1990
to 1997.[1] The restructuring of state-owned enterprise played a significant role in
the growth and distribution of shares, as well as the shares' connection to corporate
governance. Yet while privatization has increased market capitalization and the
number of shares listed on exchanges in the region, it has not left large firms listed
on domestic stock exchanges vulnerable to the market for managerial control.
Trading on these exchanges is concentrated in a few shares, and most offerings
are minority or nonvoting shares of state-owned enterprises.

In order to examine how stock has been used as both a political and economic
instrument in these economies over time, this chapter highlights the political economies of Brazil, Argentina, Chile, and Mexico. They follow the historical pattern
set out in the first section of the book insofar as they were key components of
what some historians have termed the British "informal empire" following the
disintegration of the Spanish empire between 1810 and 1824.

As a general overview, the Spanish and Portuguese empires in Latin American
disintegrated between 1810 and 1824, some 300 years after they were founded.
Historians debate whether or not the British founded their own "informal empire"
after that period.[2] It can be argued that the British did found such an empire
because they intervened in the internal affairs of these states when there had been
a breach of international law or when British property or economic interests were
threatened. The British had invested sizable amounts of capital in Latin America
extending to an early era. By 1864, British investors owned securities in 13 South
American companies.[3] British investors had a larger share of exports and retained
imports in South America from 1850 to 1913 than in any other continent or country
within their formal empire, except for India.[4]

The influence of the British matters because the British pattern of equity investment continued in Latin America much as it did in the United Kingdom. As was the case in the United Kingdom, British investors mostly invested in Latin American railroads between 1865 and 1913. Just as local, specialized exchanges developed within industries of these years in the United Kingdom, and were informally connected to each other and London, local exchanges emerged in Latin America and were informally connected to the London Stock Exchange. In time, activity on these local exchanges involved a degree of local participation.

The shocks of two world wars and the intervening Great Depression of the 1930s necessitated local production and thus import substitution. After World War II, and following the general historical pattern examined in chapter 3, import substitution strategies took further hold in Latin American with the founding of the Economic Commission for Latin America (ECLA) in 1948. Expressing the goal of fostering development in Latin America, the ECLA helped to define "development" as a concept and goal, and to found a Latin American regional identity in terms of structuralism in politics and economics.[5] As understood by the ECLA economists, structuralism accepted the basic notion of a world divided according to comparative advantage, but sought to transform it through protection from the world economy and state planning activity.[6]

The case studies show that as a group, Latin American states were the first to institute financial sector reforms as early as the 1960s. Various experiments with capital market development continued up until the debt crisis of the 1980s, when governments sold blocs of shares on these exchanges on a case-by-case basis, and eventually cross-listed securities in New York and London. An examination of domestic-level political activity shows that in many instances, organized political opposition to the sales meant that only fractions of a firm or its subsidiaries were sold. In other cases, firms that had been international before their nationalization in the 1950s and 1960s became international again. Many of these were in the telecommunications sector. In situating the firm studies within the broader institutional structure of the state's financial markets, the country studies show that firms with ownership structures from previous state development strategies coexist with those from the postprivatization era. Hence multiple forms of control structures coexist at the national level.

## Brazil

Typical of a new Latin American state within the British sphere of influence, the nineteenth century Brazilian economy was connected to the world economy through the export of coffee, sugar, and cotton. British capital played an important role in the development of this export economy; nevertheless, British investments were targeted toward three sectors: railroads, public utilities, and government loans. In the interwar period, the Brazilian state grew increasingly interventionist. When the war ended, the state continued its interventionist bent with state-sponsored growth directed at import-substituting industrialization. Toward this end, the state established bureaucratic structures to implement its industrial policies. The case study considered here, that is, Petrobras, the state oil company, was one such structure that combined the functions of economic production and regulation. The import-substituting strategies of these types of firms were mostly financed with private bank debt, which was not readily available after the debt crisis of the 1980s. Therefore when Brazil began a limited privatization program, it increasingly utilized its capital markets, which had existed since the British era.

### Stock Exchanges in Brazil

Equity trades in Brazil date to 1790 when brokers occasionally traded shares of stock in the plaza of Rio de Janeiro and other provincial centers. Formal exchanges were eventually established in Sao Paulo (1895) and Rio de Janeiro (1877), wherein brokers traded national and foreign bonds, letters of exchange, commercial loans, precious metals, and shares of stock.[7] Prompted by a growing demand for Brazilian coffee, the state passed a comprehensive piece of business legislation in 1850, the Commercial Code. The code allowed for regulation of brokerage activity and business organization, yet the joint-stock company format remained limited because a charter was difficult to obtain and because investors remained liable for the debts of companies in which they had invested, even in some instances where they had traded away the shares.[8]

Share supply increased dramatically when the new republic initiated legislative changes that lifted the unlimited liability for shareholders and lowered the capital threshold for operation. Six months after the reforms of 1890, more than 200 joint-stock companies were founded in Sao Paulo alone.[9] From the 1890s to 1905, the expansion of the Sao Paulo Bolsa drew more small investors into the capital market.[10] Nonetheless, trading was concentrated. From 60%–70% of all paid-in capital listed on the bolsa was invested in railroads, despite the small number of railroad listings in 1909.[11] After World War II, the bolsa did not play a significant role in industrial finance since the developmental state assumed the paramount role of financing exports and development. Moreover, Brazil was a major recipient of foreign direct investment during these years.

In the 1960s the Brazilian government began one of the earliest equity market development programs in Latin America. Reform of the financial system began in 1964 with three major laws: the Banking Reform law, the Housing Finance law, and the Capital Markets law. In an attempt to finance the working capital needs of companies, develop capital markets, and educate the public regarding the benefits of investing, the government passed Decree Law 157, which created fiscal investment funds. Investors could deduct a portion of the income tax they owed the government and use the deduction for the purchase of stock certificates through financial institutions that could not be withdrawn by the investor for five and a half years.[12] Although the funds were successful, a market crash in 1971 set the market back and the government did not continue that particular program.

Nonetheless, the Brazilian government did continue to pass legislation to promote capital markets. The military government of President Ernesto Geisel updated the Companies law in 1976. This legislation encouraged family businesses to offer shares, with the key provision that two-thirds of shares outstanding could be nonvoting preferred. Hence families choosing to list could retain control with as little as 16.7% of shares outstanding. Other provisions allowed for minority share-holders rights should the corporation undergo a reorganization. Therefore Brazil's capital markets remained viable in these years, albeit less developed.[13]

The earliest overtures to privatize portions of the Brazilian economy that would further augment share supply on the Brazilian exchanges resulted from the external debt crisis in 1981. At that time, the government created the Special Commission for Denationalization, and this agency privatized 20 companies over the next four years. A second wave of 18 more privatizations occurred between 1985 and 1989; however, in this second wave only small companies were privatized.[14] The third wave of privatizations associated with the administration of President Fernando Collor addressed the commanding heights of Brazilian industry, al-though Collar's resignation in 1992 slowed the pace. By 1990 Brazilian state and federal governments still controlled more than 80% of the country's power-generating capacity and most of its public utilities.[15]

Fernando Henrique Cardoso's administration renewed the momentum of the privatization program. Cardoso restructured the way it was implemented by setting up a committee of cabinet ministers, the National Privatization Council (CND), to oversee decisions about the future of privatization. At the same time, the administration moved to eliminate the constitutional distinction between foreign and Brazilian investors when a foreign company set up operations in Brazil. To tap international markets, the National Monetary Council allowed Brazilian companies to list on foreign stock exchanges through the mechanism of depository receipts.[16] By 1999, 23 had listed in New York; 15 of the 23 were concentrated in the telecommunications sector alone.[17]

Privatizations in Cardoso's administration augmented share supply because they were mostly conducted as share auctions on domestic stock exchanges. Typically the government would set a minimum price and specify the stake in the firm to be sold, and the liabilities to be transferred along with it. Bidders formed consortia to reduce risks, satisfy restrictions, and at times reduce competition. At times Brazilians participated in privatizations through offshore entities to reduce tax liabilities. Pension funds that had always been stock market participants initially participated as passive investors, but over time shifted to become active investors and owners. Although forbidden by law to buy privatized entities outright, a number of funds participated as parts of consortia. Hence the funds did not participate as long-term investors devoid of interest in running the company.[18]

### The Case of Petrobras

The case of Petrobras is significant with respect to Brazilian markets because it is the largest corporation in Brazil, one of the largest in Latin America, as well as one of the largest in the world. Petrobras was a creation of the government-business industrial structure in 1954, and its sell-off of shares represented a partial disman-tling of that structure. As an integral part of the Brazilian state sector, the Petrobras case is also significant because it was one of the most emotional privatizations in Brazilian industry. Operating under the slogan "the petroleum is ours," the state oil company had strong connections to former military leaders and had operated as a monopoly in Brazilian exploration, production, transport, and refining since it was founded. Although multinational oil companies operated service stations in Brazil, they hired Petrobras for offshore oil exploration. The coalition opposed to privatization comprised nationalist legislators, the association of Petrobras engineers, the military, and oil workers' labor unions.

As part of its early privatization efforts associated with the debt crisis of 1982, the Brazilian government offered Petrobras shares in 1985. At the time, Petrobras was experiencing credit difficulties, and Shell Oil and British Petroleum refused to sell it two large shipments of petroleum without a credit guarantee. To solve the immediate problem, the firm decided to purchase petroleum from Philbro Energy on the spot market. A longer-term problem persisted, though, as yearly profits fell to record lows and company executives argued that the loss resulted from the government's shifting of funds to cover expenses elsewhere in the debt crisis.[19] When the government offered the shares in 1985, it only included 6.6% of the firm's total capital stock. Hence the so-called privatization did not present the potential for any outside managerial influence to result. Nonetheless, the offering contributed to a boom in the secondary market for equity between 1985 and 1988. The 1985 Petrobras offer alone brought 300,000 new investors, nearly doubling the shareholder base in Brazil.[20]

When Cardoso took power 10 years later, he stated his intent to retain the monopoly held by Petrobras and not to privatize a firm he described as "unprivatizable." However, by this time the firm defined itself as a mixed-capital company, with the majority of shares held by the federal government. While the administration would not permit a single company in Brazil to purchase the firm, it would permit additional partial sales via smaller percentage blocks of shares.[21] Opposition to additional sales had organized to combat such privatization in the industry. Chiefly, the oil workers union imposed a 1% payroll levy on Petrobras's 100,000 member staff in order to form a $1 million opposition fund. When Cardoso sought further issues to open additional parts of the industry to the private sector, the government inserted a clause in a constitutional amendment that Petrobras would never be sold.[22]

Therefore the government never offered controlling interest in the firm itself. In fact, the president of Petrobras created a political uproar in 1992 by merely announcing a *hypothetical* end to the firm's federal monopoly status as part of a new 10-year strategic plan. However, a combination of state transactions did result in private operators' gaining substantive independent power over areas of the petroleum industry previously under Petrobras's exclusive control. In one group of transactions, Petrobras subsidiaries were offered publicly. For example, Petrobras Quimica SA, a petrochemical subsidiary of Petrobras, launched $200 million worth of preferred stock on the Brazilian market to raise cash to rehabilitate operating funds for the firm in 1989. Seeking to achieve maximum distribution of the stock, 30% was sold to employees of the Petrobras system and 100 financial firms participated.[23] In 1993 Petrobras sold 26.04% preferred stock in its fuel distribution network.

The result of these concessions was that the firm did not lose its monopoly status by being eliminated, but by the transfer of control to a regulating agency, the National Petroleum Agency (ANP). The ANP would handle the oil sector's business, wherein the government would sell exploration rights in areas with potential oil reserves. Petrobras would have to compete with other investors in areas where oil had already been discovered. Incidentally, similar agencies would handle business in other sectors previously dominated by the government, such as electricity and telecommunications. At that time, Petrobras's domination of the industry was finished and private-sector investment was permitted in all parts of the industry. In 1998 Petrobras announced its largest offering to date, which would reduce the state's stake in the company to 51%. Although a majority of shares would not be fully offered, more than 50% of the 1998 deal was offered to international investors.[24] As of 2002, the Federal Government of Brazil holds 55.7% of the common shares, 22.7% are offered as level III ADRs, and foreigners own 3.4% of the common shares. Of the preferred shares issued overall, foreigners own 18.8%.[25]

## The Dependent Variable

The case of Petrobras is typical of a large issue on the Brazilian market in that it is a state-created enterprise that was developed to advance the Brazilian economy in a key sector. Moreover, the case shows the shift in the government's role from active economic participant to regulator. In 1997 (prior to privatizations in the telecommunications sector), state-owned firms represented 80% of daily trading on the stock market.[26] Yet Petrobras is atypical of other firms insofar as the state had organized Petrobras as a series of subsidiaries connected to local capital and foreign firms. When these subsidiaries were sold, local groups asserted their control over companies they considered strategic to their growth. Thus, as subsidiaries of Petrobras were sold, privatization led to a concentration of ownership in some firms, and not really new forms of control.[27]

Conversely in the steel sector, the major firms' control bloc of shares was simply too expensive for any local investor to acquire single-handedly. Thus local business groups sought partnerships with other groups, pension funds, investment fund managers, banks, and foreign investors. These combinations pose an interesting potential conflict in firm governance that is usually characterized between that of majority and minority shareholders. That is, in these cases, conflict may emerge among controlling shareholders themselves.[28] In the telecommunications sector, foreign firms acquired the controlling bloc without local investors.

Therefore, prior to the privatization process, most large publicly traded firms in Brazil were either state enterprises or family-owned business groups controlling other firms through stock pyramids or dual classes of shares. The family firms had access to finance under privileged conditions. Foreign direct investment, while significant in some sectors, rarely established itself in the form of public companies, and did not depend on local capital markets for finance.

After the wave of privatizations, a variety of new ownership structures have emerged, while some of the former remain. Some firms continue under state control with a bloc of shares and some continue to be controlled by foreign owners. While family structures remain, some have operated in partnerships to concentrate their influence in a certain sector. Yet others face an important paradox in the postprivatization era, since they have lost their access to preferential finance through the state. They must either sacrifice a degree of control or fail to grow.

Thus even more ownership structures have emerged from within those that were previously typical stock pyramids or dual-class share models. For example, some family-owned business groups have sold a minority control bloc of a core firm to a foreign company. Paode Acucar Group sold 30% of its voting shares to a French company, and Organizacoes Globo Group sold 15% of its strategic cable television company to Microsoft. In these examples, the families kept the firm's growth potential and partial control, while realizing the benefits of sale to a foreign firm.[29]

Bovespa (the largest of the Brazilian exchanges) itself, however, has suffered from the circumstances of foreign versus national listings. In 1997, Bovespa's daily average was approximately US$1 billion, or about the same as Toronto's. Since that time, approximately 40% of investors have switched to holding ADRs of Brazilian firms traded in New York, where the transaction costs are approximately 165% lower. The result is that in 2002, Bovespa's volume was approximately one-sixth of Toronto's. As the exchange has attempted to attract more listings, it has sought to raise liquidity for smaller, local firms that have lost their liquidity in the interim.[30]

## Argentina

Similar to the Brazilian economy, the Argentine economy of the mid-nineteenth century was integrated with global markets as an agricultural exporter. However, the comparative advantage of development based on agriculture broke down in the world crises of the 1930s and World War II. Raw materials from the agricultural sector became part of the import substitution drive of the Populist government of Juan Peron, who used the materials together with cheap labor to fuel a growing industrial sector. As part of Peron's import-substituting strategy, the state nationalized private corporations in the railroad, energy, and telecommunications sectors, and imposed strict regulations on the economy as a whole.

The Argentine economy of the 1970s and 1980s stagnated and experienced hyperinflation. The deep national economic crisis, together with the huge fiscal deficit, led the government to attempt (unsuccessfully) its first privatization in 1987. In the early 1990s, Carlos Menem reignited the privatization drive, and pegged the Argentine peso to the U.S. dollar. Menem's plan proposed restructuring the state in such a way that the restructuring would both render short-term relief from the crisis and generate advance payment of the principal of the public foreign debt. Thus privatization involved the state's surrender of the enterprise and its monopolistic rights in exchange for the cancellation in advance of shares of public foreign debt.[31] This examination of Argentina considers the first such privatization of this type, and one of the largest transfers in the program, the telecommunications firm ENTel. Despite the failure of some earlier privatization attempts, the Menem government successfully transferred ENTel to private hands by the end of 1990. The role of equity finance here, though, did not promote an Anglo-

American style market for managerial control, but sought to address the issue of the state's indebtedness.

## Stock Exchanges in Argentina

The Stock Exchange of Buenos Aires is the oldest continuous Latin American exchange. When national and foreign businessmen formed the bolsa in 1854, they continued a tradition of share trading that extended to the end of Spanish rule. In 1810 English merchants created their own share trading organizations, but excluded Argentine nationals. In 1822 the government established a mercantile exchange, and in 1829 the Buenos Aires Commercial Room was established for both national and foreign traders.[32] By the 1930s, the Stock Exchange of Buenos Aires was comparable in size and activity to many European markets. The nationalizations of the 1950s increased listings; they increased from 266 in 1950, to 476 in 1959, to 675 in 1962. Nonetheless, the unstable economy meant that the market was prone to massive speculation and volatility.[33]

In the 1960s and 1970s the tendency was for companies on the exchange to delist and issue equity shares privately. This tendency turned around with Menem's privatization drive. In the major privatizations, a percentage of each new company was reserved for offer on the Argentine and international stock markets. Eleven Argentine companies listed on the NYSE between 1993 and 1999, including privatized state firms. In this program the government transferred controlling interests in 57 companies to the private sector and 27 public service companies to concessionaires by the end of 1993. In addition, 9 joint-venture agreements have been concluded on oil fields previously controlled by the former state oil company, and 86 concession agreements have been concluded on the exploitation of marginal oil fields. Gross revenue from the program added up to nearly US$9.1 billion in cash and US$13 billion in debt securities at nominal value.[34] ENTel was a significant privatization in the Argentine program not only because it was the first, but because the company had such a long history with the economy.

## The Case of ENTel

Originally established in 1886 by British capital, President Juan Peron purchased the majority of the Union Telefonica del Rio de la Plata (UTRP) in 1946 because it constituted, in his words, the country's "central nervous system." In the years that followed, the state forged ENTel from additional purchases of various providers, with the exception of Compania Argentina de Telefonos (CAT), which remained under the control of Swedish telecommunications equipment manufacturer Ericsson. During the period of Argentina's import substitution strategy, ENTel was required to purchase all of its equipment requirements from domestic manufacturers. The president of Argentina appointed the executive director of the firm; from the late 1950s to the late 1980s, 28 different individuals served in this role.[35]

The Alfonsin administration proposed the initial privatization of ENTel in the mid-1980s. In 1987 the government proposed selling a 40% ownership stake in

ENTel to an outside buyer, leaving 51% of the company in the hands of the state. Nine percent of total shares would be distributed to ENTel employees. However, union opposition to the plan and Alfonsin's Radical Party's loss of its Senate majority in 1987 meant that the plan was not supported in the Argentine Congress, and it fell through. The government did open up rights to other telecommunications service areas to the private sector, such as the rights to provide cellular telephone service in Buenos Aires, and the introduction of foreign vendors into the equipment purchase restrictions on ENTel.[36]

When the Menem administration took control of the government, the privatization program recommenced with renewed vigor. Menem issued a decree modifying Argentina's National Telecommunications law to eliminate the exclusive right of the state to provide and control telecommunications services. Thus, as was the case with Petrobras, the monopoly power of the firm was broken prior to the transfer of shares. Unlike Petrobras, the state went on to sell the controlling bloc of shares. Menem appointed Julio Guillan (head of the telephone workers union) as secretary of communication to encourage the union's cooperation in the revitalized privatization effort. On January 5, 1990, Menem issued another decree stipulating that ENTel would be split into two parts for the purpose of privatization: a northern and a southern company.[37]

Since the government sought expansion of service as a major goal of privatization, a license awarded to each company would entitle its owners to provide basic domestic telephone services on an exclusive basis for a limited number of years. If a license holder met certain operating performance targets during its first 7 years, its period of exclusivity could be extended for up to 10 years. The decree also included provisions affecting the pricing of services. The government anticipated that the northern and southern companies would compete for business following the end of the period of exclusivity.

Large holding groups in Argentina opposed Menem's initiatives because they made significant sums through public works contracts with the state. Suppliers also opposed the privatizations, and the sale of ENTel in particular, because they enjoyed certain privileges with state firms. The main supplier of ENTel, Siemens de Argentina, first attempted to stop the sale, and then wrote multiple contracts with ENTel prior to the sale, trying to stop it or stall it, or at least earn a degree of profit from the buyer.[38] Before the deal could be concluded, the Argentine telecommunications workers union organized a national strike and disconnected all international telecommunications links. However, Menem ordered the army to operate the phone system and fired hundreds of workers. Thus the strike, and with it any real union opposition to the privatization, ended.

When the two firms were sold, 60% of the shares in the northern and southern companies were to be sold through a competitive bidding process. Thirty percent of the shares were to be sold in subsequent public offerings. The remaining 10% were for ENTel employees.[39] On June 28, 1990, the government announced Telefonica of Spain as the victor for the southern company and Bell Atlantic as the victor for the northern company.[40] Although Bell Atlantic ultimately withdrew from the deal (its financial partner, Manufacturers Hanover, did not raise the required amount specified in the bid), a France Cable/STET consortium took over the northern portion.[41] The new southern company became known as Te-lefonica Argentina and the northern company as Telecom Argentina. The issue of debt to ENTel's suppliers was resolved after the bidders refused to assume ENTel's liabilities with its suppliers. In the end, the state assumed the bulk of the debt, and the new owners were required to honor existing contracts with Siemens, in particular, for at least two years.[42]

The government sold its remaining 30% stake in Telefonica Argentina through an international public equity offering in December 1991. It sold its remaining 30% of Telecom Argentina in March 1992. Both offerings were oversubscribed. The remaining 10% of the workers' shares continued to be held by the state through the late 1990s.[43] As a public utility, the government never completely ceded its control of the firms. For example, although the sale stipulated that the companies could set tariffs after a period of time, in January 2002, the government decided to devalue the peso. It told telephone utilities that they must keep their rates the same as before devaluation and must accept payment in pesos. These measures hit Spanish firms particularly hard since Spanish companies were the leading buyers of privatized Argentine businesses. The price of stock in many of the Spanish firms fell after the announcement.[44]

### The Dependent Variable

Prior to the privatization wave and outside the state sector, large Argentine firms were mostly family owned. Equity shares remained within the founders' portfolios, giving these groups a greater ability to navigate political and institutional unrest, as well as the inflationary environment. By keeping shares privately held, families could settle inheritance disputes; moreover, since families owned such a large percentage of shares, infringement on minority rights was negligible.[45] Within these arrangements, either state banks or a bank within the family holding company provided finance. After the wave of privatizations slowed, a large amount of mergers and acquisitions activity occurred within these large enterprises, and many of the banks in particular came under foreign control.[46] These activities have also been financed off of the public market, through private placement.

With the wave of privatizations, restructurings, and mergers and acquisitions activities that have taken place since the 1990s, Argentina has sought to foster a capital market-based financial system. A series of laws established a new legal framework to support this system. The process has changed what were previously ownership structures dominated by state-owned firms and large family-owned domestic companies to one where some family-owned domestic companies coexist with those that are foreign-owned and those that are controlled by investment funds.

Much of the equity financing activities associated with this shift, however, took place off of the Stock Exchange of Buenos Aires, and the transfers have not left the successive firms open to the market for managerial control. The privatization of ENTel is one case among many firms turned over to private, foreign control. While these firms initially made use of stock issues and public placements, and contributed to the rise in market capitalization on the stock exchange, they have subsequently financed their operations with internal capital from headquarters or from foreign institutional investors.[47]

Therefore, although the state has sold off key components of the parastatal sector, and although the stock market grew for a period, the resulting institutional structure reflects the various stages of Argentine economic development strategies dating to the end of Spanish rule. Some firms continue to be held by families, some by the state, and some are controlled by foreign capital. Since each seeks finance capital from alternate sources, a unified national financial structure along the lines of the capital market Anglo-American model has not emerged. Nonetheless, equity finance has played a significant role in these restructuring processes through private placements. When the government ended the convertibility system in 2001, and the stock exchange was closed for much of the month of December in that year, the MERVAL (El Mercado de Valores de Buenos Aires S.A.) index of shares on the exchange gained when it eventually did reopen. Individuals bought shares as a way out of the monetary crisis.[48]

## Chile

The liberal Chilean economy of the 1930s was followed by a gradual closing of the economy to foreign trade, and with it a high level of state intervention. The intervention culminated with the Marxist government of Salvador Allende from 1970 to 1973. The first stage of the Chilean "privatization" program, in fact, was after the 1973 military coup of General Augusto Pinochet, when the regime returned businesses that had been appropriated by Allende's government to their previous owners. The government transferred these firms to the private owners at no cost, under the condition that the owners not file suits against the state.

Yet Pinochet continued to transfer businesses to the private sector even after the initial return of appropriated assets, as part of a radical experimentation with neoliberal policies. In an autonomous state, Pinochet's policymakers were insulated from pressure groups. The "Chicago boys," a team of highly ideological technocrats trained in neoclassical economics, had links to a narrow range of international conglomerates that tended to concentrate their holdings in certain areas. Since the conglomerates had access to international credit and insider information concerning key policy decisions, they were able to create financial intermediation firms before other economic groups could. In addition, given their influence with, and connection to the "Chicago boys," they could buy public assets being privatized before more traditional economic groups.[49] The government transferred the assets in this phase using many methods, from auctions, to direct sales, to combinations of methods. Under the early program, taxpayers with no back taxes could buy stock on credit under favorable terms. Those who made payments when due paid only 70% of the amount due. Critics argued that in this program the benefits had been too excessive and only available to a small number of taxpayers.[50]

### Stock Exchanges in Chile

As had been the case in Brazil and Argentina, Pinochet's regime could denation-alize assets using stock because vehicles for such transfers existed. The first attempt to organize an exchange was in 1873 when 166 corporations (6 of them foreign, and mostly mines) attempted to organize themselves. Later, an organized market operated in Valparaiso. The president of Chile and the minister of finance decreed an incorporated stock exchange in Santiago in 1893.[51] The stock market was weak from 1930 to 1960 due to the collapse of the NYSE in 1929, World War II, and the subsequent developmentalist period. It grew with the Pinochet reforms.

A third phase of Pinochet's restructuring began with the economic crisis in 1982–1983. To cope with the crisis, the government intervened in the financial sector to liquidate some institutions, and to support others with the goal of restoring them to financial health in order to reprivatize them later. After the immediate economic crisis, privatization recommenced in 1984.[52] With this phase, the gov-ernment sought to address some of the problems with the earlier privatization programs and to transfer large-scale companies mostly created by the state to the private sector, exclusive of the copper industry, which remained in the hands of the state. Many of the corporations belonged to Corporacion de Fomento de la Produccion (CORFO) and were natural monopolies that delivered basic services. As a part of this process, CORFO stated that its objectives in transferring ownership were to eliminate fiscal deficits, spread ownership, increase company efficiency, diversify pension fund investments, and strengthen the capital market.

The transfer strategy chosen by CORFO was an effort to ensure that the sale price of stock was satisfactory, that ownership spread included workers, and that the process was transparent. The initial process meant placing a small volume of shares on the market while offering stock packages to workers and disseminating the results and prospects of the companies being sold through the media. As the process gained credibility and the companies improved efficiency, the price of the companies' shares rose.

The sale of stock to workers had the added benefit of ensuring the workers' opposition to any potential return of the company to state ownership. A variety of worker financing schemes were devised so that workers, and their associations, could participate. To achieve market price and presence on the stock exchange, 2.5% of stock was sold each year. When the desired price level was reached, the number of shares offered increased until the demand of institutional investors, such as pension funds, insurance companies, mutual funds, etc., was satisfied.[53] Activity associated with privatized shares on the Santiago Stock Exchange boomed, despite the fact that when the government auctioned shares of firms on the San-tiago Stock Exchange it did not generally offer enough to provide control of the enterprise. Of the stock market value in 1992, 38% represented privatized enter-prises (see table 6.1).[54]

Of the three groups of participants on the exchange—small domestic inves-tors, foreign investors, and pension funds—pension funds became important par-ticipants in the privatization effort because they created an important source of demand for the shares of privatized firms. Private pension funds began to operate

TABLE 6.1 Privatized Company Stock Transactions in Chile

|  | 1984 | 1985 | 1986 | 1987 | 1988 |
|---|---|---|---|---|---|
| Stock exchange assets (millions of US$ Dec. 1988) | 2237.0 | 2419.0 | 4625.0 | 5686.0 | 7079.0 |
| Privatized company stock transactions (millions US$) | 2.6 | 18.7 | 187.2 | 368.7 | 448.2 |
| Privatized company stock transactions (total transaction) (%) | 6.2 | 31.2 | 55.5 | 67.9 | 68.5 |

*Source*: Santiago Stock Exchange. As printed in Cristian Larroulet Vignau, "Privatization in Chile," in *Privatization: A Global Perspective*, ed. V. V. Ramanadham, New York: Routledge, 1993, p. 44.

in 1981 after reforms in the social security system. Initially they could not be invested in shares of private corporations, but after 1985 they were allowed to do so if they stayed within established limits concerning how much was invested in a corporation and what percentage of the total was invested in equity. By 1992, 24% of the accumulated pension funds were invested in publicly traded joint-stock corporations, and 86% of this amount was in shares of formerly state-owned enterprises.[55] Thus unions benefited through the liberalization program insofar as Chileans received indirect ownership of large enterprises through pension funds.

## The Case of CTC

One large firm included in the process in the late 1980s was the Chilean state telephone company, the Compania de Telefonos de Chile (CTC). It is significant because of its size and because of the sensitivity of the telecommunications sector. Yet it is also significant because these shares were the first Chilean offering on international markets in the twentieth century, and the first South American ADR issue in the United Sates in 25 years. As was the case with Petrobras and ENTel, unions protested the sale. When CORFO announced that 30% of the shares of the company would be sold to an Australian conglomerate, the State Enterprise Defense Command (an organization formed to oppose the privatization process) demonstrated in the center of Santiago by placing a coffin marked "CTC, rest in peace," in front of the metropolitan cathedral.[56] The Christian Democratic Party also protested the deal on the grounds that the government had failed to regulate the transaction properly.

Bond Corporation International (BCI) assumed management control of the company in 1988. CTC regulations stipulated that no shareholder could own more than 45% of the company, and BCI's stake was greater than 50% after other shareholders had failed to take up their rights. Under the terms of the rights issue, BCI had until August 31, 1992, to reduce its stake to less than 45%. When BCI made plans to sell the additional shares, it was experiencing serious financial difficulties of its own. By making an overseas offer of 10% of its stock in ADRs, BCI would meet the original 45% agreement, yet would also retain management control of the firm. In February 1990, BCI sold its stake in CTC to Telefonica of Spain in an attempt to prevent its own collapse from debt burden. Nonetheless, CTC proceeded with its plans to issue ADRs in the United States.

By the time the ADRs appeared on the New York market, at least seven other Chilean companies were considering trading ADRs as well. Chilean economists rationalized the foreign listings as a necessary step in the country's drive to compete internationally. A company would follow successful export strategies by establishing a presence in the export market by acquiring, or entering partnerships, with foreign companies that buy Chilean goods. Foreign listings would allow Chilean companies international recognition and would widen their shareholder base. Eventually a NYSE listing could reopen the doors to commercial bank credits that had been closed since the Latin American debt crisis of 1982.

In order to list the ADRs, the Chilean central bank needed to institute a series of foreign exchange regulations to allow the companies to operate with ADRs. Since ADRs pay dividends in dollars, the new shares were given access to the official foreign exchange market to move dollars in and out of the country. Thus foreign investors would be protected from the volatility of the parallel market. Official dollars would not be provided for private share placements on the U.S. market, that is, those shares not listed on the NYSE and traded over the counter.[57] Incidentally, non-Chileans buying shares of CTC on the Santiago Stock Exchange in July 1990 (when the ADRs were listed in New York) could not take profits out of Chile for three years.

### The Dependent Variable

The privatization of CTC is similar to the case of ENTel in that it was a telecommunications firm wherein managerial control transferred to a foreign company. However, the privatization is different from the previous examples in that it demonstrates the state's attempts to tap *international* equity markets, while allocating control through a bloc of shares. Chilean economists hoped to use foreign listings as part of an overall drive to compete internationally and widen their shareholder base, yet not to subject the firms to the market for managerial control; that is, a hostile takeover could not be accomplished through ADRs listed on the NYSE. If more foreigners sought to participate than the government had intended in the ADR issue (by buying shares on the Santiago Stock Exchange in a cross-exchange transaction, and not by buying ADRs), they could not expatriate their profits for three years. Firms in other emerging markets followed suit with listings in New York and London once the requisite domestic accommodations were made. When the ADRs were issued, they exposed Chile to the scrutiny of financial analysts in New York. This scrutiny augmented the financial profession in Chile such that reporting standards improved and pension investments could be monitored.[58] Nonetheless, the ADRs were a specific class of shares, with specific provisions attached.

### Mexico

Similar to the earlier examples of Brazil, Argentina, and Chile, Mexico progressed through an export-trade phase of economic development, a state-capitalist phase, and ultimately an export-led phase. Mining, and later oil exports, fueled economic growth. These industries were heavily dominated by foreign interests and were subsequently nationalized. Unlike the earlier examples, Mexico experienced a broad-based social revolution in the 1930s, and it never experienced military rule. Moreover, Mexico's proximity to the United States, and its obligations under the GATT and North American Free Trade Agreement (NAFTA) treaties render this example somewhat different from the others. This examination of Mexico considers the *Bolsa de Valores* and listings of domestic companies. It then considers the case of the nationalization of the state telecommunications monopoly, Telephonos de Mexico (Telmex), and the use of dual classes of shares to ensure that controlling ownership remains with a Mexican. Telmex followed a similar pattern to that of Petrobras, ENTel, and CTC. It was a significant privatization because 43% of the firm was already quoted on the bolsa at the time of the privatization sale, and these were the most active shares. When completed, the international component of the offering was the second largest global share offering for its time.[59]

### The Bolsa Mexicana de Valores

As was the case in the previous examples, Mexican equity trades date to the end of the colonial period. In 1880 groups of Mexican and foreign investors began to meet regularly to trade shares in mining companies. These meetings meant that individuals began to specialize in the securities business. In 1867 the government published a securities brokerage regulatory law. After an intervening economic crisis, the depreciation of metal prices on international markets, and the corresponding market inactivity, members of two defunct bolsas formed "la Bolsa Privada de Mexico" in 1907. The exchange later changed its name to the "Bolsa de Valores de Mexico." Thus trades have been conducted more or less constantly in Mexico since the mid-nineteenth century.

Many of the largest Mexican corporations in terms of sales are not listed on the exchange. Similar to the other Latin American examples, this lack of listing can be partially explained by fiscal policy, which until 1986 permitted corporations to deduct interest payments. It can also be partially explained by the group or family structure prevailing in Mexican industry. The group structure was favored in the import substitution years when the markets were highly protected from competition and foreign ownership was usually restricted to a 49% share.[60] When corporations do list publicly, the group controls most of the shares, leaving only a small percentage freely traded.[61] From 1997 to 2001, trading in stock accounted for only 3% of the turnover of the bolsa. While there are 35 companies included in its index, Telmex accounts for more than 26% of the market capitalization of the index. Approximately 60% of the index's market capitalization value is held in five firms: Telmex, Banamex-Accival, Telecom, WalMart de Mexico, and Cementos Mexicanos. Thus, like the other Latin American exchanges, trading is highly concentrated.

The privatization drive in the Mexican economy began in the De la Madrid presidency in the 1980s. Under De la Madrid's administration, each ministry could nominate a firm as a candidate, and the National Credit Society administered the sale. Few attractive firms were sold under this cumbersome process, although the number of public enterprises decreased considerably as small, nonmanufacturing enterprises were sold, firms were transferred to state governments, or closed. The sale of large assets occurred under the presidency of Carlos Salinas de Gortari from 1988 to 1994. Salinas and his team streamlined the process and conducted an ambitious divestiture of enterprise, with the exception of strategic sectors such as oil, electricity, and railroads.[62] Telmex was therefore a key component of Salinas's strategy.

### The Case of Telmex

The Mexican government acquired a 51% stake in Telmex in 1972 as the culmination of a 25-year process of acquiring and "Mexicanizing" shares of firms that had originally been owned by the Continental Corporation and Ericsson. When the government acquired its controlling 51% in 1972, the secretary of communications and transportation presided over the board of directors, himself chosen by the president of Mexico. Nonetheless, only 14 years later the state's control was threatened. To comply with the Uruguay round of GATT trade negotiations, the state would have to limit tariffs to 20%, remove import license requirements for telecom equipment, and remove a 5% surcharge on imports. Therefore the privatization initiative preceded the obligations under the NAFTA treaty and Salinas's presidency.

The Salinas administration announced in September 1989 that it would put a majority stake in Telmex up for sale and allow for international carriers to compete in Mexico's market. The government delayed its announcement, however, because Salinas wanted to give the union time to make an internal adjustment to the controversial decision.[63] As with the other examples, Telmex workers were organized into a union that opposed the sale out of concern that its labor contract would suffer. Unlike the example of ENTel, the government of Mexico reformed the company's tariff and tax structure prior to the sale and reduced 500 levels of salary under the former labor agreement to 41. The union agreed to allow new technology to be used by the firm. The administration later announced that the union would receive 4.4% of the newly privatized Telmex. At the time, the shares were worth approximately $10,000 per worker. Thus the union dropped its opposition to the sale.[64]

Business interests involved in the sale sought to modernize a phone system wherein the country ranked eighty-second worldwide in terms of phone lines per capita. They organized a media campaign against the workers union, blaming the lack of adequate phone service on corrupt Telmex employees. Many business interests had hesitated to invest in Telmex because they argued that the state should allow the private sector to form new telecommunications companies to compete with the utility.[65]

When sold in 1990, the government constrained buyers insofar as foreign buyers could not hold more than 10% of the firm's capital. The buyer would have to invest about US$10 billion by 1994, increase the number of public call boxes by more than 100%, and make more than 50% of the exchanges digital. Few groups, international or otherwise, had the requisite technology and capital to meet these demands.[66] The government divided Telmex's equity into 60% nonvoting

"L" shares and 40% voting "A" shares. Therefore Telmex could be controlled with 20% of the total equity, and a Mexican participant could gain control with just 10% of the total equity. Grupo Carso (a group led by Mexican businessman Carlos Slim), Southwestern Bell, and France Telecom purchased a controlling 20.4% stake in the firm. Critics argued that Telmex had been sold for less than it was worth, and that Salinas himself was the real beneficiary. Slim was widely known to be Salinas's friend, and had backed him financially before the 1988 presidential election.[67]

Regardless, the capital structure of the privatized firm satisfied Mexican nationalism, and by bringing in foreign firms in the first stage of the privatization, it served to raise the value of the stock in the second-stage global offering. In December 1990 Grupo Carso had paid just $2.04 per A share, but in May 1991 investors paid $3.41 per share. The Mexican Bolsa gained 60% as a whole in the five months following the sale, driven by foreign enthusiasm for Mexico's future.[68] At the time of the sale the secretary of communications and transportation ceased to serve as chairman of the board of Telmex, but he remained on the board until 1994. The new board has 12 Mexican investors from the Grupo Carso, 4 from Southwestern Bell, and 3 from France Telecom. The government sold its final blocs of company shares in later offerings, and in the years following the sale, Telmex has bid on telecommunication privatizations in other countries, such as Honduras.

### The Dependent Variable

Privatizations have influenced the Mexican Bolsa in a manner similar to the other large, Latin American emerging markets. The large issues of previously state-owned firms has increased market capitalization, yet the ownership structure of the resulting firms is not vulnerable to the market for managerial control. In the case of Telmex, the classes of the equity shares listed ensure that a Mexican will hold the controlling bloc. Yet there is foreign participation in the consortium. As with other Mexican business groups consisting of holding companies that invest in other companies, the holding company makes decisions on financing, dividends, fixed assets, and hiring of top managers. Individuals on top of the pyramid structure of Mexican groups generally sit on multiple boards. For example, Carlos Slim of Telmex sits on nine boards, all but one of which is from the group he controls.[69]

As the state has divested shares, multiple ownership models have emerged. Some public enterprises in strategic sectors remain under the control of the state. Some firms are foreign controlled. However, most firms have been sold to consortiums of both local and foreign investors. Of the public enterprises sold between 1987 and 1991, 98% ended up being controlled by Mexicans.[70] Many of these are situated within a family group.

## Analysis and Conclusion

In each of the four examples considered here, many of the similarities emanate from international considerations. In each of the four states, equity trades extend to the colonial era and grew during the period of British influence in the nine-

teenth century. In each case there was a degree, however small, of local participation in the local market. The early structuralist ideology of the ECLA discouraged capital market development in the region from the 1950s to 1970s in favor of
statist strategies. The debt crisis of the 1980s initiated many of the equity sell-offs,
since the crisis compelled governments to restructure their state-business bureauc-
racies. Since a history of equity trading existed, some IPOs with share auction
components were possible, particularly for large firms. Moreover, experience with
relatively sophisticated financial instruments meant that states eventually experimented with cross-listings, specifically nonvoting shares in the United States.
Hence the external influences explain one critical element of state behavior with
respect to stock markets: the listing and delisting of shares.

An examination of the individual deals in the contemporary era of state disengagement, however, explains what shares were listed and how those shares fit
into the ownership structure of the resulting firms. In some cases, controlling blocs
of shares were sold to foreign investors, in others to family business houses, and
in others, the controlling bloc remained with the state. Since variations on each
of these outcomes exist in each of the Latin American examples, no clear model
of corporate ownership with respect to the monitoring function of equity shares
has emerged. Rather, models have proliferated within a given state, and none have
developed a market for managerial control. Yet the lack of national convergence
in financial institutional structure does not mean that the state has lost its ability
to influence firm behavior.

To the contrary, the states have acted through provisions in the deals themselves, and they act in emergency situations. For example, the states set forth firm
investment targets and service requirements in each of the three telecommunications privatization deals examined here. In the Argentine economic crisis of
2001–2002, the state set forth rate guidelines and stipulated acceptable payment
currency. The Mexican government prioritized Mexican control in its nationalization of Telmex, whereas the Chilean government sought to maximize revenue
from the sale of CTC. A Mexican was thus able to control Telmex, whereas an
Australian who later sold his bloc of controlling shares controlled CTC. In the
2002 Brazilian presidential campaign, Petrobras reduced the price of cooking gas
and kept the price of gasoline 15% below world market prices to help (unsuccessfully) the electoral chances of Jose Serra.[71]

Table 6.2 summarizes the case studies examined in this chapter. It reviews
the level I (international) imperatives that initiated the sale, as well as the level II
(domestic) constituency groups required to complete the sale. In the Argentine
and Mexican cases, unions protesting the sale were promised a bloc of shares in
the new distribution. In the Chilean case, union members received individual
ownership of large enterprise through the privatized pension funds that bought
the shares of privatized firms. In the Brazilian case, the controlling interest remained with the state. Thus the case studies support the overall argument that
policymakers reconciled international and domestic considerations in concluding
privatization deals. The case studies also show that the dismantling of the state
sector through the case-by-case method has not been uniform; thus the degree of
independence from state control has likewise not been uniform. In most cases,

TABLE 6.2 Summary of Latin American Cases Examined

| State | Company privatized (year) | International imperatives (level I) | Groups protesting privatization sale (level II) | Distribution of shares | Controlling interest held by (governance structure) |
|---|---|---|---|---|---|
| Brazil | Petrobras (several sales beginning in 1985) | Credit difficulties associated with debt crisis of 1982, ongoing debt problems | Oil workers union, nationalist legislators, petroleum engineers, military | 6.6% of Petrobras total in 1985; 30% to employees when Petrobras Química, S.A. subsidiary sold; 26.04% sold as preferred stock when the Fuel Distribution Network was sold; 50% sold to international investors when Petrobras sold in 1998; as of 2002 common shares, federal government of Brazil 55.7%, 22.7% are level III ADRs, foreigners 3.4 %. | State as stakeholder (state, some offerings with classes of shares) |
| Argentina | ENTel (1990) | Hyperinflation of 1980s, debt | Telecommunications workers union, large holding groups, Siemens de Argentina (ENTel supplier) | Company split. Of total, 60% offered in a competitive bidding offer, 30% offered subsequently, 10% reserved for employees (state retained), Telefonica of Spain-controlled Southern Company, Bell Atlantic, and then a consortium led by France Cable/STET-controlled Northern Company. | Foreign managerial consortium (MNC—each consortium included MNC, Argentine group, and bank holding debt) |
| Chile | CTC (1988) | Aftereffects of economic crisis in 1982–1983, listing requirements of the New York Stock Exchange | Enterprise Defense Command and Christian Democratic Party, Argentine unions | Initially 45% to Bond Corporation International who sold to Telefonica of Spain, 10% offered as ADRs in the United States (Union members receive indirect ownership of large enterprise through privatized pension funds that bought many shares). | Foreign managerial consortium (MNC) |
| Mexico | Telmex (1990) | Uruguay Round obligations, then NAFTA | Telmex workers union | 43% already traded on the Bolsa. In 1990, 60% nonvoting "L" shares, 40% voting "A" shares. Managerial control needs 20% of total, but with a limit of 10% of the total for foreigners, a Mexican owner only needs 10% of voting shares to control a managerial consortium. Union promised 4.4% of newly privatized firm. | Consortium of national and international management, led by Mexican investor Carlos Slim (controlling minority structure with classes of shares) |

regulatory change (and not the sale of shares) broke the monopoly power of the large parastatals. However, a significant degree of ability to control the firm remains with the state.

What distinguishes the Latin American cases from some of the other regions to be considered is the degree of political support for the reforms. Much of the political science literature on privatization in Latin America has tended to emphasize the degree of insulation of reforming technocrats from vested interests. Nonetheless, others have successfully argued that shifting political coalitions allowed the privatizations to take place. For example, Corrales argues that the Argentine private-sector coalition disintegrated as a result of reordered economic institutions. Thus, without its traditional allies, the private-sector chose to acquiesce.[72] Similarly Armijo and Faucher argue that the move to markets in Brazil, Argentina, Chile, and Mexico had a degree of popular political support.[73]

The varying concessions made to domestic political groups as well as the financial limits of domestic entrepreneurs seeking to buy state enterprises explain the varying ownership structures that resulted, such as some reserving a bloc of shares for workers and others issuing dual classes of shares for foreign and domestic capital participation with domestic control. The key consideration in these cases was the ability of related labor unions to protest a given sale, to extract a percentage of shares for workers in a given offering, and to provide a method of financing these shares.

Since the dismantling of the state sector has been incomplete in this region, the price mechanism is an unlikely vehicle of control as it operates in the U.S. model—the "Wall Street Rule." The price could never drop low enough to threaten a hostile takeover. The distribution of shares seems to point to a stakeholder model, yet not a stakeholder model as operates in Europe and Japan. Rather, with the state retaining blocs of shares in some examples, the evidence points to a third "state as stakeholder" model wherein the state retains adequate shares to continue to play a role in firm governance, while allowing for some independent (i.e., nonstate) influence. This "state as stakeholder" model applies to those firms, such as Petrobras and Pemex (the Mexican oil parastatal), where the state retains the controlling shares. Moreover, even in examples such as that of Telmex, where the state eventually transferred 100% of the shares to the private sector, the price mechanism cannot threaten corporate governance in *global* markets as it does in the market model, since the terms of the privatization deal (and the terms of shares issued in various markets with and without voting rights) guarantee Mexican control.

# Asia and the Pacific

Equity products play a significant role in negotiating difficult political transitions associated with state engagement and disengagement from economic enterprise. This role in Asian emerging markets is no exception. Moreover, exchanges in this region resemble each other in that policymakers have attempted to keep the ultimate authority for decision making in large firms within the territorial confines of each given state. Nonetheless, the Asian markets have exhibited a far greater degree of diversity in individual approaches to state involvement in directing private industry than the Latin American markets did. The end result resembles Latin America because governance models proliferate and shareholders will unlikely be able to exert any degree of influence over management. Yet the individual domestic structures protecting managerial discretion vary far more among states in the region.

To examine the political and economic processes culminating in large share issues on Asian emerging markets, this chapter considers the Indian, Chinese, Korean, and Thai markets. Share trading has deep historical roots across the region for the reasons set out earlier in the book. The oldest and most active exchanges were those associated with British (and to a lesser extent Dutch) rule. The oldest of these is the Bombay Stock Exchange, established in 1875 in what was then a British colony. The highest degree of early twentieth century share trading activity, however, occurred in the international settlement area of Shanghai, where the Shanghai Sharebrokers Association was established in 1891 and the Shanghai Stock Exchange was later established in 1904. Share trading in local tea and rubber plantations began in Colombo in 1896. Shares of Dutch East Indies government agencies such as plantations were traded in colonial Jakarta. Like most of the exchanges, the Indonesian exchanges closed at the outset of World War II.[1] Since the Japanese did not begin to experiment with corporate forms until the end of the Tokugawa regime in 1868, an active share market did not grow there until the end of the nineteenth century. When it did grow, however, the Japanese floated public offerings and bonds in both Japan and Korea, where Japanese firms listed on the first organized exchange and Japanese brokers conducted most of the trading. This market likewise disintegrated with World War II.[2]

States within the region pursued radically different approaches to economic development beginning with the Communist revolution in China; however, post–World War II Asia lacked the sort of unifying developmental ideology the Latin American region possessed. Latin American ideology was more coherent across states because the institution of the ECLA had fostered it. The Asian bloc in the G-77 of the United Nations was fragmented because its member states possessed greater differences in economic development (e.g., Bangladesh and South Korea) and greater economic diversity (e.g., Iran, India, and Vietnam) than the Latin American or African bloc. Moreover, the Asians were fragmented into subregional groups, wherein the Association of South East Asian Nations and the League of Arab States (which included part of the African region as well) were the most prominent.[3] Finally, the strategic importance of Japan and Korea to U.S. foreign policy as a result of the Communist revolution in China further strained what regional unity might have developed in its absence.

Given this degree of diversity, states responded to varying level I international imperatives. They also dealt differently with their domestic constituencies on level II when issuing shares in the new era because the constituencies were differently organized. Therefore this chapter examines four exchanges that are dramatically different from those in the previous chapter, as well as from each other. The cases of India and China in particular are significant. The Communist revolution in China obliterated the history of equity trading in Shanghai. And unlike the post-Communist exchanges to be considered in the next chapter, the Chinese did not attempt any sort of restitution in their move to markets. Rather, the equity markets have been state designed and implemented down to each individual issue within a relatively short time frame.

Conversely, India has one of the oldest continually functioning exchanges in the world. Indians have participated on this exchange since its inception. Although various state development strategies have left their imprints on shares listed in Bombay, one era does not eradicate the listings and practices of all previous eras. Therefore these two exchanges show how differences in the longevity of a state's experience with equity finance contribute to the diversity of models of corporate governance. The longer the uninterrupted experience with equity finance and different development strategies in a state, the greater the variation in shareholding patterns and vulnerability to the price mechanism (of some firms within that variation) the state's market exhibits. The shorter the time frame of involvement with equity finance the state exhibits, the less the variation and the greater the consistency in shareholding patterns.

South Korea represents a third example of state intervention. On the one hand, a history of equity trades in Korea extends to the late Japanese colonial era. On the other hand, the current stock exchange owes its existence to U.S. and World Bank development assistance in the 1950s and 1960s. The initial manner of state intervention in South Korean industrial development occurred through a process of preferential credit allocation to large conglomerates, and not through state ownership of shares. The Korean exchange was closed to foreign investment until the 1980s, and grew from reasonably consistent government policies encouraging Korean firms to seek capital market finance. Finally, in the fourth example, the Thai case demonstrates states and firms offering minority shares of large enterprises in a boom.

Taken together, the Asian region shows states with expanding equity markets and growing participation. However, the region also shows the importance of considering "what is for sale" on a given exchange, and how that product fits into the ownership and control structure of the large firm.

## India

India presents one case of an emerging market where the extension of equity finance has resulted from prolonged government activity, yet privatization has not played the significant role in contributing to market capitalization and the number of firms listed that it has played elsewhere. Share trading extends to an earlier era and was highly international from its origins in British colonialism. Hence the Indian stock exchanges are deeply embedded in Indian capitalism. The historical roots and high degree of connection to society both help and hinder reforms. Hindustan Lever is a case study because it is connected to earlier Indian political economies and because it continues to play a role in the privatization era as a buyer of former government firms. Its role demonstrates how shares of large firms can, and cannot, be listed publicly. Listed on the Bombay Stock Exchange, multinational corporations such as Unilever operate alongside traditional Indian business houses and partially privatized state-controlled firms. Thus, while it appears that India is enacting reforms along the Anglo-American model, these markets will not ultimately perform the same function in corporate governance across firms as they do in the United States or United Kingdom.

### Share Trading in India

Early British involvement in the affairs of the Indian subcontinent was conducted through the British East India Company. Over time the British government became involved in the company's administration, and thus in administering the territory as well. After the 1857 Sepoy mutiny, the transfer of civil authority from the company to the British crown was completed and the City of London directed a growing amount of investment toward India. At its peak, India was second only to Canada as a recipient of investment. Approximately 18% of the total capital raised on the London stock market and placed in the British empire between 1865 and 1914 was directed to India. Significantly, much of this capital was channeled during the railroad boom, making India's share of British investment even larger at the beginning of the period when the boom in India was at its peak.[4]

Despite the large amount of British investment in India relative to other parts of the British empire, the British mostly used India as an export market. The result of British rule and competition with British manufactured imports was such that the production of indigenous artisans declined considerably and agricultural production stagnated.[5] Company law in India initially discouraged joint-stock investment, since a British corporation operating there could only receive corporate status through a royal charter, letters patent, act of the British Parliament, or act of the Indian legislature. The East India Company generally opposed such grants.[6]

After the passage of an English law requiring the registration of certain firms, the Indian Companies Act of 1850 allowed (yet did not require) every unincorporated company of seven or more persons whose shares were transferable to register.[7] Similarly following the British parliamentary lead, the Indian legislature passed an act introducing limited liability in 1857. Lawmakers in India consciously rationalized this legislation on the grounds that English and Indian law should be alike so that partnerships formed on the principle of limited liability in England, and conducting business in India, would encounter similar laws and similar risks.[8]

Prior to the formal transfer of civil authority from the British East India Company to the British government in 1858, railroad construction there had been considered too risky for private enterprise. In the 1840s, entrepreneurs had submitted a project to the company for a line from Calcutta to the northwest and another from Bombay to the Indian interior. The East India Company's charter barred it from raising a loan for these purposes and the projects were not pursued. After 1857, the government of India granted all necessary land, free of expense for 99 years, to railroad companies incorporated by an act of Parliament in England. In addition, the government guaranteed interest (approximately 5%) on capital used for these purposes. By July 1858, seven companies were formed under the guarantee system and 428.5 miles of line were opened. By 1860, 839.25 miles were open and by 1874, 6227.75 miles were open.[9] Almost all of the capital for these ventures was subscribed in London. The companies were British in origin and their boards in London controlled their operations in India.

Despite the foreign nature of railroad operations and the magnitude of railroad investments relative to manufacturing, the joint-stock form of organization came to occupy an important position in the Indian economy by the 1870s, particularly in Bombay and Calcutta. Almost all of the tea factories, jute and cotton mills, and many coal mines were organized on this basis. While foreign capital was highly concentrated in certain industries, such as jute mills, there was almost no foreign investment in the cotton industry. In the Bombay Presidency of 1911, Indians owned 92 of 129 (cotton) textile mills entirely, and exclusively non-Indian directors controlled only 12.

Along with the growth of limited liability companies, the number of brokers dealing in shares of these firms grew. And unlike the railroad example where the brokers operated in London, these brokers traded shares in India. Whereas only 6 share brokers were known in Bombay between 1840 and 1850, there were 60 in 1860 (i.e., shortly after the 1857 limited liability legislation), and 318 in 1877 (i.e., the end of the boom in cotton coinciding with the American Civil War). Indian brokers, prevented by the British from trading on their exchanges, assembled in Dalal Street in Bombay and developed an extensive, if informal, market. In July 1875 they met to draft rules for the Native Share and Stock Brokers Association in order to organize and regulate a business that had grown increasingly chaotic. Twelve years after the association was founded, it was formally constituted. Only natives of India were eligible for membership in the association.[10]

A similar assembly of brokers emerged in Calcutta, although Europeans organized and managed share dealing there. Attempts to organize the exchange in Calcutta extend to 1858, yet the Calcutta Stock Exchange was not formally constituted until 1908. First Europeans and Bengalis, then Marwaris increasingly came to dominate the scene. Both share markets were highly speculative and shared the common feature of *satta* (i.e., time bargains in which a difference in price alone is passed).

The market for shares of Indian joint-stock companies was similar to that of the metropole insofar as a local market existed for local firms and an international market existed for larger firms operating out of London. Yet the stock exchanges in India developed slowly, probably due to differences in corporate management in Britain and India. Professional management firms managed many British firms operating in India. British capitalists who sought careful supervision of their Indian investments, yet did not necessarily want to live in India, initially created the managing agencies; eventually Indian-owned companies operated under the system as well.[11] The obvious benefits of the agencies were that they were a source of managerial and technical talent, and that they mobilized capital.

But the obvious drawbacks were that the agencies created a concentration of control that at times had the effect of destroying viable firms when management was inefficient or corrupt. Moreover, the European agencies tended to employ European staffs and looked to European expertise and capital. Charlesworth argues that the managing agencies had the effect of stunting the growth of the stock exchanges precisely because managers bypassed them and looked for capital elsewhere. These managing firms were usually responsible for the initial promotion, financing, underwriting, and organizing of the joint stock. Therefore they did not need indigenous financial infrastructures such as stock exchanges, particularly the foreign firms with independent contacts and sources of capital.[12]

The number of new stock exchanges in India grew when the polity was mobilized as a supply base in World War II. For example, the Uttar Pradesh Stock Exchange Ltd. and the Nagpur Stock Exchange Ltd. were formed in 1940, and the Hyderabad Stock Exchange Ltd. was incorporated in 1944. Two other stock exchanges were floated later in Delhi in 1947.

Nonetheless, the postindependence, state-led development strategy sought industrialization insulated from the global economy, which deemphasized a role for local exchanges. Economic nationalism and interventionism in India likewise diminished their role. Several important pieces of legislation facilitated this process. Following independence in 1948, Indian leaders gave the government a monopoly in armaments, atomic energy, railroads, etc. Consequently companies in these industries delisted from the existing exchanges. The 1947 Foreign Exchange Regulation Act placed restrictions on nonresident companies and Indian companies with more than 40% of equity held by nonresidents. In 1956 the government added 17 industries to the list of industries to be conducted exclusively in the public sphere, and in so doing continued to nationalize companies. The government of the 1960s suspected private trading houses and conglomerates of manipulating markets and prices for their own profit, hence the anti-private-sector attitude persisted. The banking industry was nationalized in 1969, removing a large portion of listings from the exchanges.

Despite the high degree of state planning and restrictions on many types of economic activity, opportunities for domestic firms emerged in the independence period. The top Indian managing agents promoted new businesses by contributing a minimal amount of equity capital and then raising the rest through public offerings or from public financial institutions. A single promoter and members of his family thus gained control of a network of firms, resulting in a conglomerate or "business house." The control of the structure was in the top company, yet the firms were reasonably widely held.[13] Of privately held firms in India, the pyramid mechanism for concentrating control of family conglomerates predominates. For example, Godrej Soaps is listed on the Bombay Stock Exchange. The Godrej family holds 67% of the publicly traded shares through the privately held firm Godrej and Boyce Manufacturing Co. Further down on the pyramid, Godrej Soaps owns 65% of Godrej Agrovet (agriculture), and with the Godrej Group owns 65% of Godrej Foods (food processing).[14]

Large corporations grew during this period, but the families' control meant that they could distribute the benefits according to their own interests, and not necessarily those of noncontrolling shareholders.[15] The public financial institutions participating in the firm appointed their own nominees to the boards of these firms, however, the appointees were not to control the firm, but to protect the interests of the (Indian) shareholding public. In most instances these board members are believed to have supported existing management's decisions.[16]

The government turned toward liberalization in the 1980s, yet the turn has been more concerned with dismantling controls over private-sector activities, and in attracting foreign investment, than in privatizing state enterprises. Thus it has a "stop and go" quality, when compared with similar liberalization programs in Latin America or eastern Europe.[17] Despite the lack of large-scale sell-offs, the World Bank encouraged new issues on the Indian stock exchanges as a source of finance for the Indian private corporate sector. The bank suggested equity markets for the same reason it had suggested them elsewhere: to widen the options for savers, to increase the supply of savings for borrowers, to increase the allocative efficiency of the financial sector, and to improve the flow of financial information.[18] Many new exchanges were thus formed in the 1980s, and others that had not been recognized under the Securities Contracts Regulation Act of 1956 were established again. By 1995 the number of exchanges had grown from 8 in the independence period, to 22.

In 1991 the government recommitted itself to liberalization when low foreign exchange reserves, high deficits, and large losses of public-sector enterprises compelled it to seek assistance from the World Bank and IMF. A comprehensive reform program and changes in company law, trade, foreign investment, and industrial policy followed. The institutional legacy of the Bombay Stock Exchange impeded, as well as facilitated, these reforms. Many of the brokers on the exchange come from the Gujarati community, and in many cases their family members have worked as brokers for generations. Despite the lack of complete uniformity of the ethnicity of the exchange's membership, the sense of community allowed the brokers to form an exclusive club that maximized returns on individual transactions by manipulating the exchanges' archaic settlement system. Complicated paperwork procedures lengthened the amount of time between trades and settlement during which brokers speculated with their clients' money. Issuing companies could delay transfers as well, and had an incentive to do so if the delay minimized sales that depressed the price of their stock. The majority of the stock exchanges were closed 40%–50% of the year and even when opened, operated for only two hours a day.[19]

When the government established the Securities and Exchange Board (SEBI) of India in April 1988 to regulate the exchanges, the entity was ineffectual because any exercise of regulatory powers set SEBI against the stockbrokers. Establishing the National Stock Exchange of India (NSE) had a greater effect than the establishment of SEBI because the exchange induced a degree of competition with the Bombay Stock Exchange. The Bombay Stock Exchange had refused SEBI recommendations to admit new brokers, and Bombay Stock Exchange brokers had fought SEBI's capital adequacy norms when the NSE was incorporated in November 1992. Designed to be more investor friendly than the Bombay Stock Exchange, the trading volume of the NSE surpassed the Bombay Stock Exchange in one year.[20]

The financial reforms have had effects on India's corporate governance procedures (understood broadly). First, business associations and government officials began to issue reports and speak out on the issue. As firms sought to issue GDRs, listing requirements on world exchanges resulted in better accounting practices and reforms facilitating mergers and acquisitions in India. Second, the measures have forced corporate India to respond to pressure to meet higher standards of performance and be more responsive to the interests of shareholders. Third, the reforms associated with mergers and acquisitions have permitted hostile takeovers that could have been denied under the previous legislation if the company's management determined that the takeover was not in the company's interest. In January 1997, the bidder's price did not need to be approved by regulators. Thus there were almost no hostile takeovers prior to the reforms. Under the new code, financial institutions can invite takeover bids after companies have lost only 50% of their net worth. In February 1998, financial institutions could lend money to finance takeovers. In the spring of 1998, takeovers ensued.[21]

However, since the Bharatiya Janata Party (BJP) government that came into power in 1998 draws support from groups that oppose privatization, the pace of privatization continues to progress slowly. When the BJP attempted to proceed with its privatization program, it preferred to give priority in purchasing public-sector undertakings to Indian firms, and thus evade charges that it had allowed a "foreign takeover" of national assets. This policy put the government at odds with a department it had created itself, the Department of Disinvestment, which sought bidders globally and preferred foreign companies participation because they possessed modern technology, capital, and managerial expertise.[22]

## The Case of Unilever

One example of state-firm activity that demonstrates the historical trajectory of foreign investment, varying degree of managerial control, and stock issuance in India is the example of Unilever. William Lever registered a Lever Brothers subsidiary in India as an English company in 1913 to safeguard his brands. After that, Lever Brothers conducted its business in India as an export market and did not build local plants because management felt the Indian market was limited to those individuals who could afford imported soap.[23] The firm reconsidered the benefits of local production in the 1930s, however, and concluded that establishing a local manufacturing operation would be advantageous. At the time, Gandhi urged the boycott of foreign goods, and a new Indian tariff imposed duties of 25% *ad valorem* on imported soap. The initial proposal for the soap factory called for Indian nationals to hold 60% of the capital and for Indian nationals to serve on the board. However, management in London did not approve the initial proposal, since the establishment of a plant would result in a loss of trade with India and potentially lead to the necessity of closing a factory in England.[24] When the Indian factory eventually did open, Unilever owned all of its nominal capital, and Indians did not receive majority shareholding.

Unilever's interest in developing local manufacturing concerns in India was defensive, not offensive. The company did not undertake production there because production costs were cheaper than in Britain or Holland; labor was a small component of production costs. Rather the firm expanded to meet the threat of serious local competition from indigenous capitalists who could challenge foreign importers, combined with the tariff of 1931–1932 that demonstrated the autonomy of the Indian government to formulate economic policy in its own interests.[25]

As the Indian government grew increasingly interventionist during the World War II years, taxes grew, capital equipment and raw materials grew scarce, and production grew increasingly regulated. When the government became even more interventionist in the postindependence period, Nehru announced that foreign investors would need to provide for Indian ownership of a proportion of the capital and progressive Indianization of top management.[26] While the representation of Indians in management at Unilever had been growing since the war, the participation of Indian capital in the firm posed a greater problem.

In 1945 Unilever owned all of its subsidiaries in all countries, except in cases where it had bought an existing company. India was the first country to expect the multinational to indigenize shares, albeit not immediately. In January 1955, Unilever attempted to resolve the situation by selling nonvoting preference shares. The government would not accept this offer and demanded that Indians have a share in the equity. The next year the firm sold 20% of the shares when three Unilever companies merged to form Hindustan Lever, yet in practical terms little changed. The equity had been distributed among 16,000 separate shareholders who could do little to influence management, but expected dividends and bonus shares. Thus Hindustan Lever was forced to use its profits as dividends and to capitalize undistributed profits as bonus shares more regularly than they may have otherwise done.[27] In later years the government forced additional offerings by offering to license various projects for diversification of the business pending, and by controlling foreign exchange.

A technical problem emerged as Indian shareholding grew, in that Indians bought shares with nonconvertible rupees. If Unilever sought to expand and finance expansion in India with required imported equipment, the firm needed to pay for the equipment. Since it could not pay with rupees, it needed to provide its own foreign currency. If it did this, and the expansion was converted into shares, the balance of shareholding between Indians and non-Indians would be thrown off. The problem was not resolved until after 1965, when the government agreed to provide sufficient hard currency to pay for approved imports of capital goods by accepting rupees as payment. When the company increased its total share capital, it would sell all of the new shares to Indians. Over time, the question of ultimate control arose should Unilever's shareholding in Hindustan Lever fall below 51%.[28]

When the privatization program picked up in the late 1990s, Hindustan Lever emerged as a likely buyer for some state firms. It bought Modern Food in what was to become Vajpayee's first major full-scale privatization. In the first stage the government sold 74% of the firm's equity in January 2000. At the time, the company's employees held a rally demanding that the deal be cancelled, and later challenged it in court. In addition, employees sought reassurances with respect to their job security and working conditions. Nonetheless, the government sold the remaining 26% the next year. Employees were paid Rs4 crore against old wage settlement dues, but did not receive an allocation of shares.[29] The union leader, Govind Yadav, accused the government of selling the firm for much less than it was worth. The controversy over pricing arose from the pricing of real estate assets possessed by Modern Food.

With the sale of Modern Food, the state clearly transferred control to a transnational corporation. However, new shares were not issued. Thus the privatization program, as with this example, has not contributed to increased market listings, because one firm was sold entirely to another. However, as of March 2002, the ownership structure of the acquiring firm was as follows: Unilever owned 51.55% of the stock of Hindustan Lever, and the Indian public owned the next largest concentration of stock, with 21.28%.

*The Dependent Variable*

The function of Indian stock markets with respect to corporate governance appears to be moving in the Anglo-American direction. Shares are freely priced. Takeovers have occurred since the late 1990s, and the revision of the Indian Company Act has strengthened disclosure norms, established an Investor Education and Protection Fund, and established a National Advisory Committee on accounting standards. Moreover, while hostile takeovers are now permitted under the new regulations, firms may also buy their own shares from the stock market and conduct other activities to help fight takeover bids.[30]

Despite these indications of a shift toward the Anglo-American model, other indications point to the improbability of the market ever fully operating as the New York or London markets do. First, Indian company law favored the British model since the first law was written to provide for seamless business operations between Great Britain and India in the nineteenth century. Therefore it has always been oriented in the Anglo-American tradition relative to other countries in the region. Second, SEBI has not evolved over time into a regulatory institution in the American understanding due to resistance from both brokers and the corporate community. The latter group prefers executive power to rest with the government and not an autonomous body. Later efforts to increase SEBI's powers have resulted in the repeal of some of its early statutes.[31]

The pace and scope of the privatization program render government-owned firms an unlikely source of shares. The first government-owned enterprise to invite equity participation from the public was the Indian Petrochemicals Corporation (IPCL), which initially divested 20% of its shares and offered a further 20 million shares on the Bombay Stock Exchange in October 1992. The Disinvestment Commission recommended that the government sell a further 25% stake in IPCL in 1998, which would reduce the government's stake to less than 50%. The goal of the additional divestment was to locate a strategic buyer who would give the firm better access to raw materials, new markets, and technologies.[32] The government needs to own 26% of the equity of a given firm to block special resolutions brought by the board. Despite the pronouncements of the finance minister, the firm failed to meet its target by the end of 1998. In 2002 the government planned to sell stakes in two oil companies and an aluminum maker, Hindustan Petroleum Corporation, Bharat Petroleum Corporation, and Nalco, respectively. Nonetheless, the larger offerings planned for the years 2002–2003 were subsidiaries of transnational corporations such as Hyundai Motor and LG Electronics, of South Korea, and stakes of Bharti Tele-ventures and TCS, of the Indian Tata conglomerate.[33]

When the government does divest shares, it generally sells them either to a subsidiary of a foreign firm, as with Modern Food and Hindustan Lever, or to a domestic business group. The latter type of disinvestment raises contentious political issues as well as the former, and these issues raise questions about the future of control of privatized firms within domestic business groups. For example, Tata Group, one of India's largest conglomerates, bought 25% of the equity of India's monopoly telecommunications carrier for international calls, Videsh Sanchar Nigam Ltd. (VSNL) in 2002. Tata was then required under Indian takeover laws to make an open, public offer for an additional 20% equity to VSNL stakeholders at the same share price of its original bid.[34] When the firm finally obtained 45% of VSNL, VSNL attempted to invest US$245 million in another Tata firm in exchange for 26% equity in the Tata Company. New Delhi, which still owned 25% of VSNL accused the Tatas of "asset stripping" and threatened legal action. VSNL and the government eventually agreed to review the decision.[35]

A series of government issues in March 2004 appeared to have been prompted by upcoming federal elections, and to prove the sincerity of the BJP's intentions with respect to the broader privation program. In three weeks, the government offered stakes in three large firms: Oil and Natural Gas Corporation (84.1% government owned, 10% stake offered), Gas Authority of India (67.3% government owned, 10% stake offered), and the Dredging Corporation of India (20% stake offered). It also plans to sell its residual stakes in Indian Petrochemicals Corporation (controlled by Reliance Industries), CMC Limited (a software services company controlled by the Tata Group), and the IBP Company (a petroleum products marketing concern controlled by the Indian Oil Corporation). The sale of these shares is expected to raise $3.5 billion (US), which in turn will enable the government to reduce its budget deficit.[36]

Rather than resulting in consistent governance structures, additional listings have prompted further ambiguities with respect to takeovers within conglomerates and within transnational firms, since SEBI's enforcement has varied dramatically. For example, a division of a transnational firm may be sold to another transnational firm overseas, which would result in a transfer of controlling shares of the Indian subsidiary. It is unclear under Indian law whether or not this transaction is subject to an open offer or not. It is similarly unclear when shares are transferred within group companies, since investors may or may not be aware that a given firm is within a group.[37]

This broad mix of share offerings fails to point to one universal model of equity ownership and influence on corporate governance, pointing instead to several models existing side by side. They exist side by side because their origins differ dramatically as well. Some large firms in India such as Hindustan Lever have origins in the British colonial era, some large conglomerates such as the Tata Group and Godrej and Boyce Manufacturing Co. have origins in the colonial and interventionist eras, and a few, such as IPCL, the oil companies, and Nalco, are emerging from government privatizations. Some firms will be subject to the market for corporate control, while others will be subject to controlling minority shareholders (i.e., part of business houses), foreign corporate management, or government representation on the board.

## South Korea

The example of South Korea is an example of greater convergence at the state level. Large corporations in South Korea are conglomerates characterized by cross-ownership structures; they did not result from foreign direct investment, nor were they parastatals. These conglomerates interfaced with the state through industrial policy and preferential credit extended to those firms that implemented policy. Therefore, while the state has disengaged from its implementation of industrial policy through the banking system, this disengagement has not meant that new corporate structures have emerged. A case study of such a group, Samsung Group, is included here to describe the nature of equity growth, and the international influences on market reform and corporate governance.

### Share Trading in South Korea

The earliest organized securities market in Korea appeared during the period of Japanese rule. However, the market was suspended during World War II. After the late 1940s, South Korea entered into a period of American hegemony wherein the United States not only gave Korea military and economic aid, it deeply influenced economic programs and Korean society at large so that Korean policymakers opposed purely national solutions and pursued regional integration.[38]

One aspect of this American involvement was an ongoing, concerted effort to promote an active securities market. The Securities and Exchange Law of 1962 set forth the legal framework for a market, and the Law on Fostering the Capital Market of 1968 promoted its development by encouraging enterprises to go public, stimulating widely dispersed ownership of shares, and creating an investment climate ensuring the public's participation in enterprises. The Public Corporation Inducement Law of 1974 contained measures inducing companies to go public. Forty-one did so in 1974.

An additional aspect of these efforts was the cooperation between the World Bank, its affiliate the IFC, and South Korean administrators to develop an equity market. The ongoing nature of the relationship between the IFC and the Korean government, as well as the type of aid provided to Korea, rendered this relationship unique. For example, the IFC would, from time to time, sponsor junior officials from the Korean Securities Bureau or the Ministry of Finance to travel to Washington, DC, for a length of time to learn accounting standards, gain experience with securities commissions, or learn about stock exchanges, depending on the case. The IFC did not offer this type of informal technical assistance to all countries. The result of this ongoing partnership was that under South Korean Finance Minister Nam Duck Woo, Korea established the most comprehensive set of policies and infrastructural mechanisms found prior to that time in any emerging Asian equity market. Korea also developed the largest long-term corporate bond department in the developing world.[39]

Similar to Indian business houses, large Korean firms are conglomerates called *chaebols*, wherein a small, controlling group of shareholders exerts considerable power across industries through extensive patterns of cross-holdings. Unlike most other emerging market examples where the controlling family owns a greater percentage of shares, the Korean *chaebols* represent the most radical break between control and cash flow rights in that the controlling families in listed Korean companies have only been a fraction of the whole, and their power derives from the cross-ownership of affiliated companies. In fact, the ownership of the controlling shareholder and his family declined in the period from 8.3% in 1983 to 3.49% in 2001, yet their personal hold on the group remains formidable.[40]

In the 1970s the government implemented its industrial planning policies through state-owned commercial banks that provided low-cost loans to the *chaebols*, and by limiting the entry of multinationals. The government supported an individual company in a project for a limited time. Should the company fail to meet performance targets, it was dropped. Therefore, while patronage politics existed at the domestic level, world markets stimulated corporate competition. In this manner the government implemented its plan, and the *chaebols* funded their growth with negative real interest rates created by the government interest rate subsidies and high inflation.[41]

By the early 1980s a variety of parties hoped to expand portfolio investment on the Korean Stock Exchange. The Korean government itself was involved in a wider-scale financial liberalization project, chiefly in response to a desire to reduce the burden of default risk in a system where the state was the creditor.[42] In 1980 the Chun Doo Hwan government moved to privatize the commercial banks. Privatization meant that the government both supplied stocks to the market for sale and realized revenues when they were sold. Later, ceilings were imposed on debt-equity ratios, thereby forcing Korean firms to seek stock market financing. Whereas international securities transactions involving securities in Korea, or investment from Korea, were virtually prohibited prior to 1980, the government allowed two Korean securities investment trust companies to establish trusts for nonresident institutional investors at US$15 million each in October 1981. First Boston and Vickers da Costa of London marketed the Korea International Trust; Merrill Lynch International marketed the Korea Trust, a private placement founded by Daehan Investment Trust Company.[43] Both were increased by US$10 million to US$25 million in 1984.[44]

Private international portfolio investors shared the Korean government's growing interest in expanding foreign portfolio investment on the Korean Stock Exchange. Researchers investigating Japanese corporations as early as the 1960s and 1970s learned that Sony and Sharpe, for example, perceived their future competition to be Korean firms like Samsung and Goldstar rather than American firms like RCA and Zenith. Inquiries at the Korean Ministry of Finance in the 1970s revealed that the Koreans objected strongly to foreign ownership, particularly Japanese ownership.[45] Nonetheless, the investors remained interested in the possibilities inherent in the Korean economy and continued to search for ways investment for purposes of return, and exclusive of control, could be arranged.

Taken together, the IFC, Korean government, and investment firms had varying interests in opening opportunities for portfolio investment on the Korean Stock Exchange. The IFC hoped to further its mandate to develop domestic capital markets and provide somewhat "permanent" equity capital to the Korean market. Investment firms sought opportunities for diversification in a previously closed environment. And the Korean government sought capital. The convergence of these interests resulted in the IFC's floating of the landmark Korea Fund in 1984. The Korea Fund was notable for being the first of a string of closed-end emerging market funds listed on major exchanges such as New York or London. It was also notable for having further opened the Korean market to international portfolio investment.[46]

In 1988 the Korean Ministry of Finance required 177 companies with debts of more than US$30 million to repay them with equity financing. The ministry also ordered 598 of the *chaebol*-affiliated companies to repay bank debts with funds to be raised in the capital markets. Korean firms raised more than 20 times the previous amount of capital raised in equity markets between 1986 and 1989. The number of listed companies on the Korean Stock Exchange grew from 355 in 1986 to 626 in 1990.[47] The results of these activities, combined with the internationalization of the capital markets, were such that at the start of 1980 the South Korean stock market capitalization made up 5% of the emerging market capitalization total, and at the end of 1990 it made up 23% of the total. In 1990 it was the largest of the world's emerging markets.[48]

## The Case of Samsung Group

Samsung is a typical *chaebol* group in that its structure, management, and connection to Korean industrial policy reflect the others. It began as a small trading company that exported dried fish, vegetables, and fruit to Manchuria in 1938. It expanded into one of the largest of the South Korean *chaebols*, at times generating up to 11% of the country's exports. Along the path of this expansion, it established Samsung-Sanyo Electronics Company in 1969. Listed on the Korean Stock Exchange in 1975, the Korean government designated Samsung Electronics to be a general trading company. After that, the corporation established branches in New York, Tokyo, and Frankfurt to develop export markets in the United States, Japan, and Germany. From 1976 to 1980, the firm expanded in order to acquire access to overseas resources such as coal, oil, and wool. In the 1980s, Samsung Electronics opened production facilities in the United States, Great Britain, and Portugal in order to evade trade barriers and further develop products to meet local needs. In the late 1980s and 1990s, it opened production facilities in Southeast Asia, Latin America, and eastern European countries to exploit cheaper labor costs.[49] At its peak, the entire Samsung Group comprised more than 64 companies in almost all manufacturing and service sectors.[50] It represents approximately 20% of the shares of the Korean Stock Exchange on a given trading day.[51]

After the Asian financial crisis in late 1997, Samsung restructured itself by selling affiliated companies and reducing personnel. It reduced the number of its affiliates to 47 companies and sold 10 business units to overseas companies for US$1.5 billion, including Samsung's heavy industries construction equipment business to Volvo AB of Sweden and its forklift business unit to Clark. It also lowered its 365% debt ratio to 183% by late 1999. Seeking to lower debt in January 1998, the chairman of Samsung requested that employees gather any gold that they might have and exchange it for South Korean currency. Then the government could exchange the gold for dollars and pay down the debts of the *chaebol*.[52]

The crisis did not, however, threaten Ku Hee Lee's control of the firm his father, Byung-Chull Lee, had founded. The Lee family's share ownership in the electronics firm has declined from 8.3% in 1983 to 3.49% in June 2001, yet Lee's control of the firm remains considerable despite reforms.[53] For example, Korean board meetings generally rubber-stamp decisions of management. In the 30-year history of Samsung Electronics, no record exists of a director officially objecting to an item on the board of directors' agenda. The controlling shareholder has not attended a single Samsung Electronics board meeting from 1999 to 2002, and a key co-representative director only started to attend meetings in 2000.[54]

In December 1997, one investor in Samsung Electronics used the voting rights of shares owned by the American mutual fund Scudder, Stevens & Clark to force a meeting with Samsung's president. The men agreed that the representative would be allowed to voice his criticisms of the firm at the shareholders meeting. Prior to the shareholders meeting, however, the firm marshaled employees to fill the seats and the representative was denied entry for lack of space.[55] Although the firm later appointed some outside directors and audit committee members, minority shareholders did not propose any of the 11 that have been appointed since 1998.[56]

Since the crisis, the firm continues to be widely held, with expanded international listings. For example, Samsung SDI, a concern owned by the conglomerate, launched an affiliate in Malaysia in 2000. By listing on the Kuala Lumpur Stock Exchange rather than merely being a foreign company operating there, Samsung expected to derive the benefits of the status of a Malaysian entity.[57] Further listings have appeared on the NASDAQ and operations have commenced in China since that time. The management of the firm remains protected from the market for corporate control, however, through its interlocking ownership structure, and not from owning large blocs of shares.

## The Dependent Variable

Despite the impressive growth in market capitalization in the 1980s and the reforms following the financial crisis of the 1990s, Korean convergence on the Anglo-American model has not occurred. Korean corporate law follows the American legal structure. However, the Korean financial system, with its heavy reliance on state-directed financing, favors the German-Japanese model. Thus, according to the law, a board of directors that is unitary and solely elected by shareholders governs companies. Official stakeholder participation, such as employee participation on boards, does not exist as it does in German codetermination. Companies must have an auditor, and directors are held liable for damage to the company.[58]

The practice of management deviates from this legal framework. "Big five" accounting firms have not signed audit reports of Korean companies because the quality of the audit process does not meet international standards. Some Korean companies cannot provide revenue and cost data to potential buyers if sold because so little mergers and acquisitions activity occurred in the past, the firms lack these financial reporting capabilities.[59]

Reforms aimed at limiting the overwhelming power of the *chaebol*-controlling families imposed after the financial crisis of the late 1990s have failed to have any real effect in terms of mitigating their power, despite the dominant position of institutional investors in terms of total voting rights. This continuing control results from several features. First, foreign institutional holdings are passive by their nature as broadly diversified portfolio investment. Second, legal restrictions complicate the practice of foreign investors, in particular, voting their proxies. Third, the *chaebols* retain the power to pressure local fund managers to cooperate with their activities either because the *chaebols* are clients of the local fund managers or because a number of the insurance companies, securities companies, and banks that own the shares are themselves controlled by a *chaebol*.[60]

Efforts at increasing the transparency and accountability of the large firms have occurred, but the real effects remain ambiguous due to the scale of the problem and the lack of desire to reform. For example, Kim Woo Choong is the founder and chairman of Daewoo Group. He created Daewoo in the 1960s, and as of the Asian financial crisis was the only man still running a *chaebol* of his own creation. Daewoo annual revenues at the time represented approximately 10% of the Korean economy. Yet when asked for a chart of the whole Daewoo Group's finances in the midst of the crisis, Chairman Kim responded that the chart only existed in Chairman Kim's head.[61]

After the crisis, President Kim Dae Jung's government passed a law requiring Korean corporate accounts to be audited and companies to disclose debts. Foreigners that had been limited to a 26% stake in Korean companies would be permitted to buy companies whole.[62] Starting in 2002, companies are required to reveal the identity of directors nominated before the shareholders meeting, and not present at it. Nonetheless, determining an "outside" director of a firm is subjective and particularly complicated in sectors where professional expertise is limited.[63]

## People's Republic of China

Unlike the other postcolonial states examined, China broke dramatically with its past during the Communist revolution, both in terms of eliminating the foreign influence of the nineteenth and early twentieth centuries, and in eliminating the material basis of the small Chinese capitalist class that had existed.[64] Thus the state exerted near-complete control over the economy, and the financial sector in particular, when reforms began in the 1970s. This section depicts a stock exchange completely divorced from the market for corporate control and institutionally connected to a state that continues to own and control the means of production. As a case study of a firm listed nationally and internationally, the section considers Huaneng Power International as a part of the reform process and the reopening to international finance.

### Early Equities in Extraterritorial China, Early Equities in a Marketizing China

Although the current stock markets in China are not continuations, or resurrections, of those operating in nineteenth-century China, Shanghai was considered to have been the international financial center of the Far East during the republican period (i.e., 1911–1949).[65] Shortly after limited liability began in Great Britain, company promoters in Hong Kong and the treaty ports used the Hong Kong Chamber of Commerce to press the Hong Kong Legislative Council to adopt a similar Companies Ordinance. The promoters reasoned that registration in Hong Kong would extend the benefits of the London limited liability legislation to them without the expense of having to form a company and set up an office and board of directors in London.[66]

Although initial growth was slow in Hong Kong, a list of joint-stock companies that formed in Shanghai began to appear in a local newspaper by 1866. Many local Chinese, who themselves worked in Western trading houses and were attracted to dividends and limited liability, bought shares in these firms from the beginning.[67] Moreover, they played varying roles. For example, when the North-China Insurance Company attempted to replace a general manager, approximately

80 Chinese shareholders petitioned the board on his behalf. When the Chinese Insurance Company was established in Shanghai, indigenous Chinese supplied more than half the capital.[68] By 1860 the estimated contribution of Chinese capital to joint-stock enterprises established in Shanghai was 40% or more.[69]

Brokers sold shares of firms in various places such as the steps of the Hong Kong & Shanghai Bank, in the hall of the Shanghai Club building, or in each other's offices. However, as the business grew, 47 brokers formed the Stock and Sharebrokers Association in 1891. The association applied for registration in Hong Kong under the provisions of the Companies Ordinance. It was incorporated in 1904, at which time it formalized its membership requirements. The market was linked to Hong Kong when a telegraph cable linked Hong Kong and Shanghai. Thus prices of stocks traded in both centers followed each other. The market's outside links deepened when a Danish company established a switchboard office in Shanghai in 1882 and brokers were connected to each other and to other markets.[70] By the 1920s, the J. E. Swan offices in Shanghai had boards listing London and New York stocks and bonds, Liverpool and New Orleans cotton prices, and all of the commodities dealt on the Chicago Board of Trade. Chinese investors put through orders for buying and selling on Western markets that were cabled through and confirmed by cable on the other end. By 1941, more than one-third of the membership of the stock exchange was Chinese.[71]

When the nationalist government assumed control over Shanghai after World War II, the legal basis for the registration of companies in Shanghai was gone, as well as the means of enforcing commercial and financial contracts. The Shanghai Securities Exchange that opened for business in September 1946 excluded foreign share brokers and foreign listings; hence the foreigners moved to Hong Kong. When share registers were reestablished and a new ordinance replaced the 1932 Companies Ordinance in 1947, 193 British firms had listed in Hong Kong. Hyperinflation in Shanghai in 1948 resulted in the suspension of trading prior to the Communist takeover in 1949. Needless to say, foreign business in Shanghai was completely concluded after the Communist takeover.[72]

Therefore, while an extensive market for foreign firms in China developed, and Chinese individuals participated in it, an effective market for Chinese companies was never established. Chinese managers resisted disclosure that would require senior managers to allocate profits. Moreover, legal provisions for these firms were vague and ambiguous. The Ministry of Commerce handled disputes among them, as opposed to the court system. Each company transferred shares differently, and reporting was unreliable.[73]

In Communist China of the 1950s, state-owned banks became the sole representative of the financial sector. Yet the banks merely implemented financial directives from the new government and as such were passive players in the economy. That is, banks did not provide capital to enterprises, nor did they evaluate credit risks associated with loans and funds. The Ministry of Finance allocated all working capital to enterprises according to planned production quotas. Enterprises handed over all their operating profits, in the form of taxation and development funds, to the state treasury and relied on state budgetary allocations or extra bank loans based on their planned production quotas to finance operations. They seldom used their own assets to secure borrowing from banks, and they were not permitted to issue stocks to raise capital directly from the public, although the government did issue bonds.

Without dismantling this system, the Ministry of Finance floated State Treasury bonds in 1981 to cover budget deficits and to raise funds for a number of major construction projects. Yet shortly thereafter, small private companies issued the first corporate equities, mostly to their own employees. The rationale for issuing shares was that the private firms needed to gain additional funds necessary for expansion. The amount that firms could borrow was limited, and various discriminatory regulations imposed restrictions on the use of the funds. In fact, the shares were not true equities; they more closely resembled a cross between bonds and preferred stock insofar as they carried a guaranteed minimum interest rate and a possible dividend that most enterprises promised to pay.

Owning "shares" of either corporate bonds or any security with a participatory feature carried privileges such as priority in obtaining housing from the company (all Chinese employees legally have the right to have housing provided by the company they work for), or the nomination of a relative to join the company's staff. Some offered lottery drawings, which promised winners prizes such as TVs, washing machines, or trips to Hong Kong. The company normally guaranteed returns above existing bank deposit interest rates, and sometimes even guaranteed that the value of the stock would not fall below its par value.[74]

As corporate equities grew in popularity, the tightening of credit in 1985 gave the state-owned companies an incentive to allow shareholding companies as a legitimate experiment. The state-owned firms themselves encouraged this form of ownership because of the flexibility of the corporate shareholding structure, but more so because it rendered the securitized corporation a different identity. The board of directors and shareholders could cushion the enterprise against government intervention, which has always been a problem in state-owned firms. The equities of these companies were closer to true equities since they had no fixed interest rate and no guarantee of dividends.

Thus, in 1986, the government proceeded with a stock market experiment in Shenyang by establishing a primitive trading outlet in a building that had previously housed a bank deposit counter. At the time, two corporate bonds were available. One month later a securities trading market appeared in Shanghai. At the time, hundreds of people waited in line on opening day to buy shares. Among these individuals were young people who had no direct experience with shares, as well as the older generation who had "personal knowledge of the stock exchange in Shanghai before the founding of the People's Republic in 1949."[75] Late in 1987, Shenzhen moved to establish its own stock market, developed along the lines of the Hong Kong Stock Exchange and using the Companies Ordinance and Securities Ordinance of Hong Kong as the basis for the development of the market. The city appointed a Hong Kong company, Sung Hung Kai Securities, as its advisor.[76]

At this stage, most Chinese markets were still conducted over the counter and were promoted as an alternative source of funding for enterprises in a socialist economy. An obvious contradiction between state ownership and private ownership existed with respect to any sort of secondary market for the securities in a Communist society. The hard-line Communist Party position was that equity issuance is, in and of itself, at odds with the basic principle of public ownership.

Strict restrictions stipulated that (at the time) 70% of the shares must be retained by the state, investors could not purchase stocks exceeding a certain amount, and annual dividends could not be more than a small percentage of the share capital. To ensure that the factors of production are not turned over to private individuals, the government may only consider listing "approved" companies. In order to be approved, the company must not own the factors of production. Rather the company leases the right to manage a Chinese enterprise that owns the land, buildings, and machinery, and employs the workers, for a period of 70 years.[77]

The government instituted a freeze on the experimentation in 1989, but by 1990 the government reasserted itself and continued to develop stock markets. These would be limited to Shanghai and Shenzhen, with the goal of developing Shanghai into a bond trading center and Shenzhen into a stock trading center. By 1991 the exchanges appeared to be established economic actors. China's Premier Li Peng continued the reform process by rationalizing the use of nonsocialist development tools as necessary to propel the state into deepened socialism. Securities markets develop under the prerequisites of public ownership and adherence to a socialist orientation. Thus they are products of a planned economy where public ownership remains the norm.

The issuance of bonds and corporate equities is part of a plan developed each year by the State Planning Commission. The People's Bank of China (China's central bank) is directly responsible for the development of the securities market (i.e., the issuing and trading of securities). In the West, central banks regulate and control public finances mainly through trading state bonds in the market, with the administration and supervision of securities markets being undertaken by special regulatory commissions or agencies. At present, all markets in China are under the control of the central bank.[78]

In addition to the contradiction between state ownership and private ownership that emerged with respect to a secondary market, an additional problem emerged with respect to foreign participation. The country needed capital at the same time it feared foreign control. After a debate, the government resolved that foreigners could buy B shares, being issued by a number of companies in Shanghai and Shenzhen. While A shares are held by Chinese nationals and intended for the domestic market, B shares are denominated in Chinese currency, but are issued and traded in foreign currency based on the exchange rates in China's foreign exchange swap centers. Trading is executed on local stock exchanges, but within separate markets, because the participants are essentially a different group of people.[79]

In this manner, the Chinese government viewed the stock exchanges as a tool of growth, and not a transition to a capitalist economy. The principal shareholders are individuals and state-owned organizations. Hence the nature of Chinese enterprises has not been changed radically by the issuing of shares. Firms are not listed on the basis of the best rate of return acceptable to investors, but rather because Chinese authorities have determined the total number of issues allowed in a year and which firms can make them. Once determined, each province is allocated a subquota.

The marketization of the economy to supplement Chinese sources of capital for industrialization extended to the international community in the 1990s. In 1993 shares of Tsingtao Brewery were offered in Hong Kong. By the end of 1996, 20 companies had followed by listing H shares on the exchange. H shares are more attractive than B shares because they are not subject to an overall quota. They are large, well-known companies with major capital needs, and are able to generate sufficient foreign exchange to service dividend payments. After the initial rush to purchase the shares, however, the H shares decreased in popularity due to the operating realities of the firms: it was difficult for managers to fire excess workers and reduce their traditional welfare burdens, which meant lower profitability.

In the early 2000s, the government shifted its focus from supplying securities (i.e., listing more companies, forcing standards of corporate governance and disclosure, etc.) to developing suitable demand for them. Most of the current participants in China's stock markets are retail investors who trade on rumor. The government has opened the market to institutions such as mutual funds, insurers, and pension funds with the expectation that they will invest with a longer view, according to the balance of risk and return. The first step is to permit open-end mutual funds. Also, plans are under way for insurers to enter the market. Finally, the government will introduce modern pension funds. These institutions can potentially force further reforms in corporate governance.[80]

### The Case of Huaneng Power International, Inc.

Huaneng Power International (HPI) fits the pattern of a quasi-privatized Chinese firm supplementing its capital without releasing managerial control. Its international listing followed this logic as well. The government of China, under the auspices of the Ministry of Electrical Power, formed an organization called the China Huaneng Group to oversee electrical power generation in concert with local governments. The China Huaneng Group, in turn, formed a joint venture with foreign investors called the Huaneng Power International Development Corporation (HPIDC).[81] HPIDC would be the controlling shareholder of HPI. Specifically HPIDC would hold 53.64% of the A or domestic shares of HPI. Local government investment companies traded part of the debt that HPIDC owed to them for shares in the new company. However, the local government investment companies agreed to assign all voting rights attached to their shares to HPIDC so that the parent company's managerial control would be secure, even after the new shares were issued. HPIDC would control the election of all members to the board of directors.[82]

When selling capital, most Chinese firms that had looked outside had raised equity successfully on the Hong Kong exchange, and a few offered Hong Kong–listed shares in other countries.[83] The Hong Kong Stock Exchange even created an individual index, the Hang Seng China Enterprise Index, to track Chinese firms listed in Hong Kong. However, Chinese planners questioned the degree of saturation of the Hong Kong market with Chinese companies and the size of an issue the Hong Kong market could absorb.

U.S. markets were attractive at this particular juncture because they were large, offered high valuations, and had a high demand for emerging market issues. The NYSE had four China country funds already listed, and NASDAQ had joined the NYSE in promoting itself as an attractive place to raise capital. In 1994 Shandong Huaneng Power (a sister company to HPI) became the first company registered in China to have its primary foreign listing on a U.S. stock exchange, the NYSE. Shortly thereafter, in October 1994, HPI likewise sought a global equity issue in New York to raise funds for the construction of new power plants.

The contradiction between economic systems was apparent in the considerations for the HPI issue, as it had been in the larger context of establishing the exchanges in China. If the legal history of China was any indication, the courts would not recognize or enforce judgments obtained in U.S. or other foreign courts against a Chinese firm or its directors. Hence foreign shareholders would not be able to bring litigation against the firm if management did not act in the best interest of the shareholders.[84] Moreover, the government would not be removed from the firm's operation.

Foreign investors would need some type of incentive to risk capital on a Chinese investment. To promote foreign investment, the ministry persuaded the central government to pass legislation authorizing HPI and other electricity providers issuing international shares (such as Shandong) to guarantee a rate of return on electricity-generating assets.[85] To promote the widest possible distribution of investors, HPI listed the shares as level III ADRs. Thus the firm was required to release its financial statements in compliance with U.S. GAAP rules. It would have to fully disclose all operating results and strategic decisions. This was a higher level of disclosure than the firm would be subjected to in its home country.[86] After the international offering, investors in the global equity offering held 25% of the total, the HPIDC held 40.23%, and seven local government investment companies held 34.77%.

## The Dependent Variable

Despite the radical break with capitalism China experienced in its revolution, its current reforms seek to clarify and reassign various ownership rights among economic actors. Unlike the other examples, the post-Mao era planners did not seek to take away ownership rights from state agencies except in the agricultural sector. Rather, they systematically altered property rights with respect to control over an asset, who could appropriate returns from an asset, and who could transfer the rights of an asset to others (i.e., "exchange" rights).

Having avoided the debate over privatization in the public sphere throughout the 1980s, Communist Chinese officials remain in control of their organizations and play an active role in the economy. The labor force in the state sector remains tied almost permanently to large, government-owned firms, and continued government property rights confer power and privilege on officials at all levels.[87]

Hence the marketization of the Chinese economy without concurrent privatization means that stock exchange activity has emerged in an atmosphere where the government seeks to decentralize production and investment decisions while retaining socialist characteristics.[88]

A broader distribution of shares of Chinese enterprises has increased the amount of capital available for industrialization and has allowed for a degree of decentralization of resource allocation in China. However, the government's involvement with large-scale enterprises remains considerable. By the end of 2000, more than 90% of the 1088 firms listed on the two Chinese exchanges were transformed state-owned enterprises. More than two-thirds of the issued shares were held by the state, or state enterprises.[89] Even when the government allowed certain investment banks and funds to invest in the A-share market, China's regulators limited the amount they could use to trade, restricted capital repatriation, and limited the percentage of shares they could hold in any one company.[90]

In terms of who controls these firms, insider managers of a listed company with the support of their party ministerial associates exert the most influence, with almost no influence exerted by the nominal representatives of the dominant shareholders.[91] In theory, Chinese companies have a two-tiered board of directors: one similar to the Anglo-American board of directors, and a supervisory board with labor unions and major shareholder representation. However, the supervisory board with major shareholder representation has a very loosely defined monitoring role and has no common social or philosophical similarity with German codetermination.[92] The Chinese government and the party organization determine the chairman and members of the board of directors, chief executives, and supervisory board. When takeover battles have occurred, they have been by enterprises seeking a backdoor listing on the exchange.[93]

The Chinese firm was previously an integrated production unit within a centrally planned regime, and it is now an autonomous entity. However, the contradictions of private ownership in a Communist system complicate any role for these firms to play as agents of industrialization. That is, do they exist to create employment, provide for the workers' welfare, generate government revenue, or create a stream of profit for their shareholders? These are difficult questions to answer in any situation, without such open possibility for corruption.[94] They are particularly knotty in a situation where outside pressures on management are nearly nonexistent, and hence do not act as a check on inside managers' looting the firm. That is, the firm's reputation does not determine its future offerings, or their prices, the government does. Laws protecting shareholder rights—both minority and majority—are not feasible when the shareholder is the state.

## Thailand

Thailand's stock exchange does not have the same institutional legacy as the Bombay Stock Exchange nor past experience with a foreign financial presence as the pre-Communist Chinese exchange. Similar to the Korean Stock Exchange in many respects, it is a product of 1960s era plans to mobilize capital for national economic development. Unlike Korea, the Thai state was never involved in the financial sector to the extent that the Korean state was.[95] In fact, business-state relations in Thailand do not have systematic exchange. The diffuse, particularistic, and personalized ties are highly clientelist, and connect Chinese entrepreneurs with individual Thai officials.[96]

This complex network of relationships extends to the colonial period. Although Thailand itself was not a colony, the external threat of the colonial powers in the region forged a set of state elites that feared debt and were committed to fiscal conservatism.[97] Ethnic Chinese millers, merchants, and bankers connected small farmers to foreign markets. Thus, in the absence of a Thai landed aristocracy, the Chinese commercial class and the Thai state elites were codependent on each other. The ethnic Chinese were politically subservient to the Thai elites; the Thai elites, in turn, needed the financial resources of the Chinese-Thai class. Chinese clients received protection from individual Thai patrons in exchange for material rewards. These clientelist networks began to decline in the 1970s and 1980s as political adversity forced certain state elites out of official government positions. The Thai state-owned sector was weak, relative to others in the Asian-Pacific region; hence departing elites sought a "safe landing" in the growing number of Thai firms.[98]

This legacy has nonetheless left a Thai private sector that remains dominated by the original Thai-Chinese founding families. The control of approximately half of the firms listed on the Stock Exchange of Thailand rests with families, and the top 15 families in Thailand control 39.3% of corporate assets as a percentage of GDP.[99] Informal alliances connect the small number of these families. Pyramids and cross-holdings are relatively infrequent methods of enhanced firm control in Thailand, relative to other examples.[100] Some business groups are readily apparent and can be easily demarcated, whereas others are far less unified and identifiable. Wealthy individuals frequently invest in companies managed by friends and business associates. Thai business groups generally align themselves with high-ranking military officers, and the boards of directors in major state and nonstate enterprises generally include senior retired members of the armed forces.[101]

The formal stock exchange of Thailand emerged in the nationalist era of the 1960s, and it was developed with the active advice of the World Bank. Prior to the financial crisis of the late 1990s, the state sought to augment the supply of shares on the exchange with a privatization program. When the government sells shares, however, it generally follows the pattern of the family firms in that it retains the majority of shares. Thus ultimate control of most listed companies in Thailand remains with majority shareholders even after a large volume of shares has magnified the market capitalization. Major shareholders can appoint board members without the approval of minority shareholders through a majority vote. The stock exchange requires that there be at least two independent, nonexecutive directors on the board to monitor the management of the company, to provide a degree of independence from management, and to provide a degree of accountability to minority shareholders. However, the term "independent nonexecutive director" only excludes the firm's employees, and not friends or family of the majority shareholders.[102] Thus many of these appointees are closely connected to the majority shareholders.

The following sections trace the history of the Thai equities market through the financial crisis. It examines the privatization of Thai Airways to demonstrate the political problems associated with increasing market capitalization through a privatization program, wherein international pressures for privatization from the IMF conflict with local domestic networks. Despite several ongoing efforts to increase listings on the Stock Exchange of Thailand since the crisis, many Thai firms seek listings on other, deeper, national stock exchanges such as Singapore.

### Equities in Thailand

Plans for a Thai capital market surfaced in the 1960s when the government implemented its five-year National Economic and Social Development plans. The second of these plans proposed the establishment of a securities market; however, the first attempt to do so (i.e., the attempt to organize the Bangkok Stock Exchange privately) failed. The stock exchange closed shortly after its opening due to lack of official support and concomitant low trading volumes. In 1969 the World Bank recommended a study of the development of a Thai capital market by Sidney M. Robbins, who had served as chief economist at the SEC. Robbins's report became the master plan for the next market to open.

In 1974 the government passed the Securities Exchange of Thailand Act, BE 2517, that led to the establishment of the Securities Exchange of Thailand the next year. As with the earlier exchange, the Securities Exchange of Thailand was initially dormant. However, around 1987 the exchange began to mobilize more funds from private and corporate savings augmented by international investment on the exchange. Initial foreign direct investment had been Japanese. As it declined in the 1980s, the Thai state attracted foreign capital by liberalizing the financial sector, maintaining high domestic interest rates, and pegging the currency to the dollar.

The Securities Exchange of Thailand Act was replaced in 1992 when the government passed the Securities and Exchange Act, BE 2535, that makes provisions for a securities commission to regulate the capital market. The exchange was renamed the "Stock Exchange of Thailand" at the same time the government made the baht freely convertible, thus easing capital inflows. The exchange grew in volume to such an extent that in 1993 the World Bank concluded, "Thailand has one of the most dynamic stock exchanges in the Asia Region."[103] Much of this growth reflected the open environment for foreign investment, relatively stable political climate for investment, and appealing fiscal and monetary policies. To meet the needs of small and medium-size firms forced to operate in a gray market avoided by foreign capital, the government established an over-the-counter market in 1995. Firms listing on this market were required to meet the securities commission's requirements for public listing, but were not required to meet the stock exchange's requirements for minimum capital or proven record of profitability.[104]

As was the pattern in Korea, much of the early foreign investment entered through investment funds. The IFC invested US$9.68 million in 1987 and US$32 million in 1988 through two portfolio investment country funds. After 1989, portfolio investors from Hong Kong and Taiwan, and later from Europe and the

United States bought Thai stocks. Between 1989 and 1992 international stockbroking firms and merchant banks established a presence in Bangkok.[105]

The first Thai firms to take advantage of the growing stock market were banking firms that sold holdings in the top company of a business group. The groups reinvested revenue from the sale into new joint ventures in real estate, retail, and other domestic activities. In some of the smaller banks where controlling families failed to undertake similar measures, entrepreneurs bought undervalued stocks on the exchange.[106] One such group is the Sophonpanich family, whose primary business interest is the Bangkok Bank Public Company, and who holds sizable investments in at least 15 other companies listed on the Stock Exchange of Thailand.

The external investment in the Thai economy gravitated to the stock market, consumer financing, and real estate.[107] For example, one child of a wealthy ethnic-Chinese business leader, Anant Kanjanapas, began to acquire parcels of land near the Bangkok airport in 1990. In 1992 the family's firm, Bangkok Land, issued shares on the Thai stock exchange to raise money. A variety of funds such as the Thai International Fund, the Thai Euro Fund, and funds directed by J. Mark Mobius bought more than one million shares of Bangkok Land. The Illinois state pension fund bought shares of both the Thai International Fund and the Thai Euro Fund.[108] Bangkok Land's capitalization grew to the point where it was the largest share capitalized, with one-third of the total trading volume on the exchange. This high degree of concentration of the shares of one stock meant that the family wielded market influence in addition to its control of the firm.[109] When the stock collapsed in 1996, the share's value plunged to approximately one-ninth of its 1992 high.[110]

Prior to the financial crisis in 1997, the government had attempted to divest itself of shares of state enterprises via the exchange. The crisis made the supply of shares critical and the state's role in divesting shares more significant as a source. Nonetheless, no new listings appeared from 1998 to 2000. Exchange officials attempted to attract firms to the market in 2000 by relaxing its requirements.[111] Firms that did issue equity capital seemed to prefer to cross-list shares elsewhere, such as Singapore or the United States, an action the securities commission of Thailand lacked the power to limit. Firms listed overseas because they believed it was easier to raise capital in these markets and easier to distribute shares despite the fact that, for example, of the 13 companies that traded as ADRs in the United States, 11 traded over the counter, and 2 traded as 144A transactions.[112]

The lack of liquidity on the Thai secondary market eventually led brokers to question the wisdom of using state privatized shares to increase market capitalization. The brokers concern was that listing large government IPOs on the Stock Exchange of Thailand added to market capitalization, but failed to stimulate trading. To stimulate trading, the government would be better served to distribute the shares among a diverse group of investors, with a focus on professionals who trade actively as opposed to commercial bank depositors. Were shares offered through more traditional channels such as banks and brokers, "stock market makers" would increase the liquidity of the issued shares and could address pricing discrepancies.[113]

Therefore, while the traditional firms listed on the stock exchange were Chinese-Thai family business groups with strong links to individual Thai state patrons, economic planners have looked to state divestiture as a source of shares after the crisis. The large privatization issues, however, have followed the pattern of the family groups in that listings are minority shares that do not leave the firm vulnerable to the market for managerial control. One such ongoing case is that of Thai Airways.

### The Case of Thai Airways

The Thai Airways privatization grew out of an initial privatization program beginning prior to the stock market boom in 1988. The Thai government stalled on implementing the initial program, however, because the Thai Airways management sought to retain control of their individual fiefdoms and did not want to have to disclose company accounts publicly. The Thai Air Force controlled the firm at the time, and during these years it bought an array of aircraft and engines that did not seem to contribute to any unified master plan. The government did make an initial offering on the stock exchange in 1992, yet it only offered 7% of the company, and repeatedly delayed the sale of further tranches. Despite the introduction of some civilian managers, the company continued to perform poorly, losing more than 20% of the value of the stock.[114] Market analysts attributed the poor performance of the firm to an ongoing managerial struggle between government ministers and airline officials. The poor performance had the effect of again stalling the rest of the entire Thai privatization program.[115]

In 1993 the government requested suggestions from the World Bank for how to speed the pace of the program. Although the government had promised the IMF that it would sell the firm to a strategic partner early in 1998, the cabinet vetoed a plan proposed by the finance ministry to sell 25% of the firm to such a partner. Rather, the cabinet approved a scaled-down plan to sell 20% of the government's stake in the airline via the stock market. The government would sell 100 million new shares to be issued by the company, and those shares would not be limited to potential strategic partners. That is, the company would sell them to individuals and institutions on the exchange, leaving current management in control. In this particular round of privatization, the Ministry of Transport and Communications and the Thai Airways board of directors dominated the process of selecting underwriters for the sale, as well as timing.[116] Foreign investors were limited to owning 30% of the outstanding shares.

When the partial privatization was again stalled in August 2000, the president of the firm argued that it could not offer the shares until the stock market rebounded. When it did, the government would sell 23% of the company: 8% to the public, 5% to employees, and 10% to a strategic partner. Yet the delay in the sale affected the entire market because the government's lack of commitment to reform depressed it.[117]

### The Dependent Variable

The Thai stock exchange is thus dominated by the listings of large firms' minority shares. The state has an ongoing and active interest in these firms, yet not in the same institutional manner as in the other cases. In Thailand, the government's ties to large private business is in the individual patronage of Chinese-Thai business groups to high-ranking state officials. Initially these officials were concentrated in the military, but over time they are increasingly members of Parliament "sponsored" by a business group. Business groups maintain an extensive range of investments in many sectors, both on an active and passive basis.

As the government has sought to recover from the financial crisis of the late 1990s, it has ongoing commitments to international organizations to privatize firms, and in so doing, to increase the number of shares offered on the exchange. However, privatization has not been a historic source of shares. Between 1982 and 1996, only four major state offerings appeared: North-East Jute Mill (where the government holds less than 50% of the stock), the Krung Thai Bank, Thai Airways, and PTT Exploration and Production Public Company Ltd.[118] The Thai Airways case thus demonstrates a large state-sector firm offered publicly, yet with the same management remaining in control and not subject to the market for managerial takeover. Other firms listed on the exchange are similarly not subject to the market for managerial takeover, yet have dramatically different governance structures.

As the state divests shares, some changes in management have occurred. However, tensions within companies related to the preexisting arrangements ensue. In addition, tranches of state issues have been repeatedly stalled. In order to speed the privatization program, the government has issued a corporatization law, which prohibits changes in the existing benefits of employees of privatized firms.[119] While these initiatives may increase the supply of shares, they will not open the market for managerial control with respect to listed firms.

## Analysis and Conclusion

These four cases of stock markets and sample listings in the Asian region demonstrate many of the similarities and differences within the region. In each case, the development of a stock market has insulated management from the market for corporate control. However, each case shows management to be protected differently. In India, pyramid-style controlling-minority structures protect business families that own blocs of shares. Where foreign direct investment has occurred, and by its nature protects its own management, the Indian state promoted wider shareholding in the general population via the national stock market. Structures coexist as privatizations have progressed. In some, firms have been sold to foreign corporations, whereas in others, labor unions have been able to extract a percentage of publicly listed shares similar to the Latin American cases. In South Korea, cross-holding controlling-minority ownership structures protect the ultimate controlling family of the *chaebol* together with the institutional passivity of institutional investors. The Chinese state protects the management of Chinese firms through the distribution of shares classified with or without voting rights. Thai family ownership patterns, and patterns of government minority share divestment, protect management from the market for corporate control there.

Table 7.1 summarizes the cases of large listings examined in this chapter. The cases show that privatization has been a feature of the state's disengagement from active firm management, but it has not resulted in similar shareholding patterns.

TABLE 7.1 Summary of Asian Cases Examined

| State | Company privatized (year) | International imperatives (level I) | Groups protesting sale (level II) | Distribution of shares | Controlling interest held by (governance structure) |
|---|---|---|---|---|---|
| India | Modern food[a] (2000/ 2001) | World Bank initially suggests new issues on stock exchanges as sources of finance for Indian corporate sector. Privatizations encouraged in 1991 World Bank/IMF reform program. | Food Workers Union | 100% of firm sold to Hindustan Lever, but 49% HLL held on Indian exchange. | Hindustan Lever, which is a Unilever subsidiary (MNC, 49% of subsidiary held locally) |
| South Korea | Samsung[b] | Initial opening of Korean Stock Exchange through IFC fund, with government initiative. Following the Asian financial crisis of 1997, equity again sought to lower debt ratios. External pressure applied by foreign shareholders following crisis. | Not applicable | Not available | Mr. Lee (controlling minority) |
| China | Huaneng Electric (1994) | Tight credit in 1985 furthered initial experiments with financial reforms. In the Huaneng offering, disclosure affected by listing requirements of level III ADRs in the U.S. market. | CCP conservatives | HPIDC, 40.23%; local investment company, 34.77%; global investors, 25% | Chinese state (state) |
| Thailand | Thai Airways (1992/ 1998) | World Bank/IMF privatization plan | Current management of Thai Airways | In 1992, 7% offered on Thai Stock Exchange. In 1998, 100 million more shares sold; foreign investment limited to 30% of outstanding shares, no strategic partner selected. Current plans for privatization: 23% to be sold; 8% to the public, 5% to employees, and 10% to an as-yet-unspecified strategic partner. | Managers (state) |

[a]This case was not listed on a stock exchange.
[b]This case was not a privatization sale.

The Indian case of Modern Food was initiated by IMF and World Bank reforms, yet took several years to complete. Although the bank and the fund had encouraged the development of the Indian stock exchanges as a source of finance for Indian corporations, Modern Food did not list. It was sold to a multinational corporation that itself listed 49% of its minority shares locally. The Thai case of Thai Airways and the Chinese case of Huaneng Electric were privatizations listed on local exchanges, however, only minority shares were listed in both cases. The case of Samsung was not a privatization since the Korean state did not own the commanding heights of industry outright in the nationalist era. However, international forces propelled Samsung to change its debt-to-equity ratio following the 1997 Asian financial crisis.

As stock markets parcel out ownership of firms in these cases, the institutional setting serves to protect management from the interests of shareholders. Should any disciplining forces act to protect the interests of minority shareholders, they would have to derive from the law, and not from the market for shares. The similarity that runs through the Asian examples is that while these states may disengage from direct control of firms in the economy, they have not lost their interest in promoting development as a goal, nor in keeping control of large enterprise within the territorial confines of the state. Thus, whereas the Anglo-American model needs to reconcile the interests of short and long-term shareholders under the law, these newer models need to reconcile the interests of the state, majority, minority, national, and international investors. Discerning any common set of shareholder interests is highly complicated by these circumstances.

# 8

# Russia and Eastern Europe

This chapter specifically considers the examples of the growth and then contraction of equity markets in Hungary, Poland, Russia, and the Czech Republic. These examples elucidate the highly fluid nature of equity market functions and further call into question any conclusions concerning convergence in institutional form along the Anglo-American line of corporate governance. The Russian and eastern European emerging markets differ from the Latin American and Asian examples because the privatized firms emerged as part of a broader social revolution against Communist rule and reconfiguration of property rights. Opening, or reopening, a stock exchange to offer shares of these firms sent a symbolic political message that the Communist era had truly ended. Therefore, while the Latin Americans were addressing an international debt crisis, and the Chinese were experimenting with the market as a tool of socialist development, the Russians and eastern Europeans were addressing internal appeals for reform, as well as financial crises, in issuing private equity shares. Yet, as was the case with the Latin American and Chinese stock markets, the Russian and eastern European markets did not perform the same institutional function as their counterparts operating in other financial institutional structures, and the markets do not function similarly with respect to all firms within a given state that offer equity shares publicly.

This conclusion is less surprising in these examples than the Latin American and Asian ones because the individual transition economies experimented with a much wider variety of methods of transferring ownership to citizens during the transition from Communist rule, such as sales to outside owners, management-employee buyouts, equal-access voucher privatizations, and spontaneous privatizations. It is not immediately apparent that these exchanges fail to converge on the Anglo-American corporate governance structure, however, because regardless of the method of transfer, many states ostensibly sought to emulate it. Therefore planners initially envisioned competitive, open capital markets with industrial managers constrained by the threat of shareholders selling their shares on the capital market. Most did not envision stakeholders becoming involved in the firm's decision making.

Planned or unplanned, management did come to hold controlling blocs of shares in many cases. Banks in the Czech Republic, Hungary, and Poland did not seek to become involved in share ownership as the stakeholder model of corporate governance would require, because an active role is not cost effective when compared to the core business of relationship banking. Only some Russian banks assumed small stakes when requested to by the companies. In Hungary and Poland, banks took on restructuring roles to recover loans, but similarly avoided shareholder roles. Only when the banks realized that management was overtly driving down the value of a firm to buy it at a lower price, or when they realized a clear underexploited upside potential did they buy minority stakes of up to 20%. And even under these circumstances, banks generally only purchased shares providing there was another active shareholder, such as a foreign investor.[1]

Therefore, even if the methods of transfer sought a similar result, that is, one resembling the Anglo-American model of corporate governance, the outcome of the methods of transfer has meant that equity markets do not perform the same institutional functions as they do with the Anglo-American model. Variations in the market for managerial control in the Latin American and Asian examples stemmed from coexisting business structures created during various strategies of state development: colonial, postcolonial interventionist, and neoliberal disinvestment. In the postcolonial cases, some old reconfigured colonial firms operated alongside some state-owned, some partially state-owned, and some private firms.

Unlike the postcolonial states, Russia and eastern Europe were never formal colonies, although nineteenth-century Russia followed the import-export patterns of the European colonies insofar as it exported raw materials to the factories in England and on the continent, and imported their finished or semimanufactured goods in return.[2] As industrialization picked up in Russia, it was state led. By the end of the nineteenth century, Russia had active commodity markets and participated in world capital markets.[3] As discussed in chapter 2, although an exchange operated in St. Petersburg since the late eighteenth century, the primary market for Russian securities in the nineteenth century was the Paris Bourse.

Outside the Russian empire, industrialization had begun in the late nineteenth century Habsburg Empire as part of the economic expansion known as the *Grunderzeit*. Similar to the expansion in Latin America associated with the building of the rail networks, the railroads in the Habsburg Empire sparked the growth of the mining, iron and steel, and metalworking industries between 1867 and 1873.[4] At the end of the boom associated with this expansion, prices on the Vienna stock exchange crashed. The joint stock form of enterprise was avoided as a result, particularly in what was then Austria. The government restricted corporate charters, taxed joint-stock firms, and did not permit free incorporation until 1899. By 1907, Germany had eight times the number of joint-stock companies that Austria did, and even Russia had three times as many.[5]

Unlike the postcolonial states, and more along the lines of China, the Communist revolution in Russia and the Soviet satellites precipitated a more complete break with the ownership structures of the past, and a more radical restructuring under state planning. When the Communist takeovers occurred, the states confiscated large firms. Massive industrialization occurred along with the campaign to build communism, and thus did not utilize the joint-stock form. In the Soviet Communist system, the manager not only operated the firm for the government and its ministries, he or she also created a network to conduct their own business deals. These deals tended to benefit the manager, or an individual government official.[6] Some of these networks continue to exist alongside newer structures. Therefore any uniform system of corporate governance is difficult to discern at the national level in the contemporary era, not so much due to coexisting business forms created during various strategies of state development, but due to continuing patterns from the Soviet era. This is particularly true in Russia because of the dramatic variations in enforcement of what securities regulations do exist.

When the Communist era ended in the Russian and eastern European cases, level I international consultants and public international organizations encouraged and assisted the states in creating or re-creating stock exchanges and in designing securities market regulations. At level II, however, the "ratification" process that took place necessitated a prominent role for the managers of the former state firms. Immediately, gradually, or through outright corrupt practices, management has consolidated its control over most of the shares issued in Russia. Many firms listed on eastern European exchanges have delisted since the initial state disengagement. Thus the reciprocal causation between levels I and II has resulted in highly different ownership and control mechanisms in the twenty-first century.

## Hungary

The first post-Communist stock exchange appeared in Hungary. The original Budapest Stock Exchange was founded in 1864 and it played a role in financing the Austro-Hungarian Empire. Although the government did not permit shares to be sold abroad when the pengo's convertibility had been suspended prior to World War II, the exchange did not completely close until the Communist takeover in 1948. It did not reopen for 40 years, notwithstanding that the seeds of broader Hungarian financial reforms extended back into the Communist era. When the privatization program began in earnest, a bargained evaluation of assets, corporate owners, and positional resources resulted in what Stark terms "institutional cross-ownership."[7] The example of Ibusz demonstrates one such complex ownership structure, as well as the trajectory of many privatized Hungarian firms from public sell-off to delisting.

### The Transition from Communism in Hungary and Equity Shares

Hungary was the first state within the Soviet bloc to reform its financial system. Three new commercial banks took over the domestic commercial banking operations of the National Bank of Hungary and the State Development Bank in 1986. As part of this transition, the new commercial banks took over the loans and the deposits of their predecessors. Two years later the banks were permitted to provide foreign exchange-related services to clients. Concomitant with these developments and the passage of the Agreement on Trading in Securities of 1988, discussions concerning reopening the securities market began between the National Bank of Hungary, the Hungarian Chamber of Commerce, and 22 financial institutions. As a result of the agreement and the discussions, the institutions would meet once a week to trade bonds and to supply data on the bond market to a central information center. Companies could then issue shares, and in 1988 individuals could trade them as well.[8]

When the government planned to open a more elaborate exchange, it awarded a consulting contract to two British firms to advise on methods of price formation and trading, regulations, order routing, information required for trading, reporting and publication, and projected volumes and flows of business. The firms Garside Miller Associates and Touche Ross and Co. won the contract and offered the first eastern European course on how to run a stock exchange to 13 Hungarians and 9 Slovaks in late 1990. Led by Roger Garside, who had been the director of public affairs at the London International Stock Exchange, and Jonathan Miller, who had been the former chairman of the Society of Investment Analysts, the students in the course were mostly individuals in their mid-20s who worked in fairly junior bank jobs.[9]

In May 1990 trade union members, workers, and all parties with members in the new Hungarian parliament, including the former Communists, saw private ownership as the solution to the problems of Hungary's crisis-ridden economy. The coalition government, led by Prime Minister Jozsef Antall, sought the "privatization of privatization" through an increase in the role of international investment banks and consulting firms in the process. Problems confronting the government at this juncture were considerable. Although there was an agreement on private ownership, some believed early deals were concluded for too low a price. These criticisms were compounded when the buyers were not Hungarian, since foreign buyers gave rise to the perception that privatization amounted to "selling the country off to foreigners."[10]

Some firms were privatized at the initiative of the State Property Agency, which was charged with the legal authority to supervise the process. Yet others came about through a much more circuitous path. Directors of some public enterprises took advantage of legislation allowing state enterprises to establish joint-stock companies and limited liability companies. In these cases, the managers of the enterprise broke up the corporation into numerous corporations with individual legal identities. The state enterprises held the controlling shares of these corporate satellites in many cases. Other blocs of shares of these organizations were held by top and midlevel managers, professionals, and other staff, and in rare cases, workers. In a few cases, banks traded debt for equity shares. The resulting structure was therefore cumbersome, and involved a limited liability company owned by other limited liability companies, owned by joint-stock companies, banks, and large public enterprises, owned by the state.[11]

When the Budapest Stock Exchange reopened along Anglo-American lines on June 21, 1990, prospects appeared bright. The number of companies listed, supplied by the privatization program, grew steadily, as did their value (see table

TABLE 8.1 Growth of the Budapest Stock Exchange

|  | 90 | 91 | 92 | 93 | 94 | 95 | 96 | 97 |
|---|---|---|---|---|---|---|---|---|
| No. of equities | 6 | 20 | 23 | 28 | 40 | 42 | 45 | 49 |
| Capitalization (US$ millions) | 266.9 | 505.2 | 562.1 | 811.3 | 1,639.7 | 2,350.2 | 5,582.9 | 16,010.1 |

Source: Anna Zalewska-Mitura, "Does Market Organization Speed Up Market Stabilization? First Lessons from the Budapest and Warsaw Stock Exchanges," Centre for Economic Policy Research, Discussion Paper no. 2134, April 1999.

8.1). The international financial press promoted Hungary as a well-performing market and good choice for emerging market investment. Over time, however, the positive outlook dimmed. The privatizations slowed and the financial crisis of 1997 and 1998 slowed the pace of portfolio investment.[12]

As foreign direct investment in the Hungarian economy grew, the government increasingly used sales to foreign firms as the mechanism for privatization. Many of these sales, as well as joint ventures, could be accomplished off of the Budapest Stock Exchange through private placements. The stock exchange came to be perceived as too small for further public offers, and by the mid-1990s, some observers estimated that 90% of securities transitions took place away from it. As fewer firms list, those that might do so are discouraged by the listing requirements or by their own lack of resources or experience.[13]

### The Case of Ibusz

Ibusz is Hungary's largest travel agency, which was strategically selected by the state to open its privatization program and to demonstrate its serious commitment to the program on an ongoing basis. Operated as a state-owned firm in the Communist era, Ibusz had nonetheless been organized as a corporation. Prior to the privatization, Price Waterhouse converted the firm's last three years' financial figures into international standards and audited them. Thus Ibusz was eligible to list on both the Budapest Stock Exchange and the Vienna Stock Exchange. The flotation of shares of these two exchanges meant that Ibusz was the first eastern European firm to be listed on a Western stock exchange. The state sold roughly US$18 million in shares, which amounted to a one-third stake in the company. However, to sell the stake, the state increased its capital prior to the sale so that only 3% of the existing shares were sold.

The share allocation in the Ibusz IPO favored Hungarian and small foreign investors.[14] It was 23 times oversubscribed, and its price doubled within weeks. The initial strong performance did not, however, signal programmatic success on a grand scale. The head of the State Property Agency resigned after the sale because of criticism that he had "given the company away." Speculation from both Hungarian and Austrian holders meant that despite the firm's profitability, it consistently traded 20%–30% below its offering price.[15] Ibusz's failure to perform well in the equity market came to be seen as the reason for the lack of investor confidence in the market overall and its lack of liquidity. This perception persisted despite the fact that sales in Ibusz shares, together with two other firms, accounted for half of the total turnover in 1992.[16] Further issues of the company's shares were complicated by the stock's poor performance. Nonetheless, the company continued to issue shares, so that by 1994 foreign institutional and private investors in Ibusz owned more than 79%.[17]

By 2002 the ownership structure of Ibusz reflected the complex structure of other Hungarian firms. The parent firm owned 77.2% of Ibusz Hotels, 67.72% of Ibusz Invest, 48.17% of Ibusz Inova Invest, and Ibusz International Service. In turn, these firms owned 15.74%, 8.42%, 17.73%, and 5.52% of the parent company, respectively. When the parent company decided to delist from the stock exchange, one of the subsidiaries (Ibusz Inova Invest) increased its ownership in the parent firm by 3.74%, bringing the voting rights of the combined subsidiaries to 51%.[18] The firm delisted on March 19, 2002.

### The Dependent Variable

As Porter has observed, the Hungarian capital market at the time of the transition could not hold actors accountable in managing, buying, and selling privatized assets. However, by unintentionally controlling the pace of capital market expansion (because of the time required to value and sell each firm), the Hungarian government most likely managed to avoid many of the negative consequences of redistributing the assets through inadequate market institutions. Thus the mediocre performance of the Budapest Stock Exchange may be connected to the more-successful features of the Hungarian transition.[19] Selling firms to foreigners may have been a politically difficult course, but the strategy opened the possibility that the foreign firms would upgrade the enterprises, the cash from sales would lower Hungary's foreign debt, and the corruption based on traditional linkages among enterprises would be minimized.[20]

Hungarian firms were also the first among the eastern European firms to receive rare management pressure from minority shareholders. The pressure has been exerted through private holding companies and funds that specialize in turning around medium-size enterprises by making controlling investments. Governance here is established through concentrated ownership by institutional investors with experience in industrial restructuring. Thus scarce managerial resources can be spread across a number of enterprises, as well as diversifying the risk of investing in such industries. These forms of governance may not survive the early years of securities market formation, as alternative mechanisms may become possible.[21]

However, if the mechanism survives or not, two such investment funds, Argus Capital International (a subsidiary of the United States's Prudential Insurance) and Croesus Central European Advisors (a group that specializes in acquiring under-valued central European companies) made an unsolicited offer to buy the Hungarian packaging company Cofinec in April 1999. In addition, the majority of the management of TVK (a Hungarian chemical company) was replaced after two investment funds, one run by Croesus and the other by Templeton, secured the backing of 97.5% of shareholders for the replacement. All of the managers of a third firm, Zalakeramia (a Hungarian ceramic tile and other bathroom products manufacturer), were replaced after activism on the part of Arago, a Budapest-based team of corporate raiders that owns 15% of Zalakeramia. These actions in replacing management are significant because TVK and Zalakeramia together account for approximately 10% of the Budapest stock market's benchmark index.[22]

Therefore, while the Hungarian state initially promoted a stock exchange, and established one with input from British consultants, sales to foreigners off of the exchange became the operative method of transfer. As such, foreign management gained ultimate control of the firm in these instances according to the governance structure of the parent firm. The Budapest Stock Exchange itself has not evolved into a mechanism of corporate governance. Yet this lack of institutional function alone does not signal the failure of the privatization program, nor are managers insulated from ownership pressures.

## Poland

As did Hungary, Poland had a pre-Communist stock exchange, established in Warsaw in 1817. However, this exchange was mostly for bonds and other debt instruments, and not for equities. The reconstituted Polish state after 1918 had seven functioning exchanges, although Warsaw accounted for more than 90% of the total volume. Prior to the Nazi assault, Poland had embarked on a brief period of state capitalism that served as a useful predecessor to the rapid industrialization of the post-1945 era.[22] Yet the post-1945 industrialization was Communist led, hence the stock exchanges closed. The Polish State Treasury established the new Warsaw exchange as a joint-stock company in April 1991.

Notwithstanding its symbolic importance in the transition from Communist rule, the new exchange is somewhat different from the Hungarian, Russian, and Czech examples because it was never meant to follow the Anglo-American lead. Rather, the Polish more closely emulated German systems of corporate governance. Worker buyouts and a voucher program facilitated mass privatization, wherein citizens transferred their vouchers to 15 National Investment Funds that would invest them as intermediaries in the restructured state-owned companies and other Polish companies. In theory, the companies would eventually be transferred to individual investors through the funds. However, in practice, the state retains a significant share of large Polish enterprises, as well as influence over them through the banking system. The privatization of the Szczecin Shipyard is used to demonstrate the problems of the process, and the direction of the shift in corporate governance exclusive of a stock market.

### The Transition from Communism in Poland

Polish privatization became a political issue with the creation of the first post-Communist government in September 1989. Promising to speed a process that had begun with Jaruzelski's Polish Communist regime, the liberal government's initial successes were in privatization by liquidation. The relatively weak Polish state did not have a political party system, nor did it have partners with which to resolve key questions about mass privatization. The only organized group capable of articulating a position was the self-management system of enterprise control that the independent trade union Solidarity had forced on the Communist Party in 1981.

This decentralized management system created a strong political and psychological attachment of employees to individual firms, as well as promoted the belief that the "firms are ours."[24] When a lobby formed around the employee councils associated with the system during the transition, it advocated the interests of the workers, that is, the insiders, and de facto proposals for employee-owned enterprises. Conversely, the government proposed a more technocratic version of privatization based on the British model of selling enterprises through public offerings. Yet the financial institutional structure lacked any real capacity to supervise and monitor the behavior of firms once privatized. In the program of mass privatization announced in June 1991, 400 Polish enterprises were to be transferred in a first stage.

The employee councils' demands were met by allocating a free 10% of shares of the companies to employees of the privatized firms. Thus, without savings or credit, employees could gain a stake through their position as jobholders. To promote equality in share distribution, and to create an institutional mechanism for firm monitoring, all citizens received share vouchers from the state to be assigned to an asset manager. The manager would be responsible for exchanging the vouchers for shares in enterprises of his or her choice.[25] Thus the part of the privatization program dealing with the funds sought to create an institution that would serve an active owner function and avoid the downside of dispersed ownership. At the same time, the funds would remain the property of the State Treasury, and by extension the property of those entitled to participate in the program.[26] Workers had an effective veto over the method of privatization used, and outsiders were generally only permitted a stake in firms with a level of debt that prohibited an employee buyout.[27]

Through this program, the employee councils of the late Communist era would gradually be eliminated and the firms transformed into joint-stock companies, initially owned by the state (i.e., "commercialized"). A board of directors would be responsible for management of the companies and would answer to the state. Ultimately the firms would be sold on the open market, and in theory, resources and assets would be allocated optimally, according to neoclassical orthodoxy.

Financial markets were formed according to Western standards. Following a thorough review of several markets, the Polish Securities Commission adopted a system based on French experience. Experts from the *Societe des Bourses Francaises* and the French depository, the *Société Interprofessionnelle de Compensation de Valeurs Mobilières* (SICOVAM), assisted the implementation. Five equities listed on the Warsaw Stock Exchange when it officially reopened in 1991.[28] It joined the International Federation of Stock Exchanges (FIBV) in October 1994 (see table 8.2).

Yet as the privatization program unfolded, it became apparent that a one-time

TABLE 8.2 Growth of the Warsaw Stock Exchange

|                             | 91  | 92  | 93    | 94    | 95    | 96    | 97     |
|-----------------------------|-----|-----|-------|-------|-------|-------|--------|
| No. of equities             | 9   | 16  | 21    | 36    | 53    | 66    | 96     |
| Capitalization (US$ millions)| 147 | 222 | 2,875 | 2,954 | 4,292 | 8,054 | 10,795 |

*Source*: Anna Zalewska-Mitura, "Does Market Organization Speed Up Market Stabilization? First Lessons from the Budapest and Warsaw Stock Exchanges," Centre for Economic Policy Research, Discussion Paper no. 2134, April 1999.

political resolution of the problem of the allocation of property rights was less and less tenable. Some firms agreed to become commercialized by the state because they thought they would receive financial support or relief from the state, or that the state would find them creditors or foreign buyers. Others agreed to commercialization as a step on the way to privatization. However, once ownership rights of the firms reverted to the state, firms lost control over the choice of buyers and the terms of sale. Management was not necessarily strengthened by the state in the interim between the employee councils and independent managers. In fact, the management of many firms deteriorated by commercialization. Some managers were reluctant to introduce changes, not because they feared being fired by employee councils, but because they feared that reforms would produce unrest that would scare away potential buyers. The boards of directors did not have the authority to force managers to change policy. As a result, management-labor relations deteriorated.[29]

By 1996, 40% of the capitalization of the Warsaw Stock Exchange consisted of bank stock. The so-called easy privatizations of banks grew more complicated after the early days of the program, as the domestic stock market could only absorb so much stock from one sector. Selling bank shares overseas initially aroused nationalist sentiments. However, Poland sought entry into the European Union, which required the state to open its financial services market to free entry. Polish banks were so small in comparison to their European counterparts that planners knew they could not compete when the market would eventually open.[30] By the late 1990s, approximately two-thirds of the banking industry, measured by capital, was controlled by foreigners.[31]

### The Case of Szczecin Shipyard

At least initially, the employee councils had been seen as enemies of the process of privatization, nonetheless, they fostered many of the early instances. The case of the Szczecin Shipyard is no exception to this rule. The shipyard is the successor to three German shipyards that had been founded on the Szczecin bank of the Oder River in the nineteenth century. The German Reich converted them to submarine production in the late 1930s. Thus they had been targets for allied bombers and were mostly destroyed in the war. In the years that followed, the shift in the German-Polish border meant that the shipyards were in Polish territory.

The Communist government invested heavily in rebuilding the industry, and by the 1950s, the shipyard was once again a major industrial center.

In January 1990, the government instituted an economic restructuring plan that eliminated all government subsidies to the shipyard, which had operated at a loss. For the first time in its history the yard had to finance all new construction internally. It did so by financing production with bank credit. However, the firm had lost its main customer—the Soviet Union. As the debt burden quickly skyrocketed, rumors of the shipyard's impending bankruptcy hurt orders for future business and a crisis resulted.[32] In April 1991, a search committee of representatives from government ministries, shipyard creditors, and a panel of union members selected a long-time union activist to fill the position of managing director. The activist, Krzysztof Piotrowski, gained the support of shipyard workers who were aware that he had been fired from his job in 1985 as a result of his union activities on the workers' self-management council. Hence he had a degree of credibility with the workers that other managers may have lacked.

In September the firm was "commercialized" and management proceeded to restructure it in preparation for sale by restructuring debt, compensation, and seeking new clients. Despite the lack of profitability of the firm, it was slated for privatization in January 1993. According to the plan, 30% of the shares would be allocated to four Polish banks, 30% to shipyard employees, 9% to shipyard management, 15% to the yard's 10 largest suppliers, 10% to be retained by the state treasury, and 6% would be offered for sale. The new owners would not be permitted to sell their shares for six years in order for the firm to complete its restructuring program.[33] It was not listed on the Warsaw Stock Exchange. As was the case with similar Polish firms, the shipyard's management was uneasy with the state treasury owning 100% of the stock once it had been commercialized. Management did not have influence over stock sale decisions undertaken by the treasury, and Piotrowski feared that the government would sell the shipyard to a foreign investor who would reduce it to a role as low-cost provider of prefabricated keels for a large Western shipyard. The six-year requirement reduced the near-term threat.[34]

Walesa's government stalled the privatization in 1993, against the wishes of Piotrowski and other local unions. Nonetheless, once it did occur, the shipyard sought to create a Japanese-style industrial group by diversifying into other sectors such as food, financial services, and other industries.[35] Specifically, the shipyard sought to include the Cegielski Works in Poznan (where it purchased 17 of the 34 ships' engines produced there in 1993) and the Huta Czestochowa Steelworks in the industrial group. However, the plans to diversify into these firms were stalled by the uncertain inclusion of the firms in the privatization program, as well as by competition from the two other main Polish shipyards (i.e., Gdansk and Gdynia) that also sought to buy them.[36]

By 1996 Szczecin was the only profitable Polish ship producer. In order to take a majority stake and management control over the Gdynia shipyard (and thereby end the competition) and the Cegielski marine engine company, it had to compensate the government by agreeing to transfer the construction of five bulk tankers for the state-owned PZM Shipping Company to the Gdansk yard. With the transfer of the order, Marek Belha (the Polish finance minister) transferred the Polish Treasury's 47% in Gdynia to Szczecin. The Polish banks, as well as the European Bank for Reconstruction and Development (EBRD) supported the transfers.[37] Despite considerable successes after the privatization, the company's fortunes reversed in the economic downturn of 2002. The strong Polish zloty hurt exports, the price of ships dropped 25%, and the Polish government had dropped its subsidies to the industry. Salaries grew at a time when labor efficiency declined. The firm's management argued that the company made large investments and paid a large amount in taxes to the national budget, which contributed to the bankruptcy. Conversely, the banks lending money to the shipyard argued that the investments diverted to build a holding company, and not ships, were responsible. In March 2002 the firm halted production, and an investigation concerning securities fraud (related to further undisclosed debt) began in May.

For the first time, the Polish government considered the option of renationalizing a firm by taking a 35% stake, up from the 10% it had retained in the privatization. In exchange for the stake, the government would provide loan guarantees for the company to restart production. Prime Minister Leszek Miller argued that only by renationalizing the shipyard and playing a more active role in appointing company management and supervisory boards could the government participate in solving its problems. Only one of the four opposition parties represented in the Sejm, the Civic Platform, opposed the plan.[38]

### The Dependent Variable

The Polish privatization program sought to move the country toward a stakeholder model of corporate governance, with concentrated blocks of owners actively involved in formulating firm policies and business strategies. Individual firms, such as the Szczecin Shipyard, likewise sought to forge industrial groups along Japanese lines, which could withstand intense foreign competition. Therefore the Polish stock market's lack of institutional function in corporate governance was by design. Although the government established a securities market in 1991, and with it the appropriate regulating commission, it did not seek a corporate monitoring function for the market. Privatized companies, passing from management by workers councils to being commercialized firms, have a supervisory board as the ultimate governing body. Similar to the German model, workers are legally guaranteed participation in management, and industrial strategic investors hold blocs of shares. However, the Polish structure is unlike the German one in that the Polish banks have preferred to play a passive investment role. And foreigners control Polish banks overwhelmingly.

Moreover, the German model of corporate governance emerged as part of German industrialization and state formation. The Polish model (if a unified model exists) is emerging from state disengagement in large-scale state enterprises, with possible reengagement when the private ventures collapse. Thus a firm can be restructured and privatized, and be renationalized under political pressure from workers losing their jobs in an economic downturn. Moreover, Poland is the recipient of a growing degree of foreign direct investment. In the years 2000–2003, it attracted the largest amount of any ex-Communist state, including Russia.

## Russia

The post-Communist Russian equities market comprises three main sections.[39] The initial section consists of stocks of companies that brokers initially sold in 1990. These were primarily banks, commodities exchanges, and insurance companies. The second section emerged in 1993–1994 when firms began to issue bearer shares, many in classic pyramid schemes that used the profits from the sale of the shares to pay dividends to the buyers of previously issued shares. The third section is the professional market for corporate equities, in which ownership of shares is recorded in registries, and which passed into private hands through mass privatization schemes. Some firms within this category include large privatized enterprises that have not been attractive to outside investors, and where insiders control most shares. However, other firms within this sector have attracted outside investors. Most trading of these latter shares takes place on the Russian Trading System (RTS).[40] Since many of the scandals of the 1990s Russian equities market were associated with the bearer market, as well as the disreputable brokerage firms that had conducted the trades, stock exchanges in Russia acquired an untrustworthy reputation. Many brokerages avoid trading on the exchanges at all.[41] Hence the large volume of over-the-counter trading complicates any measurement of the total market capitalization in Russia.

Russian securities law has been modeled on the Anglo-American corporate governance structure. However, the lack of a liquid, well-regulated, secondary market for equity shares has eliminated the potential for the equities market to perform any function in the monitoring of, and market for, corporate management. The case study of the Cherkizovsky Group included in this section demonstrates the continuity and change inherent in the management of Russian firms from the Communist era. Given the evolutionary nature of stock markets in Russia, a more coherent picture of corporate governance may emerge. However, at present it is uneven and subject to a variety of pressures from the state, workers, and organized crime.

### The Transition from Communism in Russia

After the initial experience with communism from 1918 to 1921, the Soviet state embarked on the New Economic Policy in an attempt to combine market forces with socialism. During this period, large-scale industry remained nationalized, yet was divided into two categories. The commanding heights (e.g., fuel, metallurgy, war industries, transport, banking, and foreign trade) remained part of the state budget, and depended on centralized allocations of state supplies. However, the remaining nationalized enterprises became increasingly autonomous from the state. They could federate into trusts such that by 1923, 75% of all workers employed in nationalized industries worked in the 478 chartered trusts.[42] In most factories in the Soviet era, Moscow would set production targets, yet often did not provide the necessary inputs. Thus managers cut deals on the side in order to fulfill the plan and created their own networks to increase their access to required goods. Since most social services were also provided through the workplace, managers also cut deals to improve the living conditions of their workers.[43]

At the official end of the Communist era, the first phase of the Russian mass privatization program commenced from 1992 to 1994. However, prior to the 1992 program, unknown numbers of "spontaneous" privatizations had occurred. Johnson, Kroll, and Eder define spontaneous privatization as occurring "when managers acquire, on their own initiative, residual rights of control over their firms."[44] In some cases, enterprises previously leased by their workers' collectives bought out the assets using installment payments. These buyouts could later be transformed into partnerships with limited liability. Whereas some analysts argue that spontaneous privatizations amounted to nothing more than theft benefiting the old Communist *nomenklatura*, others argued that such privatizations were the only feasible way forward for state enterprises. When the formal privatization program eventually began, it did not seek any of the features of the Japanese or German governance structure, emulating the Anglo-American structure instead.

In the formal program, 80% of industrial output was transferred after a 1992 presidential decree required all large enterprises with more than 1000 employees to privatize. Medium-size firms could choose to do the same. By mid-1994, approximately 19,000 enterprises had registered as joint-stock companies. Russians could use vouchers (introduced in 1992) to purchase shares in the companies through an auction system or through preferential employee stock-ownership programs. In addition, voucher investment funds could acquire and invest both vouchers and cash on behalf of individuals. While the goal of phase one was to break up large state industries and satisfy demands for social justice, the method had the effect of distributing payoffs to managers and other employees in the form of equity shares. It did not bring new capital into firms, nor introduce anything more than a change in ownership.[45] In almost all cases the workers and managers acquired more than 50% of the shares of their workplace.[46]

Under phase two of the program, the government sold residual shares of its firms for cash, and not for vouchers. However, by this phase, outsiders did not want to purchase blocks of shares for cash in enterprises insiders controlled.[47] Therefore the resulting Russian ownership structure continued to protect workers and managers. Workers, who owned a majority of shares, did not perceive their interests to be aligned with the value of the company, but rather with their job security. Without any real knowledge of the potential stock ownership implies for control of underperforming management, they did not conceptualize the possibility of replacing Soviet-trained managers at this point in the Communist transition. Thus they began to sell their stock. Given an underdeveloped securities market, their shares were not liquid and the most immediate buyers were managers and other inside investors. In addition, workers often gave their shares to managers in return for a promise that they would not lose their jobs.[48] Hence, as the workers gave or sold their shares to the managers, the balance of ownership gradually shifted as managements' ownership became more concentrated.[49]

Following the transfer of assets, the Russian Duma adopted the Law on Stock Companies and the Law on the Securities Market in 1995. These laws came into effect in 1996 to strengthen corporate governance, but immediately encountered serious discrepancies in enforcement. One significant problem existed with respect to establishing a clear title to share certificates. Russian law does not currently require companies to issue share certificates. Companies themselves can control their own share registers, which are at times the only proof of ownership, opening countless possibilities for conflicts of interest and outright fraud. Some independent registrars have been established, and the IFC established the National Registry Company in 1995 to attempt to address this problem. Nonetheless, the share registers make it nearly impossible for shareholders to sell their shares without having to go through management. At times, managements have tried to prevent workers from selling shares to outsiders. Some managers have transferred assets to other firms under their control.[50] Continuing legal attempts to address the problem of register control and manipulation by management insiders have been frustrated by lack of enforcement.[51] In 2003 the Prime Minister of Russia, Mikhail Kasyanov, assured the Russian business community that the government would not investigate the origins of the fortunes made during its privatization program.[52]

Therefore the large ownership stakes by insiders (managers and workers) and the lack of institutional concentration of outside ownership resulted in a lack of effective governance of these firms along either an Anglo-American or Continental model. The phase one voucher investment funds that could have been the basis for institutional ownership failed to gain controlling stakes, or to monitor management as intended, because they lacked liquidity, access to company registers, and an enforcement mechanism that would guarantee their ownership. Moreover, after having bought shares without a legal foundation to support them in struggles with directors, and a tax code that discouraged them from restructuring their portfolio shares, the funds proved to be inadequate mechanisms.

### The Case of Cherkizovsky Group

One example of a privatized firm with continuity in management from the Soviet era is the Cherkizovsky Group. Igor Babaev, the firm's manager, was appointed chief engineer of the Cherkizovsky Meat Processing Plant in Moscow. In this position, Babaev had proximity to the planning bureaus and party authorities. He became president of the plant in 1991 and continued in the role through the privatization process, when, as in the other cases, ownership was transferred to the management and workers. To accomplish the transfer of the processing plant, Babaev formed a limited liability company with 600 employees in December 1991. Each worker received shares in proportion to the length of his or her employment. In February 1992 Cherkizovsky Ltd. entered a lease agreement with the city of Moscow, and various agencies of the Moscow city government made a passive investment of $15 million in the firm.

Over the next two years, Babaev made additional investments in the company and bought many shares from employees. With a $5 million bank loan, he increased his stake to more than 60%. In interviews, Babaev stated that the banks lent him the money because they were "immersed in a socialist mindset, so they usually lent money without any sense" or they "liked me because I created things."[53] In December 1993, the firm and the city restructured their venture into the Cherkizovsky Meat Processing Plant Joint Stock Company, wherein the firm owned 82% and the Moscow government owned 18%. By 1993 the workforce had increased to approximately 3000 individuals, yet shareholders were limited to the original 600 employees. Babaev continued to buy their shares, as well as the government's shares.

Reflecting the shifting balance between management and employees in Russian ownership structures, Babaev held 82% of the firm, the Moscow government 12%, and employees 6% in 1997.[54] By this time the Cherkizovsky Meat Processing Works was Moscow's leading meat producer, led by Babaev; an engineer who reorganized the production process, Musheg Mamikonyan; and an American expatriate consultant, Mike Harman. It led a coalition of meat producers to limit foreign meat imports from Poland and the European Union. Managerial problems within the company emerged with respect to additional firms purchased by Babaev, yet not integrated into the system, because the managers tended to identify closely with their own entities and not with the overall conglomerate. In addition, the firm found it difficult to attract foreign capital, given the business and political climate. Yet the firm rebounded after the financial crisis in 1998 and successfully traded equity shares for credits with the Agency for Restructuring of Crediting Organizations, Morgan Stanley, and Canadian trading company Ronald Chisholm International. In May 2003 it planned to sell a 25% stake in its shares in an IPO in either London or New York.[55]

### The Dependent Variable

The Cherkizovsky Group is similar to other Russian firms that needed cash following the 1998 financial crisis. The crisis caused the state to revisit again the issue of corporate governance because the banking sector collapsed and foreign investment appeared to be the only source of investment capital. Relative to other states, Russia received less foreign direct investment than Hungary, and a fraction of what China received. A lack of investor confidence in governance structures appears to prohibit a strategy of massive foreign investment in the short to medium term.[56]

The managerial control of most Russian companies is concentrated in the hands of a few individuals, often significantly disproportionate to their ownership stakes. Unlike the three controlling-minority structures proposed at the start of this section, the Russian structures rest on managers' ability to control share registers and operate in the absence of a liquid secondary market for shares. At times, managers can refuse to register share transactions. At other times, managers can change share registration from common to preferred stock in order to prevent shareholders from exercising voting rights. In the extreme, there have been instances of corporations preventing foreign investors from exercising their voting rights or preventing a foreign firm from taking control of a Russian firm by refusing to recognize Russian Federal Court decisions.[57]

The manner of retaining control through minority structures, however, is not systematic. In addition to the earlier examples, in some instances, managers have followed former Soviet practices of using factory capacity and warehouse space for "special deals" conducted off of the company's books. In other instances, workers have been compensated for their votes at stockholders meetings when such votes were required to approve the deals. Workers in these conditions have few good options. Leaving their jobs or selling their shares to the sole buyer (i.e., management) are among the bad options.[58]

Therefore there is no real consensus on the goal of corporate governance in Russia: to maximize shareholder wealth, to develop the state, or to provide for the workers. The role of the state as a stakeholder has decreased since the privatization program in 1991, and enterprises routinely ignore decrees from the central Russian government. However, the role of the state has not been completely eliminated. It can influence the firm where the State Property Fund retains a large share-holding in some individual firms (as in the Cherkizovsky Group), or where it holds a "golden" share, effectively vetoing takeovers in others.[59] Few shares are transferred on organized stock markets in Russia, and a real market has only developed for approximately 100 of the largest enterprises.

## The Czech Republic

As was the case with Hungary and Poland, Czech commodities exchanges appeared in Prague in the nineteenth century. The trading of securities on an organized exchange picked up in the interim between the two world wars, at which time the Prague market boomed. However, the exchange did not reopen after the war, when Czechoslovakia became a Soviet satellite. The new exchange was formed in connection with the transition from communism in 1992.[60] Although the Czech transfer of assets began later than the Hungarian and Polish programs did, the Czech mass privatization program progressed much more rapidly. Unlike other transition economies, where companies were individually valued and sold to either domestic or foreign investors or workers, the Czech program turned over assets through a program of vouchers assigned to individual citizens. The program distributed assets equitably, but did not realize revenue for the state. A group of investment funds, loosely modeled after Western mutual funds, emerged as part of the transition to manage individual citizens' choice of firms. This section considers Harvard Capital, one of the more controversial of these funds, and its connection to equity market growth and firm management in the Czech Republic.

### The Transition from Communism in
### the Czech Republic

Financial restructuring in the Czech Republic began in 1991 when the Ministry of Finance and National Property Fund founded the Consolidation Bank. Komerica Bank and Ivesticni Bank transferred their loans and credits to the Consolidation Bank in order to renegotiate the terms of the loans and to pursue collections. In November 1991, the state-owned National Property Fund transferred bonds to the Consolidation Bank in order to cushion the effects of bankruptcy in subsequent years and to write down a degree of debt. Next, finance minister Vaclav Klaus sought quick privatization of industrial assets to begin prior to the June 1992 elections.

In order to transfer ownership of industry, the Czech authorities distributed more than 50% of the equity of large public enterprises through a citizen voucher scheme. Each citizen received vouchers equal to 1000 investment points. The points could be exchanged for shares in the enterprises designated for privatization at a price (in points) the state initially determined. A share of more prominent firms would cost more (in points) than a share of less prominent firms. The privatizations took place in rounds, with the final prices (in points) determined by supply and demand for shares.[61] With this system, the government seemed to be moving toward an Anglo-American-style system of raising investment funds through markets. The point of the voucher auction was to transfer shares to private hands so that they could be bought and sold on a market. Thus the leadership of the Czech Republic was willing to allow dispersed ownership, at least initially. It did not specifically favor the managers of the firms to be sold.[62]

Trading opened on the new Prague Stock Exchange in only seven securities in April 1993. Market capitalization shot up two months later, however, when the first wave of coupon privatization was launched and 622 new share issues were listed. The next month, 333 additional shares were listed after the first wave of coupon privatization. In March 1995, 674 more shares were issued with the second wave of coupon privatization. By this time, more than half of the state's assets had been privatized and the Prague market was among the largest in Europe. Although it opened after the Budapest and Warsaw markets, the Prague market's capitalization quickly surpassed the others. Conversely, most of the Czech shares were not liquid, whereas the Hungarian and Polish shares were.

As part of the process of privatization, more than two-thirds of Czech voucher holders had placed their vouchers with competing investment funds. The 10 largest of these funds obtained more than 40% of all vouchers in the two waves of privatization. The funds pooled the vouchers and invested them on the owners' behalf. Yet their role in corporate governance is unclear. The Civic Forum refused to enact managerial codetermination along German lines in 1990. The larger of the investment funds are affiliated with the major, state-owned banks, yet the banks are not themselves privatized. Hence the funds did not function within a German-type system. Investors try to build up controlling stakes in firms off of the formal exchanges. As was the case with Hungary, analysts estimate that 80%–90% of the shares of the Czech Republic are traded in blocs in this way. The following case of Harvard Capital further depicts the ambiguous role of the funds in corporate governance.

### The Case of Harvard Capital

Harvard Capital evolved as part of the privatization program itself. When the government announced the first program, it required citizens to spend roughly US$37 (one week's wages) to buy and register a book of the vouchers. Given the complexity of the program, and the fee, only about 700,000 citizens had registered by the end of 1991. In January 1992, the pace of the registration increased when Harvard Capital began to advertise five times a day on television. The advertisements promised citizens a 10-fold return on their investment in one year if they would turn the management of the vouchers over to the fund. A Czech native who had defected in 1980 and graduated from Harvard University, Viktor Kozeny, would manage it. Twenty-two thousand agents bought voucher books at local post offices where registration took place, and by the end of the month more than two million had registered their shares.

Other funds emerged, competed with Harvard Capital, and likewise promised spectacular returns. By March, more than 80% of the population (i.e., 8.6 million people) had bought the vouchers. In response to the funds, Privatization Ministry officials prepared legislation to require the funds to diversify their investment in at least 10 companies and not to acquire more than 20% of a given company's equity.[63] Even with the legislation, ministers feared the companies' entry into the privatization scheme because so many funds had promised such great returns in such a short amount of time.

Harvard Capital was somewhat unlike the other investment companies in that it openly planned to manage the firms in which it invested. Kozeny had worked at the merchant bank Robert Fleming and had some Western managerial experience despite his young age — 28 years old in 1992. Moreover, he planned to import 250 managers to help run the firms.[64] By 1993 Harvard Capital had concentrated its holdings in 51 of the former Czechoslovakia's most significant companies. Notwithstanding the legal prohibition against owning more than 20% of a firm's equity, Kozeny could claim to control 30 of the top 50 firms because with dispersed ownership, his holding was the largest bloc. It operated with large foreign investors in 12 firms. Moreover, Harvard Capital made temporary deals to represent other shareholders, and asserted itself in general. In 12 firms it operated with large foreign investors. Taken together, one observer noted that Kozeny was "in effect chairman of the board of half of the fifty leading Czech companies."[65]

Kozeny planned to cut workforces and liquidate underperforming firms. Yet before he could accomplish any restructuring on a massive scale, he left the Czech Republic and managed the fund from the Bahamas. The reasons for his departure are somewhat uncertain. Public sentiment had certainly turned against him in 1993 due to his involvement with a Communist-era secret service agent, Vaclav Wallis. Rumors circulated that Kozeny had used Wallis to gain inside information on privatization decisions that had helped to drive up the investment company's stake in the large enterprises. Kozeny admitted that he paid Wallis a retainer, but he denied having access to inside information.[66] Since 1997 the Harvard Capital funds have been in liquidation, and Kozeny was indicted in 2003 on charges that he stole $182 million from some former clients. The Manhattan district attorney started extradition proceedings he hoped would force Kozeny to return to the United States in October of that year.[67]

### The Dependent Variable

At the end of the massive wave of privatizations, the ownership structure of Czech firms had been atomized and aggregated. Since citizens diversified their individual risk by investing their vouchers in the funds, the funds owned large or controlling stakes in many firms. This ownership structure impeded efficient corporate governance, and blocked the market for managerial control, when considered in relation to the other Czech financial market participants. Unlike the Harvard Capital fund, the major domestic banks owned the majority of the rest of the funds. The banks were in turn controlled by the state. Hence the funds did not treat the poorly performing firms aggressively, since to do so would require bank owners to write down debt to these firms. The state-influenced banks tended to extend credit to poor firms and roll over credit long after bankruptcy was necessary. Managers loaded firms with debt, then took the cash and vanished, leaving the firm saddled with debt it had not used for restructuring.[68]

Therefore, while some observers have argued that with concentrated ownership through the funds the Czech Republic's corporate governance structure resembles the German one, several key differences have emerged specifically with respect to the investment funds, and continued state involvement, that belies this conclusion. Chiefly, the state, operating through the Fund of National Property, remained the controlling shareholder of the largest five financial institutions from the Communist regime. Although investment funds are not permitted to own shares of their own or other banks, owning subsidiaries allows banks to circumvent this regulation. After the first round of privatizations in June 1993, the degree of interlocking shareholdings in Czech financial institutions had grown considerably.[69] In addition, the Fund of National Property held a controlling interest in the 50 very large enterprises the government had designated as "strategic" (e.g., Aero Holding, Czech Airlines, West Bohemian Mines, Vitkovice Stell Works, etc.).[70]

The poor performance of the funds can be partially attributed to faulty pricing of the underlying assets of the funds. Yet it can also be attributed to the tight relationship between the funds management, the banks, and large enterprises (which are the banks' creditors). With this relationship, fund managers act to keep the funds' price low, allow the brokerage firms to buy out the small shareholders of the funds, and benefit former ranking members of the banking-industrial *nomenklatura*.[71]

Therefore the continuing problems with opacity and mistrust extending from the Communist era have meant that the Prague stock market never evolved into the type of institution envisioned when the government handed shares over to citizens. As early as 1995, the Prague Stock Exchange was considered to be of such low transparency that it was an "insiders market" only. Companies gutted by corrupt managers, or manipulated by inside trades, have produced ongoing scandals and contributed to the lack of trust. A total of 1700 state-owned enterprises were converted to publicly traded companies in the privatization process, yet 1301 shares were withdrawn from the Prague market in 1997 due to lack of liquidity. So many have fallen apart and delisted that only seven listed domestic stocks were considered "investment grade" in March 2002, and the main stock index only contained 37 issues.[72]

Given this lack of managerial function, the performance of the economy overall remains to be seen. Although small stockholders may not benefit from the relationship among banks, the funds, and enterprise management, dominant ownerships of large corporations may emerge to perform the monitoring function. In that case, the Czech Republic would more closely resemble the German model, and overall productivity may improve.

## Analysis and Conclusion

The ownership of what industrialization had already occurred in Russia and eastern Europe prior to the Communist takeover was reorganized after the takeovers. The command economies did not allow for private ownership of large-scale industrial enterprise, thus the joint-stock company business did not continue to function (unless the shares were held by the state), nor did primary or secondary securities markets for large-firms' securities. Therefore establishing stock exchanges when the Communist era ended was an important symbolic move, particularly in states where an exchange had existed in the former era. Consultants from international organizations and from private firms assisted in the transition and promoted outwardly Western business practices and stock exchange functions.

Nevertheless, fostering effective financial institution functions in the transition economies has been a much more complicated task. Table 8.3 summarizes the case studies of eastern European and Russian firms in this chapter. Individual case studies show that the state remains heavily involved in the management of these firms, despite the relatively higher degree of popular domestic political support for the privatization programs than existed in the Latin American and Asian regions. Hence level I and level II political influences produced a completely different result in terms of distribution of shares than they did in the Latin American and Asian regions. Level I imperatives concern the accessibility of foreign exchanges and the emulation of Western business practices and securities laws. The external influences came from consultants provided by international financial organizations. The initiative to privatize, however, did not come from these organizations. Rather it originated in the broad-based social movements opposed to Soviet-backed regimes.

Level II domestic constituencies did not protest the transfer of ownership, as in the other regions, at least as much as it was a part of the transition from communism. Some did protest sales to outsiders. The time frame for reforms was very short once the change was definitive. Over time, the financial institutional structure has settled into more consistent patterns in these states (compared to Latin America and Asia), yet the former Communist management has been able to use its advantage to construct control along lines that resemble a blending of past and present practices, and not so much a break with the past. In some extreme cases, renationalization may occur.

In the Polish example, the state emulated the German-Japanese model of corporate governance. Thus the exchange does not function in the market for managerial control by design. The Polish result, however, does not resemble the German structure, and is not uniform across industries. One key difference between the Polish result and the German model is in the banking system: Poland is the recipient of a large amount of foreign direct investment, particularly in its banking industry; hence these banks have not played the same monitoring function

TABLE 8.3 Summary of Russian and Eastern European Cases Examined

| State | Company privatized (year) | International imperative (level I) | Groups active in sale (level II) | Distribution of shares | Controlling interest held by (governance structure) |
|---|---|---|---|---|---|
| Hungary | Ibusz (1990) | Listing requirements of Vienna stock exchange (e.g., the firm's books were audited by Western accountants prior to the sale to allow cross-listing). London firms advised when exchange was created. | The head of the State Property Agency resigned after the sale due to criticism that he had "given the company away." Perceptions that the firm did not perform well led to a lack of future listings. | Firm increased its capitalization so that only 3% of the existing shares were sold. At first, the state held 63%. Later, cross-holdings with subsidiaries. The firm delisted from the stock exchange in 2002. | Institutional cross-ownership (cross-holdings) |
| Poland | Szczecin Shipyard (1993)[a] | Experts from the French Bourse assisted when the exchange was setup. Shipyard seeks privatization after losing its main customer (the USSR) and needing bank credit. | Former union activist became manager. Later, groups sought renationalization. | 30% banks, 30% employees, 9% management, 15% to ten largest suppliers, 10% state Treasury, 6% public sale. | Krzysztof Piotrowski (former union activist) |
| Russia | Cherkozorsky Group (1993–1997) | Firm plans to make an international offering. | Firm management consolidated shares following privatization. | 82% Igor Babaev, 12% Moscow government, 6% employees. | Igor Babaev (former manager, majority shareholder) |
| Czech Republic | Harvard Capital[b] (1992) | Government sought Anglo-American style system. | Funds consolidated controlling stakes in privatized firms. | Voting rights of shares turned over to fund | Viktor Kozeny (fund manger) |

[a]These shares were not listed on a stock exchange.

[b]This case was not itself a privatization sale, but consolidated shares from other sales in a massive and rapid privatization.

their German counterparts do. In addition, the result is not uniform because large-scale Polish industry may be subject to renationalization, as the case of the Szczecin Shipyard showed. Firms whose managerial control was transferred outside the state are subject to the governance structures of a parent company located in another state, such as Germany.

The Hungarian, Russian, and Czech examples sought to emulate the Anglo-American corporate governance model, yet none of these states have achieved financial institutions functioning in the market for managerial control, as do the New York or London markets. Insider managers have control over most large Russian firms. The lack of a liquid, well-regulated secondary market for shares reinforces their hold, since a hostile takeover is not possible in these circumstances. Hungary and the Czech Republic attempted to create liquid primary and secondary securities markets, yet elaborate cross-holding structures tended to reinforce managers' power. In the Hungarian example, it was not the stock exchange that challenged managers' power as much as outside investors. In the example of the Czech Republic, the relationship among the banks, investment funds, and the state prevented any one of the three from taking on a monitoring role or from leaving management open to the market for corporate control.

# Africa and the Middle East

A frican stock markets represent opposite ends of the spectrum of emerging markets. At one end of the spectrum, old, highly integrated exchanges remain from the British era. The Johannesburg exchange was only reclassified by the IFC as "emerging" after the free elections held in the postapartheid era. At the other end of the spectrum, new exchanges, designed specifically to enable mass privatization programs, have been created in the 1990s with the active involvement of international financial institutions. The Accra exchange in Ghana opened in 1990 and has handled many such deals. Nonetheless, the African exchanges examined in this chapter are similar to other emerging markets in that they have been political as well as economic institutions from their inception. The politics of how shares come to be issued on African exchanges are a similar reconciliation of international and domestic forces. States issuing shares may have done so to respond to international pressure; nonetheless, the domestic "ratification" process results in ownership and control structures that render shareholder influence nearly meaningless.

Africa, as a continent, differs from other territories of the postcolonial world because it has had a much shorter history with the state system. European powers did not consolidate their hold on African interior territories until after the Berlin Congo Conference of the late nineteenth century, and even then the European urban areas were generally situated on the coasts. The African countryside had few continuous political systems. Only areas with significant concentrations of white settler populations, such as South Africa, had somewhat comprehensive colonial states.[1] The multinational corporations operating in Africa were generally involved in trading, and not local production, because the political units were so thinly populated that deep consumer markets could not develop unless they were heavily protected. Moreover, local poverty limited the demand for consumer goods, except for the cheapest types that offered low profit margins.[2]

When investment did occur, Europeans imported capital-intensive new technology such as steamships, railways, deep-level mining, and mechanized processing capabilities for plantations. They paid for the technology with currency that could be readily converted into that of their home country. The vastly different technologies, monetary systems, and eventually legal systems created the basis for self-perpetuating enclaves of external influence.[3] If stocks needed to be issued or traded to finance investment, they were generally issued and traded in the colonial metropole. However, there were two significant exceptions to this rule: South Africa and Egypt. Both of these markets grew to the extent that they were among the largest in the world for their time.

As was the case with the other postcolonial exchanges, the independence period was accompanied by intensive strategies of state-led development and de-emphasis on equity finance. Thus, in the cases where new exchanges appeared, the state used the exchange as a symbol of financial sophistication and as a tool of state intervention through joint ownership of many of the old colonial firms. Where an exchange appeared, firms were usually required to list shares. In most cases the state did not even establish an exchange because it was both owner and manager of large-scale industrial concerns. Hence a stock exchange was not necessary. In the two cases where extensive trading occurred, the South African exchange developed into one with extensive cross-holdings of domestic firms and few foreign listings. The Egyptian markets expanded and underwent an intensive "Egyptianization" project, yet were effectively closed under Nasser's mass nationalization program.

Along with the dramatic changes accompanying the debt crisis of the 1980s and 1990s, the privatization era in Africa has unfolded somewhat differently than in the other regions. In the Latin American and Asian examples, political interest groups may not have agreed on the merits of state disinvestment, but certain domestic interests did back some strategies. In Russia and eastern Europe, establishing a stock exchange sent a symbolic message, particularly where a pre-Communist exchange had operated. Conversely, the new African stock exchanges are much more analogous to international development projects like the pre-1980s World Bank projects for steel mills, to encourage industry, and the pre-1980s World Bank projects for small farmers, to encourage agricultural development, than they are to any statement of a shift in policy orientation.

The African exchanges thus differ from the others because of their lack of domestic political support, the complete lack of securities market infrastructure (in most cases), and the notably slow pace and small size of privatizations. The average size of an African sell-off is US$1 million, and the most common method of sale has been through a competitive tender, whether of shares or assets. In the cases where a stock market exists, some privatizations have been offered publicly. Yet even in these cases, the sale has been part of an integrated strategy involving the sale of a block of shares to a strategic investor.

While the privatization programs lack widespread domestic political support, African states do not have many viable alternatives. The conditionality requirements of structural adjustment loans tied the physical resources of Africa more firmly into the global economy. Simultaneously, structural adjustment facilitated the financial machinery necessary to transport wealth into and out of the region. Privatization has been an important component of these programs, and privatization itself requires the financial machinery of a stock exchange to continue on a large scale, and to include local capital as minority shares.[4] From the perspective of the international financial organizations, stock exchanges improve the allocative efficiency of capital and make it possible to restore lending in situations where private interest rates have skyrocketed.

This situation means that in the current era, African stock exchanges such as those in Cairo and Alexandria that extend to the colonial era have been reborn with new listings. The original Abidjan Bourse, an exchange created in the nationalist era to indigenize shares, was deepened with new listings and broadened with the inclusion of other states to create a regional exchange. In a third category, some states created new exchanges *de novo* to handle privatizations and accommodate new banking regulations associated with structural adjustment programs. An example of this type would be the Accra Stock Exchange. Nonetheless, these new and revitalized exchanges coexist with the older structures. That is, the new exchanges have emerged in an environment where the possibility of cross-listing in the old colonial metropole still exists for companies large enough to meet the requirements of the heavily capitalized, transnational exchanges.

This chapter begins with the example of South Africa because it has been significant both in the history of the continent and in the history of the international political economy. However, the inclusion of South Africa is admittedly problematic because it was only recently reclassified as an emerging market exchange. The chapter then examines the Egyptian exchanges and their evolution from colonial, to postcolonial, to contemporary markets. Next, it turns to the example of Senegal, a former French colony that has forgone establishing a national exchange and has listed its privatized shares on a regional market. Finally, the chapter considers the example of Ghana as one where an exchange was created *de novo*.

## South Africa

As with the South African state, the South African equities market exhibits contradictory characteristics of both a developed and developing market. Similar to the developed, industrial exchanges, it is one of the oldest and largest in the world, and it operates within a deeply embedded institutional equity culture. Nevertheless, the exchange is characterized by listings of large, family-controlled firms that hold large numbers of shares of other firms. Thus it does not play a role in the market for managerial control. Corporate governance reforms associated with the end of the nationalist apartheid regime have sought to minimize excessive corporate governance abuses; yet at the same time, the new, open environment has enticed many large firms to move their headquarters to London and change their primary listing. This section uses the example of the Anglo-American conglomerate to demonstrate operations of one firm on the exchange and the reconfiguration of the exchange as some firms delist and some large firms migrate to London.

### Share Trading in South Africa

Similar to other developing regions, European powers imported the business form of the joint-stock company to South Africa. It was not an indigenous business form. And similar to other developing regions with colonial-era stock exchanges, South Africa was an area that attracted a strong pattern of transnational investment under Dutch and then direct British control. Demonstrating both the longstanding and the international nature of the equity market, an early joint-stock company for the purpose of catching whales and seals on the African coast was floated both in Amsterdam and Cape Town under the Peace of Amiens, when the colony of the Cape of Good Hope was returned to the Netherlands.[5] The share market grew to the extent that in 1854, fourteen firms of brokers operated in Cape Town.

When political authority for the territory was transferred to Great Britain, the City of London initially directed most of its capital to South Africa through the joint-stock colonial banks. Nonetheless, share trading in South Africa received a boost, as it had in Great Britain and India, from the introduction of limited liability. The 1861 act "to limit the liability of members of certain Joint Stock Companies" put an end to the need to apply each time for special legislation in Parliament to create a joint-stock company and gave anonymous shareholders a sense of security from bad investments. The law helped to stimulate joint-stock investment in South Africa from overseas, which would become important when diamonds were discovered on the northern frontier of the Cape Colony in 1867. Unlike some other colonial exchanges, such as Bombay, Cairo, and Alexandria, indigenous Africans did not participate in equity trades.

The amalgamation of the various Kimberley private diamond mining companies and small holdings into joint-stock mining companies by late 1880–1881 marks the starting point for a torrent of capital to South African mining that came to be the hallmark of the Johannesburg exchange. Capital issues rose from £0.4 million in 1880 to £40 million in 1891, and £140 million in 1901. The Rand syndicates raised this capital by filtering the shares through their London offices, particularly those of Wernher Beit & Co. and Barnato Bros.[6] Historians disagree as to the proportion of colonial versus metropole capital speculated in the mines.[7] Some estimate that in the first 15 years of production, diamond mines were financed out of company surplus and inflation on the cape. However, other observers note that 15 of the 71 companies formed in 1881 were incorporated in London and Paris. These 15 companies represent one-third of the total nominal capital of the mines.[8] Speculation had been outlawed on German bourses, with the result that speculative business was conducted elsewhere, especially London.[9]

A limited arbitrage existed between Kimberley and London, particularly for companies registered in Europe. In February 1881, the Royal Stock Exchange was established in Kimberley so that brokers and others could meet for business without going to the camps to ask for shares, or make offers for sale.[10] Several other rival stock exchanges were also established in the Kimberley share boom of 1881. When gold was discovered on the Witwatersrand Ridge in 1886, the discovery increased the number of South African mining firms exponentially. Benjamin Woollan founded the Johannesburg Stock Exchange in November 1887 for the same reasons as the Kimberley exchange had been founded: the sheer number of mining and financial companies necessitated a facility through which to buy and sell shares.

By 1889 the European population numbered approximately 500,000 and there were 750 stockbroking firms. Thus three years after the proclamation of the Rand goldfield, the European community of South Africa could arguably claim the highest proportion of stockbrokers to population in the world.[11] This proportion was short-lived, however. In 1888 DeBeers Consolidated mines was established, and the number of shares quoted in Kimberley was reduced considerably. Although other types of companies (e.g., water and electricity) were quoted there, many members switched their operations to Johannesburg. The Kimberley market eventually closed.[12]

By the end of the 1890s, the Rand goldfield was the largest single producer of gold, with more than one-fourth of all world output. By 1906–1910, gold accounted for about two-thirds of the value of South Africa's exports. French and German investors invested in the mines as well, but the British share was about 60%–80% of the total.[13] This concentration of production, and its connection to Britain, led to an uneasy relationship between the City of London and imperialists operating in South Africa, such as Cecil Rhodes. Since most of the early capital invested in the Rand was generated internally, in Kimberley, and in several trading towns, Rothschilds and other merchant banks were unable to impose their will on any of Rhodes's companies or on the state of Transvaal.[14]

Nonetheless, the gold boom in South Africa is a prime example of the formation of corporations attracting widespread investment interest and the subsequent transformation of local securities into international securities. At the peak of the boom, the shares of the principle mining companies were traded on exchanges of various sizes, ranging from London, to Constantinople, to Cairo.[15] The effects of the global spread of South African shares were concentrated, however, in only one of several European interest groups in the region. Tensions among these groups eventually erupted in a particularly cruel war from 1899–1902.

The British were victorious in what came to be known as the Anglo-Boer War, and thus formed the Union of South Africa; nonetheless, internal divisions persisted among political groups beneath the outward displays of unity after it ended. Afrikaners sympathized with the German cause in World War I, and mobilized their own capital in the interwar years. Hence, agricultural, small-scale manufacturing, and white working-class interests forged a political-economic consciousness in opposition to the United Party, comprising financial, mining, large-scale manufacturing, and "English" capital interests. The Afrikaner consciousness ascended along with the victory of the Nationalist party in 1948. After coming into power, the Nationalists controlled state capital, pursued a program of apartheid, and used the wider state apparatus to promote Afrikaner interests throughout the political economy.

With apartheid controlling African labor and preventing black African participation on the stock exchange, the National Party government expanded the public sector, and with it Afrikaner economic advancement. It established a number of agricultural control boards and public enterprises such as ESCOM (electricity), South African Railways and Harbours, Armscor (armaments), FOSKOR (fertilizers), etc. The effect of this expansion was to increase Afrikaner participation in the private sector and diminish English and foreign control. At the same time, the program expanded secondary industry and made the country less reliant on mining. The country experienced an economic boom during the 1960s, due in part to the high degree of involvement of transnational firms. The British government, in particular, was directly engaged in the economy through its nationalized corporations such as British Steel and British Leyland.[16]

The Johannesburg stock exchange itself remained heavily focused on mining shares. The shares of the Anglo-American conglomerate alone (including companies in which it has a large stake) accounted for half the value of the entire exchange in 1982. This group is also typical of many other large enterprises in South Africa in that it was controlled by the Oppenheimer family from its founding in 1917 until 1982. The founder's grandson, Nicholas Oppenheimer, is the president of DeBeers as of this writing. Although a rash of new listings on the exchange appeared in 1987 (211 companies) and again in 1998 (101 companies), it has had a historical problem with insider trading. No one has ever been successfully prosecuted for insider trading in South Africa, and previously existing laws have been considered unenforceable. New regulations to address this issue came into effect in 1999.[17]

### The Case of Anglo-American

Anglo-American follows the history of joint-stock companies in South Africa in that it was a family-controlled, foreign-financed mining company in the colonial era, then a widely diversified conglomerate within the nationalist economy, and then a refocused international enterprise in the postapartheid era. Sir Ernest Oppenheimer established Anglo-American in 1917 to exploit the gold mining industry of the East Rand after he had already consolidated his hold on the diamond industry through DeBeers. He financed Anglo-American with investments from the United States and the United Kingdom.

Under Sir Ernest's management, Anglo-American diversified in the 1950s and 1960s by buying interests in all aspects of South African life: gold mines, shopping centers, fertilizers, motorways, wine, sugar production, banking, insurance, car dealerships, car assembly plants, and travel services. However, despite the fact that it was the largest mining group in the world, it was not an international firm since it was so heavily concentrated in the economy of one state. Upon Sir Ernest's death in 1957, his son, Harry Oppenheimer, took over the chairmanship. Harry Oppenheimer defended Anglo's tacit support for the apartheid regime, arguing that economic growth in South Africa would be an engine for change.

The Oppenheimer family maintained its managerial hold on Anglo-American through a cross-holding, minority-controlling ownership structure. That is, the Oppenheimer family's private company, E. Oppenheimer and Son, controlled only 8.3% of Anglo-American. A South African insurance firm held the second largest stake as a portfolio investment. The family also held a 7% share of Minorco, Anglo's foreign investment arm. Of the four holding companies with interlocking shares, DeBeers had the largest stake in Anglo itself.[18] In the 1980s, however, the power of the family was diluted as 15 large associates and subsidiaries came to hold increasing proportions of Anglo's investments. Executives from the firm could not travel to the United States because the Justice Department had charged DeBeers with price fixing.

Gavin Relly took over Anglo-American's management in 1982. He shocked the Nationalist regime at the time by traveling to Zambia to meet with Oliver Tambo and other African National Congress (ANC) leaders in exile to negotiate the country's future. When the ANC took over the government, nationalization was no longer an issue. Yet when Julian Ogilvie Thompson took over from Relly in 1990, he redirected the postapartheid firm away from South Africa and onto the world stage. Initially seeking the approval of Thambo Mbeke (then the ANC deputy president) and Trevor Manuel (the finance minister), he merged the firm with Minorco and moved its headquarters to London in 1999.[19]

The firm sought a London listing for financial reasons. London represents a much larger capital market, and as a British firm, funds restricted to investing in British firms can invest in Anglo. Moreover, in London, Anglo-American is included in the Financial Times Stock Exchange (FTSE) index. Thus funds indexed to the FTSE will buy shares out of necessity. The move to London has also meant a restructuring and a refocus. Anglo is no longer the highly diversified conglomerate it was in the "old" South Africa. Currently it is a mining and natural resources group divided according to product lines: Anglo Platinum (platinum), Anglo Gold (gold), De Beers (diamonds), Anglo Coal (coal), Mondi Europe (forest products), Anglo Industrial Minerals (industrial minerals), Anglo Ferrous Metals and Industries (ferrous metals), and Anglo Base Metals (base metals). To transform itself, it has sold its assets in other domestic South African companies.[20]

The transformation has changed the ownership structure, yet concentrated the hold of the Oppenheimer family in the diamonds sector. In May 2001, shareholders voted to turn DeBeers into an unlisted subsidiary of Anglo-American. Thus the firm began to unscramble its large cross-holdings. DeBeers had first listed publicly in 1893, yet it delisted from the Johannesburg exchange with this transaction in 2001. As a result of the transaction, the Oppenheimer family received 45% of DeBeers, with managerial control (up from its ownership of 2.6% before), Anglo-American received 45% of DeBeers, and Debswana (a joint venture between DeBeers and the Botswana government) received 10%. The delisting took away 15% of the turnover of the Johannesburg Stock Exchange and 8.5% of its market capitalization.[21] While South African stock traders may have been hurt by lower transaction volume from the delisting, the Oppenheimer family gained a much more solid grasp of the firm. In addition, Anglo-American benefited from the delisting because in increasing its stake in DeBeers to 45%, DeBeers in turn made its 35% of Anglo-American available to investors, thus freeing those shares for trading. With more shares trading, Anglo's weight in the FTSE 100 was not reduced.

### The Dependent Variable

The interlocking ownership structure of Anglo-American Corporation is typical for firms listed on the Johannesburg Stock Exchange, although current efforts at reform seek to curb the practice in the future.[22] In November 2000, four companies (Anglo-American Corporation, Sanlam, SA Mutual, and Rembrandt) controlled 56.2% of the market capitalization of the exchange. The family influence associated with these firms is formidable. The Hertzog and Rupert families controlled

Rembrandt, which controlled 10.8% of the market capitalization in 2000.[23] Unlike some other emerging exchanges, where foreign investment is sizable, foreign entities control only 3.8% of the market capitalization in Johannesburg. When overseas investors invest, they tend to do so through wholly owned private or public companies that are not listed on the exchange.

The decision to list overseas has also been made by several other large South African firms. For example, in 1997 Gencor, the former South African General Mining Corporation, became Billiton, P.L.C., and listed in London. In July 1999, Old Mutual, a South African insurance firm, likewise switched its listing.[24] As a result of the globalization of trading since 2000, any real market for managerial control of South African firms has emerged overseas, since more merger and acquisition activities have taken place offshore than in the purely domestic market.[25] The unbundling and restructuring of companies has resulted more from scrutiny by the London Stock Exchange than the Johannesburg exchange. Plans continue to develop for collaboration between the London and Johannesburg exchanges, such as the provision of core technology services by the London exchange to the Johannesburg exchange.

Proposals for reform of the domestic market reflect the ongoing politics of resolving the apartheid legacy. In the British tradition, the South African banking system does not monitor corporate clients. What outside monitoring does take place, takes place through regulatory authorities enforcing company and labor law. Here the state has made serious attempts at reform, beginning with the publication of the King Report on corporate governance. The first King Report argued that a sophisticated system of stakeholder identification would be required to clarify corporate governance principles. It rejected the notion of accountability to all, arguing that this would effectively amount to accountability to none.[26] Nonetheless, competing views over what constitutes the fundamentals of corporate governance became apparent with the publication of the 2001 Institute of Directors Report on corporate governance for South Africa.

This report included in its concept of good corporate governance notions of "African personality fundamentals," such as spiritual collectiveness, consensus, humility, morality based on historical precedent, and optimism stemming from a belief in a superior being. In this context, the board of directors defines the purpose and values of the corporation and identifies stakeholders. Then the board should ensure and monitor the implementation of any associated strategies by management.[27] As of this writing, the government plans to transfer ultimate ownership of the country's mining resources to the state, which will in turn transfer licenses to companies in a manner similar to Australia, Chile, Canada, and Peru. However, the proposals place a distinct emphasis on the responsibility of companies for social development in mining communities, and on black participation in ownership and management. As currently understood, the Minerals and Petroleum Resources Development Bill would change the focus of the firm from strictly maximizing profits for shareholders (in the Anglo-American tradition) to building schools, clinics, and roads in the communities where they mine.[28] To comply with the new regulations, three mining companies announced in November 2003 that they would create the country's largest black-owned diversified mining company.[29]

Given these conflicts over principles, any unifying system of corporate governance with respect to the institutional functions of the domestic stock exchange may grow ambiguous in the future. On the one hand, large mining concerns have moved their headquarters overseas and are, to an extent, subject to the functions of those markets. On the other hand, the remaining firms listed in Johannesburg operate in a fluid environment where the goals and norms of corporate governance in the African context continue to be worked out among participants.

## Egypt

The stock market in Egypt has had a long history. Similar to the Johannesburg market, the combined Cairo and Alexandria markets have at times been among the largest in the world. Unlike the Johannesburg market, the Alexandria exchange in particular had brokers of diverse origins by the 1950s. When the stock market was resurrected in the current era, increased listings of minority shares of both public and private shares propelled its growth. This section considers one of these firms, the Olympic Group, which has operated along the lines of a stock pyramid ownership structure. Olympic is one of the few firms that added to its size by successfully buying a controlling stake in a former state firm. The institutional result of increased listings of this type, together with minority shares of privatized firms, has meant that while market capitalization has grown, the listed firms are not subject to the market for managerial control.

### Stock Markets in Egypt

The Alexandria exchange was not formally established until 1888, yet the futures market for cotton had begun to record transactions in Alexandria as early as 1865. Cotton forward contracts were legalized in 1909 as Egypt recovered from a financial crash in 1907. Cairo merchants and brokers formed a bourse in 1903.

In the years prior to World War I, three groups dominated the Egyptian political economy: the British political and military establishment, the Egyptian landed oligarchy, and metropolitan capital. As a particularly diverse and fragmented group, metropolitan capital was represented by many nationalities. Nonetheless, European economic power was pervasive and resented. Most visibly manifested through foreign banks, three major European powers had invested massive sums in Egypt. Each connected Egypt to the international economy differently. French money and managerial talent were focused on a few heavily capitalized firms—the Suez Canal Company, the Credit Foncier Egyptien, and the Sugar Company. Individuals in the field generally managed the French firms. Belgian firms exercised the tightest control over their operations in Egypt, yet Belgian companies were not as highly capitalized as the French. The British firms were the most numerous. They specialized in electricity, public utilities, and railroads. Boards consisting of persons living in Great Britain administered most of the British firms, although local British entrepreneurs managed a few.[30]

Egyptian political autonomy grew after the end of World War I with a series of pronouncements and treaties designed to loosen British controls. World War II motivated the domestic Egyptian bourgeoisie decisively because during the war Egypt had been cut off from its traditional European trading and investment partners and hence had been forced to rely on its own resources.[31] When the war ended, nationalist activities with respect to joint-stock companies continued with Nasser's rise to power.

In 1947 and 1948, the state passed a series of decrees bringing the joint-stock companies under greater state control and forcing a larger role for Egyptian nationals in their management. For example, a 1947 law required 40% of the board members of companies to be Egyptian, 51% of the stock of new companies to be held by nationals, 75% of the white-collar employees to be Egyptian and receive 65% of the salaries, and 90% of the workers to be Egyptian and receive 80% of the wages.[32] Particular nationalist attention in Egypt at the time focused on foreign concessionaires, many of which had been established in the late nineteenth century to attract European capital and business firms into the country.[33] Nonetheless, the stock market of these years continued to prosper. In the 1940s the combined exchanges were ranked fourth globally, and in the 1950s they were the predominant source of funding for business.

In addition to the 1947 and 1948 legislation, Egyptians' purchases of stock and their appointment to directorships accelerated the Egyptianization of joint-stock companies. The two exchanges merged in the 1950s. The pace of reform, however, was not enough to keep up with the very serious social problems of the postwar years. When the Nasser military faction came to power in late 1952, it initiated land reforms attempting to transfer capital from the agrarian to industrial sector. After the British, French, and Israeli invasion in 1956, the military nationalized the assets of British, French, and Jewish nationals. The government nationalized Belgian holdings in 1960, following the first Congo crisis. By the early 1960s, the military government had taken over almost all large-scale industrial and commercial firms. The central planning and socialist policies of the Nasser regime led to dormancy on the stock exchanges from 1961 to 1992, when the government's restructuring and economic reform program revived them.

Thirty years after the Nasser era nationalizations, the Egyptian state sector was particularly well entrenched in the economy. The debate over privatization initially emerged as part of a debate over exactly what the term meant. Interpretations varied, from the concept of "selling the public sector," to "encouraging the private sector," to "encouraging private capital." At extreme ends of the spectrum, some commentators advocated a massive sell-off of state-industries regardless of the economic efficiency or social value, and others advocated no sell-off at all.[34] Early initiatives to reform the state sector came from Egypt's 1987 IMF agreement designed to deal with the public-sector deficit, inflation, and exchange rate depreciation. Although the 1987 IMF program failed, the debate over how much and how to privatize the state sector persisted. Given the involvement of the bank and the fund, and despite the Mubarak administration's open statements concerning the need to privatize, the level of the government's commitment to dismantling the state sector has been an ongoing question.

Several problems plague the Egyptian privatization program. One has been how the government should divest its shares. Another has been the questionable future of thousands of surplus workers employed by state agencies. Should these individuals lose their jobs, either alternative jobs would need to be found or the government would need to expand its social safety net. Either course is complicated when the economy is weak. Furthermore, the Egyptian government taxed investments in stocks and bonds, but not bank deposits and interest income. When interest rates on Egyptian pound deposits neared 20%, investors had no incentive to switch to riskier investments that would not likely meet that rate of return.

An additional problem concerned the cost of pricing the firms. The costs associated with keeping the state sector solvent are themselves open to question. State enterprises receive benefits such as cheaper inputs, subsidized loans, and tax credits that are not available to the private sector. Price controls on electricity, oil, and gas mean that Egyptian state textile manufacturers receive 26% lower fuel costs than their international competitors in Southeast Asia and Europe. As global competition intensified in the 1980s, the list of benefits grew longer and became better hidden. Unlike direct government spending, the public cost of these loans, loan guarantees, and tax benefits cannot be measured because most of the items are not indicated in the state budget. Nor are they explicitly authorized and appropriated as part of the budgeting process. Hence public officials can easily manipulate these benefits to create the appearance of lower public spending than is actually taking place.[35] Nonetheless, an accurate accounting of these costs is necessary for a prospective buyer to analyze a state enterprise as an investment.

As the ongoing economic crisis worsened in the 1990s, the government negotiated another agreement with the IMF and the World Bank. Since the IMF hoped to avoid the failure of the 1987 agreement, it insisted on the government's carrying out of certain reforms in advance of its approval of the $372 million stand-by credit facility. Once again, privatization and public enterprise reform emerged as structural reforms included in the package. Although the commitment of the government continued to be questionable, the U.S. Agency for International Development (USAID) and the World Bank presented Egypt with a detailed securities market study as a blueprint for overhauling the country's financial markets. Specific elements of the World Bank aid were funds for computer technology necessary to operate an active stock market, and training for Egypt's supervisory Capital Market Authority.[36]

In 1992 the government drafted a new stock exchange law in order to facilitate the sale of shares of state-sector firms, particularly those already listed due to some degree of existing minority private participation, yet broader privatization continued to progress at a particularly slow rate. The first wholly state-owned industrial company was not privatized until April 1997, when the government sold the Egyptian Bottling Company (EBC) to a joint venture between a Cairo-based export-import group of companies and a major Pepsi bottler in Saudi Arabia. Under the terms of the agreement, the privatized firm would be required to retain its 4000 employees for three years and to make large investments into the operation over the first two years. Ten percent of the stock was reserved for the workers and 30% was to be put on the stock exchange in two years.[37]

Yet in 1996, the pace of the program continued to drag. In May of that year, only 5 fully owned public enterprises of the 314 earmarked for sale passed to private control. Seventeen others were privatized by the state's releasing of 10% minority stakes.[38] In 1998 the state had sold shares in 84 companies, but remained the largest shareholder in 29 of the 34 companies in which more than half the shares had been sold. In the eight companies where it sold less than half the shares, it retained an average of 70%.[39]

The Egyptian stock markets encountered an additional problem: the supply of attractive stocks. The government planned to use the proceeds from the sale of the initial companies to restructure the loss-making ones, thus making them more attractive prospects for sale. Yet this plan would take years to effect. The government encountered difficulty selling additional blocs of companies in which blocs had already been sold.[40] In 2001 the market dropped with the international decline in telecom shares, prompting the government to postpone another large issue.

## The Case of Olympic Group Financial Investment (OGFI)

The Olympic Group demonstrates the tension between public and private interests in Egypt over privatization. Founded in the years between the 1952 revolution and the nationalization program of the 1960s, Olympic experienced zero growth until 1975, when it was returned to the Sallam family. Egypt's leading manufacturer of domestic heaters, Olympic operates on a pyramid ownership structure. When equity finance became a more attractive mechanism for raising capital in 1995, the family sold 14% of its holding company in a private placement to local and foreign institutions, including Commercial International Bank, Concord International Investments, Goldman Sachs, and HSBC's James Capel. It later raised £E25.5 million by selling 16.7% of its Cairo Precision Industries subsidiary on the Cairo stock exchange in January 1997. This was the first public flotation by a private-sector manufacturer.[41] Olympic held stakes of between 65% and 92% in five other companies and quickly made plans to offer public shares in each.

Seeking to expand as the state sold off enterprises, Olympic Group sought international partners with whom they could bid on, take over, and restructure as many as four state-owned appliance companies.[42] In January 1998 it was successful in purchasing a controlling stake in a public-sector firm that manufactured washing machines and refrigerators, and was the government's monopoly supplier of office furniture. The US$69 million deal was only the second of its kind to a strategic investor. In the January 1998 transaction, Olympic acquired 75% of the Ideal Company from the state. The state sold the rest of its shares to individuals, banks, investment funds, and the company's stockholders.

Yet despite the sale of a majority of shares, the Egyptian state would not allow Olympic to dispose of land occupied by Ideal's four production sites when Olympic sought to consolidate its production facilities outside Cairo.[43] Since the privatization deal stipulated that no employees could be fired, Olympic had to train 5000 of the 6800 employees. With the deal, the company inherited US$2.3 million due from public-sector companies that had accumulated debts with Ideal prior to the transfer.[44] Thus, although Olympic was one of the few buyers successful in acquiring managerial control of a state enterprise, it was not free to manage the firm as it saw fit. Nor was it completely severed from the state, since it became a creditor to other public-sector companies.

### The Dependent Variable

Given the piecemeal manner of Egyptian privatization on the Cairo Stock Exchange, a market for corporate management has not emerged in privatized firms. Many firms have not been privatized at all, for both political and economic reasons. An example of a difficult-to-privatize, large firm is that of the Alexandria Shipyard. Built with the help of the former Soviet Union in the 1960s, the shipyard was considered to be a "sell-off prize" of Egyptian industry early in the program. It was well situated on the east-west trade route and was staffed by relatively inexpensive labor. Industrial labor relations were relatively good, if for no other reason than Egyptian law did not allow strikes.

Yet it was also apparent early on that the shipyard was unlikely to be privatized because of its strategic value to the government as a naval as well as a merchant shipbuilder. Were it to be privatized, the government would likely restrict its future.[45] When the government ultimately put it up for sale in 1992, it was offered as a full or partial takeover. Yet only one investor took an interest beyond the initial contact stage. Without having been sold, the firm attempted to restructure its workforce and debt burden in 1997 so that it could attract a buyer.[46] Nonetheless, in 1999 the minister of public business admitted that the ministry had received few bids for the shipyard and that privatization would again be postponed. In the interim, the management would be transferred to the private sector for a specific period of time in exchange for a profit share and interest. The government would construct necessary infrastructure facilities such as roads, ports, docks, and warehousing facilities.[47]

Of the firms that have been sold, the state has preferred to sell minority stakes. As the example of Olympic group shows, pyramid ownership structures insulate family-controlled firms from the market for corporate control. Therefore, while the stock market has been used as a vehicle to raise capital, and to transfer shares, it has not assumed a role in corporate governance as the Anglo-American model would predict. The state remains the dominant economic actor.

## Senegal

Senegal represents an example of an African state that did not develop a local equity market in the colonial period, nor in the nationalist period that followed. Nonetheless, as a member of the West African Monetary Union, it was a member state of the *Bourse Regionale Des Valeurs Mobilieres* (BRVM) when it replaced the former Abidjan Bourse in 1998. This examination of Senegalese participation in the BRVM uses the case of the telecommunications firm Sonatel, which made the BRVM a truly regional bourse with the first transnational listing in 1998.

## Senegal and the Abidjan Regional Bourse

French colonial rule drew the early contours of the French West African financial institutional structure. The French state governed territory now comprising Senegal, Mali, Burkina Faso, Niger, Mauritania, Benin, Cote d'Ivoire, and Guinea as a vast unit with a common tariff structure, administered from Dakar, Senegal. Within this single trading zone (the Federation of French West Africa), the French pursued what Boone has described as a rudimentary and mercantile form of colonial economic development wherein participants would buy African commodities at the lowest possible price and sell French manufactured goods in return at the highest possible price. Manufacturing activity in the federation was nearly nonexistent before World War II. French trading houses controlled all levels and aspects of the West African export-import trade. When French commercial banks were eventually established in French West Africa, they joined forces with the colonial administration and the trading houses to block independent traders' access to credit.[48]

The federation did not issue individual colonial or national currencies, nor did it develop a local securities market. Rather, some colonial and postcolonial firms listed shares on a "second board" of the Paris Bourse, and the French established a system of chartered banks to issue money in Africa. In 1946 a separate currency for the colonies was established when the government decided to consolidate the francs circulating in the region. At that time the French Treasury guaranteed that the CFA (French colonies of Africa) franc would be directly convertible into the French franc at a 50-to-1 ratio. When two regional banks were created to manage monetary policy in the franc zone, their headquarters were located in Paris. When the colonies of the federation became independent states, 14 remained in the CFA franc zone. Many retained the tie because they were poorer and more dependent on aid than the former British colonies.[49] Thus the region has been much more integrated than any other in Africa.

In the late 1970s the commodity price boom ended, and when it did, coffee and cocoa prices declined. Governments that had borrowed to invest in state enterprises experienced a crisis as these companies failed. By the early 1980s, West African governments were forced to continue to borrow to sustain spending levels. The crisis worsened for francophone countries using the CFA franc when the proportion of debt from multilateral institutions denominated in dollars grew and the proportion of CFA-denominated (i.e., French franc) debt declined. When the debt had been denominated in francs, and parity had been fixed, parity was not an issue. However, as the dollar-denominated proportion grew, parity with the dollar (which was not fixed after the Bretton Woods fixed system ended) became an issue. By 1987 a significant liquidity crisis resulted and capital flight became a major problem throughout the zone.[50]

As a result of these dire economic circumstances and the concomitant lack of short-term, long-term, equity, or debt financial market access, the West African central bank (BCEAO) monetary authorities reopened longstanding discussions on the creation of a regional bourse. In December 1992 the Council of Ministers of the Union mandated that the BCEAO begin operations. This initiative was part and parcel of several other economic integration initiatives under way at the time, which all received a boost from the CFA franc devaluation of 50% in January 1994. Participants in the devaluation (i.e., the World Bank, French representatives, and BCEAO member states) reasoned that the currency area would not be viable in the long run unless it were to be grounded in an equivalent economic area with goods and factor mobility, and a high degree of convergence of economic and policy performance.[51]

Thus, shortly after the devaluation, member states revised the West African Monetary Union treaty, enlarged its scope of activities to include economic integration, and defined new institutions and their activities. The renamed union, *Union Economique et Monétaire de l'Afrique de l'Ouest* (UEMOA), installed a seven member commission to serve as the executive authority and a court of justice to serve as the judiciary authority in 1995. Work began on creating a common external tariff and tax harmonization. Accounting and insurance codes have since been standardized in the broader region of the franc zone. Along with these developments, members of the BCEAO reached an agreement on a regional stock market on December 18, 1996.

The market, which subsumed the former Abidjan (Cote d'Ivoire) Bourse, opened nearly two years later, on September 16, 1998. The Canadian International Development Agency (CIDA) provided technical assistance and a grant for the final creation of the BRVM. A team of consultants led by a former Montreal exchange executive, then with Pricewaterhouse Coopers, advised the project. They hired staff, wrote trading regulations, set up a clearing and settlement mechanism, and organized the selection of computer software and telecommunications systems.[52] The BRVM became a truly regional market with the introduction of the Senegalese telecommunications firm Sonatel on October 2, 1998. Rather than each state creating its own market, each instituted a national antenna of the bourse which centralizes the transmission of orders, provides information, and organizes local promotion of the regional market.[53]

The BRVM has an electronic trading and competitive settlement system that takes "buy" and "sell" orders and matches them electronically. Share prices cannot increase or decrease by more than 7.5% per session. Trading takes place three days a week (Monday, Wednesday, and Friday) from 9:30 A.M. to 10:30 A.M. While no investment limits have been officially established with respect to foreign ownership, the states do retain the right (through their ministries of finance) to set a purchase limit to favor local ownership in IPO operations.[54]

Despite the creation of the regional stock exchange, Senegal itself remains a state wherein the government is the largest employer and consumer. It launched its nationalization drive in the early to mid-1970s with takeovers of the water and electric utilities, and by becoming the majority shareholder in companies in key sectors of the economy, including mining and peanut oil manufacturing and marketing. In addition, financing from foreign donors helped the state create 70 new parastatals.[55] By the end of the 1970s, the parastatals came to be viewed negatively by both the World Bank and the political opposition within the country. In 1980 the Senegalese National Assembly voted to abolish the peanut marketing board.

The state began its first liberalization program with the IMF in 1980. The second program in 1985 was essentially an acceleration of the first program. In its 1986 structural adjustment loan with the World Bank, the state agreed to privatize 27 enterprises. Despite numerous commitments to privatize firms in the interim, and despite the formation of the Commission for State Disengagement in 1987, by 1994 only 16 enterprises had actually been sold, and they were mostly small enterprises.[56]

The slow pace of the privatization program in these years is generally not attributed to fears that the leading sectors would revert to foreign owners. Foreign investors were not interested in buying the enterprises, and the government restricted the shares that foreigners could buy. Rather, the state sought to retain its control of the leading industry sectors.[57] Moreover, the pool from which to select privatization candidates was relatively small despite its magnitude in relation to the economy overall. At the beginning of the program, the parastatal sector consisted of 62 wholly or majority-owned enterprises and 24 public agencies. In addition, the state held an indirect stake in 46 companies, mostly through the banking system. Of these, the telecommunications parastatal was one enterprise that was privatized, yet remained under the influence of government authorities.

## The Case of Sonatel

Created in 1985 by the fusion of two entities previously charged with internal and external telecommunications development, Sonatel forged one of the continent's most extensive telecommunications infrastructures, second only to that in South Africa. The Senegalese state authorized the privatization of Sonatel in 1996. Initial negotiations began with an American-Swedish consortium, but fell apart when the parties failed to agree on the role to be played by each in the development of the firm. In 1998 the firm was privatized with a controlling 42.33% share going to France Telecom. As of FY2001, the Senegalese state owned 27.76%, employees and former employees owned 10%, institutional investors and the general public owned 20%, and France Telecom held 42.33%.[58] Both a representative of the Senegalese state and the armed forces held seats on the board. With approximately one-quarter of the capitalization of the bourse, Sonatel is the largest firm listed on the BRVM. It represents one-third of the BRVM 10 index.

Despite the strong financial performance of the company since privatization, it is not without its critics. Business owners, investors, internet providers, and others argue that the firm has been able to realize its high profit margin because of the unfair advantages granted to it by the state, and that this monopoly status (through 2017) results in extraordinary profits that revert to France, since France Telecom is the controlling owner. Differences have emerged between Sonatel and the state as well, as the government has demanded that thousands of rural villages be connected.[59] The company has responded to its critics by trying to promote its role in development. It created the Sonatel Foundation, for art, culture, and education. Moreover, by investing in new technologies, information, and communication, it seeks to aid the development of these sectors in Senegal.[60]

### The Dependent Variable

Establishing any clear pattern of corporate governance in Senegal is complicated by the government's ongoing participation in large-scale concerns. A former French colony, the state retains a clear interventionist orientation. The poor performance of some privatized firms has led to state renationalization. For example, Abdou Diouf, the president of Senegal in the mid-1990s, sold stakes in the main utilities. However, his successor, President Abdoulaye Wade, has argued that some of the bigger deals in the last years of Diouf's rule were not appropriate.

The state had sold one-third of the shares of the electricity company, Senelec, to a consortium of French and Canadian companies, Elyo and Hydro-Quebec, with a highly unionized staff. At the privatization, the management had a free hand in that it was only required to keep 5 of the 12 members of the board of administration. The consortium spent little on maintenance and continued to operate the firm with equipment that was so old, one turbine allegedly dated to 1954. With such equipment, one blackout in Dakar was allegedly caused by the incineration of a vulture. The consortium hired expatriate managers who required higher salaries than local Senegalese, and it used foreign suppliers instead of local ones.

In September 2000, the Wade regime took back control of the firm. When service improved under state control, rumors surfaced that the unions had sabotaged supplies to the privatized company. However, the consortium was willing to leave, most likely because it had underestimated the investment that would be required when it took control. Hydro-Quebec and Elyo did not want to make further major investments unless they could buy more shares of the firm.[61] As of this writing, the government is seeking a new consortium to run the electricity firm.

As the sole enterprise created from a privatized entity that did offer public shares, and given that the BRVM is an illiquid market, and that such a small percentage of Sonatel shares were offered, the stock market plays no role in the market for corporate governance. Ultimate governing authority for the firm rests with France Telecom in Paris and with the Senegalese state through the board of directors. Of the other Senegalese firms that have been sold, a pattern has emerged similar to the Egyptian one, wherein the state sells partial stakes in firms and seeks to continue to influence the direction of the firm with its stake. For example, in 1999 the state sold 51% of Air Senegal to Royal Air Maroc. This firm was not listed on the BRVM, but the plan at the time was for a percentage of Royal Air Maroc to be offered on the Casablanca Stock Exchange when the parent firm was privatized.

Therefore, despite the creation of a regional outlet for selling equity shares denominated in CFA francs, only one firm from all of the West African member states (exclusive of Cote d'Ivoire) has taken advantage of the opportunity. By offering a percentage of Sonatel shares on the BRVM publicly, the firm's employees and small Senegalese shareholders have the opportunity to buy shares they otherwise would have to buy overseas (i.e., as shares of France Telecom). Nonetheless, the BRVM does not play a role in the market for managerial control of Senegalese firms currently, nor is it likely to in the future. Rather, the Senegalese state remains the dominant economic actor.

## Ghana

The Ghana Stock Exchange is representative of many others on the African continent in that it is relatively new (1990), has relatively few firms listed (21), and only one firm (Ashanti Goldfields Company) is cross-listed on major world exchanges. Ashanti Goldfields itself is representative of many African privatizations because it followed the pattern of colonial firm to nationalized firm to privatized firm. It currently represents 55% of market capitalization on the stock exchange in Accra.

### The Birth of the Accra Bourse

British colonial rule in West Africa had less of an impact on the future financial infrastructure than French colonial rule, since the British officials, committed to indirect rule, did not perceive their chief purpose to be in advancing the interests of British-based firms. Later, the postcolonial period presented a dramatic break with British free-market liberal orthodoxy. Nonetheless, certain commercial interests forged important ties during this period that would extend to the present. Low-yielding portfolios made it impossible for local banks to offer attractive returns on deposits and to mobilize African savings, which was left to the Post Office Savings Bank. Similar to the French, the British in West Africa did not extend credit to indigenous Africans.[62]

The free-trade tariff system of British West Africa discouraged potential local manufacturers since the duty on imported industrial raw materials balanced the import duties on products such as soap. Thus there was no tariff advantage in locally manufacturing items dependent on imported materials. British multinational firms operating in the Gold Coast had no incentive to establish local operations, and operated through trade instead. One such major firm, Unilever, did not establish a plant in Ghana until the 1960s.[63] Colonial firms seeking a stock exchange listing listed in London. For example, the Ashanti Goldfields Company (AGC) was listed on the London Stock Exchange in 1897.

The political leaders that followed independence experimented with a variety of development strategies. Notably, Nkrumah embarked on a program of state intervention in the economy with the goal of rapid industrialization. While Nkrumah was publicly committed to pan-Africanism, he moved to strengthen Ghanaian distinctness at the expense of regional arrangements.[64] Later leaders used approaches ranging from liberal to more interventionist. However, by the late 1970s, the accumulated state sector supplied 60% of all goods and services to the economy.

Although one individual regime or development strategy cannot be held to blame for the state of the Ghanaian economy, it is clear that by the 1980s the level of the economic crisis had reached catastrophic proportions. Real per capita income had declined by 30% of its 1970 levels, real export earnings declined by

52%, and GDP declined by 20% of its 1974 level. The real minimum wage fell to 10% of its 1975 level, inflation rose to 123%, and the parallel market *cedi* rate was more than 3000% the official rate.[65] On December 31, 1981, Jerry Rawlings, who had previously come to power during the 1979 Armed Forces Revolutionary Council (AFRC) takeover, returned to power as the leader of the Provisional National Defense Council (PNDC). He immediately sought to separate Ghana from its African neighbors and receive assistance from Libya. When this plan failed, he turned to the IMF.

Rawlings's shift did not signal a united "political will" in favor of an IMF agreement. To the contrary, much infighting occurred in his regime during the negotiations prior to 1983. However, the internal disagreements worked in his favor insofar as he was able to rid the government of anti-IMF individuals who had attempted coups as the negotiations progressed. Therefore, when the government and the IMF reached their agreement, the PNDC had lost almost all of its anti-IMF members. Most of the remaining political leaders believed that there were no alternatives to the IMF reforms, and that the economic benefits of the program outweighed its problematic political consequences. The same senior economic team remained throughout, which resulted in greater continuity of policies, a smoother implementation experience, and greater credibility with the public. In total, a clear policymaking structure meant that agreements were easily concluded and implemented. What opposition to the IMF plans remained was disorganized and leaderless.[66]

Immediately prior to the 1983 IMF accord, the Rawlings junta devalued the *cedi*. As part of the $382 million program that followed, the government agreed to end exchange controls, legalize the parallel currency market through independent foreign exchange bureaus, remove restrictions on imports, withdraw subsidies in areas such as health and education, and privatize state economic interests.[67] When the sell-off of state interests began, it signaled a change in the country's economy. However, it progressed slowly and was handicapped by the questionable commitment of the Rawlings regime to the process, and the lack of a stock exchange in order to attract foreign investment and any potential Ghanaian shareholders.

As part of the financial sector adjustment package, the IFC commissioned a study of Ghana's capital markets in 1987, culminating in the establishment of the stock exchange. The CIDA augmented the IFC's efforts in the initial study by contributing $700,000 to the project, and the UN Development Program contributed the rest of the capital necessary to complete it. Toronto-based Coopers & Lybrand Canada developed the market infrastructure by preparing rigorous rules for when and if the market does expand. For example, dealers must put clients' funds in an omnibus trust and cannot mix them with their own funds. The rules prohibit selling short, and there are other rules to prevent insider trading.[68] They became law in an apparent response to the World Bank conditionalities.[69] The exchange began operations in November 1990 with trading in 11 securities.[70]

The first new listing on the exchange was Super Paper Products, a manufacturing company that listed approximately a year and a half after the exchange opened. At that time, however, significant obstacles remained to foreigners and nonresident Ghanaians attempting to participate in the market. To eliminate some of these obstacles, the government passed the Investment Promotion Center Act in 1994. The act eliminated the need for formal government approval for foreigners to invest, and reduced the minimum foreign capital requirements to encourage joint ventures between foreign investors and domestic small-scale enterprises. Moreover, exchange officials attempted to promote the idea of the market to Ghanaians. Toward this end, they explained its principles on a "road show" in 11 ethnic languages. They conducted the market in the Ashanti capital of Kumasi so that individuals could observe its operation. Billboards in Accra and television ads promoting the advantages of investment in securities as a form of savings appeared as well.[71]

The biggest boost to the market's development came when the government sold shares of the Ashanti Goldfields Company it had acquired in the interventionist 1960s. The export promotion of gold had been a prominent feature of the structural adjustment program the regime concluded with the IMF and World Bank. As part of its efforts to put a new and comprehensive mining regime into place, the government established a Minerals Commission as an advisory and mining promotion body.

### The Case of Ashanti Goldfields

The Ashanti Goldfields Company (AGC) was listed on the London Stock Exchange in 1897. The London Rhodesia Mining and Land Company (Lonrho) bought the firm in 1967, at which time the government acquired a 20% interest with an option to acquire an additional 20%. At that time, the firm delisted from the London exchange. Similar to the other nationalizations of the 1960s and 1970s, the military government acquired a 55% equity interest in all mining companies, including Ashanti Goldfields, by legislative order in 1972. The headquarters then moved from London to Accra.[72] Gold production declined in the following years.

In 1983 the Rawlings junta launched the IMF-World Bank-sponsored Structural Adjustment Program. The stock exchange's creation followed. Despite a court challenge by some Ghanaian citizens, the government eventually sold more than half of its 55% equity interest in AGC to the private sector, which lifted the Accra market capitalization from US$30 million (at inception) to US$2.1 billion by the end of May 1994.[73] Each of the company's 10,000 employees received five free shares. At the time, Ashanti represented approximately 90% of the total capitalization. On February 22, 1996, AGC cross-listed on the NYSE, making it the only sub-Saharan African company outside of South Africa to list on the "big board."

Prior to the state's sell-off, the government had been deeply involved in the management of the firm. The president appointed the chief executive officer (CEO) of AGC. The head of state also commissioned some of the major shafts at the company, and individuals associated with it drafted mining rules. The head of the company served on the board of the Minerals Commission and other boards of state-owned enterprises. Since privatization, however, the president of Ghana can no longer fire the CEO of AGC. Lonmin (which inherited Lonrho's shares) hires and fires the CEO of the firm. When approximately half of the members of the AGC board who had been government representatives retired in early 2000, two former ministers in the British and American governments were appointed as replacements. While the company is registered in Ghana, and subject to Ghanaian laws, the majority of its shareholders are not Ghanaian.

Although the managerial power of the president was mitigated with privatization and the distribution of shares globally, a true "market-oriented" system of corporate governance did not result. The government retains a golden share and can rebuff takeover bids if it so desires. Tensions over labor and environmental issues have called for new government activity with respect to the firm.[74] For example, management and workers collaborated successfully after privatization, likely because expanded output meant that few workers lost their jobs, and some received bonuses. However, the first strike occurred for two weeks in 1999 over labor cutbacks and wages. The government attempted to arbitrate the situation as a neutral broker, but workers called for a more activist role on their behalf.

The firm considered declaring bankruptcy in 1999 following the gold price run, but chose instead to restructure its balance sheet. It has lobbied the government to release the golden share; since Lonmin has indicated its willingness to sell its stake at the right value, Ashanti will undoubtedly be taken over. Sam Jonah, the CEO, has attempted to talk around the issue of the golden share by arguing that if the right deal came along, the government would not exercise its rights.[75]

*The Dependent Variable*

The Ghanaian market has been used for corporate restructuring, fundraising, and for the development of indigenous companies. For example, Unilever restructured and reorganized its interests in Ghana and developed UTC Estates, a property and real estate development company. New issues such as Mechanical Lloyd (car distribution) and Housing Finance (April 1995) have also appeared. Yet the driving force behind the development of the stock market has been the government's ongoing privatization program. The average Ghanaian private company remains a closed, thinly capitalized, debt-laden family business that is often under the control of the family patriarch. Many multinational corporations doing business in Ghana do business as private firms (e.g., Shell and TotalfinaElf). Only Mobil Oil (Ghana) Limited operates as a public company.[76]

## Analysis and Conclusion

Stock exchanges are financial institutions transplanted relatively recently from the West into African societies. By participating in the transplant, states do not so much retreat against the market and societal forces, but shift to create some markets to cope with international political and economic pressures. In so doing, they reconfigure the relationship between themselves and society.[77] Stocks play a role in this process by reconciling the international and national political and economic demands.

Table 9.1 reviews the cases presented in this chapter. Although the case of Anglo-American was not a privatization issue, the restructuring of ownership fol-

TABLE 9.1 Summary of African and Middle Eastern Cases Examined

| State | Company privatized (year) | International imperatives (level I) | Groups protesting sale (level II) | Distribution of shares | Controlling interest held by (governance structure) |
|---|---|---|---|---|---|
| South Africa | Anglo-American[a] | Initially, strong international sanctions and U.S. antitrust laws drove share-owning pattern. Later, London listing requirements drove a restructuring of the shares. | Not applicable | As of March 12, 2002, the company reported the following interests in 3% or more of its ordinary share capital: PLC Nominees (Pty) Limited, 31.00%; Old Mutual Plc, 6.40%; Central Holdings Ltd., 4.58%; Butterfield Trust (Guernsey) Limited, 3.90% | Holding company (cross-ownership) |
| Senegal/ Cote d'Ivoire | Sonatel | IMF/World Bank stabilization program | Telecom users and others protest monopoly status | France Telecom, 42.33%; Senegalese state, 27.76%; employees/former employees, 10%; institutional investors, general public, 20% | France Telecom (foreign corporation, state retains seats on board of subsidiary) |
| Ghana | Ashanti Goldfields | IMF/World Bank stabilization program | Group of Ghanaian citizens challenge sale in court (1994) | Lonmin, PLC, 31.88%; Government of Ghana, 19.46%; Depository for Global Depository Receipts, 40.73%; others 7.2% | Lonmin (foreign corporation, government retains golden share) |
| Egypt | Ideal Company | IMF/World Bank stabilization program | Not available | Olympic Group, 75%; individuals, banks, investment funds, 25% | Olympic Group (domestic pyramid conglomerate, restrictions on land use and employee job retention in deal) |

[a]This case was not a privatization sale, but represents a considerable percentage of shares traded in Johannesburg.

lowing the apartheid era to facilitate listing in London demonstrates the powerful interplay of international and domestic political forces. The company had been restricted by international sanctions, imposed by states seeking to end the apartheid regime in the nationalist era. It has also been restricted by U.S. antitrust laws. It was a highly diversified conglomerate, involved in many sectors of South African society. Domestic share issues were large in volume, yet did not leave the Oppenheimer family vulnerable to the market for managerial control. As the international pressures associated with apartheid have lifted, firms have sought the deeper capital markets of London. In Anglo's case, this has meant a consolidation of the family's hold over the diamond sector and a delisting of DeBeers from the Johannesburg exchange.

The other three cases demonstrate more typical divestment examples of the sale of shares, with ongoing government intervention of various types. Level I pressures generally emanated from IMF and World Bank stabilization programs, which called for privatization. At level II, states divested shares on local exchanges and retained a degree of local control through different mechanisms. The Senegalese state retained a stake in Sonatel, with seats on the board of the newly created subsidiary of France Telecom. The Egyptian state restricted the activities of the Olympic Group in managing the Ideal Company after its sale with respect to employees and land use. Moreover, in selling the firm to a domestic conglomerate, the privatized firm was not left vulnerable to a managerial takeover, since the Sallam family controlled the conglomerate through a pyramid scheme. Finally, the Egyptian state retained a relationship to the Ideal Company as a debtor and through the receivables of other state-owned firms. The Ghanaian state retained a "golden share," that is, restricted takeovers of the privatized Ashanti Goldfields.

South Africa is atypical of the other African exchanges because it has had a different kind of connection, both in terms of volume and quality of transactions, to the international market since its inception. In the South African example, the state is moving to increase its involvement in the mining sector—by asserting mineral ownership rights—not to decrease its involvement as the others are ostensibly doing. South Africa has sought to develop corporate governance regulations to lessen instances of insider trading, but these initiatives, as well as initiatives to promote the exchange, have come from international stock exchange requirements such as the London Stock Exchange. Thus they have not occurred in response to IMF/World Bank structural adjustment pressures.

The Egyptian, Senegalese, and Ghanaian examples are more typical of others on the African continent, although Egypt had considerable experience with equity finance prior to the Nasser nationalizations. Like most African states addressing IMF/World Bank requirements, Senegal and Ghana both needed to create the opportunity for local listings: in Senegal this came through the regionalization of the Abidjan (Cote d'Ivoire) Bourse; in Ghana it came through the creation of the Accra Bourse *de novo*. Shares issued from privatizations drove the growth in market capitalization on all three exchanges, yet the results of the drive are far from conclusive.

# PART III

# CONCLUSION

# Stock Markets in the Global Political Economy

In their analysis of the revolution in public enterprise taking place in the United States of the 1930s, Adolf Berle and Gardiner Means remarked that growth in size does not single-handedly transform the social significance of corporations. The use of an open market for the securities of these corporations transforms the relationships among managers, workers, owners, consumers, and the state.[1] Likewise in the late twentieth century, the growth in size of firms in emerging markets alone has not transformed their social significance. The rise of open markets for the securities of these firms has contributed to the transformation of relationships among present-day workers, owners, and consumers. Unlike the U.S. securities markets of Berle and Means's day, an interstate dimension characterizes the present emerging market transformation since contemporary securities markets cross state boundaries. Each state ultimately seeks to retain the greatest degree of control of economic enterprise within its territory as is possible; hence the interstate dimension involves a relative power dimension in addition to its economic dimension.

The international and domestic political aspects of equity financial products are not new. They have changed over time, however, because states and transnational firms constantly reconfigure the authority relationships among one another. In the earliest years, the distribution of shares did not have an international political dimension because it was not feasible for investors from one country to seize control of a firm in another by buying shares. The first transnational corporation, the Dutch East India Company, failed to abide by the disclosure requirements in its charter, and the Dutch government supported the firm. For some years after, the company operated as an extension of the state overseas, and anonymous shares of the company were transferred freely among Dutch citizens as a store of value. Local markets for equities eventually appeared in the Dutch, British, and Japanese colonies, yet the legal systems that made limited liability possible were part and parcel of the colonial states. Indigenous peoples rarely participated in stock exchange transactions. Therefore, when issuing shares, individuals in the metropole did not need to seek political ratification in the colonial state because the colonial political structure was not sovereign. In Russia and the Latin American cases where the states were juridically sovereign, local exchanges had a distinctly international character. Much of the volume on the nineteenth-century Russian, Argentine, Chilean, Mexican, Brazilian, and Chinese bourses channeled foreign investment for large enterprise. Yet investments were generally managed within the host state by British or French firms.

The distribution of power in the international system shifted conclusively after World War II. When it did, sovereign states replaced colonies, and stock markets took on a new, nationalist character. Nonetheless, stock markets were not significant institutions for raising capital in these areas because U.S. foreign direct investment replaced British investment as the means of economic penetration into what was then called the third world. The transnational firm had a variety of financing options available to it and was not reliant on local equity markets. During the same years, capital transfers to Russia and eastern Europe halted with the Bolshevik revolution. Therefore the use of equity securities generally declined across the postcolonial world and ceased in the Eastern bloc. When the new states established securities markets in this era, they did so to obtain a degree of control in the asymmetrical power relationships that now existed among sovereign states. A national stock exchange represented financial sophistication; moreover, it provided a means of indigenizing shares of foreign corporations. Nonetheless, few shares were listed on these exchanges, and little trading occurred.

A subsequent shift in the distribution of power in the international system occurred with the debt crisis of the 1980s, the rise of neoliberal economic ideology, and the collapse of communism. Although states remained juridically sovereign, the conditionality requirements of public international lenders altered the nature of their sovereignty and ushered in a host of new international imperatives. The debt crisis meant that the endpoint for economic decision making was frequently not within the polity, but was shared with international agencies. The collapse of communism meant that when Russia and the eastern European economies reentered the international financial system, they did so as competitors of the former third world for the resources of the international lending agencies and not as partners of the third world in protesting capitalist institutions. For their part, the agencies advocated that states take neoliberal paths to economic development, that is, one with a vision of a distinct separation between public- and private-sector activities.

Therefore the efforts of the international lending agencies sought to transform the relationships among managers, workers, and owners in economic enterprise by separating these groups from the state. Along with the strong set of international imperatives for action related to debt, an increasingly unified set of international standards for equity transactions appeared. If states sought to access global markets, or to encourage private firms within their territories to do so, they needed to meet these international standards. When global markets become an option, social relationships among managers, workers, and owners are not neatly sorted out in states whose industrial history charted such different courses from those in the West. Indeed, equity markets in these states do transform the relationships among groups, as they do in the West. Yet they must also sort out additional dimensions to these relations, chiefly relationships among foreign managers, foreign owners, and foreign consumers vis-à-vis the domestic groups.

On level I, international lending agencies promote equity financial instruments by virtue of their economic functions. Divestment of government shares leads to more efficient enterprises and deeper financial market institutions. Hence equity issues are mechanisms for the state to raise capital, enhance managerial efficiency in (former) parastatals, and reduce debt exposure. Equity markets should contribute to the state's future economic growth by making additional forms of capital available. As private firms eventually look to equity markets to raise funds, additional level I imperatives contribute to convergence in behavior, chiefly because international issues must comply with the listing requirements of transnational exchanges.

Yet the level II political goals in issuing equity stock are much wider in scope and contribute to a broad divergence in behavior. Goals include guaranteeing the ownership of large enterprise to citizens of the state in question, guaranteeing the continuing managerial authority of previous state managers, allowing a continuing role for the state in directing the enterprise, and limiting the transfer discretion of a transnational controller. Some shares are issued without voting rights. Some blocs are issued that are small enough that the state retains control. Controlling blocs of others are sold to domestic business groups that are insulated from the market for managerial control. In some instances new managers gained control, while in others the old managers became even more entrenched. In some instances the state lost direct control, while in others the restructured enterprises acquired shares of other firms themselves, both inside and outside the home state. These effects only become apparent with an analysis of the politics of particular issues.

Hence the notion that issuers must reconcile national and international criteria bears relevance because systemic influences may effect convergence in practice, yet the necessity of complying with local demands effects results that are far from homogeneous. Since trading on most local exchanges is concentrated in a few large firms, and each of the large firms may well have appeared as a result of reconciling vastly different political interests, the resulting structure of ownership does not tend to leave management vulnerable to the market for managerial control at the domestic level, let alone the international level, although an individual firm may be vulnerable. Thus, while an exchange may grow in absolute volume, its function with respect to the price mechanism varies according to the firms listed on it. This is a dramatic contrast to financial market institutions in the West, where the states experienced a more direct industrialization process and firms issuing shares have followed the functional paths of their predecessors.

When emerging markets are analyzed strictly according to economic (i.e., price and profit) criteria, the macro-level economic benefits of a given exchange may appear to have failed. However, the political goals of shares issued may well have succeeded. For example, in economic terms, most shares issued on the Prague Bourse as part of the voucher distribution schemes were never liquid, did not perform well in terms of dividends and growth in value, and eventually delisted. Nonetheless, many of the initial political goals of the transfer were met (i.e., speed, equality of distribution, and the symbolism of opening the stock exchange). While the shareholders lost value in relation to their holdings, analysts are divided as to the future of the Czech financial system. The state-controlled banking sector that controls the investment funds may perform a role in providing soft financing to firms that would otherwise cease operations. In this way, the verdict on the future of the financial system is still out

## Implications for the Future

This book has detailed the political and economic dimensions of the growth of equity finance in emerging markets, but one outstanding question remains: Are stock markets good or bad for individuals who live in the South? The answer that has been implied throughout the book is that it is impossible to generalize the merits or demerits across entire populations because issues on these markets result from intensely political processes. By their nature, political processes have winners and losers. Equity issues in emerging markets have an international political dimension, hence they have an additional layer of winners and losers. Nonetheless, there are three sets of implications that can be generalized from this study, which speak to the broader issue of stock markets' contribution to society at large: domestic political, international political, and analytical.

The first set of implications for this study concerns the domestic political aspects of emerging markets. These implications call for a reassessment of how to monitor firms effectively, when private-sector firms are expected to shoulder the responsibility for economic development in lieu of states. The proliferation of structures within an emerging market needs to be addressed, notwithstanding that the political issues attached to various shareholder arrangements will complicate this task.

In general, monitoring systems correspond to the corporate governance system in place within a state. Corporations with a few, large blocs of shareholders are monitored internally by these shareholders and through their boards of directors. Conversely, corporations with a large number of small shareholders are generally monitored through the market for corporate control, the market for managers, and the market for products and services. While "codes of good corporate governance" increasingly attempt to articulate norms to regulate the behavior and structure of the boards of directors, legal systems can either enhance or detract from enforcement of these codes. In a common law legal system, as operates in Anglo-Saxon countries, judges have the discretion to apply codes of good governance broadly, that is, "in the spirit of the law."

Judges are far more constrained in states with a civil law legal system, as operates in the continental European tradition. In these states, the judge must only apply the codes according to the "letter of the law." Parliamentary action to provide for an array of contingencies takes time, and inhibits a flexible response. Thus these systems are much less effective.[2] Judicial systems plagued by endemic corruption, lack of respect for the rule of law, and gross asymmetries of information are similarly rendered less effective, regardless of the adoption of one code or another.[3]

As a remedy for the enforcement weakness inherent in certain judicial and legal systems, some commentators have proposed expanding the market control mechanism. Cuervo, for example, advocates expanding market control mechanisms to facilitate the maximization of firm value in continental Europe, as opposed to promoting codes of good governance.[4] Loredo and Suarez advocate expanding the market for corporate control from the national to the international level in the privatized British electricity utilities industry in order to introduce appropriate incentives for good corporate governance practices. They argue that nationalist privatization practices (in their case involving a golden share) benefit domestic agents at the expense of firms headquartered elsewhere. These firms distort the balance of power within firms and industries when rival domestic companies do not possess the required resources to acquire the privatized firm.[5]

Evidence from this study demonstrates that one of these proposed solutions alone will not resolve problems in corporate governance inherent in many emerging markets. Greater compliance with international "best practice" norms will enhance the governance practices of some, market mechanisms will work for others, and legal codes will be necessary for others. As Reed points out, additional features of corporate governance will also need to be attached to firms in emerging markets tending toward Anglo-American governance systems to address political inequalities.[6] For example, South African firms will continue to need strong affirmative action programs in the coming years to address the institutional legacy of apartheid. Moreover, a degree of firm monitoring will be required at the international level to protect both international investors as well as citizens in countries that host transnational firms.

The second set of implications for this study has to do with international political aspects of emerging markets, and specifically the future role of the IMF and World Bank in the broader international financial architecture. Interpretations of international organizations range from those who view them as mere instruments of powerful states to those who argue that they have a degree of autonomy from their member states and can act independently.[7] The interpretation matters because these organizations have been increasingly criticized for their activities in recent financial crises. When attacked from the right, international organizations are said to contribute to periodic financial crises by creating a problem of moral hazard through state-supported bailouts. When attacked from the left, they are said to contribute to the evisceration of the world's poor through the onerous conditionality requirements attached to their loans.

The view of the organizations offered here is one of agencies that acted (consciously or not) to benefit investors in their most prominent member states. In particular, the IFC's activities were not as much causes of the rise of equity finance, but evidence of ideological and material changes that had occurred elsewhere and that benefited a transnational class of investors. The power of these organizations is normative insofar as they can introduce standards of corporate conduct or the infrastructure of equity markets to entice foreign capital to enter societies otherwise lacking such investment. Nonetheless, local conditions, such as the legal system, presence of institutional investors, and other institutional legacies, also act to shape the operations of these corporations and markets.

Thus this study charts a middle course in criticizing public international organizations. While agreeing with critics who point to the mistakes these organizations have made in handling the ongoing debt crisis, as well as the organizations' lack of transparency and accountability, the study invites intensive reform, and not abandonment, of these organizations. Indeed, these organizations have at times been insensitive to some of the most vulnerable members of the world community. Nonetheless, without public-sector organizations, only the wealthiest emerging markets would have offered enough of a financial incentive for private-sector actors to create the necessary infrastructure for some financial activities to occur. Individuals advising a government drawn exclusively from the private sector would operate exclusively according to the profit motive, and devoid of any development motive. Despite the mistakes international financial institutions have made in recent times, they have been able to promote foreign investment where it would not have been possible in the absence of public-sector actors. They have done this by at least attempting to take developmental goals into consideration.

The third set of implications for this study is analytical in nature. Analysts question if stock markets are good or bad for an emerging market economy because they function outside the industrial core (i.e., relatively more powerful countries) of the world economy. Whereas political science has a reasonably well-developed literature on the activities of large firms, these have mostly examined the activities of large firms headquartered in the industrial core.[8] Thus these studies did not question whether stock markets were good or bad, because that question was examined in other political literature on the distribution of wealth in an individual country. Nonetheless, studies from political science do make a strong case that where a transnational firm is headquartered matters. Pauly and Reich argue that corporate governance and financial patterns, in particular, are linked to the home country.[9] Peter Evans's study of Brazilian development shows how differing interests, power, and capabilities of groups have produced a system promoting industrialization, but excluding the majority of the population from the benefits of growth, in the parastatal sector in a variety of industries.[10]

This study has added an interstate dimension to the analysis. Any interstate consideration should include an assessment of the states' position in the overall structure. Early evidence from the case studies included in this study indicate that activities of firms headquartered in the south, and purchasing other firms in the south, will grow in significance in the years to come. Foreign managerial consortiums bought two of the three Latin American telecommunications companies examined in this book (i.e., in Argentina and Chile), and a domestic managerial consortium bought the third (i.e., in Mexico). As the 2002–2003 economic crisis in Argentina deepened, the leader of the Mexican consortium, Carlos Slim, appeared interested in purchasing Telecom Argentina. At the same time, Petrobras, the Brazilian firm in which the state remains the ultimate owner, announced that it would buy a 58.6% stake in Perez Companc, S.A., from its Argentine family owners, and Petrobras expected to purchase Santa Fe, another Argentine oil company, soon thereafter.

The rationale for one state-owned firm purchasing another firm, in another state, when private international investors hesitate to do so, has to do with the state-to-state relationship. The president of Brazil had been a vocal supporter of international assistance for Argentina during the 2002–2003 crisis. When polled, residents of Buenos Aires responded that they preferred that U.S., Brazilian, and Spanish companies invest, in that order. Nonetheless, a state-owned firm is perceived as being better equipped to handle property rights in another state lacking a solid legal framework for business.[11]

Additional analytical implications from this study have to do with the similarities and differences between emerging stock markets and the international exchanges themselves, yet they also speak to the interstate and relative power dimensions of equity finance. Each of the characteristics associated with emerging markets, for example, golden shares, classes of shares, and other controlling minority structures, appears in firms listed in large industrial centers of the world economy. Nestle, for example, is perhaps one of the most internationalized of all companies, with only 5% of its assets and employees located in Switzerland. Yet Nestle limits its non-Swiss voting rights to 3% of the total.[12] Ford Motor Company has a share structure that gives special voting rights to a select few shareholders, and similar arrangements are common in media groups. However, American and British stock exchanges usually discourage these arrangements as criteria for listing, and the shares generally trade at lower prices than similar ones with voting rights.[13]

Despite having some of the same characteristics in shares, the models of corporate governance have tighter convergence in the West because the states followed more consistent development paths, and remained within a more consistent position in the structure of the world economy. Peripheral states are more permeable to global influences and have experienced a greater variety of political structures (e.g., colonial, developmental state, etc.) interacting with global firms than their counterparts in the core have experienced. The growth of conglomerates in developing states has resulted from organic growth in unrelated fields, whereas in the United States and the United Kingdom it results more from takeover activity of existing firms. Thus, when firms in the United States and United Kingdom go to the stock market, they are generally acquiring an existing corporation and its assets. When developing country firms go to the stock market, they are generally financing new investments.[14] These differences are not absolute, however. Key differences exist among developed countries as well.

The European trend has been toward stock market integration among states and demutualization of these exchanges. The birth of the Euro reduced trading margins and opportunities for currency and interest rate arbitrage desks. A merging of stock markets reduces operating costs by using one trading platform and offers the benefits of an integrated trading and clearing system. Whereas the exchanges were traditionally owned by members who had an array of vested interests, the demutualized exchanges operate for the interests of shareholders and can thus better respond to competition from other exchanges. Stockholm demutualized and began to float its own shares in 1992. Amsterdam and Milan followed, and Paris's Societies Bourses Francaises merged with the domestic derivatives market (Matif). It is considering restructuring its ownerships and selling its shares as of this writing.

Despite the intensity of the merger and demutualization activity in Europe, political issues remain highly contentious. Golden shares and other forms of government involvement in firm management are particularly controversial topics within the European Union. The European Commission recently examined Volkswagen of Germany and the Dutch government's representation on the board of the Dutch telecommunications group KPN as 2 of 10 examples of potential violations of the law ensuring the free movement of capital within the union. The European Court of First Instance in Luxembourg struck these governance arrangements down in 2002.[15]

The role of stock markets continues to evolve in the United States as well. Although stock issuance is generally not a political event in the U.S. system, stock ownership is increasingly political, particularly as broader cross sections of the American public own shares. The separation of ownership and control in U.S. corporations has rendered the shareholder bereft of any real control or influence exclusive of the "Wall Street Walk." Nonetheless, activists have advanced proposals to increase the role of stockholders and directors, and decrease the role of corporate officers in patterns of corporate governance because some investors (such as large pension funds) are too large to merely sell their position in a company. The collapses of Enron and WorldCom in the United States have only hastened this activity.[16]

Therefore exchanges may join forces and operate across state boundaries, and eventually emerging market exchanges may even join the network, yet these links only tell half of the story. The other half of the story concerns the shareholding arrangements of the listed firms and the characteristics of the securities themselves. Although they may all act similarly with respect to a trading system, or a clearance mechanism, they do not all function similarly within the territory of the state to which they are attached. Thus any analysis of the merits and demerits of stock markets must consider the role of shares in corporate governance.

## Emerging Stock Markets and Globalization

Activities on emerging stock markets figure prominently in discussions of globalization because state sell-offs appear to lessen all states' power in the face of market forces, and because three commonly accepted dimensions of economic globalization intersect with respect to equity markets: international trade, international financial flows, and transnational corporations. Nonetheless, as this book has shown, a lack of precision about exactly what activities take place on these markets can lead to the wrong conclusions about how emerging markets themselves participate in economic globalization. These discussions need to incorporate notions of ownership and control through equity markets, as well as the activities of transnational firms headquartered in regions of the South, in order to arrive at more meaningful conclusions.

Globalization literature raises compelling questions concerning state territory in the contemporary era, and its connection to state power. For Hoogvelt, and Hardt and Negri in particular, a social division of the world economy has replaced what was formerly a geographical hierarchy of "first and third worlds, center and periphery, North and South."[17] For these authors, the new social division is such that various nations and regions contain different proportions of what used to be considered a first world and third world, center and periphery, North and South. The social dimension of stock markets would seem to lend credence to this argument, since generally only a small percentage of the local population participates, and the exchanges are an urban phenomenon.

Nonetheless, the historical dimension of this study cautions against conclusions separating the old global hierarchy from geography. It points out that firms can be nationalized, privatized, and renationalized. The shares can be listed in London, moved to Johannesburg, and moved back to London. The financial reports of many firms continue to give lip service to their role in the development of the state. When shares are issued that can only be held by resident citizens of the state, the state asserts itself in the face of market forces. Although emerging stock markets may have been designed with an economic motive in mind, they do not function well in most economic respects. They do not promote an egalitarian distribution of wealth in society, and they leave small economies vulnerable to speculative capital flows. They fail to provide effective firm monitoring through the price mechanism. Nonetheless, emerging markets do fulfill many political goals left unexamined by aggregate studies of the exchanges and their connection to economic development. They reserve a proportion of ownership of assets, and the stream of income connected to those assets, for a group of individuals living within the territorial confines of the state. Some shareholding arrangements allow for citizens of the state to achieve control of an economic enterprise without owning a majority of shares.

Hoogvelt highlights the negative role of privatization, writing "while national stock markets are still small and in the process of being formed (in Africa), these privatization policies ensured that foreign investors got a large slice of the action. The under-capitalization of the emerging stock markets provided an attractive hunting ground for the active money managers of core countries' investment funds and more speculative instruments such as hedge funds."[18] As the book has shown, speculative capital did indeed enter some African markets during the period in the 1990s Hoogvelt describes. Yet the bulk of this money targeted South Africa simply because there was so little to buy on the other African exchanges. Much of the capital was channeled through closed-end mutual funds that traded at a discount to their NAVs, and the managers encountered serious difficulty locating American and European investors who were willing to buy the funds. Even when foreign transnational corporations purchased controlling blocs, the state retained a degree of control over most of the large African enterprises. Contrary to being instruments of globalization, these illiquid markets allowed for a degree of local participation that would otherwise not have been available, since Africans own a sizable percentage of shares.[19]

Therefore the globalization literature is correct in that the wealth that is generated on these exchanges may indeed raise the proportion of first world characteristics in the former third world. However, those first world characteristics (i.e., stock exchanges) have existed since the nineteenth century in many emerging markets. The fragmentation of national models of corporate governance vis-à-vis the price mechanism did not result merely from new globalization forces and structural influences, but are the relics of a variety of global and structural configurations and reconfigurations occurring over the past centuries.

In sum, this book has shown the world to be a place where, as Cooper writes, "economic and political relations are very uneven; it is filled with lumps, places where power coalesces surrounded by those where it does not. . . ."[20] Rather than understanding globalization as an unmitigated good where capital is free to seek its most efficient use, or as an unmitigated evil where national politics are marginalized, this book argues that globalization is far from a homogeneous, systematic phenomenon, particularly in the issue area of equity finance. Given this world, it is likely that states of varying capacities will continue to mediate global forces for some time to come.

# Appendix

## IFC Involvement in Financial Sector and Privatization Projects, by EM Country Examples

Argentina: IFC's Advising on Single-Enterprise Privatization

| Project | Financial year | Description and IFC task |
|---|---|---|
| Aerolineas Argentinas | 1989 | IFC advised the government of Argentina on valuation in the partial privatization of Aerolineas Argentinas. |
| Altos Hornos Zapla | 1991–1992 | IFC advised the Ministry of Defense on the privatization of Altos Hornos Zapla, an integrated steel producer, arranging a tender process, preparing the sales documentation, and marketing the opportunity. Implemented through phase II and succeeded. |
| ECA | 1992–1993 | IFC advised the Ministry of Defense on structuring and implementing the sale of ECA, a copper slabs, cable, and wire manufacturer. |

Argentina: IFC's Financial Sector Activities Board Approvals FY71–97

| Institution | Year | Net amount (US$ millions) | Project name |
|---|---|---|---|
| Venture capital fund | 1985 | 2.05 | SA de Inversiones de Cap de Riesgo/ SADICAR |
| Commercial bank | 1986 | 10.00 | Banco Roberts I AL |
| Commercial bank | 1987 | 10.00 | Banco General de Negocios, SA I AL |
| Commercial bank | 1987 | 30.00 | Banco Rio de la Plata I |
| Commercial bank | 1989 | 15.00 | Banco Frances del Rio de la Plata SA I |
|  |  |  | (*continued*) |

Sources for information in this appendix are as follows: IFC *Privitization: Principles and Practice*, Washington, DC: World Bank, 1995; IFC *Financial Institutions*, Washington, DC: World Bank, 1998.

Argentina: IFC's Financial Sector Activities Board Approvals FY71–97 (*continued*)

| Institution | Year | Net amount (US$ millions) | Project name |
|---|---|---|---|
| Commercial bank | 1989 | 10.00 | Banco General de Negocios, SA II AL |
| Commercial bank | 1989 | 10.00 | Banco Roberts II AL |
| Portfolio equity fund | 1989 | 2.10 | Argentina Investment Corporation/AIC |
| Fund management company | 1990 | 0.08 | Corp. de Inversiones y Priv/CIP/APDT |
| Commercial bank | 1991 | 6.00 | Banco Roberts III AL |
| Commercial bank | 1992 | 20.00 | Banco Rio de la Plata II |
| Securities brokerage | 1992 | 0.18 | MBA Sociedad de Bolsa SA |
| Private equity fund | 1993 | 4.00 | Argentine Equity Investments Ltd./AEIL I |
| Commercial bank | 1994 | 15.00 | Banco General de Negocios SA |
| Insurance company | 1994 | 3.30 | Roberts AFJP Group-LBAV |
| Insurance company | 1994 | 1.32 | Roberts AFJP; LBAR |
| Pension fund management company | 1994 | 10.78 | Roberts AFJP; Maxima I |
| Commercial bank | 1995 | 20.00 | Banco Roberts SA Subordinated Loan |
| Fund management company | 1995 | 0.15 | The Tower Investment Management Company |
| Pension fund management company | 1995 | 4.00 | Roberts AFJP; Maxima II |
| Private equity fund | 1995 | 20.00 | Roberts Argentina Investment Capital Fund LP |
| Commercial bank | 1996 | 40.00 | Banco Frances del Rio de la Plata SA II |
| Commercial bank | 1996 | 25.00 | Bansud CL |
| Industrial/manufacturing company | 1996 | 15.00 | Alpargatas SAIC-USCP Facility |
| Multipurpose bank | 1996 | 30.00 | Banco de Galicia y Buenos Aires SA |
| Securities brokerage | 1996 | — | MBA Bolsa/Merchant Bankers Asociados SA |
| Commercial bank | 1997 | 10.00 | Banco del Suquia Subordinated Convertible Loan |
| Commercial bank | 1997 | 30.00 | Banco Roberts NOA Credit Line |
| Pension fund management company | 1997 | 4.20 | Maxima SA AFJP-Maxima EQ Rights Issue |
| Securitization of assets | 1997 | 35.40 | Argie Mae Mortgage Securitization Warehousing Facility GF |

Argentina: IFC's Investments in Privatization Projects

| Project | Financial year | Project value (US$ millions) | Description and IFC role |
|---|---|---|---|
| Chirete I | 1987 | 33.0 | IFC took a 15% equity stake in exploration joint ventures in the Chirete/Morillo/Olleros blocks, one with a local company and one with a foreign investor. The blocks had been offered as part of an effort by the state oil company, YPF, to attract private investment in oil exploration. |
| Chirete II | 1991 | 9.2 | This second investment was to finance the discovery of a small field within the Olleros Block. Overall, however, the exploration project was not commercially successful. |

Argentina: IFC's Investments in Privatization Projects (*continued*)

| | | | |
|---|---|---|---|
| Chihuidos | 1989 | 32.40 | With a group of foreign and domestic private investors, IFC took a 5% equity stake in this exploration concession and granted a part of YPF efforts to increase private participation in the sector. IFC's role was in filling a financing gap left by the withdrawal of an earlier participant concerned about country risk. The first three wells produced no major discoveries and IFC withdrew from the project in 1992. |
| Astra Capsa II | 1989 | 97.00 | IFC initially lent US$25 million and arranged financing for the three-year investment program of this local company involving expenditures to develop existing oil and gas fields in response to the improved incentives introduced by the Argentine government under the Olivos Plan. |
| Astra Capsa III | 1991 | 171.00 | IFC subsequently extended another loan, part of which was converted to equity for further development of existing fields and new joint venture participation in developing and operating primary and secondary fields sold off by YPF. Results have been very satisfactory and the company has expanded to participate in privatizations in other sectors. |
| CIP | 1990 | 0.5 | This project involved a small investment with two large commercial banks to establish a fund management company for the Argentina Private Development Trust (APDT). The APDT, in turn, was capitalized by the conversion of Argentina's public-sector debt into equity holdings in newly privatized companies. The program was successful. Debt-holding banks subscribed to it and all of APDT's debt had been converted to good-quality equity by the end of 1993. CIP has been highly profitable and is now helping APDT to develop a strategy for the future, including an exit mechanism for some of the banks. |
| Bridas | 1992 | 238.00 | IFC provided a loan and equity and mobilized other financing to assist in this local company's development program, allowing it to take part in the privatization and break-up of YPF in 1992–93. This has contributed to the company's growth and additional downstream activities are being pursued, both in Argentina and abroad. A subsidiary has interests in Russia and Turkmenistan. |
| FEPSA | 1992 | 54.8 | IFC provided financing for the US$56.2 million rehabilitation program for the 5300 km FEPSA network, the first private rail concession to be awarded by the Argentine government. The privatization involved an annual rental fee and commitment to an investment program in exchange for rights to provide freight on an exclusive basis for 30 years. IFC played a key role in financing and resource mobilization. Though it has experi- |

(*continued*)

Argentina: IFC's Investments in Privatization Projects (*continued*)

| Project | Financial year | Project value (US$ millions) | Description and IFC role |
|---|---|---|---|
| | | | enced difficulties associated with natural disasters and vigorous competition from road operators, the project has improved labor productivity and clients have benefited from lower prices. It was followed by four other railroad privatizations. |
| Huantraico/San Jorge | 1992 | 60.00 | IFC took an equity participation for up to US$17 million in the Huantraico Block jointly with a relatively small local independent. Three discoveries were made and YPF subsequently accorded the venture increased exploration and development rights in the block. |
| Huantraico/San Jorge II | 1992 | 180.4 | A subsequent equity/loan/syndication package was arranged to help finance the development of the El Trapial discovery, the largest ever made by a local company, and step-out exploration. The investment has been highly successful. |
| Cadipsa | 1993 | 83.00 | IFC provided equity financing, a loan, and syndicated financing for the development programs of five oil field concessions acquired by this local company in a joint venture with foreign partners under the breakup of YPF. While the project was moderately successful technically, financial difficulties have led to a recent takeover. |
| NCA Railway | 1993 | 62.2 | This project involved the rehabilitation of the recently privatized Mitre Railway line, Argentina's most utilized export freight line. The NCA consortium of local and U.S. investors, with 15% IFC participation, was awarded a 30-year concession to operate the line in return for a comprehensive US$61 million investment program. Though heavy rains and competition from truckers have affected railway performance, freight volume has grown and new markets have been accessed. |
| Yacylec | 1993 | 134.7 | In 1992, after a competitive bidding process, the Argentine government awarded a concession to Yaclec, a consortium of foreign and local power companies, to construct, operate, and maintain for a period of 95 years, a 273 km, 500 kV transmission line in northern Argentina. This was one of the first instances of private involvement in electricity transmission in the world. IFC lent to and mobilized term financing for the project; commercial banks would only lend under the "B" loan umbrella. The project was competed on schedule and is operating satisfactorily. |
| Edenor | 1994 | 402.4 | Edenor was formed in the breakup and privatization of the Buenos Aires electric utility and has the exclusive concession to provide electricity distribution services to about two million customers in the northern greater Buenos Aires area. A 51% |

Argentina: IFC's Investments in Privatization Projects (*continued*)

|  |  |  |  |
|---|---|---|---|
|  |  |  | controlling interest was sold to a consortium of local and foreign investors. IFC's role was to provide and mobilize the term financing necessary for an investment program to improve electricity distribution, reduce prices, and lessen energy waste and loss. |
| Edenor II | 1995 | 3.5 | IFC subsequently approved the arrangement of an interest rate swap on the project for a total exposure of up to US$3.5 million. |
| Aguas Argentinas | 1994 | 329.00 | Aguas Argentinas, an international consortium was awarded a 30-year concession, after competitive bidding, to operate the greater Buenos Aires water and sewage network—the first such major concession in this sector in the developing world. In addition to helping finance the required investments, IFC's role in the project included assistance in financial structuring and provision of comfort to long-term lenders, as well as the mobilization of financing. Consumers have benefited from lower tariffs, better quality service, and new connections; government has eliminated a budgetary drain; and the private operator is making a profit. |
| Agua Argentinas Syndication | 1995 | 52.00 | The syndication of finance planned under the first Agua project was oversubscribed and the company decided to extend the size of the loan, enabling its investment program to be accelerated. IFC approved the increase under its "B" loan umbrella. |
| Aguas Argentinas II | 1995 | 540.00 | IFC approved a further loan of US$150 million, of which US$40 million was for its own account to finance the ongoing investment program. The intention is to interest nontraditional lenders, such as insurance companies and pension funds, in the "B" loan element, thus broadening and diversifying the company's sources of financing and, simultaneously, Argentina's capital markets. |
| REC Highway | 1995 | 161.00 | This privatization involved improvement of the Buenos Aires airport road, construction of a new road, and their operation and maintenance on a toll concession basis for 23 years by a consortium of foreign and local investors. IFC has approved up to US$81 million in financing, including US$20 million for its own account—critical, given the term financing needs of such a project. It has also been involved in the design of the security and financing package and risk mitigation. |
| Terminales Portuarios Argentinos | 1995 | 50.30 | This project involves a concession to redevelop and operate a terminal in Buenos Aires Port, secured by a consortium of local and foreign companies after competitive bidding. IFC has approved support for the privatization with US$10 million in term financing and a 17% equity participation. |

## Brazil: IFC Advising on Single-Enterprise Privatization

| Project | Financial year | Description and IFC task |
|---|---|---|
| Oxitero, S.A. & Ultraquimica Participacoes, S.A. | 1991 | IFC assisted in the restructuring and merger of the core businesses of these two leading Brazilian petrochemical companies, resulting in a lowering of the government's shareholding. |

## Brazil: IFC's Financial Sector Activities Board Approvals FY71–97

| Institution | Year | Net amount (US$ millions) | Project name |
|---|---|---|---|
| Securities brokerage | 1973 | 5.00 | Capital Market Development Fund/ FUMCAP |
| Venture capital fund | 1981 | 1.5 | Brasilpar SA |
| Leasing company | 1982 | 10.45 | Banco de Investimento Planibanc SA |
| Venture capital fund | 1982 | 1.00 | Companhia Riograndense de Participacoes |
| Commercial bank | 1988 | 80.00 | Uniao de Bancos Brasileiros, S.A./Unibanco I |
| Portfolio equity fund | 1988 | 17.50 | Equity Fund of Brazil |
| Portfolio equity fund | 1988 | 10.00 | Equitypar |
| Portfolio equity fund | 1988 | — | Brazil Fund—Underwriting |
| Commercial bank | 1991 | 60.00 | Banco Bradesco SA AL |
| Fund management company | 1992 | 0.03 | CR Management Co. |
| Industrial/manufacturing company | 1992 | — | Riocell SA I |
| Portfolio equity fund | 1992 | 3.00 | Brazil Investment Fund Inc. |
| Venture capital fund | 1992 | 2.00 | CRP-Caderi Capital de Risco |
| Commercial bank | 1994 | 25.00 | Uniao de Bancos Brasileiros, S.A./Unibanco II |
| Private equity fund | 1994 | 20.00 | GP Capital Partners LP |
| Commercial bank | 1996 | 40.00 | Banco Bradesco SA—Syndicated Credit Line |
| Commercial bank | 1996 | — | Uniao de Bancos Brasileiros, S.A./Unibanco III |
| Investment bank | 1996 | 10.00 | Banco Liberal SA |

## Chile: IFC's Financial Sector Activities Board Approvals FY71–97

| Institution | Year | Net amount (US$ millions) | Project name |
|---|---|---|---|
| Investment bank | 1982 | 0.20 | Compania Chilena de Inversiones SA/Inverchile |
| Portfolio equity fund | 1988 | 7.56 | Chile Investment Company/CIC |
| Portfolio equity fund | 1989 | 7.26 | International Invest Corp of Chile/IICC |
| Leasing company | 1990 | 5.00 | Leasing Andino I |

Chile: IFC's Financial Sector Activities Board Approvals FY71–97 (*continued*)

| | | | |
|---|---|---|---|
| Portfolio equity fund | 1990 | — | Five Arrows Chile Fund, Ltd. |
| Development finance company | 1991 | 10.00 | Banco Bice |
| Development finance company | 1991 | 10.00 | Banco O'Higgins Credit Agency Line |
| Fund management company | 1994 | 0.20 | Moneda Asset Management SA I |
| Leasing company | 1994 | 15.00 | Leasing Andino II |
| Portfolio equity fund | 1994 | 10.00 | Pionero Fondo de Inversion Mobiliaria |
| Fund management company | 1996 | 0.13 | Moneda Asset Management SA II RI |
| Venture capital fund | 1996 | 10.00 | Proa Fondo de Inversion de Desarrollo de Empresas |
| Fund management company | 1997 | 0.14 | Moneda Asset Management III RI |

Chile: IFC's Investments in Privatization Projects

| Project | Financial year | Project value (US$ millions) | Description and IFC role |
|---|---|---|---|
| CTC I | 1990 | 1104.00 | Compania de Telefonos de Chile (CTC), the recently privatized Chilean telecommunications company, was doubling the number of phone lines in service and further increasing and diversifying its telecommunications services. IFC initially lent US$80 million for its own account and syndicated US$50 million for other banks in the three-year investment program, as well as underwriting an ADR issue on the New York Stock Exchange. The program has been a success, technically and economically; performance targets have been exceeded. |
| CTC II | 1992 | — | IFC arranged an additional syndication of US$63 million because the expansion was more rapid than had been predicated. |
| CTC III | 1993 | — | IFC's board approved an interest rate hedging facility of up to US$173 million (with a maximum IFC exposure of US$13.8 million). The facility has not been taken up by CTC to date. |

China: IFC's Advising on Single-Enterprise Privatizations

| Project | Financial year | Description and IFC task |
|---|---|---|
| Shenzen Nanya | 1994 | IFC advised this company on the feasibility of establishing a postconsumer polyethylene terephthalate plastic recycling plant in southern China. |

## China: IFC's Financial Sector Board Approvals FY71–97

| Institution | Year | Net amount (US$ millions) | Project name |
|---|---|---|---|
| Venture capital fund | 1987 | 3.04 | JF China Investment Fund |
| Commercial bank | 1993 | 7.5 | JV Commercial Bank |
| Fund management company | 1994 | 0.01 | China Walden Mgmt. Ltd. |
| Fund management company | 1994 | — | H&Q Fund Management Company |
| Venture capital fund | 1994 | 20.00 | China Dynamic Growth Fund LP/Dynamic Fund |
| Venture capital fund | 1994 | 7.50 | China Walden Venture Investment Ltd. |
| Venture capital fund | 1995 | 10.00 | Newbridge Investment Partners LP |
| Development finance company | 1997 | 10.00 | Orient Finance Company—Loan Facility |

## Czech Republic: IFC's Advising on Single-Enterprise Privatizations

| Project | Financial year | Descriptions and IFC task |
|---|---|---|
| CKD Kompresory | 1991–1992 | A leading manufacturer of large-scale compressors has restructured and set up a joint venture with a foreign partner with IFC's assistance. |
| Grand Hotel Pupp | 1991–1992 | IFC designed and implemented a privatization strategy for this historic spa resort and assisted in the selection of a foreign partner to invest in the refurbishment and upgrading of the hotel. The deal did not go through and ultimately the hotel was privatized through vouchers. |
| Skoda Plzen | 1991–1992 | IFC designed a privatization strategy for Skoda Plzen, Czechoslovakia's largest industrial company, and assisted in the selection of a foreign partner for the company's electrical and locomotive manufacturing units. Although an agreement in principle was signed with Siemens, changes in government and management led to its breakdown. Ultimately privatized by voucher. |
| Elitex Usti & Elitex Chrastava | 1992 | IFC advised these textile machinery manufacturers on privatization, identifying potential investors, and assisting in negotiations. The sale finally went ahead, with a Swiss company acquiring 94% of the company. |
| Kavalier Glassworks | 1992 | This speciality glassware manufacturer retained IFC to assess its strategic strengths and weaknesses, restructuring needs, and privatization options. |
| First Brno | 1992–1993 | IFC has assisted this manufacturing group in reviewing its operations in preparation for privatization, preparing sale documents, and evaluating proposals, and successfully concluded negotiations with a major Swedish-Swiss investor as a joint venture partner. |

Czech Republic: IFC's Financial Sector Activities Board Approval FY71–97

| Institution | Year | Net amount (US$ millions) | Project name |
|---|---|---|---|
| Commercial bank | 1992 | 6.49 | Zivnostenska Banka I |
| Factoring company | 1992 | 0.21 | OB Heller AS |
| Leasing company | 1992 | 0.57 | OB Sogelease AS |
| Commercial bank | 1995 | 9.07 | Zivnostenska Banka II |

Czech Republic: IFC's Investments in Privatization Projects

| Project | Financial year | Project value (US$ millions) | Description and IFC role |
|---|---|---|---|
| C. S. Cabot | 1992 | 87.10 | This project involved the transfer of the carbon black operations of Deza Ltd., an important European coal tar distributor, to a new joint venture in which Cabot, a leading world producer of carbon black, acquired 52% of the company, with Deza retaining 48%. The project involved the modernization and expansion of operations, and was completed in mid-1994. Early performance is promising. IFC financed 25% of the project, which included expansion of capacity and product improvement. This was one of the first privatization undertakings of its size in the country. |
| Mokra | 1992 | 38.00 | This project involved the privatization and modernization of the largest cement producer in the Czech Republic. A Belgian cement producer was the successful buyer. Privatization was effected by a combination of direct purchase of shares by the strategic investor and IFC from the National Assets Fund (FNA), a capital increase which diluted FNA's share further, and divestiture by FNA of its shares to the Czech public via a coupon scheme. The investment plan is on track, production has been streamlined, downstream business has been expanded, and the plant has been upgraded environmentally. |
| Zivnostenska Banka | 1992 | 50.00 | The oldest bank in the Czech Republic was the first bank privatization in eastern Europe and IFC's first investment in (then) Czechoslovakia. IFC advised on the initial sale of 40% of the bank to a strategic investor and on the choice of purchaser, and established a relationship as an honest broker which led to a request for its continued participation as a shareholder for a stake of 12%. The subsequent sale of 48% of the bank of the general public has been completed. The bank has witnessed rapid growth and healthy profitability. |
| Zivnostenska Banka II | 1995 | 60.9 | In order to sustain its growth, the bank is to increase its capital through a convertible bond issue, one of the first in the country, and IFC's board has approved that IFC exercise its rights to take a share of this. |
| Plzensky Prazdroj | 1995 | 171.5 | This major Czech brewery was privatized by coupon in 1992 and is controlled by four investment funds. IFC |

(*continued*)

Czech Republic: IFC's Investments in Privatization Projects (*continued*)

| Project | Financial year | Project value (US$ millions) | Description and IFC role |
|---|---|---|---|
| | | | is arranging a total of US$64 million in senior loans, syndication, and quasi-equity to complete the company's modernization program. IFC's role is to help a locally owned company in its postprivatization phase with a combination of technical advice and an umbrella for long-term lending by domestic banks. |
| Autokola Nova Hut | 1994 | 63.00 | This investment supported a joint venture between a U.S. investor and Nova Hut Ostrava, a Czech steel producer, then wholly owned by the National Assets Fund, to expand production of car wheels. IFC helped by providing term financing and brokering between the partners. The project is proceeding well. |
| Mafra | 1994 | 39.2 | The project entailed the privatization and modernization of one of the leading daily newspapers in the Czech Republic through the creation of a joint venture with Socpresse, France (48%), and the Czech government (52%). IFC's role was defined by nonavailability of alternative commercial sources of long-term financing on the terms required. |

Egypt: IFC's Financial Sector Activities Board Approvals FY71–97

| Institution | Year | Net amount (US$ millions) | Project name |
|---|---|---|---|
| Securities brokerage | 1985 | 1.86 | Misr. Financial Investment Co. |
| Private equity fund | 1991 | 2.43 | Egypt Tourism Investment Co. |
| Commercial bank | 1993 | 16.5 | Commercial International Bank |
| Fund management company | 1993 | .01 | Horus Investments Ltd. |
| Venture capital fund | 1993 | 6.00 | International Egyptian Investments |
| Investment bank | 1996 | 4.50 | Commercial International Investment Co. |
| Leasing company | 1996 | 5.88 | ORIX Leasing EGT |
| Merchant bank | 1996 | 10.00 | National Bank of Egypt RMF |
| Industrial/manufacturing company | 1997 | 30.00 | ANSDK GDR |
| Portfolio equity fund | 1997 | 5.00 | The Egypt Trust |

Egypt: IFC's Investments in Privatization Projects

| Project | Financial year | Project value (US$ millions) | Description and IFC role |
|---|---|---|---|
| Commercial international bank | 1993 | 100.00 | This divestiture was among the first in Egypt and involved the privatization of CIB by public issue. The issue involved employees, a public offer on the domestic stock exchange, and sales to primarily institutional international investors. IFC also took a 5% stake. It was the first new securi- |

Egypt: IFC's Investments in Privatization Projects *(continued)*

|  |  |  | ties issue on the domestic stock exchange and IFC assisted in reviewing the securities place-ment legislation and developing the modalities of the placement. The project has had an impor-tant demonstration effect. The bank has since performed well, and with IFC advice has diversi-fied its corporate finance and financial services activities. |
|---|---|---|---|
| ANSDK | 1994 | 225.5 | ANSDK was set up in 1982 as a joint venture be-tween Egyptian public institutions (with a sub-stantial shareholding majority), a consortium of Japanese investors, and IFC to produce reinforc-ing steel bars, mainly for domestic consumption. In 1992 IFC was awarded the mandate to advise on its expansion and privatization involving re-structuring, manner of sale, and technical con-figuration. This was designed in two stages; the first, a dilution of the existing public-sector shar-eholding through a capital increase, and the sec-ond, a direct divestment by the public sector. In 1994 IFC provided equity investment, a loan, and guarantees associated with the first-phase ex-pansion. ANSDK is currently performing very strongly and there is considerable appetite for the shares. |

Ghana: IFC's Advising on Single-Enterprise Privatization

| Project | Financial year | Description and IFC task |
|---|---|---|
| Ashanti Goldfields Corp. Ltd. | 1994 | IFC advised the government on the value of the company in the context of the sale of part of its interest in this corporation. |

Ghana: IFC's Financial Sector Activities Board Approvals FY71–97

| Institution | Year | Net amount (US$ millions) | Project name |
|---|---|---|---|
| Merchant bank | 1989 | 0.98 | Continental Acceptances I |
| Merchant bank | 1991 | 3.00 | Continental Acceptances II |
| Other securities market players, niches | 1991 | 0.23 | Securities Discount Co. Ltd. |
| Leasing company | 1992 | 0.60 | Ghana Leasing I |
| Leasing company | 1993 | 5.00 | Ghana Leasing III |
| Leasing company | 1993 | 0.15 | Ghana Leasing II |
| Merchant bank | 1993 | 5.00 | Continental Acceptances III |
| Merchant bank | 1993 | 6.00 | Ecobank Ghana Ltd. I |
| Merchant bank | 1996 | 5.00 | Ecobank Ghana Ltd. II |

Hungary: IFC's Financial Sector Activities Board Approvals FY71–97

| Institution | Year | Net amount (US$ millions) | Project name |
|---|---|---|---|
| Commercial bank | 1987 | 3.14 | Unicbank Rt I |
| Fund management company | 1990 | 7.50 | First Hungarian Investment Advisory Rt/FHIA |
| Insurance company | 1991 | 3.26 | First American Hungarian Insurance Co. Rt. |
| Investment bank | 1991 | 1.63 | Nomura Magyar Beefektetesi Bank Rt/NMBB |
| Commercial bank | 1992 | 10.00 | Unicbank Rt II |
| Venture capital fund | 1992 | 2.74 | Euroventures Hungary BV |
| Venture capital fund | 1995 | 2.50 | Creditanstalt |
| Commercial bank | 1996 | 10.00 | Inter-Europa Bank RT CL |

Hungary: IFC's Investments in Privatization Projects

| Project | Financial year | Project value (US$ millions) | Description and IFC role |
|---|---|---|---|
| Hungarian Telecom. Co. | 1994 | 470.2 | In an unusual arrangement, IFC invested US$28.6 million in preference shares of HTC, Hungary's national telecommunications carrier, prior to its privatization to enable it to complete its 1993 investment program agreed upon under World Bank auspices. IFC (and EBRD) then worked closely with HTC to develop the structure needed for a successful privatization. At the end of 1993, 30.29% was sold to a strategic investor, who also took operational management control. IFC's shares converted to common stock. This was the first telecommunications privatization in central and eastern Europe. |

India: IFC's Advising on Single-Enterprise Privatization

| Project | Financial year | Description and IFC task |
|---|---|---|
| Hindustan Machine Tools Ltd | 1994 | IFC assisted this company, one of India's largest government-owned conglomerates, in finding a joint venture partner for its core business. With the support of its Technical Assistance Trust Funds Program, IFC provided advisory services on restructuring for the company. Privatization did not materialize. |

India: IFC's Financial Sector Activities Board Approvals FY71–97

| Institution | Year | Net amount (US$ millions) | Project name |
|---|---|---|---|
| Housing finance company | 1978 | 5.21 | Housing Development Finance Corp./HDFC I |
| Leasing company | 1983 | 5.45 | India Equipment Leasing Ltd. I |

India: IFC's Financial Sector Activities Board Approvals FY71–97 (*continued*)

| | | | |
|---|---|---|---|
| Leasing company | 1983 | 5.46 | Leasing Corporation of India Ltd. |
| Housing finance company | 1985 | 0.20 | Gujarat Rural Housing Finance |
| Leasing company | 1985 | 5.41 | India Lease Development I |
| Housing finance company | 1987 | 0.39 | Housing Development Finance Corp/ HDFC II |
| Securities brokerage | 1989 | 0.55 | JM Share & Stock Brokers Ltd/JSB India I |
| Leasing company | 1990 | 3.94 | India Lease Development II |
| Leasing company | 1990 | 16.95 | Infra Leasing/IL & FS I |
| Venture capital fund | 1990 | 2.87 | TDICI-VECAUS II |
| Housing finance company | 1991 | 44.80 | Housing Development Finance Corp./ HDFC IV |
| Housing finance company | 1991 | 0.51 | Housing Development Finance Corp/ HDFC III RI |
| Fund management company | 1992 | 0.51 | Creditcapital Venture Fund Mgmt Co. I |
| Fund management company | 1992 | 0.01 | Indus Venture Capital Mgmt Co. |
| Leasing company | 1992 | 0.8 | Kotak Mahindra Finance Limited |
| Leasing company | 1992 | 3.25 | Nicco-Uco Financial Services Ltd. |
| Venture capital fund | 1992 | 1.16 | Indus Venture Capital Fund/Indus VCF I |
| Venture capital fund | 1992 | 0.74 | Info Tech Fund |
| Housing finance company | 1993 | 2.29 | Housing Development Finance Corp/HDFC V RI |
| Leasing company | 1993 | 8.00 | 20th Century Finance Corp Ltd. I |
| Leasing company | 1993 | 3.0 | India Equipment Leasing Ltd. II |
| Leasing company | 1993 | 3.71 | Infra Leasing/JL & FS II |
| Commercial bank | 1994 | 3.19 | Global Trust Bank |
| Fund management company | 1994 | 0.16 | Twentieth Century Asset Management Corp. |
| Fund management company | 1994 | 0.32 | Creditcapital Asset Mgmt Co. |
| Industrial/manufacturing company | 1994 | — | Gujarat Ambuja Cements Ltd. II Convertible Bond Issue |
| Industrial/manufacturing company | 1994 | — | India International Securities Issues |
| Industrial/manufacturing company | 1994 | — | TISCO—Tata Iron and Steel Co. Securities Issue |
| Leasing company | 1994 | 25.00 | Infra Leasing (IL & FS) III |
| Leasing company | 1994 | 0.14 | India Equipment Leasing Ltd. III |
| Leasing company | 1994 | 0.3 | India Lease Development III |
| Unit trust/mutual fund company | 1994 | 2.39 | Centurion Growth Scheme |
| Unit trust/mutual fund company | 1994 | 7.17 | Taurus the Starshare/Cubic Growth Fund/CGF |
| Commercial bank | 1995 | 5.41 | Centurion Bank Ltd/CBL |
| Fund management company | 1995 | 0.6 | Creditcapital Venture Mgmt. Co. II |
| Leasing company | 1995 | 20.00 | SRF Finance Ltd. |
| Leasing company | 1995 | 0.33 | India Equipment Leasing Ltd. IV RI |
| Securities brokerage | 1995 | 2.45 | JM Share & Stock Brokers Ltd/JSB India II |
| Securities brokerage | 1995 | 0.64 | IL&FS Stockbroking and Investment Co/SIC |
| Venture capital fund | 1995 | 7.97 | South Asia Regional Apex Fund |
| Commercial bank | 1996 | 1.89 | Development Credit Bank |
| Industrial/manufacturing company | 1996 | 2.17 | Indo Rama Synthetics Ltd. |
| Venture capital fund | 1996 | 8.00 | Creditcapital Venture Fund Ltd. AL |
| Venture capital fund | 1996 | 7.50 | India Direct Fund |
| Venture capital fund | 1996 | 5.00 | Indus II |
| Fund management company | 1997 | 0.08 | Walden-Nikko India Ventures Company/Walden Management |

(*continued*)

India: IFC's Financial Sector Activities Board Approvals FY71–97 (*continued*)

| Institution | Year | Net amount (US$ millions) | Project name |
|---|---|---|---|
| Leasing company | 1997 | 15.00 | 20th Century Finance Corp. Ltd. II |
| Leasing company | 1997 | 20.00 | CEAT Financial Services |
| Leasing company | 1997 | 10.00 | India Infrastructure & Export Leasing Project WIPRO Finance Ltd. CL |
| Leasing company | 1997 | 30.00 | ITC Classic |
| Leasing company | 1997 | 5.00 | Nicco Uco Financial Services Ltd./NUFSL |
| Leasing company | 1997 | 18.00 | SREI International Finance Ltd. |
| Leasing company | 1997 | 0.13 | Nicco-Uco Financial Services Ltd.–Roghts Issue II |
| Venture capital fund | 1997 | 6.00 | Walden-Nikko Indian Ventures Company/ WIV |

Korea: IFC's Financial Sector Activities Board Approvals FY71–97

| Institution | Year | Net amount (US$ millions) | Project name |
|---|---|---|---|
| Commercial bank | 1971 | 0.7 | Hana Bank I |
| Commercial bank | 1974 | 0.34 | Hana Bank II |
| Development finance company | 1974 | 0.36 | Korea Long Term Credit Bank II |
| Other securities market players, niches | 1975 | 5.58 | Korea Securities Finance Co. I |
| Commercial bank | 1976 | 0.4 | Hana Bank III |
| Development finance company | 1976 | 8.91 | Korea Long Term Credit Bank III |
| Development finance company | 1977 | 0.29 | Korea Long Term Credit Bank IV |
| Leasing company | 1977 | 5.37 | Korea Development Leasing Corporation I |
| Other securities market players, niches | 1977 | 0.5 | Korea Securities Finance Co. II |
| Development finance company | 1978 | 1.08 | Korea Long Term Credit Bank V |
| Commercial bank | 1979 | 0.59 | Hana Bank IV |
| Leasing company | 1979 | 0.25 | Korea Development Leasing Corporation I |
| Commercial bank | 1980 | 0.63 | Hana Bank V |
| Development finance company | 1980 | 2.24 | Korea Long Term Credit Bank VI |
| Other securities market players, niches | 1980 | 0.82 | Korea Securities Finance Co. III |
| Commercial bank | 1982 | 0.66 | Hana Bank VI |
| Other securities market players, niches | 1982 | 0.35 | Korea Securities Finance Co. IV |
| Other securities market players, niches | 1983 | 1.18 | Korea Securities Finance Co. V |
| Venture capital fund | 1983 | 0.98 | Korea Development Investment Corporation II |
| Portfolio equity fund | 1984 | 21.80 | Korea Fund Inc. I |
| Commercial bank | 1985 | 0.54 | Hana Bank VII |
| Venture capital fund | 1985 | 5.00 | Korea Development Investment Corporation ACL |
| Portfolio equity fund | 1986 | 1.73 | Korea Fund Inc. II |
| Leasing company | 1987 | 0.25 | Korea Development Leasing Corporation II |

Korea: IFC's Financial Sector Activities Board Approvals FY71–97 *(continued)*

| | | | |
|---|---|---|---|
| Other securities market players, niches | 1987 | 0.19 | Korea Business Research & Information |
| Development finance company | 1988 | 2.73 | Korea Long Term Credit Bank IX FI |
| Commercial Bank | 1989 | 2.70 | Hana Bank VIII |
| Commercial bank | 1989 | 2.18 | Hana Bank XI |
| Development finance company | 1990 | 15.98 | Korea Long Term Credit Bank VII |
| Leasing company | 1990 | 0.9 | Korea Development Leasing Corporation IV |
| Commercial bank | 1991 | 4.48 | Hana Bank IX |
| Venture capital fund | 1991 | 0.89 | Korea Development Corporation II |
| Commercial bank | 1994 | 2.10 | Hana Bank X RI |
| Development finance company | 1994 | 7.42 | Korea Long Term Credit Bank VIII |
| Commercial bank | 1997 | 0.65 | Hana Bank XI RI |

Mexico: IFC's Financial Sector Activities Board Approvals FY71–97

| Institution | Year | Net amount (US$ millions) | Project name |
|---|---|---|---|
| Industrial/manufacturing company | 1982 | 10.50 | Vitro Sociedad Anonima (VISA) ADS Bond Issue |
| Industrial/manufacturing company | 1986 | 20.00 | CICASA Constr. Guarantee Facility |
| Commercial bank | 1989 | 60.00 | Banca Serfin I |
| Commercial bank | 1990 | 60.00 | Banco Nacional de Mexico/BANAMEX I |
| Commercial bank | 1990 | 20.00 | Bancomer, S.N.C. |
| Commercial bank | 1990 | 6.50 | Banca Serfin II RMF |
| Portfolio equity fund | 1991 | — | Mexico Equity & Income Fund |
| Commercial bank | 1992 | 20.00 | Banorte, C.V. Multi product ACL |
| Commercial bank | 1992 | 40.00 | Banco Nacional de Mexico/BANAMEX II RMF |
| Merchant bank | 1992 | 7.50 | Grupo Financiero Probursa I |
| Fund management company | 1993 | 0.15 | Inversiones de Capital Bancomer, SA de CV |
| Industrial/manufacturing company | 1993 | 11.43 | APASCO IV |
| Venture capital fund | 1993 | 9.85 | Kapta Integracion Capitales SA de CV |
| Factoring company | 1994 | 0.98 | Aurum-Heller Factoraje, SA de CV I |
| Fund management company | 1995 | 0.15 | Baring Venture Partners de Mexico SA de CV I |
| Venture capital fund | 1995 | 10.00 | Baring Venture Mexico Fund I |
| Commercial bank | 1996 | 100.00 | Banco Nacional |
| Factoring company | 1996 | 0.97 | Aurum-Heller Factoraje, SA de CV II CRP |
| Fund management company | 1996 | 0.03 | Baring Venture Partners de Mexico SA de CV II RI |
| Industrial/manufacturing company | 1996 | 40.00 | Grupo Irsa, SA de CV I—USCP Facility |
| Merchant bank | 1996 | 0.80 | Grupo Financiero Probursa II RI |
| Merchant bank | 1996 | 0.23 | Grupo Financiero Probursa III RI |
| Commercial bank | 1997 | 110.00 | Banca Bilbao Vizcaya (BBV) Mexico SA |

*(continued)*

Mexico: IFC's Financial Sector Activities Board Approvals FY71–97 (*continued*)

| Institution | Year | Net amount (US$ millions) | Project name |
|---|---|---|---|
| Fund management company | 1997 | 0.02 | Chiapas Fund Management Company |
| Housing finance company | 1997 | 2.50 | General Hipotecaria |
| Merchant bank | 1997 | 0.35 | Grupo Financiero Probursa IV RI (subscr) |
| Merchant bank | 1997 | 0.25 | Grupo Financiero Probursa V RI |
| Venture capital fund | 1997 | 5.00 | Fondo Chiapas SA de CV Sociedad de Inversiones de Capitales |
| Venture capital fund | 1997 | 20.00 | Mexico Partners Trust |

Mexico: IFC's Investments in Privatization Projects

| Project | Financial year | Project value (US$ millions) | Description and IFC role |
|---|---|---|---|
| MCTTR | 1992 | 312.7 | The private holder of a concession to operate and collect tolls from a 22 km toll road from Mexico to Toluca sought to raise US$200 million through placement of a 10-year Euro-Bond issue secured by assignment of toll proceeds. The funds were then used to pay off construction debt, extend the concession, and finance construction of other toll roads. IFC underwrote 5% of the issue and purchased 5% of the issue for its account. The project has operated well with traffic levels above forecasts. |
| GOTM | 1993 | 21.00 | IFC provided equity, loan, syndication, and interest rate swap support for the second and major phase of the expansion of Altamira port's liquid storage facility terminal following the agreement of a 12-year concession between government and GOTM, a consortium representing Mexican and foreign investors. The project involved additional storage tanks, improved truck-handling facilities, and the acquisition of land. This was the second privately operated port terminal built in Mexico. |
| GOTM II | 1995 | — | IFC has subsequently approved participation in a rights issue in GOTM. |

Poland: IFC's Advising on Single-Enterprise Privatization

| Project | Financial year | Description and IFC task |
|---|---|---|
| International Foundation for Capital Market Development and Ownership Changes | 1990–1991 | IFC provided the government of Poland with general advice on the legal, regulatory, and institutional framework for privatization. IFC has also played a key role in establishing the foundation and helped raise funding from the European Community for the foundation's operations. |

## Poland: IFC's Advising on Single-Enterprise Privatization (*continued*)

| | | |
|---|---|---|
| Swarzedzkie Fabryki Mebli S.A. (SFM) | 1991–1992 | IFC was retained by the government of Poland to design and implement a privatization strategy for SFM, a major furniture company with 3,200 employees. IFC designed and implemented a financial restructuring of the company prior to managing its sale through public offering and listing on the Warsaw Stock Exchange. As part of this assignment, IFC designed a new share distribution mechanism for Poland. |
| Cement and lime sector strategies | 1991–1992 | On behalf of the Polish Ministry of Privatization, IFC carried out a strategic review of the cement and lime sectors, including appraisals of 19 cement plants and 10 lime plants. Based on this work, IFC prepared a restructuring and privatization strategy for the sectors. |
| Gorazdze S.A. Strzelce Opolskie S.A., Odra S.A., Opolwal S.A., KCW Warta S.A., Wojcieszow Sp. Zoo, KCW Kujawy S.A. | 1992–1995 | Subsequently IFC has assisted in implementing this strategy, managing the sale of the seven companies listed and providing ongoing advice in two more. |

## Poland: IFC's Financial Sector Activities Board Approvals FY71–97

| Institution | Year | Net amount (US$ millions) | Project name |
|---|---|---|---|
| Commercial bank | 1991 | 3.20 | International Bank in Poland I |
| Venture capital fund | 1993 | 2.50 | Advent PEF; Poland Inv Fund |
| Factoring company | 1994 | .60 | Handlowy-Heller |
| Housing finance company | 1996 | 15.00 | Polish American Mortgage Bank |
| Commercial bank | 1997 | 4.00 | International Bank in Poland II |
| Venture capital fund | 1997 | 5.00 | Central Poland Fund |

## Poland: IFC's Investments in Privatization Projects

| Project | Financial year | Project value (US$ millions) | Description and IFC role |
|---|---|---|---|
| Bristol Hotel | 1990 | 36.2 | The US$36 million project involved the privatization and renovation of Poland's most famous hotel, which had been closed for nine years. IFC's role was to help catalyze one of Poland's first joint ventures on a project of national stature by providing loan financing and help to structure a complex deal. A glut of hotel building in Warsaw has produced strong competition. |
| Philips Lighting Poland | 1992 | 60.00 | The project involved the privatization and modernization of Polam Pila, the largest manufacturer of lighting products in Poland, by bringing in Philips Lighting (Netherlands) as a majority shareholder (86%). The project is performing well and financial targets have been exceeded. |

(*continued*)

Poland: IFC's Investments in Privatization Projects (*continued*)

| Project | Financial year | Project value (US$ millions) | Description and IFC role |
|---|---|---|---|
| Huta L. W. | 1993 | 299.1 | IFC took a 5% equity stake and made a loan of ECU 30 million in the privatization and modernization of Huta Warszawa, the largest producer of special and alloy steels in Poland, with an Italian strategic investor controlling an effective majority. IFC's role was to provide reassurance to Polish banks who had swapped debt for equity in the project and were unfamiliar with such transactions, and to the foreign sponsor, entering Poland for the first time. The modernization has been delayed while land title problems have been resolved, but is now ready to proceed. |
| Pilkington Sandoglass | 1993 | 171.5 | This privatization was set up in 1993 as a joint venture with Pilkington of the United Kingdom and involved the privatization of the country's largest sheet glass manufacturer and the construction of a new float glass plant. IFC helped bring the government and strategic investor together and to provide third-party advice on dealings during and after privatization. The project also involved the largest-ever syndicated loan for a private company in Poland. The performance of the sheet glass business has improved since privatization and the float glass plant is now in production. |
| Kwidzyn | 1994 | 328.0 | An IFC loan was approved to support the 1993–96 investment program of this paper mill from the Polish government by a U.S. investor in 1992. |
| PPMs Opole/Peters | 1994 | 18.0 | This state-owned meat processing plant was privatized by sale to a foreign strategic investor, bringing with it an infusion of capital and new management. There had been limited previous privatization in the sector, which in contrast had been through lease of assets to employees, resulting in fragmentation. IFC provided long-term debt financing and equity. The death of the principal owner has led to restructuring efforts, including introduction of a new strategic foreign partner. |

Russian Federation: IFC's Advising on Single-Enterprise Privatization

| Project | Financial year | Description and IFC task |
|---|---|---|
| A/O Vostok | 1994 | IFC is assisting A/O Vostok, a leading Russian manufacturer and distributor of disposable syringes, to identify and negotiate a collaborative arrangement with a strategic foreign partner. |
| Beta Air | 1994 | IFC is assisting Beta Air, a Russian aerospace joint venture, to negotiate a partnership agreement with a foreign-industry investor. |
| Pilot initial public offering | 1995 | Following its support in conducting voucher privatization auctions for medium and large-scale enterprises, IFC is assisting two companies in the Nizhny Novgorod oblast arrange initial public offerings of equity capital on the domestic capital markets. |

Russian Federation: IFC's Advisory Work Relating to Privatization (projects designed to serve as models for the rapid transfer of ownership from public to private hands)

| Project | Financial year | Description and IFC role |
|---|---|---|
| Small-scale privatization | 1992–1995 | IFC developed a model for the privatization of small enterprises, mainly in the retail sector, by auction in Nizhny Novgorod, and rolled these out in many other cities in Russia. |
| Trucking privatizations | 1993–1995 | IFC developed a model for privatization of the trucking sector in Nizhny Novgorod, involving the break-up of the monopoly and a mixture of voucher certificates and cash-based auctions. |
| Medium and large privatization | 1993–1994 | IFC developed a model for privatization of medium and large-scale enterprises using an auction system centered around the national privatization certificates. This was first undertaken in Volgograd and then rolled out to other Russian cities. |
| Land privatization | 1993–1995 | IFC developed a model in Nizhny Novgorod for the simultaneous break-up and privatization of state and collective farms using a system of land and machinery entitlement certificates for all farm workers. This model is also currently being replicated in other Russian oblasts. |

Russian Federation: IFC's Financial Sector Activities Board Approvals FY71–97

| Institution | Year | Net amount (US$ millions) | Project name |
|---|---|---|---|
| Commercial bank | 1993 | 15.00 | International Moscow Bank |
| Commercial bank | 1994 | 5.00 | Tokobank RMF |
| Venture capital fund | 1994 | 8.00 | Framlington Russian Investment Fund |
| Fund management company | 1995 | 0.47 | Sector Capital Development Company Ltd. |
| Other securities market players, niches | 1995 | 1.5 | National Registry Company/Russia Registry |
| Trade finance company | 1995 | 10.00 | Russian Trade Enhancement Facility |
| Venture capital fund | 1995 | 15.00 | First NIS Regional Federation Fund |
| Venture capital fund | 1995 | 2.00 | Russian Technology Fund |
| Venture capital fund | 1995 | 4.55 | Sector Capital Fund Ltd. |
| Commercial bank | 1996 | 15.00 | United Export Import Bank/ UNEXIM Bank |
| Fund management company | 1996 | 4.00 | Pioneer First Russia Inc. |
| Other securities market players, niches | 1997 | 2.99 | Troika Dialog |
| Securities brokerage | 1997 | 7.01 | Nikitas Brokerage |

Russian Federation: IFC's Investments in Privatization Projects

| Project | Financial year | Project value (US$ millions) | Description and IFC role |
|---|---|---|---|
| Tula Apple | 1995 | 19.4 | This project involves a loan and equity participation in a joint venture between two Italian companies and a Russian closed joint stock company comprising 33 former collective farms. Ownership of the farms had already been vested in the workers by law, but in practical terms this project constituted the real step to privatization. |
| AO Volga | 1995 | 371.00 | This newsprint paper mill was privatized under Russia's Mass Privatization program in 1994, leaving ownership divided primarily among employees, U.S. institutional investors and the German sponsor. The project involves upgrading existing facilities and providing working capital, and is the first example of nonportfolio foreign investment in the manufacturing sector in Russia. Ownership will be consolidated by a capital increase and the strategic investor will take management control. IFC has played a lead structuring role and mobilized finance. |

Senegal: IFC's Financial Sector Activities Board Approvals FY71–97

| Institution | Year | Net amount (US$ millions) | Project name |
|---|---|---|---|
| Development finance company | 1974 | 0.21 | Sofisedit I |
| Housing finance company | 1980 | 0.46 | Banque de l'Habitat du Senegal/BHS |
| Development finance company | 1981 | 0.17 | Sofisedit II |
| Leasing company | 1994 | 1.18 | Societe Generale de Credit Automobile/SOGECA I |
| Leasing company | 1996 | 0.18 | Societe Generale de Credit Automobile/SOGECA III RI |
| Leasing company | 1996 | 1.18 | Societe Generale de Credit Automobile/SOGECA II (rev) GF |

South Africa: IFC's Financial Sector Activities Board Approvals FY71–97

| Institution | Year | Net amount (US$ Millions) | Project name |
|---|---|---|---|
| Fund management company | 1995 | 0.06 | South Africa Franchise Fund Mgmt. Co. Ltd. |
| Insurance company | 1995 | 11.70 | Africa Life Assurance Co. Ltd. I |
| Venture capital fund | 1995 | 20.00 | South Africa Capital Growth Fund |
| Venture capital fund | 1995 | 3.52 | South Africa Franchise Equity Fund Ltd. |
| Insurance company | 1996 | 3.17 | Africa Life Assurance Co. Ltd. II RI |
| Merchant bank | 1996 | 2.53 | Cashbank Subordinated Loan |

Thailand: IFC's Financial Sector Activities Board Approvals FY71–97

| Institution | Year | Net amount (US$ millions) | Project name |
|---|---|---|---|
| Unit trust/mutual fund company | 1977 | 0.29 | Mutual Fund Co. Ltd. Of Thailand I |
| Development finance company | 1978 | 2.00 | Siam Commercial Bank |
| Leasing company | 1979 | 0.15 | Thai Orient Leasing Co. |
| Venture capital fund | 1984 | 1.00 | SEAVI Thailand I |
| Portfolio equity fund | 1987 | — | Thai Fund |
| Portfolio equity fund | 1988 | — | Thai Fund Inc. |
| Portfolio equity fund | 1989 | — | Thai Prime Fund |
| Unit trust/mutual fund company | 1990 | 0.26 | Mutual Fund Co. Ltd of Thailand II |
| Leasing company | 1991 | 0.23 | Ayudhya Development Leasing Co. Ltd/ADLC I |
| Venture capital fund | 1991 | 1.50 | SEAVI Thailand II |
| Commercial bank | 1992 | 5.93 | Bank of Asia I |
| Leasing company | 1992 | 0.35 | Krung Thai IBJ |
| Commercial bank | 1993 | 0.49 | Bank of Asia II |
| Leasing company | 1993 | 0.36 | Ayudhya Development Leasing Co. Ltd./ADLC II |
| Other securities market players, niches | 1994 | 30.00 | Dhana Siam Finance & Securities Company |
| Commercial bank | 1995 | 30.00 | Finance One USCP |
| Commercial bank | 1995 | 1.10 | Bank of Asia III RI |
| Investment bank | 1996 | 40.00 | National Finance & Public Securities Ltd. |
| Leasing company | 1996 | 10.00 | Ayudhya Development Leasing Co. Ltd./ADLC IV |
| Leasing company | 1996 | 0.89 | Ayudhya Development Leasing Co. Ltd/ADLC III RI |
| Securities brokerage | 1997 | 13.04 | Phatra Thanakit Public Co. Ltd. |

# Notes

## Introduction

1. Saul Hansell, "At Morgan, New Markets and a Rohatyn Emerge," *New York Times*, February 28, 1994.
2. Gerri Willis, "Burned, but Not Shy, Lenders Go Abroad," *Crain's New York Business*, January 10, 1994.
3. Joan Ogden, "Merrill Gets Serious About Emerging Markets," *Global Finance*, December 1995, 44–47.
4. David Crane, "World's Economic Balance is Shifting Emerging Economies," *Toronto Star*, January 10, 1993.
5. N. Rohatyn quoted in Hansell, "At Morgan."
6. Statistics used from World Bank, *1999 World Development Indicators*. Washington, DC: World Bank.
7. For some samples of editorials on the question of the IMF, see Steve H. Hanke, "The IMF: Immune from (Frequent) Failure," *Wall Street Journal*, August 25, 1997; Jeffrey Sachs, "IMF is a Power Unto Itself," *Financial Times*, December 11, 1997; Soren Ambrose, "Checking the Balance of the IMF," *Washington Post National Weekly Edition*, May 4, 1998; Jeffrey E. Garten, "Needed: A Fed for the World," *New York Times*, September 23, 1998.

## Chapter 1

1. This study uses the term "emerging markets" despite the fact that for many markets it is euphemistic, at best. For some reviews of the origins of the term, and problems with its use, see James Derrick Sidaway and Michael Pryke, "The Strange Geographies of 'Emerging Markets,' " *Transactions* 25 (2000): 187–201; James D. Sidaway and John R. Bryson, "Constructing Knowledges of 'Emerging Markets': UK-Based Investment Managers and Their Overseas Connections," *Environment and Planning A* 34 (March 2002): 401–416.
2. Jack D. Glen and Mariusz A. Sumlinski, "Trends in Private Investment in Developing Countries: Statistics for 1970–1996," IFC Discussion Paper 34 (Washington, DC: World Bank, 1997).

3. While shares can be traded without a formal exchange, it is difficult for a deep and liquid capital market to develop in a state without one. A variety of definitions for the term "stock exchange" exist. For a comprehensive review, see Ruben Lee, *What Is an Exchange? The Automation, Management and Regulation of Financial Markets* (New York: Oxford University Press, 1998), Appendix 2.

4. For some examples from the economics literature, see Andrea Calamanti, *The Securities Market and Underdevelopment* (Milan: Giuffre, 1983); Ajit Singh, "The Stock-Market and Economic Development: Should Developing Countries Encourage Stock-Markets?" *UNCTAD Review* 4 (1993): 1–28; Makoto Nagaishi, "Stock Market Development and Economic Growth: Dubious Relationship," *Economic and Political Weekly* 34 (July 17, 1999): 2004–2012. While continuing the tendency to aggregate data, some economic literature has begun to look at other factors, such as historical and cultural, to understand stock market development. See Geert Bekaert and Campbell R. Harvey, "Research in Emerging Markets Finance: Looking to the Future," *Emerging Markets Review* 3 (2002): 429–448.

5. For some examples of this literature, see Peter J. Katzenstein, ed., *Between Power and Plenty: Foreign Economic Policies of Advanced Industrial States* (Madison, WI: University of Wisconsin Press, 1978); John Zysman, *Governments, Markets and Growth* (Ithaca, NY: Cornell University Press, 1983); Sylvia Maxfield, *Governing Capital* (Ithaca, NY: Cornell University Press, 1990); Michael Loriaux, *France After Hegemony* (Ithaca, NY: Cornell University Press, 1991); Jung-eun Woo, *Race to the Swift* (New York: Columbia University Press, 1991); Stephan Haggard, Chung Lee, and Sylvia Maxfield, eds., *The Politics of Finance in Developing Countries* (Ithaca, NY: Cornell University Press, 1993); Michael Loriaux, Meredith Woo-Cumings, Kent E. Calder, Sylvia Maxfield, and Sophia Perez, eds., *Capital Ungoverned: Liberalizing Finance in Interventionist States* (Ithaca, NY: Cornell University Press, 1997); Sylvia Maxfield and Ben Ross Schneider, *Business and the State in Developing Countries* (Ithaca, NY: Cornell University Press, 1997); Sophia Perez, "Systemic Explanations, Divergent Outcomes: The Politics of Financial Liberalization in France and Spain," *International Studies Quarterly* 42 (December 1998): 755–784.

6. Saskia Sassen, "Global Financial Centers," *Foreign Affairs* 78 (January/February 1999): 75–87. See also Randall D. Germain, *The International Organization of Credit: States and Global Finance in the World-Economy* (Cambridge: Cambridge University Press, 1997).

7. For some examples from the literature in comparative political economy that questions national institutional economic convergence, see Suzanne Berger and Ronald Dore, eds., *National Diversity and Global Capitalism* (Ithaca, NY: Cornell University Press, 1996), 60–88. See also Peter A. Hall and David Soskice, eds., *Varieties of Capitalism: The Institutional Foundations of Comparative Advantage* (New York: Oxford University Press, 2001).

8. Darryl Reed, "Corporate Governance Reforms in Developing Countries," *Journal of Business Ethics* 37 (2002): 233.

9. A. M. Honore, "Ownership," in *Oxford Essays in Jurisprudence*, 1st series (Oxford: Oxford University Press, 1961), 107–147.

10. A. A. Berle and G. C. Means, *The Modern Corporation and Private Property*, rev. ed. (New York: Harcourt, Brace & World, 1968).

11. G. Visentini, "Compatibility and Competition Between European and American Corporate Governance: Which Model of Capitalism?" *Brooklyn Journal of International Law* 23 (1998): 833–851.

12. Variations of disintermediated forms of capital exist. For example, preferred shares of stock blur the distinction between the two major classes of securities. Preferred shares have a prior claim on the company's dividends and/or assets should the company dissolve. Thus they combine some of the characteristics of a bond and a stock insofar as some

preferred shares are rated and some have parallel price trends with high-quality, long-term bonds. Yet even with their "senior security" status, preferred stocks are fundamentally equity securities. The issuer can change the dividend at any time and the holder does not share the legal rights of a creditor should the company be dissolved. See Jeffrey B. Little and Lucien Rhodes, *Understanding Wall Street*, 3rd ed. (New York: Liberty Hall Press, 1991).

13. Ian H. Giddy, "Global Capital Markets: What Do They Mean?" in *Financial Markets and Development: The Crisis in Emerging Markets*, eds. Alison Harwood, Robert E. Litan, and Michael Pomerleano, 219 (Washington, DC: Brookings Institution Press, 1999).

14. See Douglass C. North, "Institutions and Economic Growth: An Historical Introduction," *World Development* 17 (1989): 1319–1332.

15. For some examples in political science, see John Zysman, *Governments, Markets, and Growth*; Jung-eun Woo, *Race to the Swift*; Suzanne Berger and Ronald Dore, *National Diversity and Global Capitalism*; Sigurt Vitols, "Varieties of Corporate Governance: Comparing Germany and the UK," in *Varieties of Capitalism: The Institutional Foundations of Comparative Advantage*, eds. Peter A. Hall and David Soskice, 337–360 (New York: Oxford University Press, 2001). For some examples in the business literature, see Jeroen Weimer and Joost C. Pape, "A Taxonomy of Systems of Corporate Governance," *Corporate Governance* 7 (April 1999): 152–166; Enrique Loredo and Eugenia Suarez, "Privatization and Deregulation: Corporate Governance Consequences in a Global Economy," *Corporate Governance* 8 (January 2000): 65–74; Alvaro Cuervo, "Corporate Governance Mechanisms: A Plea for Less Code of Good Governance and More Market Control," *Corporate Governance* 10 (April 2002): 84–93; Darryl Reed, "Corporate Governance Reforms in Developing Countries," *Journal of Business Ethics* 37 (2002): 223–247. For some examples in the legal literature, see G. Visentini, "Compatibility and Competition"; L. A. Cunningham, "Commonalities and Prescriptions in the Vertical Dimension of Global Corporate Governance," *Cornell Law Review* 84 (1999): 1133–1194.

16. E. J. Hobsbawm, *Industry and Empire* (New York: Penguin Books, 1969), 119.

17. M. J. Roe, *Strong Managers, Weak Owners: The Political Roots of American Corporate Finance* (Princeton, NJ: Princeton University Press, 1994).

18. See G. Visentini, "Compatibility and Competition"; L. A. Cunningham, "Commonalities and Prescriptions"; J. Zysman, *Governments, Markets, and Growth*.

19. A. Gerschenkron, *Economic Backwardness in Historical Perspective* (Cambridge, MA: Harvard University Press, 1962).

20. Albert O. Hirschman, "The Political Economy of Import-Substituting Industrialization in Latin America," *Quarterly Journal of Economics* 82 (1968): 1–32.

21. Ibid.

22. Cunningham, "Commonalities and Prescriptions," 1140.

23. See Gerschenkron, *Economic Backwardness in Historical Perspective*, and Hirschman, "Political Economy of Import-Substituting Industrialization in Latin America."

24. Peter Gourevitch, "The Second Image Reversed: The International Sources of Domestic Politics," *International Organization* 32 (Autumn 1978): 888.

25. Hall and Soskice, *Varieties of Capitalism: The Institutional Foundations of Comparative Advantage*.

26. Rafael La Porta, Florencio Lopez-de-Silanes, and Andrei Shleifer, "Corporate Ownership Around the World," *Journal of Finance* 54 (April 1999): 471–517.

27. Mark Granovetter, "Business Groups," in *Handbook of Economic Sociology*, eds. Neil Smelser and Richard Swedberg, 453–475 (Princeton, NJ: Princeton University Press, 1994).

28. For example, a new company may not be able to obtain a bond rating and may

therefore sell equity, as was the case with many Internet initial public offerings (IPOs) in the late 1990s.

29. For some reviews in the business literature, see Juliet D'Souza and William L. Megginson, "The Financial and Operating Performance of Newly Privatized Firms in the 1990s," *Journal of Finance* 54 (August 1999): 1397–1438; William L. Megginson and Maria K. Boutchkova, "Privatization and the Rise of Global Capital Markets," *Financial Management* 29 (Winter 2000): 31–76.

30. Kenneth E. Scott, "Corporate Governance and East Asia: Korea, Indonesia, Malaysia, and Thailand," in *Financial Markets and Development: The Crisis in Emerging Markets*, eds. Alison Harwood, Robert E. Litan, and Michael Pomerleano, 336 (Washington, DC: Brookings Institution Press, 1999).

31. William D. Coleman and Tony Porter, "Regulating International Banking and Securities: Emerging Co-operation among National Authorities," in *Political Economy and the Changing Global Order*, eds. Richard Stubbs and Geoffrey R. D. Underhill, 195 (New York: St. Martin's Press, 1994). Coleman and Porter cite as a statistical source Michael Howell and Angela Cozzini, *Games Without Frontiers: Global Equity Markets in the 1990s* (New York: Salomon Brothers, 1991). A London listing, for example, makes it easier to raise capital to finance global expansion plans, and it removes the "political risk premium" a company pays for being in a country like South Africa, where the cost of capital is significantly higher. Moreover, a London listing means a company could be in the *Financial Times* 100 stock index, which is the British equivalent of the Dow Jones industrial average. Index listing improves visibility among investors and it forces index fund managers to buy its shares. Finally, listing in London may force greater disclosure on a company and ease the suspicion some international investors have with respect to firms in certain regions.

32. The term ADR is used interchangeably for the certificate and the securities themselves. The term "ordinary" or "ord" represents the local or underlying share.

33. Nobel Gulati, *ADR Monitor: The Key to the World*, September 1999 (New York: Salomon Smith Barney, 1999), 8.

34. Funds can also be distinguished by four broad categories of investment purpose. International portfolio investment funds mainly buy securities listed on local stock exchanges, and some ADRs. Private equity funds buy significant minority equity stakes in unlisted companies. Venture capital (VC) funds buy private equity stakes in smaller and newer enterprises. VC funds historically have been small. Domestic mutual funds, or unit trusts, raise money from local investors and buy securities listed on the domestic stock market. See L. W. Carter, *IFC's Experience in Promoting Emerging Market Investment Funds* (Washington, DC: World Bank, 1996), 8.

35. Historians credit King William I of the Netherlands with forming the first closed-end fund in Belgium in 1822. This form of investment became popular with British investors in the late 1800s. The first important postwar country fund was the Japan Fund, listed in New York in 1964. See David Gill, "Two Decades of Change in Emerging Markets," in *The World's Emerging Stock Markets: Structure, Developments, Regulations and Opportunities*, eds. Keith Park and Antoine Van Agtmael, 47–56 (Chicago: Probus Publishing, 1993); see also L. W. Carter, *IFC's Experience*.

36. Ralph Dahrendorf, *Class and Class Conflict in Industrial Society* (Stanford, CA: Stanford University Press, 1959).

37. Geert Bekaert, "Market Integration and Investment Barriers in Emerging Equity Markets," *World Bank Economic Review* 9 (January 1995): 75–107. Investment banks do not conduct business with the public. They are intermediaries between corporate, governmental, and quasi-governmental bodies and the institutional investing public. The effectiveness of an investment bank has to do with its "placing power," or its ability to underwrite

risk securities and then sell them on to investment clients for a fee. Usually this ability is most directly linked to securities markets where certain investment banks, because of substantial client contacts, are able to sell new issues of stocks and/or bonds to clients of long or close standing. In more traditional merchant banking, however, the ability is still evident but more often seen in private transactions, where the intermediary will bring two clients together in order to initiate and complete a transaction. Knowledge of both the markets and specific clients needs are in fact placing power to a merchant bank, even if it does not always involve itself in the securities markets. American investment banking involves both the underwriting of securities and the maintaining of a secondary market in many of them, especially if they are bonds or equities listed over the counter. This trading function is also known as the "market-making" function. See Charles R. Geisst, *A Guide to Financial Institutions* (New York: St. Martin's Press, 1988).

38. See David E. Van Zandt, "The Regulatory and Institutional Conditions for an International Securities Market," *Virginia Journal of International Law* 32 (1991): 68; Gary Humphreys, "Closing the Time-Lag in Settlements," *Euromoney*, March 1989, 31 (Global Custody: Speeding the Paper Chase, special supplement). Van Zandt cites Humphreys's statistics.

39. See Craig Doidge, G. Andrew Karolyi, and Rene M. Stulz, "Why Are Foreign Firms Listed in the U.S. Worth More?" National Bureau of Economic Research Working Paper 8538, http://www.nber.org/papers/w8538 (accessed December 19, 2003).

40. Van Zandt, "Regulatory and Institutional Conditions."

41. Woo, *Race to the Swift*, 174.

42. Capital structure is the mix of debt and equity instruments in a given firm. Modigliani and Miller asserted that in an idealized world without taxes, the value of a firm is independent of its debt-equity mix. The value of a firm depends only on the cash flows it generates and not on the manner in which those flows are distributed between mixes of debt and equity finance. Hence capital structure is irrelevant unless tax structure intervenes. See Franco Modigliani and Merton Miller, "The Cost of Capital, Corporation Finance, and the Theory of Investment," *American Economic Review*, June 1958, 261–297.

43. Jack Glen and Brian Pinto, "Debt or Equity? How Firms in Developing Countries Choose," IFC Discussion Paper 22 (Washington, DC: World Bank, 1994), 4.

44. Ibid. See also Stewart Myers, "The Capital Structure Puzzle," *Journal of Finance* 39 (1984): 575–592.

45. John H. Boyd and Bruce D. Smith, "The Evolution of Debt and Equity Markets in Economic Development," *Economic Theory* 12 (1998): 519–560.

46. Christian Tyler, "Third World Tunes into Capitalism," *Foreign Times*, June 11, 1987, 37.

47. Yoon Je Cho, "Inefficiencies from Financial Liberalization in the Absence of Well-Functioning Equity Markets," *Journal of Money, Credit and Banking* 18 (May 1986): 197.

48. Robert J. Shiller, *Irrational Exuberance* (Princeton, NJ: Princeton University Press, 2000).

49. Raghuram G. Rajan and Luigi Zingales, "The Great Reversals: The Politics of Financial Development in the Twentieth Century," *Journal of Financial Economics* 69 (2003): 5–50.

50. Calamanti, *Securities Market and Underdevelopment*.

51. Singh, "The Stock-Market and Economic Development: Should Developing Countries Encourage Stock-Markets?" *UNCTAD Review* 4 (1993): 1–28. Ajit Singh is an economist at UNCTAD. See also various articles in the South Centre's "Financing Development," 1, no. 30 (1998) of the *South Letter*.

52. Nagaishi, "Stock Market Development and Economic Growth."

53. Edward B. Flowers, "Merging But Different, Emerging Markets Persist," in *Inter-locking Global Business Systems: The Restructuring of Industries, Economies and Capital Markets*, eds. Edward B. Flowers, Thomas P. Chen, and Jonchi Shyu, 75–92 (Westport, CT: Quorum Books).

54. Ian Domowitz, Jack Glen, and Ananth Madhavan, "International Cross-Listing and Order Flow Migration: Evidence from an Emerging Market," *Journal of Finance* 53 (December 1998): 2001–2027.

55. Robert B. Dickie, "Development of Third World Securities Markets: An Analysis of General Principles and a Case Study of the Indonesian Market," *Law and Policy in International Business* 13 (1981): 177–222.

56. Robert D. Putnam, "Diplomacy and Domestic Politics: The Logic of Two-Level Games," *International Organization* 42 (Summer 1988): 427–460. See also Peter B. Evans, Harold K. Jacobson, and Robert D. Putnam, eds., *Double-Edged Diplomacy: International Bargaining and Domestic Politics* (Berkeley: University of California Press, 1993). For a similar argument, albeit not one that uses the two-level game analogy, see Yves Tiberghien, "State Mediation of Global Financial Forces: Different Paths of Structural Reforms in Japan and South Korea," *Journal of East Asian Studies* 2 (2002): 103–141.

57. Each exchange also has its own method of order execution. For example, trading can be accomplished by a two-way auction process, specialist system, or by direct negotiations.

58. Historians refer to this empire as "informal" because Britain never sought territorial rights on the South American mainland with the exception of Guyana. Nonetheless, the British did intervene in the internal affairs of these states when international law had been broken, when British property was threatened, and when its economic interests were threatened. See P. J. Cain and A. G. Hopkins, *British Imperialism: Innovation and Expansion, 1688–1914* (New York: Longman, 1993).

59. Eric Helleiner, "From Bretton Woods to Global Finance: A World Turned Upside Down," in *Political Economy and the Changing Global Order*, eds. Richard Stubbs and Geoffrey R. D. Underhill, 163–175 (New York: St. Martin's Press, 1994).

60. Germain, *The International Organization of Credit*.

61. Transparency is the degree in which real-time trade and quote information becomes available to market participants. Transparency is needed to assess value. Capital adequacy refers to having enough capital to settle daily transactions. Disclosure refers to the fact that when foreign issuers make public offerings of securities to U.S. retail investors, they must reveal the same financial information as the U.S. firms do.

## Chapter 2

1. U.S. Department of Commerce, *International Direct Investment: Global Trends and the U.S. Role* (Washington, DC: U.S. Government Printing Office, 1984).

2. Herman M. Schwartz, *States Versus Markets: History, Geography, and the Development of the International Political Economy* (New York: St. Martin's Press, 1994), 13.

3. Contemporary estimates of foreign direct investment often exclude reinvested profits. Dunning argues that by assembling widely disparate estimates of both inward and outward direct capital stakes of countries, by 1914 approximately three-fifths of the total foreign capital stake was directed at today's "developing" countries; if we use "all areas outside the Europe and United States" as a definition of developing countries, more than four-fifths was directed there. See John H. Dunning, "Changes in the Level and Structure of International Production: The Last One Hundred Years," in *The Growth of International Business*, ed. Mark Casson, 84–139 (Boston: George Allen & Unwin, 1983).

4. M. M. Postan, *Medieval Trade and Finance* (New York: Cambridge University Press, 1973), 49.

5. Kenneth R. Andrews, *Trade, Plunder and Settlement: Maritime Enterprise and the Genesis of the British Empire, 1480–1630* (New York: Cambridge University Press, 1984), 262.

6. William Robert Scott, *The Constitution and Finance of English, Scottish and Irish Joint-Stock Companies to 1720* (Cambridge: Cambridge University Press, 1912). See also Theodore K. Rabb, *Enterprise and Empire* (Cambridge, MA: Harvard University Press, 1967).

7. Raymond W. Goldsmith, *Premodern Financial Systems: A Historical Comparative Study* (New York: Cambridge University Press, 1987).

8. Niels Steensgaard, "The Dutch East India Company as an Institutional Innovation," in *Dutch Capitalism and World Capitalism*, ed. Maurice Aymard, 246 (New York: Cambridge University Press, 1982).

9. Scott, *Constitution and Finance*, 197.

10. Steensgaard, "Dutch East India Company," 237.

11. Ibid., 247. The second of the two issuers of corporate shares in the United Provinces, the Dutch West India Company, was a different type of organization both in terms of its (lack of) success and its social basis of support. Whereas Amsterdam merchants had controlled the East India Company, their opponents, the "party" of Orangists, Calvinists, Zeelanders, and southern Netherlander migrants resettled in the north, controlled the West India Company. A struggle between different interests took place inside the West India Company, mostly between the economically weaker Zeelanders, with their reliance on the company's monopoly in privateering, and the Amsterdam merchants, who were willing to take a cut of the privateering of any Dutch entrepreneur. After the company was founded in 1621, the Dutch sought to expand in the Atlantic by founding New Amsterdam, conquering northeast Brazil, and capturing Elmina in West Africa and then Luanda in Angola. Although they lost several of these territories shortly thereafter and the company did not play the same role in corporate history as the East India Company, the Dutch did launch sugar cultivation in the Americas and conduct a slave trade to furnish manpower for the sugar plantations in association with the West India Company. These activities had important historical ramifications, albeit not for equity securities. See Immanuel Wallerstein, *The Modern World-System II: Mercantilism and the Consolidation of the European World-Economy, 1600–1750* (New York: Academic Press, 1980), 50–51.

12. Bruce G. Carruthers, *City of Capital: Politics and Markets in the English Financial Revolution* (Princeton, NJ: Princeton University Press, 1996), 171.

13. Edward Victor Morgan and W. A. Thomas, *The Stock Exchange: Its History and Functions* (London: Elek Books, 1969), 23.

14. P. J. Cain and A. G. Hopkins, *British Imperialism: Innovation and Expansion, 1688–1914* (New York: Longman, 1993), 60.

15. Ibid., 168.

16. Ibid., 169.

17. Morgan and Thomas, *Stock Exchange*, 49.

18. D. C. M. Platt, *Finance, Trade and Politics in British Foreign Policy* (Oxford: Clarendon Press, 1968).

19. E. J. Hobsbawm, *Industry and Empire* (New York: Penguin Books, 1969), 110.

20. Ibid., 118.

21. Ibid., 119.

22. R. C. Michie, *The London and New York Stock Exchanges: 1850–1914* (Boston: Allen & Unwin, 1987), 110.

23. Ibid.

24. Ibid., 6.

25. Ibid., 38.

26. Ibid.

27. The work of the British merchant banking industry was overwhelmingly accepting of house activities. Few houses made issues. Moreover, only a small number of houses earned income from retailing a share of issues passed on by big names—as opposed to making their own issues. The problem for the merchant banks in issuing stock was in assessing the price and market for a particular issue. Pricing could mean life or death to the house in question because the capital of most merchant banks was actually quite modest. Nor did merchant banks have sufficient capital or deposits to finance development loans.

Rather, foreigners subscribed most of the foreign loans raised in London because they recognized the name of the London issue as a guarantee of the soundness of the bonds bought. In this way the merchant bank could act as a catalyst for the generation of capital from the particular country or locality where it was needed. Britain benefited from these capital exporting activities since much of the capital returned in orders for British manufacturers. Particularly in the industrializing world, the British could sell their industrial surplus at a time when the industrializing country could not pay for these products with adequate exports. See S. D. Chapman, *The Rise of Merchant Banking* (Boston: Allen & Unwin, 1984).

28. C. K. Hobson, *The Export of Capital* (New York: MacMillan, 1914), 113. See also Alfred Colling, *La Prodigieuse Histoire de la Bourse* (Paris: Societe d'Editions Economiques et Financieres, 1949).

29. Platt, *Finance, Trade and Politics*, 7.

30. See William Parker, *The Paris Bourse and French Finance* (New York: AMS Press, 1967); see also Hobson, *Export of Capital*.

31. Parker, *Paris Bourse*, 59.

32. Alexander Gerschenkron, *Europe in the Russian Mirror* (Cambridge: Cambridge University Press, 1970), 102–103.

33. Roger Munting, "Industrial Revolution in Russia," in *The Industrial Revolution in National Context: Europe and the USA*, eds. Mikulas Teich and Roy Porter, 334 (Cambridge: Cambridge University Press, 1996).

34. William L. Blackwell, *The Beginnings of Russian Industrialization: 1800–1860* (Princeton, NJ: Princeton University Press, 1968).

35. Olga Crisp, *Studies in the Russian Economy Before 1914* (New York: Harper & Row, 1976), 149.

36. Ibid., 161.

37. Ibid., 159.

38. For examples of the connection between imperialism and industrialization, see John A. Hobson, *Imperialism, A Study* (London: Allen & Unwin, 1938); Vladimir I. Lenin, *Imperialism, the Highest Stage of Capitalism* (New York: International Publishers, 1939); Joseph Schumpeter, *Capitalism, Socialism, and Democracy* (New York: Harper Torchbooks, 1950); Joseph Schumpeter, "The Sociology of Imperialism," in *Imperialism and Social Classes* (Cleveland: World Publishing, 1955). See also Crawford Young, "The African Colonial State and its Political Legacy," in *The Precarious Balance: State and Society in Africa*, eds. Donald Rothchild and Naomi Chazan, 25–66 (Boulder, CO: Westview Press, 1988).

39. Paul S. Reinsch, *Colonial Administration* (New York: MacMillan, 1905).

40. Ibid., 199.

41. Morgan and Thomas, *Stock Exchange*, 97–98.

42. Michie, *London and New York*, 74.

43. International Finance Corporation, *Emerging Stock Markets Factbook* 1999 (Washington, DC: World Bank, 1998).

44. Economist Publications, *Directory of World Stock Exchanges* (Baltimore: Johns Hopkins University Press, 1988), 307.

45. Morgan and Thomas, *Stock Exchange*, 80.

46. Hobson, *Export of Capital*.

47. Jeffrey Herbst, "The Creation and Maintenance of National Boundaries in Africa," *International Organization* 43 (Fall 1989): 673–692.

48. Ralph A. Austen, *African Economic History: Internal Development and External Dependency* (Portsmouth, NH: Heinemann, 1987).

49. Ibid., 128.

50. Ibid., 127.

51. Reinsch, *Colonial Administration*, 188.

52. The federation comprised Senegal, Mali, Burkina Faso, Niger, Mauritania, Benin, Cote d'Ivoire, and Guinea.

53. Catherine Boone, *Merchant Capital and the Roots of State Power in Senegal, 1930–1985* (New York: Cambridge University Press, 1992).

54. Ibid., 45.

55. August Gachter, "Finance Capital and Peasants in Colonial West Africa: A Comment on Cowen and Shenton," *Journal of Peasant Studies* 20 (July 1993): 674.

56. Munting, "Industrial Revolution," 344.

*Chapter 3*

1. Robert Gilpin, *War and Change in World Politics* (New York: Cambridge University Press, 1990).

2. John Gerard Ruggie, "Multilateralism: The Anatomy of an Institution," in *Multilateralism Matters: The Theory and Praxis of an Institutional Form*, ed. John Gerard Ruggie, 3–47 (New York: Columbia University Press, 1993).

3. P. J. Cain and A. G. Hopkins, *British Imperialism: Crisis and Deconstruction, 1914–1990* (New York: Longman, 1993), 16.

4. Ibid., 18.

5. Ibid., 19.

6. M. J. Roe, *Strong Managers, Weak Owners: The Political Roots of American Corporate Finance* (Princeton, NJ: Princeton University Press, 1994), 94–95.

7. Ibid. See also Adolf A. Berle Jr. and Gardiner C. Means, *The Modern Corporation and Private Property* (New York: Macmillan, 1933), 111.

8. Roe, *Strong Managers*, 96–97.

9. Alfonso Quiroz, *Domestic and Foreign Finance in Modern Peru, 1850–1950: Financing Visions of Development* (Pittsburgh, PA: University of Pittsburgh Press, 1993), 212.

10. Ibid., 211.

11. Andrea Calamanti, *The Securities Market and Underdevelopment* (Milan: Giuffre, 1983).

12. Lawrence Krause, "Private International Finance," *International Organization* 25 (1975): 523–540.

13. Chakravarth Raghavan, *Recolonization, GATT, the Uruguay Round and the Third World* (Atlantic Highlands, NJ: Zed Books, 1990), 51.

14. B. E. Matecki, *The Establishment of the International Finance Corporation and United States Policy* (New York: Praeger, 1957).

15. Ibid.

16. Ibid.

17. Jonas Haralz, "The International Finance Corporation," in *The World Bank, Its First Half Century*, eds. Devesh Kapur, John P. Lewis, and Richard Webb, 820 (Washington, DC: Brookings Institution Press, 1997).

18. Ibid.

19. Ibid., 845.

20. See Karl Polanyi, *The Great Transformation*, 6th printing (Boston: Beacon Press, 1965). See also John Gerard Ruggie, "International Regimes, Transactions, and Change: Embedded Liberalism in the Postwar Economic Order," in *International Regimes*, ed. Stephen Krasner, 204–214 (Ithaca, NY: Cornell University Press, 1983).

21. See Arturo Escobar, "Power and Visibility: Development and the Invention and Management of the Third World," *Cultural Anthropology* 3 (November 1988): 428–443, and Arturo Escobar, "Reflections on 'Development,' Grassroots Approaches and Alternative Politics in the Third World," *Futures*, June 1992, 411–436.

22. See Frank Partnoy, *F.I.A.S.C.O. Blood in the Water on Wall Street* (New York: Norton, 1997).

23. Robert Gilpin, *The Political Economy of International Relations* (Princeton, NJ: Princeton University Press, 1987), 238. Incidentally, this form of long-term capital export favored by the United States has various definitions. Economics texts commonly reference "portfolio" investment and "direct foreign" investment in terms of the element of control. This distinction is somewhat imprecise, however, because different texts associate different financial vehicles with each form. For example, Ellsworth and Leith associate portfolio investment with bonds bearing a specific rate of interest, and direct investment with business firms expanding their operations into others by buying controlling interests of stocks or building plants. The question of direct, yet noncontrolling, interests of stocks is left open. Kenen defines portfolio investment as holdings or stocks *or* bonds designed to earn dividends and interest rather than exercise control over the use of foreign facilities. "International direct investment" is generally considered to be the purchase by residents in one country of a substantial ownership and management share of a business enterprise or real property in another country, or an increase in the amount of an already existing investment. Other forms are portfolio, commercial bank lending, and international holding of official government reserves. In general, the stock of direct investments consists of the net book value of a parent company's share of equity in, and net outstanding loans to, its foreign affiliates. Some countries use 50% of ownership of voting stock of foreign affiliates as "direct investment" where some degree of control is exercised. Others consider 25% or 10% adequate to have some control. Also, the definition of an indirectly owned affiliate (foreign affiliate owned by another foreign affiliate in turn owned by a domestic parent) differs. Also, stock estimates can be understated because many Organization for Economic Development and Cooperation (OECD) countries (Germany, Italy, Norway, Portugal until 1975, Spain, and the United Kingdom) do not collect or consider data on reinvested earnings of foreign affiliates in their direct investment balance of payments flow estimates. See P. T. Ellsworth and J. C. Leith, *The International Economy* (New York: Macmillan, 1984); Peter B. Kenen, *The International Economy* (New York: Cambridge University Press, 1994); U.S. Department of Commerce, *International Direct Investment: Global Trends and the U.S. Role* (Washington, DC: U.S. Government Printing Office, 1984).

24. Randall D. Germain, *The International Organization of Credit: States and Global Finance in the World-Economy* (Cambridge: Cambridge University Press, 1997).

25. See, for example, Raymond Vernon, *Sovereignty at Bay* (New York: Basic Books, 1971).

26. John Stopford and Susan Strange, *Rival States, Rival Firms: Competition for World Market Shares* (Cambridge: Cambridge University Press, 1991).

27. U.S. Department of Commerce, *International Direct Investment.*

28. OECD, *International Investment and Multinational Enterprises* (Paris: OECD, 1981). See also U.S. Department of Commerce, *International Direct Investment*, 17.

29. Robert B. Dickie, "Development of Third World Securities Markets: An Analysis of General Principles and a Case Study of the Indonesian Market," *Law and Policy in International Business* 13 (1981): 178–179.

30. Ibid., 200–201.

31. Ibid., 202.

32. David D. Hale, "Stock Markets in the New World Order," *Columbia Journal of World Business* XXIX (Summer 1994): 16.

33. David Gill, "Two Decades of Change in Emerging Markets," in *The World's Emerging Stock Markets: Structure, Developments, Regulations and Opportunities*, eds. Keith Park and Antoine Van Agtmael, 51 (Chicago: Probus Publishing, 1993).

34. Khalid A. Mirza, "Pakistan," in *The World's Emerging Stock Markets: Structure, Developments, Regulations and Opportunities*, eds. Keith Park and Antoine Van Agtmael, 197–222 (Chicago: Probus Publishing, 1993).

35. Nick Seaward, "Malaysia," in *The World's Emerging Stock Markets: Structure, Developments, Regulations and Opportunities*, eds. Keith Park and Antoine Van Agtmael, 143–159 (Chicago: Probus Publishing, 1993).

36. Calamanti, *The Securities Market.*

37. Ibid.

38. Ibid., 184.

39. Douglas Gustafson, "The Development of Nigeria's Stock Exchange," in *Financing African Development*, ed. Tom J. Farer, 144–156 (Cambridge, MA: MIT Press, 1965).

40. Calamanti, *The Securities Market.*

41. Roy C. Smith and Ingo Walter, *Global Banking* (New York: Oxford University Press, 1997).

42. Charles R. Geisst, *A Guide to Financial Institutions* (New York: St. Martin's Press, 1988).

43. See Norman S. Poser, *International Securities Regulation: London's "Big Bang" and the European Securities Markets* (Boston: Little, Brown, 1991).

*Chapter 4*

1. David D. Hale, "Stock Markets in the New World Order," *Columbia Journal of World Business* XXIX (Summer 1994): 15.

2. As discussed in chapter 1, the metaphor draws on Robert Putnam's understanding of the interaction between international and domestic forces. See Robert D. Putnam, "Diplomacy and Domestic Politics: The Logic of Two-Level Games," *International Organization* 42 (Summer 1988): 427–460.

3. Charles Lipson, "International Debt and International Institutions," in *The Politics of International Debt*, ed. Miles Kahler (Ithaca, NY: Cornell University Press, 1986).

4. The sister institution of the IMF, the World Bank, had been a third "pillar" of the Bretton Woods system, yet in the peculiar role of both bank and development agency. In this role it had a traditional strength in lending for specific development projects prior to 1982. Upon Robert McNamara's appointment as president in 1968, the bank directed its lending toward agriculture, particularly toward the small farmer. The aim was to increase production among poorer segments of the developing world's population without loss to

the wealthier segments. The degree of effectiveness of these lending programs to actually produce benefits accruing to the poor, however, was widely debated prior to 1982.

5. See International Finance Corporation, *Lessons of Experience: Financial Institutions*, no. 6 (Washington, DC: International Finance Corporation, 1998), 24.

6. Charles Lipson, "The International Organization of Third World Debt," in *Toward a Political Economy of Development*, ed. Robert Bates (Berkeley: University of California Press, 1988).

7. Ibid., 22–23. Lipson cites *World Financial Markets* 4 (January 1981), Table 5.

8. Lipson, "International Debt," 235. See also "The Latin American Debt Crisis," in *The World Bank: Its First Half Century, Volume I: History*, eds. Devesh Kapur, John P. Lewis, and Richard Webb, 595–682 (Washington, DC: Brookings Institution Press, 1997).

9. David F. Gordon, "Debt, Conditionality and Reform: The International Relations of Economic Restructuring in Sub-Saharan Africa," in *Hemmed In: Responses to Africa's Economic Decline*, eds. Thomas M. Callaghy and John Ravenhill, 105 (New York: Columbia University Press, 1993).

10. Jonas Haralz, "The International Finance Corporation," in *The World Bank: Its First Half Century, Volume I: History*, eds. Devesh Kapur, John P. Lewis, and Richard Webb, 814 (Washington, DC: Brookings Institution Press, 1997).

11. Ibid., 838.

12. Ibid., 847.

13. David Gill, "Two Decades of Change in Emerging Markets," in *The World's Emerging Stock Markets: Structure, Developments, Regulations and Opportunities*, eds. Keith Park and Antoine Van Agtmael, 50–51 (Chicago: Probus Publishing, 1993).

14. Raymond W. Goldsmith, *Financial Structure and Development* (New Haven, CT: Yale University Press, 1969).

15. Haralz, "The International Finance Corporation," 864.

16. IFC, *Lessons of Experience: Financial Institutions*, no. 6 (Washington, DC: International Finance Corporation, 1998), 33.

17. Brian Lorin Sudweeks, *Equity Market Development in Developing Countries* (New York: Praeger, 1989), 33.

18. Jack Glen, "An Introduction to the Microstructure of Emerging Markets," IFC Discussion Paper 24 (Washington, DC: World Bank, 1994), 1.

19. Haralz, "The International Finance Corporation," 891. As the two organizations function together, the IFC acts either as an advisor *or* an investor in member government's privatization. It cannot both advise and invest because its articles prevent it from acting as a project sponsor. Thus others must develop a proposal, and the IFC appraises it. It accommodates political objectives and overcomes political impediments to privatization. It develops techniques custom-tailored to the political market that allow privatizations to be concluded and maximize the economic gains to be realized.

20. L. W. Carter, *IFC's Experience in Promoting Emerging Market Investment Funds* (Washington, DC: World Bank, 1996), 19.

21. See Kathryn C. Lavelle, "International Financial Institutions and Emerging Capital Markets in Africa," *Review of International Political Economy* 6 (Summer 1999): 200–224, and "The International Finance Corporation and the Emerging Market Funds Industry," *Third World Quarterly* 21 (2000): 193–213.

22. Nicholas Bratt, Scudder Kemper Investments, interviewed by author, September 30, 1998.

23. Korea Fund, Inc., "Prospectus of the Korea Fund," August 22, 1984 (New York: First Boston Corporation, Lehman Brothers, International Finance Corporation, 1984). Nonetheless, the Korea Fund does vote its proxies. The Korea Fund and others recently

elected some independent directors to the board of SK Telecom, which was a significant development.

24. Carter, *Promoting Emerging Market Investment Funds*, 19.

25. According to World Bank regulations, deals must have the approval of the host country government. This particular deal was concluded after First Boston stepped in when the IFC was removed.

26. Clyde H. Farnsworth, "Agency Proposes Fund of Stocks in Third World," *New York Times*, December 20, 1985.

27. William Hall, "Looking for Third World Winners: William Hall on a World Bank Investment Concept," *Financial Times* (London), February 18, 1986.

28. Carter, *Promoting Emerging Market Investment Funds*.

29. World Bank, *Private Capital Flows to Developing Countries* (New York: Oxford University Press, 1997), 106.

30. CDA/Wiesenberger Investment Companies Service, *Investment Companies Yearbook 1998* (Rockville, MD: CDA/Wiesenberger, 1998), 30. The lack of redemption risk gives closed-end portfolio managers more freedom to invest in securities that would not be prudent in an open-end fund. Nonetheless, this structure is not marketed as aggressively by investment banks, nor is it as profitable for them. Therefore their numbers have declined dramatically.

31. Carter, *Promoting Emerging Market Investment Funds*, 19.

32. The Non-Aligned Movement ad hoc Advisory Group of Experts on Debt, *The Continuing Debt Crisis of the Developing Countries* (August 1994). See also, the "Ministerial Meeting of Non-Aligned Countries on Debt and Development: Sharing of Experiences," Jakarta, Indonesia (August 13–15, 1994).

33. The World Bank classifies debtor countries into three categories: severely indebted, moderately indebted, and less indebted. About 53 countries are currently classified as severely indebted. However, the World Bank includes three eastern European countries in this classification, therefore 50 developing countries are conceptually comparable to the 55 to 60 used in this chapter as reported in the Non-Aligned Movement report. UNCTAD listed 57 developing countries and 4 in transition that were experiencing debt servicing difficulties.

34. See Non-Aligned Movement, "Meeting of Non-Aligned Countries" (August 13–15, 1994).

35. Concessional debt has a grant element of at least 25%.

36. Non-Aligned Movement, *Continuing Debt Crisis*, 26.

37. IFC, *Financial Institutions*, 23.

38. IFC, *Financial Institutions*, 36.

39. The central bank governors of the Group of Ten countries founded the Basle Committee on Banking Supervision in late 1974 in response to the secondary banking crisis in Britain and the collapses of both the Franklin National Bank in the United States and the Herstatt Bank in Germany. The Bank for International Settlements (BIS) in Basle, Switzerland, provides the secretariat for the committee and it meets 10 times a year at BIS headquarters. The committee concluded the Basle Concordat in 1974 which established the principle of international banking regulation that the home country is responsible for supervising the global operation of international banks in its jurisdiction on the basis of a consolidated balance sheet.

40. See Takatoshi Ito and David Folkerts-Landau, *International Capital Markets: Developments, Prospects, and Key Policy Issues* (Washington, DC: International Monetary Fund, 1996).

41. Michael H. Sutton, "International Harmonization of Accounting Standards: Per-

spectives from the Securities and Exchange Commission" (remarks to the International Accounting Association, August 17, 1997), http://www.sec.gov/news/speeches/spch174.txt.

42. Incidentally, a U.S. investor can buy shares of a non-U.S. firm on its home exchange by using a U.S. broker, however, the commission costs are higher than if the investor is trading U.S. equities.

*Chapter 5*

1. International Finance Corporation, *Privatization: Principles and Practice* (Washington, DC: World Bank, 1995), 13.

2. OECD, *Financial Market Trends: February 1995*, no. 60 (Paris: OECD), 14.

3. OECD, *Financial Market Trends: June 2000*, no. 76 (Paris: OECD), 63.

4. OECD, *Financial Market Trends: February 1999*, no. 72 (Paris: OECD), 140.

5. OECD, *Financial Market Trends*, no. 60, 26.

6. Mary Shirley and Ahmed Galal, *Bureaucrats in Business: The Economics and Politics of Government Ownership* (Washington, DC: World Bank, 1995), 8.

7. OECD, *Financial Market Trends*, no. 60, 22.

8. L. Bouton and M. A. Sumlinski, "Trends in Private Investment in Developing Countries: Statistics for 1970–95," IFC Discussion Paper 31, rev. ed. (Washington, DC: International Finance Corporation, 1997).

9. For a discussion of the problems associated with accounting for stock market listings, see Stijn Claessens, Daniela Klingebiel, and Sergio L. Schmukler, "Explaining the Migration of Stocks from Exchanges in Emerging Economies to International Centers," World Bank Working Paper 2816 (Washington, DC: World Bank, 2002), 8. A certain degree of limited comparisons are possible, depending on the problem explored. However, the comparisons are not possible across a large number of countries.

10. World Bank, *World Development Indicators, 1999* (Washington, DC: World Bank, 1999), 277.

11. Francis N. Botchway, "Privatization and State Control: The Case of Ashanti Goldfields Company," unpublished manuscript.

12. Itzhak Goldberg, Gregory Jedrzejczak, and Michael Fuchs, "The IPO-Plus: A New Approach to Privatization," World Bank Working Paper 1821 (Washington, DC: World Bank, 1997).

13. Enrico C. Perotti and Serhat E. Guney, "The Structure of Privatization Plans," *Financial Management* 22 (Spring 1993): 84–98.

14. Enrico C. Perotti and Serhat E. Guney, "The Structure of Privatization Plans," (Graduate School of Management and Department of Economics, Boston University, photocopy). 10.

15. OECD, *Financial Market Trends*, no. 60, 21.

16. Some would argue that when the French state has retained a majority or controlling interest, it seeks a graduated approach, more than a desire to maintain itself as the major shareholder in competitive sectors. That is, the state seeks to take into account the social, political, and stock market context. This view is evidenced by France Telecom's floating of a second block of capital in November 1998. See OECD, *Economic Surveys, 1999 France* (Paris: OECD), 75.

17. World Bank, *World Development Report 1996: From Plan to Market* (New York: Oxford University Press, 1996), 56.

18. Eva Thiel Blommestein, "The Development of Securities Markets in Transition Economies—Policy Issues and Country Experience," in OECD, *Corporate Governance, State-Owned Enterprises and Privatization* (Paris: OECD, 1998), 18.

19. T. Jenkinson, "Corporate Governance and Privatisation Via Initial Public Offering (IPO)," in OECD, *Corporate Governance, State-Owned Enterprises and Privatization* (Paris: OECD, 1998).

20. International Finance Corporation, *Privatization*, 28.

21. See I. Domowitz, J. Glen, and A. Madhavan, "International Cross-Listing and Order Flow Migration: Evidence from an Emerging Market," *Journal of Finance* 53 (1998): 2001–2027.

22. Botchway, "Privatization and State Control."

23. See Rafael La Porta, Florencio Lopez-de-Silanes, and Andrei Shleifer, "Corporate Ownership Around the World," *Journal of Finance* 54 (April 1999): 471–517.

24. For an elaboration of the concept of controlling-minority structures in corporate governance, see Lucian Arye Bebchuk, Reinier Kraakman, and George G. Triantis, "Stock Pyramids, Cross-Ownership, and Dual Class Equity: The Mechanisms and Agency Costs of Separating Control from Cash-Flow Rights," in *Concentrated Corporate Ownership*, ed. Randall K. Morck (Chicago: University of Chicago Press, 2000).

25. Ibid., 298.

26. Ibid., 299.

27. Ibid., 316.

28. Boniface Ahunwan, "Corporate Governance in Nigeria," *Journal of Business Ethics* 37 (2002): 276.

29. See Enrique Loredo and Eugenia Suarez, "Privatisation and Deregulation; Corporate Governance Consequences in a Global Economy," *Corporate Governance* 8 (January 2000), 65–74.

*Chapter 6*

1. Alejandro Lopez-Mejia, "Large Capital Flows: Causes, Consequences, and Policy Responses," *Finance and Development*, September 1999, 28.

2. For examples of the literature on this debate, see J. Gallagher and R. Robinson, "The Imperialism of Free Trade," *Economic History Review, Second Series VI* (1953): 8; D. C. M. Platt, *Finance, Trade and Politics in British Foreign Policy* (Oxford: Clarendon Press, 1968); P. J. Cain and A. G. Hopkins, *British Imperialism: Innovation and Expansion, 1688–1914* (New York: Longman, 1993), 276.

3. Irving Stone, *The Composition and Distribution of British Investment in Latin America, 1865 to 1913* (New York: Garland Publishing, 1987), 197.

4. Cain and Hopkins, *Innovation and Expansion*.

5. Anil Hira, *Ideas and Economic Policy in Latin America* (Westport, CT: Praeger, 1998), 36.

6. Ibid., 40.

7. David K. Eiteman, *Stock Exchanges in Latin America*, Michigan International Business Studies no. 7 (Ann Arbor: University of Michigan Press, 1966).

8. Anne Hanley, "Business Finance and the Sao Paulo Bolsa, 1886–1917," in *Latin America and the World Economy Since 1800*, eds. John H. Coatsworth and Alan M. Taylor, 117 (Cambridge, MA: Harvard University Press, 1998).

9. Ibid., 119.

10. Ibid., 120.

11. Ibid., 122.

12. Brian Lorin Sudweeks, *Equity Market Development in Developing Countries* (New York: Praeger, 1989), 114.

13. Leslie Elliott Armijo and Walter L. Ness Jr., "Modernizing Brazil's Capital Markets,

1985–2001: Pragmatism and Democratic Adjustment" (paper presented at the annual meeting of the International Studies Association, New Orleans, LA, March 2002), 2.

14. Pankaj Ghemawat, "Note on Privatization in Brazil," Harvard Business School Case 9-799-025, rev. 29 (September 1998), 2.

15. Ibid.

16. Armijo and Ness, "Modernizing Brazil's Capital Markets," 9.

17. New York Stock Exchange, available at www.nyse.com.

18. Ghemawat, "Privatization in Brazil," 7.

19. James Bruce, "Petrobras Latest Victim of Brazil's Debt Crisis," *Journal of Commerce*, August 28, 1987.

20. Ghemawat, "Privatization in Brazil," 7.

21. George Hawrylyshyn, "Dress Rehearsal Towards Flexibility," *Lloyd's List*, October 19, 1994.

22. Jonathan Wheatley, "Everyone a Winner as Monopoly Ends" *Financial Times* (London), May 26, 1998.

23. James Bruce, "Petroquisa Stock Sale Announced in Brazil," *Journal of Commerce*, November 27, 1989.

24. Edward Luce, "Petrobras Offering Seen by October," *Financial Times* (London), June 11, 1998.

25. Petrobras, *Annual Report of Petrobras*, 2001.

26. Flavio M. Rabelo and Flavio C. Vasconcelos, "Corporate Governance in Brazil," *Journal of Business Ethics* 37 (2002): 330.

27. Ibid., 326.

28. Ibid., 327.

29. Ibid., 328.

30. Tony Smith, "Stoking a Stock Market 'Revolution'," *New York Times*, July 30, 2002.

31. Alejandra Herrera, "The Privatization of Telecommunications Services: The Case of Argentina," *Columbia Journal of World Business* 1 (Spring 1993): 48.

32. Eiteman, *Stock Exchanges in Latin America*.

33. Eduardo Tapia, "Argentina," in *The World's Emerging Stock Markets: Structure, Developments, Regulations and Opportunities*, eds. Keith Park and Antoine Van Agtmael, 321–343 (Chicago: Probus Publishing, 1993).

34. Guillermo Harteneck and Brian McMahon, "Privatisation in Argentina," in *Privatisation in Asia, Europe and Latin America* (Paris: OECD, 1996), 67–85.

35. Willis Emmons, "ENTel and the Privatization of Argentine Telecommunications," Harvard Business School Case 796-065, rev. 29 (April 3, 1996), 3.

36. Ibid., 4.

37. The split was intended to foster competition. However, the only way a customer could switch services was to move to the other region.

38. Javier Corrales, "Coalitions and Corporate Choices in Argentina," *Studies in Comparative International Development* 32 (Winter 1998): 30.

39. Emmons, "ENTel," 6.

40. At the time, the government of Spain owned 40% of the shares of Telefonica of Spain.

41. Each of the consortiums had at least one telephone company, an Argentine financial conglomerate, and a U.S. bank. In both cases, the U.S. banks were one of Argentina's principal foreign creditors. See Herrera, "Privatization of Telecommunications Services," 49.

42. Corrales, "Coalitions and Corporate Choices," 30.

43. Emmons, "ENTel," 10.

44. Emma Daly, "Argentina Devalues, and the Spanish Feel the Loss," *New York Times*, January 8, 2002.

45. Rololfo Apreda, "Corporate Governance in Argentina: The Outcome of Economic Freedom," *Corporate Governance* 9 (October 2001): 299.

46. Ibid., 302.

47. Ibid., 307.

48. Jennifer L. Rich, "Argentine Stock Exchange is Re-opened," *New York Times*, January 18, 2002.

49. Eduardo Silva, "Business Elites and the State in Chile," in *Business and the State in Developing Countries*, eds. Sylvia Maxfield and Ben Ross Schneider, 152–188 (Ithaca, NY: Cornell University Press, 1997).

50. Cristian Larroulet Vignau, "Privatization in Chile," in *Privatization: A Global Perspective*, ed. V. V. Ramanadham, 233–253 (New York: Routledge, 1993).

51. Eiteman, *Stock Exchanges in Latin America*.

52. Tomislav Mandakovic and Marcos Lima, "Privatization in Chile: Management Effectiveness Analysis," in *Privatization and Deregulation in Global Perspective*, eds. Dennis J. Gayle and Jonathan N. Goodrich, 177–197 (New York: Quorum Books, 1990).

53. Vignau, "Privatization in Chile," 242–243.

54. Raul E. Saez, "Financial Aspects of Privatization in Chile," in *Privatisation in Asia, Europe and Latin America* (Paris: OECD, 1996), 181.

55. Ibid., 177.

56. "Chilean Telephones Stake for Bond Group," *Latin American Markets*, January 15, 1988.

57. Leslie Crawford, "Santiago's High-Flyers Turn to Wall Street," *Financial Times* (London), July 3, 1990.

58. T. Khanna and K. Palepu, "The Right Way to Restructure Conglomerates in Emerging Markets," *Harvard Business Review* 77 (July–August 1999): 127.

59. Damian Fraser, "Mexico Succeeds in a Fair Exchange," *Financial Times* (London), May 17, 1991.

60. Bryan W. Husted and Carlos Serrano, "Corporate Governance in Mexico," *Journal of Business Ethics* 37 (2002): 337.

61. Miguel Hakim, *The Efficiency of the Mexican Stock Market* (New York: Garland Publishing, 1992).

62. Mark Eric Williams, "Market Reforms, Technocrats, and Institutional Innovation," *World Development* 30 (2002): 395–412.

63. Larry Rohter, "Mexico Set to Sell its Phone Unit," *New York Times*, September 19, 1989.

64. Fraser, "Mexico Succeeds." Control of the shares remained with the workers union. In addition, other incentives compelled acceptance, such as the guarantee that jobs would not be lost despite management's desire to cut them. The treatment of the telecommunications workers union contrasted sharply with Salinas's treatment of some of the other unions involved in privatizations during this period. See Judith Clifton, *The Politics of Telecommunications in Mexico* (New York: St. Martin's Press, 2000).

65. Rohter, "Mexico Set."

66. "Telmex Privatisation Headaches," *Latin American Markets*, February 9, 1990.

67. Clifton, *Telecommunications in Mexico*, 161.

68. Fraser, "Mexico Succeeds."

69. Husted and Serrano, "Corporate Governance," 343.

70. Clifton, *Telecommunications in Mexico*, 148.

71. Tony Smith, "Brazilian Oil Company Twists in Political Wind," *New York Times*, October 2, 2002.

72. Corrales, "Coalitions and Corporate Choices."

73. Leslie Elliott Armijo and Philippe Faucher, "We Have a Consensus: Explaining Political Support for Market Reforms in Latin America," *Latin American Politics and Society* 44 (Summer 2002): 1–40.

## Chapter 7

1. John R. Niepold, "Indonesia," in *The World's Emerging Stock Markets: Structure, Developments, Regulations and Opportunities*, eds. Keith Park and Antoine Van Agtmael, 161–180 (Chicago: Probus Publishing, 1993).

2. Raymond W. Goldsmith, *The Financial Development of Japan, 1868–1977* (New Haven, CT: Yale University Press, 1983).

3. Karl P. Sauvant, *G-77: Evolution, Structure, Organization* (New York: Oceana, 1981), 37.

4. P. J. Cain and A. G. Hopkins, *British Imperialism: Innovation and Expansion, 1688–1914* (New York: Longman, 1993), 338.

5. See Atul Kohli, *The State and Poverty in India: The Politics of Reform* (Cambridge: Cambridge University Press, 1987). See also Lloyd I. Rudolph and Susanne Hoeber Rudolph, *In Pursuit of Lakshmi: The Political Economy of the Indian State* (Chicago: University of Chicago Press, 1987).

6. Radhe Shyam Rungta, *The Rise of Business Corporations in India, 1851–1900* (London: Cambridge University Press, 1970), 36.

7. Ibid., 45.

8. Ibid., 68.

9. C. K. Hobson, *The Export of Capital* (New York: MacMillan, 1914), 135.

10. Rungta, *Rise of Business Corporations*, 211.

11. Blair B. Kling, "The Origin of the Managing Agency System in India," *Journal of Asian Studies* 26 (November 1966): 37–47.

12. Neil Charlesworth, *British Rule and the Indian Economy, 1800–1914* (London: MacMillan, 1982).

13. Ananya Mukherjee Reed, "Corporate Governance Reforms in India," *Journal of Business Ethics* 37 (2002): 253.

14. Lucian Arye Bebchuk, Reinier Kraakman, and George G. Triantis, "Stock Pyramids, Cross-Ownership, and Dual Class Equity: The Mechanisms and Agency Costs of Separating Control from Cash-Flow Rights," in *Concentrated Corporate Ownership*, ed. Randall K. Morck, 299 (Chicago: University of Chicago Press).

15. Reed, "Corporate Governance Reforms in India," 256.

16. Ibid., 254.

17. See Atsi Tarun Sheth, *Emerging Market, Emerging Contradictions: The Politics of Economic Liberalization in India*, Ph.D. dissertation, Northwestern University, 1997.

18. See World Bank, *India: Structural Change and Development Perspectives—Volume I* (Washington, DC: World Bank, 1985), 6–9. See also World Bank, *World Development Report, 1987* (Washington, DC: World Bank, 1987), 122.

19. John Echeverri-Gent, "India: Financial Globalization, Liberal Norms, and the Ambiguities of Democracy," in *Financial Globalization and Democracy in Emerging Markets*, ed. Leslie Elliott Armijo, 213–214 (New York: St. Martin's Press, 1999).

20. Ibid., 216.

21. John Echeverri-Gent, "Economic Governance Regimes and the Reform of India's

Stock Exchanges," paper presented to the International Political Science World Congress, Quebec City, August 2000, Special Session 97, 18.

22. Rakesh Joshi, "Indians First," *Business India*, August 6, 2001.

23. D. K. Fieldhouse, *Unilever Overseas: The Anatomy of a Multinational: 1895–1965* (Stanford, CA: Hoover Institution Press, 1978).

24. Ibid., 167.

25. Ibid., 174.

26. Ibid., 186.

27. Ibid., 200.

28. Ibid., 204.

29. "Decks Cleared for Complete Privatisation of Modern Food," *Global News Wire* Indian Express, February 20, 2002.

30. Reed, "Corporate Governance Reforms in India," 257.

31. Ibid., 257.

32. Baldave Singh, "Faster Privatization for IPCL," *Chemicalweek Asia* 3 (April 15, 1998), 1.

33. Saritha Rai, "Big Flood of Offerings Stirs Hopes in India," *New York Times*, July 3, 2002.

34. Josey Puliyenthuruthel, "India Picks Winners in Privatization Deals," *Daily Deal*, February 5, 2002.

35. Josey Puliyenthuruthel, "Tata Group, New Delhi End Dispute," *Daily Deal*, June 12, 2002.

36. Saritha Rai, "India Hopes Sale of Assets Raises $3.5 Billion," *New York Times*, March 5, 2004. See also Saritha Rai, "As India's Economy Rises, So Do Expectations," *New York Times*, January 30, 2004.

37. See S. Vaidya Nathan, "Grey Areas in Takeover Code," *Hindu Business Line*, April 21, 2002, and S. Vaidya Nathan, "Takeover Code—Straighten out the Global Angle," *Hindu Business Line*, November 5, 2000.

38. Bruce Cumings, "The Origins and Development of the Northeast Asian Political Economy: Industrial Sectors, Product Cycles, and Political Consequences," *International Organization* 38 (1984): 1–40; Bruce Cumings, *The Origins of the Korean War: Volume II, The Roaring of the Cataract, 1947–1950* (Princeton, NJ: Princeton University Press, 1990).

39. David Gill, "Two Decades of Change in Emerging Markets," in *The World's Emerging Stock Markets: Structure, Developments, Regulations and Opportunities*, eds. Keith Park and Antoine Van Agtmael, 47–56 (Chicago: Probus Publishing, 1993).

40. Hasung Jang and Joongi Kim, "Nascent Stages of Corporate Governance in an Emerging Market: Regulatory Change, Shareholder Activism and Samsung Electronics," *Corporate Governance* 10 (April 2002): 96.

41. Keith K. H. Park, "Growing Pains of the Korean Equity Market," in *The World's Emerging Stock Markets: Structure, Developments, Regulations and Opportunities*, eds. Keith K. H. Park and Antoine Van Agtmael, 483–497 (Chicago: Probus Publishing, 1993).

42. Jung-eun Woo, *Race to the Swift* (New York: Columbia University Press, 1991).

43. The Korea International Trust invested 80% of its portfolio in the equities of 39 companies, including 16.5% electronics, 17.5% construction, 10% finance, 11% trading houses, 8% chemicals, and 6% textiles. The Korea Trust put its money into construction companies, machinery and equipment manufacturers, petrochemicals, and wholesaling. See Ann Charters, "South Korea Sells Equities Abroad," *Financial Times* (London), April 16, 1982; Y. D. Euh and J. C. Baker, *The Korean Banking System and Foreign Influence* (New York: Routledge, 1990).

44. D. Medland, "Useful Ways to Bring in Foreign Currency," *Financial Times* (London), October 21, 1987.

45. Nicholas Bratt, Scudder Kemper Investments, interview with the author, September 30, 1998.

46. See Kathryn C. Lavelle, "The International Finance Corporation and the Emerging Market Funds Industry," *Third World Quarterly* 21 (2000): 193–213.

47. Park, "Growing Pains," 491.

48. Ibid., 484.

49. Chol Lee, "Globalization of a Korean Firm: The Case of Samsung," in *Corporate Strategies in the Pacific Rim: Global Versus Regional Trends*, ed. Denis Fred Simon, 251 (New York: Routledge, 1995).

50. See Chul-Kyu Kang, "Diversification Process and the Ownership Structure of Samsung Chaebol," in *Beyond the Firm: Business Groups in International and Historical Perspective*, eds. Takao Shiba and Masahiro Shimotani, 31–58 (New York: Oxford University Press, 1997).

51. Don Kirk, "Profits at Samsung Electronics Rise but Disappoint Investors," *New York Times*, January 17, 2003.

52. When the Koreans delivered the gold, the price of gold on world markets declined to record lows. See Michael Lewis, "Going Out of Business Sale," *New York Times Magazine*, May 31, 1998.

53. Jang and Kim, "Nascent Stages," 96.

54. Ibid., 97.

55. Lewis, "Going Out of Business Sale," 64.

56. Jang and Kim, "Nascent Stages," 98.

57. Francis Fernandez, "Samsung Unit Working on an IPO," *Business Times* (Malaysia), November 7, 2000.

58. Jang and Kim, "Nascent Stages," 95.

59. T. Khanna and K Palepu, "The Right Way to Restructure Conglomerates in Emerging Markets," *Harvard Business Review* 77 (July–August 1999): 127.

60. Jang and Kim, "Nascent Stages," 99.

61. Lewis, "Going Out of Business Sale," 40.

62. Ibid., 41.

63. Jane Fuller, "Push Toward Clear, Clean Management," *Financial Times* (London), October 19, 2000.

64. Margaret M. Pearson, *Joint Ventures in the People's Republic of China: The Control of Foreign Direct Investment Under Socialism* (Princeton, NJ: Princeton University Press, 1991).

65. See Ellen Hertz, *The Trading Crowd: An Ethnography of the Shanghai Stock Market* (Cambridge: Cambridge University Press, 1998). See also Elisabeth Koll, *From Cotton Mill to Business Empire: The Emergence of Regional Enterprises in Modern China* (Cambridge, MA: Harvard University Press, 2004).

66. W. A. Thomas, *Western Capitalism in China* (Burlington, VT: Ashgate, 2001).

67. Ibid., 86.

68. Ibid., 88.

69. Ibid., 90.

70. Ibid., 107.

71. Ibid., 112.

72. Ibid., 234. See also Hu Yebi, *China's Capital Market* (Hong Kong: Chinese University Press, 1993), 4.

73. Thomas, *Western Capitalism*, 247.

74. Yebi, *China's Capital Market*, 10.

75. Thomas, *Western Capitalism*, 278.

76. Yebi, *China's Capital Market*, 14.

77. Ibid., 70.

78. Ibid., 69.

79. For a detailed elaboration of the shares structure, see Chengxi Yao, *Stock Market and Futures Market in the People's Republic of China* (New York: Oxford University Press, 1998). See also Matthew C. J. Rudolph, "The Diversity of Convergence: Global Finance, Capital Control, and the Politics of Securitization in China," paper presented to the annual meeting of the International Studies Association, New Orleans, LA, March 2002. As of February 2001, domestic residents may trade B shares as well. The government's objective in allowing this change was to utilize the growing private foreign exchange savings in the country.

80. "Fools in Need of Institutions," *Economist*, June 30, 2001.

81. Jerry White, Steve Foerster, and Andrew Karolyi, "Huaneng Power International Inc. Raising Capital in Global Markets," Richard Ivey School of Business, University of Western Ontario, 9A98N001 (1998), 6.

82. The global issue would consist of a foreign class of shares in HPI for sale only outside of China to non-Chinese citizens. The new issue would only represent 25% of the company. See White, Foerster, and Karolyi, "Huaneng Power," 7.

83. Ibid.

84. Ibid., 5.

85. Ibid., 9.

86. The alternative would have been to list under Rule 144A and not be subject to the reporting requirements. However, this type of listing would have limited the individuals who could invest to qualified institutional buyers (QIBs). Other Chinese firms have considered this less expensive option. See White, Foerster, and Karolyi, "Huaneng Power," 12.

87. Andrew G. Walder, "Corporate Organization and Local Government Property Rights in China," in *Changing Political Economies: Privatization in Post-Communist and Reforming Communist States*, ed. Vedat Milor, 53–66 (Boulder, CO: Lynne Rienner, 1994).

88. Yebi, *China's Capital Market*, 4.

89. On Kit Tam, "Ethical Issues in the Evolution of Corporate Governance in China," *Journal of Business Ethics* 37 (2002): 305.

90. Chris Buckley, "China's Main Stock Market Opens to Foreigners," *New York Times*, July 10, 2003.

91. Tam, "Ethical Issues," 307.

92. Ibid., 310.

93. Ibid. See also Hertz, *Trading Crowd*, 55.

94. See Tam, "Ethical Issues," 312.

95. See Richard Doner and Daniel Unger, "The Politics of Finance in Thai Economic Development," in *The Politics of Finance in Developing Countries*, eds. Stephan Haggard, Chung H. Lee, and Sylvia Maxfield, 93–122 (Ithaca, NY: Cornell University Press, 1993).

96. Richard F. Doner and Ansil Ramsay, "Competitive Clientelism and Economic Governance: The Case of Thailand," in *Business and the State in Developing Countries*, eds. Sylvia Maxfield and Ben Ross Schneider, 237–276 (Ithaca, NY: Cornell University Press, 1997).

97. Ibid., 240.

98. Ibid., 263.

99. Gordon Walker and Mark Fox, "Corporate Governance Reform in East Asia," *Corporate Governance* 2 (2002): 7.

100. See Stijn Claessens, Simeon Djankov, and Larry H. P. Lang, "Corporate Ownership and Valuation: Evidence from East Asia," in *Financial Markets and Development: The Crisis in Emerging Markets*, eds. Alison Harwood, Robert E. Litan, and Michael Pomerleano, 159–178 (Washington, DC: Brookings Institution Press, 1999), and Kenneth E. Scott, "Corporate Governance and East Asia: Korea, Indonesia, Malaysia, and Thailand," in *Financial Markets and Development: The Crisis in Emerging Markets*, eds. Alison Harwood, Robert E. Litan, and Michael Pomerleano, 356 (Washington, DC: Brookings Institution Press, 1999).

101. "Southeast Asia in Focus: Features of the Thai Private Sector and Characteristics of Thai Companies," *Connector Asia*, April 15, 2001.

102. Saravuth Pitiyasak, "Corporate Governance in Family Controlled Companies: A Comparative Study between Hong Kong and Thailand," *Thailand Law Forum*, http://members.tripod.com/asialaw/articles/governance.html (accessed March 19, 2003).

103. Manimai Vudthitornetiraks, "The Privatisation Experience in Thailand," in *Privatisation in Asia, Europe and Latin America* (Paris: OECD, 1996), 92.

104. Ted Bardacke, "Trading Starts on Thailand's OTC Market," *Financial Times* (London), November 15, 1995.

105. Pasuk Phongpaichit and Chris Baker, *Thailand: Economy and Politics* (New York: Oxford University Press, 1995), 158–159.

106. Ibid., 167.

107. "The End of the Asian Miracle," *Inside Asia*, no. 53, April–June 1998, http://www.insideindonesia.org/edit54/walden.htm (accessed March 19, 2003).

108. Nicholas D. Kristof and David Sanger, "How US Wooed Asia to Let Cash Flow In," *New York Times*, February 16, 1999.

109. Victor Mallet, "Bangkok Land Valued at Dollars 3.6bn in Stock Exchange Debut," *Financial Times* (London), February 6, 1992.

110. Pete Engardio and Robert Horn, "An Embarrassment of Scandals—Even for Thailand," *Business Week*, September 2, 1996.

111. Amy Louise Kazmin, "Thailand Tries to Polish Up Its Act," *Financial Times* (London), July 3, 2000.

112. These types of offerings in the United States are significantly less liquid than a listing on a major exchange.

113. Kochakorn Boonlai, "Stock Market: State Firm IPOs No Cure-all: Trading Liquidity Will Be Key to Success," Global News Wire, *Bangkok Post*, April 14, 2001.

114. Victor Mallet and William Barnets, "Thai State Sell-offs Prove to be a Half-hearted Business," *Financial Times* (London), October 12, 1994.

115. Alan Boyd, "Thai Privatisation Back on Track with New Listing Plans," *Business Times* (Singapore), July 6, 1993.

116. Ted Bardacke, "Thais Scale Down Airline Sell-Off," *Financial Times* (London), June 10, 1998.

117. Maria Cheng and Julian Gearing, "Slow-Motion Reform: Why Bangkok's Delay in Selling Part of Thai Airways is Bad News," *Asiaweek.com* 26 (30), August 4, 2000.

118. Vudthitornetiraks, "Privatisation Experience in Thailand," 89.

119. See Investor Relations Asia—The Stock Exchange of Thailand, "Working Group Join Forces to Revive Thai Capital Market," http://203.194.162.10/regbod/th/set/press/p010331.htm (accessed March 19, 2003).

*Chapter 8*

1. Peter Dittus, "Why East European Banks Don't Want Equity," *European Economic Review* 40 (April 1996): 655–662.

2. William L. Blackwell, *The Beginnings of Russian Industrialization: 1800–1860* (Princeton, NJ: Princeton University Press, 1968), 72.

3. Paul R. Gregory, *Before Command: An Economic History of Russia from Emancipation to the First Five-Year Plan* (Princeton, NJ: Princeton University Press, 1994), 82. See also Alexander Gerschenkron, *Europe in the Russian Mirror* (Cambridge: Cambridge University Press, 1970).

4. David F. Good, *The Economic Rise of the Habsburg Empire, 1750–1914* (University of California Press, 1984), 164.

5. Richard L. Rudolph, *Banking and Industrialization in Austria-Hungary* (New York: Cambridge University Press, 1976), 77.

6. Linda M. Randall, *Reluctant Capitalists: Russia's Journey Through Market Transition* (New York: Routledge, 2000), 67.

7. David Stark, "Path Dependence and Privatization Strategies in East-Central Europe," in *Changing Political Economies: Privatization in Post-Communist and Reforming Communist States*, ed. Vedat Milor, 130 (Boulder, CO: Lynne Rienner, 1994).

8. Tony Porter, "The Budapest Stock Exchange and the Global Political Economy," paper presented at the annual meeting of the International Studies Association, New Orleans, LA, March 27, 2002.

9. See "UK Consultants Win Contract to Advise Budapest Stock Exchange," *MTI Hungarian News Agency*, December 10, 1990. See also Stephen Aris, "Making Eastern Yuppies," *Sunday Telegraph*, May 26, 1991.

10. Paul Neuburg, "Hungary Goes for Hard Sell in Privatisation," *Sunday Times*, May 20, 1990.

11. Stark, "Path Dependence," 132–133.

12. Porter, "Budapest Stock Exchange," 4.

13. Ibid., 5.

14. Kalman Meszaros, "Evolution of the Hungarian Capital Market," in *Privatization in the Transition to a Market Economy*, eds. John S. Earle, Roman Frydman, and Andrzej Rapaczynski, 193 (New York: St. Martin's Press, 1993).

15. John Marino, "Hotel Sale Epitomizes Hungary's Sometimes Painful Privatization," *Mergers and Acquisitions Report* 5 (June 22, 1992): 14.

16. "The Long Slumber—Share Trading is Non-existent on the Budapest Stock Exchange which Has Failed to Live up to High Expectations," *Banker* 143 (July 1, 1993).

17. Nicholas Denton, "The Painful Road to Privatisation," *Financial Times* (London), 5 November 1991.

18. "Ibusz Group Profits Down 51% in 2001," *Hungarian News Agency*, February 14, 2002.

19. Porter, "Budapest Stock Exchange," 11.

20. Ibid., 10.

21. "Restructuring, Privatisation and Financial Deepening (Part 1 of 2)," *EBRD Transition Report* (October 1994): 49.

22. "Getting Hostile," *Economist*, May 22, 1999.

23. Joseph Rothschild, *East Central Europe Between the Two World Wars* (Seattle: University of Washington Press, 1974), 69.

24. Jan Szomburg, "The Decision-Making Structure of Polish Privatization," in *Pri-*

*vatization in the Transition to a Market Economy*, eds. John S. Earle, Roman Frydman, and Andrzej Rapaczynski (New York: St. Martin's Press, 1993), 78.

25. Stark, "Path Dependence," 128. See also Szomburg, "The Decision-Making Structure," 77.

26. Izabela Koladkiewicz, "Building of a Corporate Governance System in Poland: Initial Experiences," *Corporate Governance* 9 (July 2001): 233.

27. Chris Mallin and Ranko Jelic, "Developments in Corporate Governance in Central and Eastern Europe," *Corporate Governance* 8 (January 2000): 46.

28. The first Warsaw Stock Exchange opened in 1817. It closed in 1939.

29. Anthony Levitas, "Privatization in Poland," in *Changing Political Economies: Privatization in Post-Communist and Reforming Communist States*, ed. Vedat Milor, 108 (Boulder, CO: Lynne Rienner, 1994).

30. Robert Patterson, "Poland: Out with the Body Builders," *Banker* 146 (May 1, 1996).

31. Colin Jones, "In Foreign Hands," *Banker* 149 (November 1, 1999).

32. The discussion of the Szczecin Shipyard relies heavily on David T. Kotchen, "The Szczecin Shipyard: State Enterprise Restructuring in Poland," Harvard Business School Case Study 9-693-089, July 8, 1997.

33. Ibid., 13.

34. Ibid.

35. Christopher Bobinski, "Polish Row Over Shipyard Selloff," *Financial Times* (London), May 25, 1993.

36. "Shipyard Continues Diversification," *Finance East Europe* (September 9, 1994).

37. Christopher Bobinski and Anthony Robinson, "Polish Shipyards Seek to Chart More Hopeful Courses," *Financial Times* (London), March 27, 1997.

38. Robert Wylot, "Renationalization Project Popular Across Party Lines," *Warsaw Business Journal*, May 20, 2002. See also Ian Fisher, "As Poland Endures Hard Times, Capitalism Comes Under Attack," *New York Times*, June 12, 2002.

39. The classification of the Russian equities market is borrowed from Timothy Frye, *Brokers and Bureaucrats: Building Market Institutions in Russia* (Ann Arbor, MI: University of Michigan Press, 2000).

40. The RTS is a computerized, screen-based trading system similar to the NASDAQ or SEAQ.

41. Frye, *Brokers and Bureaucrats*, 125.

42. Gregory, *Before Command*, 88.

43. See Merle Fainsod, *How Russia is Ruled* (Cambridge, MA: Harvard University Press, 1953).

44. For a discussion of spontaneous privatization, see Simon Johnson, Heidi Kroll, and Santiago Eder, "Strategy, Structure, and Spontaneous Privatization in Russia and Ukraine," in *Changing Political Economies: Privatization in Post-Communist and Reforming Communist States*, ed. Vedat Milor, 147 (Boulder, CO: Lynne Rienner, 1993).

45. Trevor Buck, Igor Filatotchev, and Mike Wright, "Agents, Stakeholders and Corporate Governance in Russian Firms," *Journal of Management Studies* 35 (January 1998): 90.

46. *EBRD Transition Report*, 49.

47. Itzhak Goldberg, Gregory Jedrzejczak, and Michael Fuchs, "A New Approach to Privatization: The 'IPO Plus,'" World Bank Working Paper 1821 (Washington, DC: World Bank).

48. See Hilary Appel, "Voucher Privatisation in Russia: Structural Consequences and Mass Response in the Second Period of Reform," *Europe-Asia Studies* 49 (1997): 1433–1449.

49. Randall, *Reluctant Capitalists*, 76–77.

50. World Bank, *World Development Report 1996: From Plan to Market* (New York: Oxford University Press, 1996), 56.

51. Randall, *Reluctant Capitalists*, 82.

52. Sabrina Tavernise, "Russia Says it Won't Seek Origins of Elite's Wealth," *New York Times*, July 18, 2003. The government later announced plans to review the entire privatization process; however, Vladimir Putin stated that he would not reverse any sales. See Mara D. Bellaby, "Russia Plans Review of Privatization Deals," *Plain Dealer* (Cleveland), December 23, 2003.

53. Babaev quoted in Harold F. Hogan, "The Cherkizovsky Group," Harvard Business School Case 9-399-119, October 20, 1999.

54. Ibid.

55. Interviews and Opinions, "Cherkizovsky Plans to Raise $150 mil through IPO," *Prime-Tass.com*, http://www.prime-tass.com/news/65/opened/2003/324129.asp (accessed November 5, 2003).

56. Fianna Jesover, "Corporate Governance in the Russian Federation: The Relevance of the OECD Principles on Shareholder Rights and Equitable Treatment," *Corporate Governance* 9 (April 2001): 80.

57. Ibid., 85. Frye takes a more sanguine view of the share registration process, arguing that it was often exaggerated in the press. See Frye, *Brokers and Bureaucrats*, 139.

58. Randall, *Reluctant Capitalists*, 78.

59. Buck, Filatotchev, and Wright, "Agents, Stakeholders and Corporate Governance," 98.

60. A second exchange opened in Bratislava, to serve the Slovak transition after the "velvet divorce" between the Czech and Slovak republics.

61. Stark, "Path Dependence," 125.

62. Ibid., 126–127. See also Hilary Appel, "The Ideological Determinants of Liberal Economic Reform: The Case of Privatization," *World Politics* 52 (July 2000): 520–549.

63. Ariane Genillard, "Czechoslovaks Queue To Cash in on Capitalism," *Financial Times* (London), January 29, 1992.

64. Francine Kiefer, "Czechoslovakians Buy Capitalism," *Christian Science Monitor*, March 4, 1992.

65. "East European Privatisation: Making it Work," *Economist*, March 13, 1993.

66. Vincent Boland, "Czech Privatisation Pioneer Seeks Peace," *Financial Times* (London), April 3, 1995.

67. Gretchen Morgenson, "Seller of Privatization Securities Is Indicted in the US," *New York Times*, October 3, 2003.

68. John Nellis, "Time to Rethink Privatization in Transition Economies?" IFC Discussion Paper 38 (Washington, DC: World Bank, 1999), 11.

69. Kristian Palda, "Czech Privatization and Corporate Governance," *Communist and Post-Communist Studies* 30 (1997): 91. *See also* Peter Kenway and Jiri Chlumsky, "The Influence of Owners on Voucher Privatized Firms in the Czech Republic," *Economics of Transition* 5 (1997): 185–193; Danes Brzica, "International Comparison of Corporate Governance and Keiretsu Structures: The Case of the Slovak Republic, the Czech Republic and Japan in the Mid-90s," *Ekonomickay Casopis* 47 (1999): 714–741.

70. Palda, "Czech Privatization," 92.

71. Ibid., 89.

72. Peter S. Green, "Rumors Roil Shaky Prague Market," *New York Times*, March 22, 2002.

*Chapter 9*

1. Jeffrey Herbst, *States and Power in Africa* (Princeton, NJ: Princeton University Press, 2000), 17.

2. D. K. Herbst, *Unilever Overseas: The Anatomy of a Multinational, 1895–1965* (Stanford, CA: Hoover Institution Press, 1978), 417.

3. Ralph A. Austen, *African Economic History: Internal Development and External Dependency* (Portsmouth, NH: Heinemann, 1987), 130.

4. Ankie Hoogvelt, *Globalization and the Postcolonial World: The New Political Economy of Development*, 2nd ed. (Baltimore: Johns Hopkins University Press, 2001), 184.

5. Eric Rosenthal, *On Change Through the Years: A History of Share Dealing in South Africa* (Cape Town: Flesch Financial Publications, 1968), 20.

6. S. Chapman, "Rhodes and the City of London: Another View of Imperialism," *Historical Journal* 28 (1985): 662.

7. See Robert Vicat Turrell, *Capital and Labour on the Kimberley Diamond Fields, 1871–1890* (New York: Cambridge University Press, 1987), 105; see also Chapman, "Rhodes and the City."

8. Nonetheless, this distribution indicates where some company promoters hoped to raise capital, and not where they did actually raise it. Shares were not taken up by the public and remained restricted to the diamond brokers and merchants of Hatton Garden. The London Stock Exchange required that 50% of the capital of a company be offered to the public to be listed, and few mining companies satisfied that rule. Although trades of shares of unquoted companies occurred from time to time, few diamond mining companies listed on the London Stock Exchange. Rather, shares traded in Hatton Garden, where diamond importers and jewelers did their business. The Hatton Garden share market was thus an outside, street market with few formalities and little protection. See Turrell, *Capital and Labour*, 106, 110.

9. Robert Vicat Turrell with Jean-Jacques Van Helten, "The Rothschilds, the Exploration Company and Mining Finance," *Business History* 23 (April 1986): 181.

10. As quoted in Rosenthal, *On Change*, 60.

11. Ibid., 134.

12. Ibid., 73.

13. P. J. Cain and A. G. Hopkins, *British Imperialism: Innovation and Expansion, 1688–1914* (New York: Longman, 1993), 373.

14. Chapman, "Rhodes and the City," and Robert Vicat Turrell, "Review Article: 'Finance . . . The Governor of the Imperial Entine': Hobson and the Case of Rothschild and Rhodes," *Journal of Southern African Studies* 13 (April 1987): 417–432. The Rhodes-Rothschild connection is complex. At first Rhodes admired Lord Rothschild, but later thought of him as "honest but without sufficient brains." By 1892 Rothschild's activities in South Africa moved into line with their traditional interest in state loans. They raised a loan in London for the Transvaal government for vital railway links. See Chapman, "Rhodes and the City," 653, 659. Rhodes was chronically short of development capital, and consequently more or less dependent on Beit, Barnato, Rothschild, and Eckstein. Eckstein was Wernher, Beit & Co.'s principal representative in Johannesburg in the 1890s.

15. R. C. Michie, *The London and New York Stock Exchanges: 1850–1914* (Boston: Allen & Unwin, 1987), 56.

16. Roger J. Southall, "South Africa," in *The Political Economy of African Foreign Policy*, eds. Timothy M. Shaw and Olajide Aluko, 221–262 (New York: St. Martin's Press, 1984).

17. "Johannesburg Stock Exchange (JSE)," *Mbendi: Information for Africa*, http://mbendi.co.za/exjs.htm (accessed May 4, 2000).

18. Bill Jamieson, "Oppenheimer Dynasty Set for a Succession," *Sunday Telegraph*, November 29, 1992.

19. Victor Mallet, "Anglo Goes Global," *Financial Times* (London), October 16, 1998.

20. See James Lamont, "Changing the Colour of Money," *Financial Times* (London), April 10, 2002.

21. Nicol Degli Innocenti and James Lamont, "Oppenheimers Buy Back Control of Family Jewels," *Financial Times* (London), May 21, 2001.

22. Jos Gerson, "Should the State Attempt to Reshape South Africa's Corporate and Financial Structures?" in *State and Market in Post Apartheid South Africa*, eds. Merle Lipton and Charles Simkins, 161–201 (Boulder, CO: Westview Press, 1993).

23. G. J. Rossouw, A. van der Watt, and D. P. Malan, "Corporate Governance in South Africa," *Journal of Business Ethics* 37 (2002): 289–302.

24. See Donald G. McNeil Jr., "South African Industrial Giant Moving to London," *New York Times*, October 16, 1998.

25. G. J. Rossouw, van der Watt, and Malan, "Corporate Governance," 293.

26. Ibid., 301.

27. Ibid.

28. Henri E. Cauvin, "A Radical Overhaul for South African Mining," *New York Times*, June 4, 2002.

29. Nicole Itano, "South African Mines in a 3-Way Deal," *New York Times*, November 14, 2003.

30. Robert L. Tignor, *State, Private Enterprise and Economic Change in Egypt, 1918–1952* (Princeton, NJ: Princeton University Press, 1984).

31. Ibid.

32. Ibid., 180.

33. Concessionaires differed from other joint-stock companies because the state conferred economic privileges on them, such as territory or exclusive markets, in their acts of incorporation; the best known of the concessions was the one granted to the Suez Canal Company in 1854 and 1856.

34. Hassan A. W. El-Hayawan and Denis J. Sullivan, "Privatization in Egypt," in *Privatization: A Global Perspective*, ed. V. V. Ramanadham, 340–341 (New York: Routledge, 1993).

35. Tony Walker, "Privatisation as a Panacea," *Financial Times* (London), April 4, 1990.

36. Tony Walker, "On the Road to Reform in Cairo's Markets," *Financial Times* (London), October 22, 1991.

37. "Privatisation Rolls With Pepsi," *Al-Ahram Weekly*, April 21, 1994.

38. James Whittington, "Egypt Inches Towards Privatization," *Financial Times* (London), May 8, 1996.

39. Mark Huband, "Choosy Investors Play Wait and See," *Financial Times* (London), March 26, 1998.

40. David Butter, "Choosing the Path to Privatization," *Middle East Economic Digest*, June 30, 1995.

41. Mark Huband, "Egyptian Groups Take the Public Road," *Financial Post* (Toronto), April 4, 1997.

42. "In Brief," *Middle East Economic Digest*, November 21, 1997.

43. Huband, "Choosy Investors."

44. Mark Huband, "Political Anxiety Stalls Egyptian IPOs," *Financial Times* (London), January 14, 1999.

45. David Mott, "Special Report on Egypt: Alexandria Shipyard is Sell-off Prize," *Lloyd's List*, August 30, 1993.

46. Dee Rissik, "Alexandria Yard a Model Privatization," *Lloyds List*, December 22, 1997.

47. "Privatization of Alexandria Shipyard Postponed," *Middle East News Items*, January 14, 1999.

48. Catherine Boone, *Merchant Capital and the Roots of State Power in Senegal, 1930–1985* (New York: Cambridge University Press, 1992), 45.

49. Ibid., 220.

50. Jean A. P. Clement with Johannes Mueller, Stephane Cosse, and Jean le Dem, "Aftermath of the CFA Franc Devaluation," IMF Occasional Paper 138 (Washington, DC: International Monetary Fund, 1996), 1.

51. Ibid., 25.

52. Don Macdonald, "Yankee Know-How, But in French," *The Gazette* (Montreal), August 1, 1998.

53. Bourse Regionale des Valeurs Mobilieres, *Revue Trimestrielle*, no. 1 (September 16, 1998–December 31, 1998). See also Bourse des Valeurs d'Abidjan, "Organisation du Marche Financier en Cote d'Ivoire," Cellule des Etudes et Statistiques (July 1996).

54. Hudson Finance, "Information on the Cote d'Ivoire Market," unpublished document, 1999.

55. Sheldon Gellar, *Senegal: An African Nation Between Islam and the West* (Boulder, CO: Westview Press, 1995), 66.

56. Ibid., 67. See also Nicholas Woodsworth, "Senegal Bows to the Shifting Sands of Monetarism" *Financial Times* (London), November 3, 1987.

57. Geller, *Senegal*, 68.

58. Sonatel, *Rapport Annuel*, Abidjan (2001), 9.

59. William Wallis, "Senegal: Second Thoughts on State Sell-Offs," *Financial Times* (London), November 13, 2000.

60. A. Coly, "Image: La Sonatel decide de mieux communiquer," *franconnex.com*, July 3, 2002. See also Stephane Foucart, "La Combattante du Web Africain," *Le Monde*, May 9, 2001.

61. William Wallis, "Second Thoughts on State Sell-offs," *Financial Times* (London), November 13, 2000.

62. August Gachter, "Finance Capital and Peasants in Colonial West Africa: A Comment on Cowen and Shenton," *Journal of Peasant Studies* 20 (July 1993): 674.

63. D. K. Fieldhouse, *Unilever Overseas: The Anatomy of a Multinational: 1895–1965* (Stanford, CA: Hoover Institution Press, 1978), 406.

64. Herbst, *States and Power*, 214.

65. Jonathan R. Magnusen, "Structural Adjustment Policies and the Evolution of a New Legal Framework for Economic Activity in Ghana," in *Emerging Financial Markets and the Role of International Financial Organizations*, eds. Joseph J. Norton and Mads Andenas, 81–114 (Boston: Kluwer Law International, 1996).

66. Matthew Martin, "Neither Phoenix Nor Icarus: Negotiating Economic Reform in Ghana and Zambia, 1983–1992," in *Hemmed In: Responses to Africa's Economic Decline*, eds. Thomas M. Callaghy and John Ravenhill, 136–137 (New York: Columbia University Press, 1993).

67. Francis N. Botchway, "Privatization and State Control: The Case of Ashanti Gold-

fields Company," manuscript, 15. See also Richard Grant, "Liberalization Policies and Foreign Companies in Accra, Ghana," *Environment and Planning* 33 (2001): 997–1014.

68. Robert McDonald, "New Stock Exchange in Ghana Helped by Toronto Consultants," *Toronto Star*, December 7, 1992.

69. Magnusen, "Structural Adjustment Policies," 107.

70. Michael Holman, "Survey of Ghana," *Financial Times*, August 4, 1995.

71. McDonald, "New Stock Exchange."

72. Botchway, "Ashanti Goldfields Company."

73. Ibid.

74. Ibid.

75. David Mckay, "AAGM: Government Veto Won't Stop Ashanti Deal," *Miningweb* (South Africa), February 12, 2002.

76. H. Kwasi Prempeh, "AAGM: The Private Sector Control and the Gross Undercapitalisation of Companies," *Financial Times Information*, February 19, 2002.

77. For a discussion of this concept with respect to privatization, see Beatrice Hibou, "Retrait ou redeploiement de l'etat?" *Critique Internationale* 1 (Autumn 1998): 151–168.

*Chapter 10*

1. Adolf A. Berle Jr. and Gardiner C. Means, *The Modern Corporation and Private Property* (New York: Macmillan, 1933).

2. Alvaro Cuervo, "Corporate Governance Mechanisms: A Plea for Less Code of Good Governance and More Market Control," *Corporate Governance* 10 (April 2002): 84–93.

3. Boniface Ahunwan, "Corporate Governance in Nigeria," *Journal of Business Ethics* 37 (2002): 269–287.

4. See Cuervo, "Corporate Governance Mechanisms."

5. Enrique Loredo and Eugenia Suarez, "Privatisation and Deregulation: Corporate Governance Consequences in a Global Economy," *Corporate Governance* 8 (January 2000): 65–74.

6. Darryl Reed, "Corporate Governance Reforms in Developing Countries," *Journal of Business Ethics* 37 (2002): 223–247.

7. See Margaret P. Karns and Karen A. Mingst, *The United States and Multilateral Institutions: Patterns of Changing Instrumentality and Influence* (Boston: Unwin Hyman, 1990.) See also Miles Kahler, *International Institutions and the Political Economy of Integration* (Washington, DC: Brookings Institution Press, 1995).

8. See Robert Gilpin, *US Power and the Multinational Corporation: The Political Economy of Foreign Direct Investment* (New York: Basic Books, 1975), and John Stopford and Susan Strange with John S. Henley, *Rival States, Rival Firms: Competition for World Market Shares* (Cambridge: Cambridge University Press, 1991).

9. See Louis W. Pauly and Simon Reich, "National Structures and Multinational Corporate Behavior: Enduring Differences in the Age of Globalization," *International Organization* 51 (Winter 1997): 1–30. See also Paul N. Doremus, William W. Keller, Louis W. Pauly, and Simon Reich, *The Myth of the Global Corporation* (Princeton, NJ: Princeton University Press, 1998); Robert Wade, "Globalization and Its Limits: Reports of the Death of the National Economy Are Greatly Exaggerated," in *National Diversity and Global Capitalism*, eds. Suzanne Berger and Ronald Dore, 60–88 (Ithaca, NY: Cornell University Press, 1996).

10. Peter Evans, *Dependent Development: The Alliance of Multinational, State, and Local Capital in Brazil* (Princeton, NJ: Princeton University Press, 1979).

11. See Tony Smith, "Latin Companies Are Bargain Hunting in Argentina," *New York Times*, July 24, 2002. See also "Petrobras Paying $1.1 Billion for Argentine Oil Company," *New York Times*, July 23, 2002.

12. Wade, "Globalization and Its Limits," 79.

13. See "Families in the Boardroom: Under the Influence," *Economist*, November 17, 2001.

14. Incidentally, many large firms in the United States remain under the control of the founding family. See Ajit Singh, *Corporate Financial Patterns in Industrializing Economies* (Washington, DC: World Bank, 1995).

15. "Germany: Golden Share Cases Examined," *New York Times*, June 21, 2002.

16. See Riva D. Atlas, "Big Board Issues Its Ideas on Corporate Governance," *New York Times*, June 7, 2002.

17. Ankie Hoogvelt, *Globalization and the Postcolonial World: The New Political Economy of Development*, 2nd ed. (Baltimore: Johns Hopkins University Press, 2001); Michael Hardt and Antonio Negri, *Empire* (Cambridge, MA: Harvard University Press, 2000).

18. Hoogvelt, *Globalization*, 184.

19. See Kathryn C. Lavelle, "Architecture of Equity Markets: The Abidjan Regional Bourse," *International Organization* 55 (Summer 2001): 717–742.

20. Frederick Cooper, "What is the Concept of Globalization Good For? An African Historian's Perspective," *African Affairs* 100 (2001): 190.

# Bibliography

Newspapers and Magazines .

*Al-Ahram Weekly*
*Bangkok Post*
*The Banker*
*Business India*
*Business Times*
*Business Week*
*Chemicalweek Asia*
*Christian Science Monitor*
*Connector Asia*
*EBRD Transition Report*
*The Economist*
*Euromoney*
*Finance and Development*
*Finance East Europe*
*Financial Post* (Toronto)
*Financial Times* (London)
*Foreign Times*
*The Gazette* (Montreal)
*Global News Wire*
*Hindu Business Line*
*Hungarian News Agency*
*Inside Asia*
*Journal of Commerce*
*Latin American Markets*
*Le Monde*
*Lloyd's List*
*Mbendi: Information for Africa*
*Middle East Economic Digest*

*Middle East News Items*
*Miningweb*
*MTI Hungarian News Agency*
*New York Times*
*Plain Dealer* (Cleveland)
*Sunday Telegraph*
*Toronto Star*
*Wall Street Journal*
*Warsaw Business Journal*


Official Sources

*Bourse Regionale des Valeurs Mobilieres*

"Organisation du Marche Financier en Cote d'Ivoire" Cellule des Etudes et Statistiques (July 1996).
*Revue Trimestrielle* no. 1 (September 16, 1998–December 31, 1998).


*IMF and World Bank*

Glen, Jack, and Brian Pinto. "Debt or Equity? How Firms in Developing Countries Choose." IFC Discussion Paper 22. Washington, DC: World Bank, 1994.

Glen, Jack D. "An Introduction to the Microstructure of Emerging Markets." IFC Discussion Paper 24. Washington, DC: World Bank, 1994.

Glen, Jack D. and Mariusz A. Sumlinski. "Trends in Private Investment in Developing Countries: Statistics for 1970–1996." IFC Discussion Paper 34. Washington, DC: World Bank, 1997.

Goldberg, Itzhak Gregory Jedrzejczak, and Michael Fuchs. "The IPO-Plus: A New Approach to Privatization." World Bank Working Paper 1821. Washington, DC: World Bank, 1997.

International Finance Corporation. *Emerging Stock Markets Factbook 1999*. Washington, DC: World Bank, 1998.

———. *Lessons of Experience: Financial Institutions*, no. 6. Washington, DC: World Bank, 1998.

———. *Privatization: Principles and Practice*. Washington, DC: World Bank, 1995.

Ito, Takatoshi and David Folkerts-Landau. *International Capital Markets: Developments, Prospects, and Key Policy Issues*. Washington, DC: International Monetary Fund, 1996.

Nellis, John. "Time to Rethink Privatization in Transition Economies?" IFC Discussion Paper 38. Washington, DC: World Bank, 1999.

Shirley, Mary and Ahmed Galal. *Bureaucrats in Business: The Economics and Politics of Government Ownership*. Washington, DC: World Bank, 1995.

World Bank. *India: Structural Change and Development Perspectives—Volume I*. Washington, DC: World Bank, 1985.

———. *Private Capital Flows to Developing Countries*. New York: Oxford University Press, 1997.

———. *World Development Indicators, 1999*. Washington, DC: World Bank, 1999.

———. *World Development Report, 1987*. Washington, DC: World Bank, 1987.

———. *World Development Report 1996: From Plan to Market*. New York: Oxford University Press, 1996.

## Non-Aligned Movement

Non-Aligned Movement ad hoc Advisory Group of Experts on Debt. "Ministerial Meeting of Non-Aligned Countries on Debt and Development: Sharing of Experiences." Jakarta, Indonesia (August 13–15, 1994).

————. *The Continuing Debt Crisis of the Developing Countries* (August 1994).

## Organization for Economic Cooperation and Development (OECD)

OECD. *Corporate Governance, State-Owned Enterprises and Privatization* (Paris: OECD, 1998).

————. *Economic Surveys, 1999 France* (Paris: OECD).

————. *Financial Market Trends: February 1995*, no. 60 (Paris: OECD).

————. *Financial Market Trends: February 1999*, no. 72 (Paris: OECD).

————. *Financial Market Trends: June 2000*, no. 76 (Paris: OECD).

————. *International Investment and Multinational Enterprises* (Paris: OECD, 1981).

*Privatisation in Asia, Europe and Latin America*, edited by OECD (Paris: OECD, 1996).

## U.S. Department of Commerce

U.S. Department of Commerce. *International Direct Investment: Global Trends and the U.S. Role* (Washington, DC: U.S. Government Printing Office, 1984).

## Books, Journal Articles, and Unpublished Manuscripts

Ahunwan, Boniface. "Corporate Governance in Nigeria." *Journal of Business Ethics* 37 (2002): 269–287.

Anderson, Terry L., and Peter J. Hill, eds. *The Privatization Process: A Worldwide Perspective*. Lanham, MD: Rowman & Littlefield, 1996.

Andrews, Kenneth R. *Trade, Plunder and Settlement: Maritime Enterprise and the Genesis of the British Empire, 1480–1630*. New York: Cambridge University Press, 1984.

Appel, Hilary. "Voucher Privatisation in Russia: Structural Consequences and Mass Response in the Second Period of Reform." *Europe-Asia Studies* 49 (1997): 1433–1449.

————. "The Ideological Determinants of Liberal Economic Reform: The Case of Privatization." *World Politics* 52 (July 2000): 520–549.

Apreda, Rololfo. "Corporate Governance in Argentina: The Outcome of Economic Freedom." *Corporate Governance* 9 (October 2001): 298–310.

Armijo, Leslie Elliott, and Philippe Faucher. "We Have a Consensus: Explaining Political Support for Market Reforms in Latin America." *Latin American Politics and Society* 44 (Summer 2002): 1–40.

Armijo, Leslie Elliott, and Walter L. Ness Jr. "Modernizing Brazil's Capital Markets, 1985–2001: Pragmatism and Democratic Adjustment." Paper presented at the annual meeting of the International Studies Association, New Orleans, LA, March 2002.

Austen, Ralph A. *African Economic History: Internal Development and External Dependency*. Portsmouth, NH: Heinemann, 1987.

Bebchuk, Lucian Arye, Reinier Kraakman, and George G. Triantis. "Stock Pyramids, Cross-Ownership, and Dual Class Equity: The Mechanisms and Agency Costs of Separating Control from Cash-Flow Rights." In *Concentrated Corporate Ownership*, edited by Randall K. Morck. Chicago: University of Chicago Press, 2000.

Bekaert, Geert. "Market Integration and Investment Barriers in Emerging Equity Markets." *World Bank Economic Review* 9 (January 1995): 75–107.

Bekaert, Geert, and Campbell R. Harvey. "Research in Emerging Markets Finance: Looking to the Future." *Emerging Markets Review* 3 (2002): 429–448.

Berger, Suzanne, and Ronald Dore, eds. *National Diversity and Global Capitalism.* Ithaca, NY: Cornell University Press, 1996.

Berle, Adolf A. Jr., and Gardiner C. Means. *The Modern Corporation and Private Property.* New York: Macmillan, 1933.

Blackwell, William L. *The Beginnings of Russian Industrialization: 1800–1860.* Princeton, NJ: Princeton University Press, 1968.

Blommestein, Eva Thiel. "The Development of Securities Markets in Transition Economies—Policy Issues and Country Experience." In OECD, *Corporate Governance, State-Owned Enterprises and Privatization.* Paris: OECD, 1998.

Boone, Catherine. *Merchant Capital and the Roots of State Power in Senegal, 1930–1985.* New York: Cambridge University Press, 1992.

Botchway, Francis N. "Privatization and State Control: The Case of Ashanti Goldfields Company" (manuscript).

Bouton, L., and M. A. Sumlinski. "Trends in Private Investment in Developing Countries: Statistics for 1970–95." IFC Discussion Paper 31, rev. ed. Washington, DC: World Bank, 1997.

Boyd, John H., and Bruce D. Smith. "The Evolution of Debt and Equity Markets in Economic Development." *Economic Theory* 12 (1998): 519–560.

Brzica, Danes. "International Comparison of Corporate Governance and Keiretsu Structures: The Case of the Slovak Republic, the Czech Republic and Japan in the Mid-90s." *Ekonomickay Casopis* 47 (1999): 714–741.

Buck, Trevor Igor Filatotchev, and Mike Wright. "Agents, Stakeholders and Corporate Governance in Russian Firms." *Journal of Management Studies* 35 (January 1998): 81–104.

Cain, P. J., and A. G. Hopkins. *British Imperialism: Innovation and Expansion, 1688–1914.* New York: Longman, 1993.

———. *British Imperialism: Crisis and Deconstruction, 1914–1990.* New York: Longman, 1993.

Calamanti, Andrea. *The Securities Market and Underdevelopment.* Milan: Giuffre, 1983.

Carruthers, Bruce G. *City of Capital: Politics and Markets in the English Financial Revolution.* Princeton, NJ: Princeton University Press, 1996.

Carter, L. W. *IFC's Experience in Promoting Emerging Market Investment Funds.* Washington, DC: World Bank, 1996.

CDA/Wiesenberger Investment Companies Service. *Investment Companies Yearbook 1998.* Rockville, MD: CDA/Wiesenberger, 1998.

Chapman, S. D. *The Rise of Merchant Banking.* Boston: Allen & Unwin, 1984.

———. "Rhodes and the City of London: Another View of Imperialism." *Historical Journal* 28 (1985): 647–666.

Charlesworth, Neil. *British Rule and the Indian Economy, 1800–1914.* London: MacMillan, 1982.

Cho, Yoon Je. "Inefficiencies from Financial Liberalization in the Absence of Well-Functioning Equity Markets." *Journal of Money, Credit and Banking* 18 (May 1986): 191–199.

Claessens, Stijn, Simeon Djankov, and Larry H. P. Lang. "Corporate Ownership and Valuation: Evidence from East Asia." In *Financial Markets and Development: The Crisis in Emerging Markets,* edited by Alison Harwood, Robert E. Litan, and Michael Pomerleano, 159–178. Washington, DC: Brookings Institution Press, 1999.

Claessens, Stijn, Daniela Klingebiel, and Sergio L. Schmukler. "Explaining the Migration of Stocks from Exchanges in Emerging Economies to International Centers." World Bank Working Paper 2816. Washington, DC: World Bank, 2002.

Clement, Jean A. P., with Johannes Mueller, Stephane Cosse, and Jean le Dem. "Aftermath of the CFA Franc Devaluation." IMF Occasional Paper 138. Washington, DC: International Monetary Fund, 1996.

Clifton, Judith. *The Politics of Telecommunications in Mexico.* New York: St. Martin's Press, 2000.

Coleman, William D., and Tony Porter. "Regulating International Banking and Securities: Emerging Co-operation among National Authorities." In *Political Economy and the Changing Global Order,* edited by Richard Stubbs and Geoffrey R. D. Underhill, 190–203. New York: St. Martin's Press, 1994.

Colling, Alfred. *La Prodigieuse Histoire de la Bourse.* Paris: Societe d'Editions Economiques et Financieres, 1949.

Cooper, Frederick. "What is the Concept of Globalization Good For? An African Historian's Perspective." *African Affairs* 100 (2001): 189–213.

Corrales, Javier. "Coalitions and Corporate Choices in Argentina." *Studies in Comparative International Development* 32(Winter 1998): 24–51.

Crisp, Olga. *Studies in the Russian Economy Before 1914.* New York: Harper & Row, 1976.

Cuervo, Alvaro. "Corporate Governance Mechanisms: A Plea for Less Code of Good Governance and More Market Control." *Corporate Governance* 10 (April 2002): 84–93.

Cumings, Bruce. "The Origins and Development of the Northeast Asian Political Economy: Industrial Sectors, Product Cycles, and Political Consequences." *International Organization* 38 (1984): 1–40.

———. *The Origins of the Korean War: Volume II, The Roaring of the Cataract, 1947–1950.* Princeton, NJ: Princeton University Press, 1990.

Cunningham, L. A. "Commonalities and Prescriptions in the Vertical Dimension of Global Corporate Governance." *Cornell Law Review* 84 (1999): 1133–1194.

Dahrendorf, Ralph. *Class and Class Conflict in Industrial Society.* Stanford, CA: Stanford University Press, 1959.

Dickie, Robert B. "Development of Third World Securities Markets: An Analysis of General Principles and a Case Study of the Indonesian Market." *Law and Policy in International Business* 13 (1981): 178–222.

Dittus, Peter. "Why East European Banks Don't Want Equity." *European Economic Review* 40 (April 1996): 655–662.

Doidge, Craig, G. Andrew Karolyi, and Rene M. Stulz. "Why Are Foreign Firms Listed in the U.S. Worth More?" National Bureau of Economic Research Working Paper 8538, October 2001, http://papers.nber.org/papers/w8538 (accessed December 19, 2003).

Domowitz, I. J. Glen, and A. Madhavan. "International Cross-Listing and Order Flow Migration: Evidence from an Emerging Market." *Journal of Finance* 53 (1998): 2001–2027.

Doner, Richard F., and Ansil Ramsay. "Competitive Clientelism and Economic Governance: The Case of Thailand." In *Business and the State in Developing Countries,* edited by Sylvia Maxfield and Ben Ross Schneider, 237–276. Ithaca, NY: Cornell University Press, 1997.

Doner, Richard and Daniel Unger. "The Politics of Finance in Thai Economic Development." In *The Politics of Finance in Developing Countries,* edited by Stephan Haggard, Chung H. Lee, and Sylvia Maxfield, 93–122. Ithaca, NY: Cornell University Press, 1993.

Doremus, Paul N. William W. Keller, Louis W. Pauly, and Simon Reich. *The Myth of the Global Corporation.* Princeton, NJ: Princeton University Press, 1998.

D'Souza, Juliet, and William L. Megginson. "The Financial and Operating Performance of Newly Privatized Firms in the 1990s." *Journal of Finance* 54 (August 1999): 1397–1438.

Dunning, John H. "Changes in the Level and Structure of International Production: The

Last One Hundred Years." In *The Growth of International Business*, edited by Mark Casson, 84–139. Boston: Allen & Unwin, 1983.

Echeverri-Gent, John. "India: Financial Globalization, Liberal Norms, and the Ambiguities of Democracy." In *Financial Globalization and Democracy in Emerging Markets*, edited by Leslie Elliott Armijo, 213–214. New York: St. Martin's Press, 1999.

———. "Economic Governance Regimes and the Reform of India's Stock Exchanges." Paper presented to the International Political Science World Congress, Quebec City, August 2000, Special Session 97.

Economist Publications. *Directory of World Stock Exchanges*. Baltimore, MD: Johns Hopkins University Press, 1988.

Eiteman, David K. *Stock Exchanges in Latin America*. Michigan International Business Studies no. 7. Ann Arbor: University of Michigan Press, 1966.

El-Hayawan, Hassan A. W., and Denis J. Sullivan. "Privatization in Egypt." In *Privatization: A Global Perspective*, edited by V. V. Ramanadham, 337–353. New York: Routledge, 1993.

Ellsworth, P. T., and J. C. Leith. *The International Economy*. New York: Macmillan, 1984.

Emmons, Willis. "ENTel and the Privatization of Argentine Telecommunications." Harvard Business School Case 796-065, rev. 29 (April 3, 1996).

Escobar, Arturo. "Power and Visibility: Development and the Invention and Management of the Third World." *Cultural Anthropology* 3 (November 1988): 428–443.

———. "Reflections on 'Development,' Grassroots Approaches and Alternative Politics in the Third World." *Futures* 24 (June 1992): 411–436.

Euh, Y. D., and J. C. Baker. *The Korean Banking System and Foreign Influence*. New York: Routledge, 1990.

Evans, Peter. *Dependent Development: The Alliance of Multinational, State, and Local Capital in Brazil*. Princeton, NJ: Princeton University Press, 1979.

Evans, Peter B., Harold K. Jacobson, and Robert D. Putnam, eds. *Double-Edged Diplomacy: International Bargaining and Domestic Politics*. Berkeley: University of California Press, 1993.

Fainsod, Merle. *How Russia is Ruled*. Cambridge, MA: Harvard University Press, 1953.

Fieldhouse, D. K. *Unilever Overseas: The Anatomy of a Multinational: 1895–1965*. Stanford, CA: Hoover Institution Press, 1978.

Flowers, Edward B. "Merging But Different, Emerging Markets Persist." In *Interlocking Global Business Systems: The Restructuring of Industries, Economies and Capital Markets*, edited by Edward B. Flowers, Thomas P. Chen, and Jonchi Shyu, 75–92. Westport, CT: Quorum Books.

Frye, Timothy. *Brokers and Bureaucrats: Building Market Institutions in Russia*. Ann Arbor, MI: University of Michigan Press, 2000.

Gachter, August. "Finance Capital and Peasants in Colonial West Africa: A Comment on Cowen and Shenton." *Journal of Peasant Studies* 20 (July 1993): 669–680.

Gallagher, J., and R. Robinson. "The Imperialism of Free Trade." *Economic History Review, Second Series* VI (1953): 8.

Geisst, Charles R. *A Guide to Financial Institutions*. New York: St. Martin's Press, 1988.

Gellar, Sheldon. *Senegal: An African Nation Between Islam and the West*. Boulder, CO: Westview Press, 1995.

Germain, Randall D. *The International Organization of Credit: States and Global Finance in the World-Economy*. Cambridge: Cambridge University Press, 1997.

Gerschenkron, Alexander. *Economic Backwardness in Historical Perspective*. Cambridge, MA: Harvard University Press, 1962.

———. *Europe in the Russian Mirror*. Cambridge: Cambridge University Press, 1970.

Gerson, Jos. "Should the State Attempt to Reshape South Africa's Corporate and Financial Structures?" In *State and Market in Post Apartheid South Africa*, edited by Merle Lipton and Charles Simkins, 161–201. Boulder, CO: Westview Press, 1993.

Ghemawat, Pankaj. "Note on Privatization in Brazil," Harvard Business School Case 9-799-025, rev. 29 (September 1998).

Giddy, Ian H. "Global Capital Markets: What Do They Mean?" In *Financial Markets and Development: The Crisis in Emerging Markets*, edited by Alison Harwood, Robert E. Litan, and Michael Pomerleano, 219–242. Washington, DC: Brookings Institution Press, 1999.

Gill, David. "Two Decades of Change in Emerging Markets." In *The World's Emerging Stock Markets: Structure, Developments, Regulations and Opportunities*, edited by Keith Park and Antoine Van Agtmael, 47–56. Chicago: Probus Publishing, 1993.

Gilpin, Robert. *US Power and the Multinational Corporation: The Political Economy of Foreign Direct Investment.* New York: Basic Books, 1975.

———. *The Political Economy of International Relations.* Princeton, NJ: Princeton University Press, 1987.

———. *War and Change in World Politics.* New York: Cambridge University Press, 1990.

Goldsmith, Raymond W. *Financial Structure and Development.* New Haven, CT: Yale University Press, 1969.

———. *The Financial Development of Japan, 1868–1977.* New Haven, CT: Yale University Press, 1983.

———. *Premodern Financial Systems: A Historical Comparative Study.* New York: Cambridge University Press, 1987.

Good, David F. *The Economic Rise of the Habsburg Empire, 1750–1914.* University of California Press, 1984.

Gordon, David F. "Debt, Conditionality and Reform: The International Relations of Economic Restructuring in Sub-Saharan Africa." In *Hemmed In: Responses to Africa's Economic Decline*, edited by Thomas M. Callaghy and John Ravenhill, 90–129. New York: Columbia University Press, 1993.

Gourevitch, Peter. "The Second Image Reversed: The International Sources of Domestic Politics." *International Organization* 32 (Autumn 1978): 881–911.

Granovetter, Mark. "Business Groups." In *Handbook of Economic Sociology*, edited by Neil Smelser and Richard Swedberg, 453–475. Princeton, NJ: Princeton University Press, 1994.

Grant, Richard. "Liberalization Policies and Foreign Companies in Accra, Ghana." *Environment and Planning* 33 (2001): 997–1014.

Gregory, Paul R. *Before Command: An Economic History of Russia from Emancipation to the First Five-Year Plan.* Princeton, NJ: Princeton University Press, 1994), 82.

Gulati, Nobel. *ADR Monitor: The Key to the World, September 1999.* New York: Salomon Smith Barney, 1999.

Gustafson, Douglas. "The Development of Nigeria's Stock Exchange." In *Financing African Development*, edited by Tom J. Farer, 144–156. Cambridge, MA: MIT Press, 1965.

Haggard, Stephan, Chung Lee, and Sylvia Maxfield, eds. *The Politics of Finance in Developing Countries.* Ithaca, NY: Cornell University Press, 1993.

Hakim, Miguel. *The Efficiency of the Mexican Stock Market.* New York: Garland Publishing, 1992.

Hale, David D. "Stock Markets in the New World Order." *Columbia Journal of World Business* XXIX (Summer 1994): 14–29.

Hall, Peter A., and David Soskice, eds. *Varieties of Capitalism: The Institutional Foundations of Comparative Advantage.* New York: Oxford University Press, 2001.

Hanley, Anne. "Business Finance and the Sao Paulo Bolsa, 1886–1917." In *Latin America and the World Economy Since 1800*, edited by John H. Coatsworth and Alan M. Taylor, 115–138. Cambridge, MA: Harvard University Press, 1998.

Haralz, Jonas. "The International Finance Corporation." In *The World Bank, Its First Half Century*, edited by Devesh Kapur, John P. Lewis, and Richard Webb, 805–899. Washington, DC: Brookings Institution Press, 1997.

Hardt, Michael, and Antonio Negri. *Empire*. Cambridge, MA: Harvard University Press, 2000.

Harris, Lawrence E. *Liquidity, Trading Rules, and Electronic Trading Series*. New York: New York University Salomon Center, 1991.

Harteneck, Guillermo, and Brian McMahon. "Privatisation in Argentina." In *Privatisation in Asia, Europe and Latin America*. Paris: OECD, 1996.

Hawrylyshyn, George. "Dress Rehearsal Towards Flexibility." *Lloyd's List*, October 19, 1994.

Helleiner, Eric. "From Bretton Woods to Global Finance: A World Turned Upside Down." In *Political Economy and the Changing Global Order*, edited by Richard Stubbs and Geoffrey R. D. Underhill, 163–175. New York: St. Martin's Press, 1994.

Herbst, D. K. *Unilever Overseas: The Anatomy of a Multinational, 1895–1965*. Stanford, CA: Hoover Institution Press, 1978.

Herbst, Jeffrey. "The Creationand Maintenance of National Boundaries in Africa." *International Organization* 43 (Fall 1989): 673–692.

———. *States and Power in Africa*. Princeton, NJ: Princeton University Press, 2000.

Herrera, Alejandra. "The Privatization of Telecommunications Services: The Case of Argentina." *Columbia Journal of World Business* Spring 1993): 46–61.

Hertz, Ellen. *The Trading Crowd: An Ethnography of the Shanghai Stock Market*. Cambridge: Cambridge University Press, 1998.

Hibou, Beatrice. "Retrait ou redeploiement de l'etat?" *Critique Internationale* 1 (Autumn 1998): 151–168.

Hira, Anil. *Ideas and Economic Policy in Latin America*. Westport, CT: Praeger, 1998.

Hirschman, Albert O. "The Political Economy of Import-Substituting Industrialization in Latin America." *Quarterly Journal of Economics* 82 (1968): 1–32.

Hobsbawm, E. J. *Industry and Empire*. New York: Penguin Books, 1969.

Hobson, Charles K. *The Export of Capital*. New York: MacMillan, 1914.

Hobson, John A. *Imperialism, A Study*. London: Allen & Unwin, 1938.

Hogan, Harold F. "The Cherkizovsky Group." Harvard Business School Case 9-399-119 (October 20, 1999).

Honore, A. M. "Ownership." In *Oxford Essays in Jurisprudence*, 1st series, 107–147. Oxford: Oxford University Press, 1961.

Hoogvelt, Ankie. *Globalization and the Postcolonial World: The New Political Economy of Development*, 2nd ed. Baltimore, MD: Johns Hopkins University Press, 2001.

Howell, Michael, and Angela Cozzini. *Games Without Frontiers: Global Equity Markets in the 1990s*. New York: Salomon Brothers, 1991.

Hudson Finance. "Information on the Cote d'Ivoire Market" (unpublished document), 1999.

Humphreys, Gary. "Closing the Time-Lag in Settlements," *Euromoney* March 1989, 31 (Global Custody: Speeding the Paper Chase, special supplement).

Husted, Bryan W., and Carlos Serrano. "Corporate Governance in Mexico." *Journal of Business Ethics* 37 (2002): 337–348.

Jang, Hasung, and Joongi Kim. "Nascent Stages of Corporate Governance in an Emerging Market: Regulatory Change, Shareholder Activism and Samsung Electronics." *Corporate Governance* 10 (April 2002): 94–105.

Jenkinson T. "Corporate Governance and Privatisation Via Initial Public Offering (IPO)." In *Corporate Governance, State-Owned Enterprises and Privatization*. Paris: OECD, 1998.

Jesover, Fianna. "Corporate Governance in the Russian Federation: The Relevance of the OECD Principles on Shareholder Rights and Equitable Treatment." *Corporate Governance* 9 (April 2001): 79–88.

Johnson, Simon, Heidi Kroll, and Santiago Eder. "Strategy, Structure, and Spontaneous Privatization in Russia and Ukraine." In *Changing Political Economies: Privatization in Post-Communist and Reforming Communist States*, edited by Vedat Milor. Boulder, CO: Lynne Rienner, 1993.

Kahler, Miles. *International Institutions and the Political Economy of Integration.* Washington, DC: Brookings Institution Press, 1995.

Kang, Chul-Kyu. "Diversification Process and the Ownership Structure of Samsung Chaebol." In *Beyond the Firm: Business Groups in International and Historical Perspective*, edited by Takao Shiba and Masahiro Shimotani, 31–58. New York: Oxford University Press, 1997.

Kapur, Devesh, John P. Lewis, and Richard Webb, eds. *The World Bank: Its First Half Century, Volume I: History*. Washington, DC: Brookings Institution Press, 1997.

Karns, Margaret P., and Karen A. Mingst. *The United States and Multilateral Institutions: Patterns of Changing Instrumentality and Influence.* Boston: Unwin Hyman, 1990.

Katzenstein, Peter J., ed. *Between Power and Plenty: Foreign Economic Policies of Advanced Industrial States.* Madison, WI: University of Wisconsin Press, 1978.

Kenen, Peter B. *The International Economy.* New York: Cambridge University Press, 1994.

Kenway, Peter, and Jiri Chlumsky. "The Influence of Owners on Voucher Privatized Firms in the Czech Republic." *Economics of Transition* 5 (1997): 185–193.

Khanna, T., and K. Palepu. "The Right Way to Restructure Conglomerates in Emerging Markets." *Harvard Business Review* 77 (July–August 1999): 125–127.

Kling, Blair B. "The Origin of the Managing Agency System in India." *Journal of Asian Studies* 26 (November 1966): 37–47.

Kohli, Atul. *The State and Poverty in India: The Politics of Reform.* Cambridge: Cambridge University Press, 1987.

Koladkiewicz, Izabela. "Building of a Corporate Governance System in Poland: Initial Experiences." *Corporate Governance* 9 (July 2001): 228–237.

Koll, Elisabeth. *From Cotton Mill to Business Empire: The Emergence of Regional Enterprises in Modern China.* Cambridge, MA: Harvard University Press, 2004.

Korea Fund, Inc. "Prospectus of the Korea Fund" (August 22, 1984). New York: First Boston Corporation, Lehman Brothers, International Finance Corporation, 1984.

Kotchen, David T. "The Szczecin Shipyard: State Enterprise Restructuring in Poland." Harvard Business School Case 9-693-089 (July 8, 1997).

Krause, Lawrence. "Private International Finance." *International Organization* 25 (1975): 523–540.

La Porta, Rafael, Florencio Lopez-de-Silanes, and Andrei Shleifer. "Corporate Ownership Around the World." *Journal of Finance* 54 (April 1999): 471–517.

Lavelle, Kathryn C. "International Financial Institutions and Emerging Capital Markets in Africa." *Review of International Political Economy* 6 (Summer 1999): 200–224.

———. "The International Finance Corporation and the Emerging Market Funds Industry." *Third World Quarterly* 21 (2000): 193–213.

———. "Architecture of Equity Markets: The Abidjan Regional Bourse." *International Organization* 55 (Summer 2001): 717–742.

Lee, Chol. "Globalization of a Korean Firm: The Case of Samsung." In *Corporate Strat-*

egies in the Pacific Rim: Global Versus Regional Trends, edited by Denis Fred Simon. New York: Routledge, 1995.

Lee, Ruben. What is an Exchange? The Automation, Management and Regulation of Financial Markets. New York: Oxford University Press, 1998.

Lenin, Vladimir I. Imperialism, the Highest Stage of Capitalism. New York: International Publishers, 1939.

Levitas, Anthony. "Privatization in Poland." In Changing Political Economies: Privatization in Post-Communist and Reforming Communist States, edited by Vedat Milor. Boulder, CO: Lynne Rienner, 1994.

Lipson, Charles. "International Debt and International Institutions." In The Politics of International Debt, edited by Miles Kahler. Ithaca, NY: Cornell University Press, 1986.

———. "The International Organization of Third World Debt." In Toward a Political Economy of Development, edited by Robert Bates. Berkeley: University of California Press, 1988.

Little, Jeffrey B., and Lucien Rhodes. Understanding Wall Street, 3rd ed. New York: Liberty Hall Press, 1991.

Loredo, Enrique, and Eugenia Suarez. "Privatization and Deregulation: Corporate Governance Consequences in a Global Economy." Corporate Governance 8 (January 2000): 65–74.

Loriaux, Michael. France After Hegemony. Ithaca, NY: Cornell University Press, 1991.

Loriaux, Michael, Meredith Woo-Cumings, Kent E. Calder, Sylvia Maxfield, and Sophia Perez, eds. Capital Ungoverned: Liberalizing Finance in Interventionist States. Ithaca, NY: Cornell University Press, 1997.

Lopez-Mejia, Alejandro. "Large Capital Flows: Causes, Consequences, and Policy Responses," Finance and Development, September 1999, 28.

Magnusen, Jonathan R. "Structural Adjustment Policies and the Evolution of a New Legal Framework for Economic Activity in Ghana." In Emerging Financial Markets and the Role of International Financial Organizations, edited by Joseph J. Norton and Mads Andenas, 81–114. Boston: Kluwer Law International, 1996.

Mallin, Chris, and Ranko Jelic. "Developments in Corporate Governance in Central and Eastern Europe." Corporate Governance 8 (January 2000): 43–51.

Mandakovic, Tomislav, and Marcos Lima. "Privatization in Chile: Management Effectiveness Analysis." In Privatization and Deregulation in Global Perspective, edited by Dennis J. Gayle and Jonathan N. Goodrich, 177–197. New York: Quorum Books, 1990.

Marino, John. "Hotel Sale Epitomizes Hungary's Sometimes Painful Privatization." Mergers and Acquisitions Report 5 (June 22, 1992): 14.

Martin, Matthew. "Neither Phoenix Nor Icarus: Negotiating Economic Reform in Ghana and Zambia, 1983–1992." In Hemmed In: Responses to Africa's Economic Decline, edited by Thomas M. Callaghy and John Ravenhill, 130–179. New York: Columbia University Press, 1993.

Matecki, B. E. The Establishment of the International Finance Corporation and United States Policy. New York: Praeger, 1957.

Maxfield, Sylvia. Governing Capital. Ithaca, NY: Cornell University Press, 1990.

Maxfield, Sylvia, and Ben Ross Schneider. Business and the State in Developing Countries. Ithaca, NY: Cornell University Press, 1997.

Megginson, William L., and Maria K. Boutchkova. "Privatization and the Rise of Global Capital Markets." Financial Management 29 (Winter 2000): 31–76.

Meszaros, Kalman. "Evolution of the Hungarian Capital Market." In Privatization in the Transition to a Market Economy, edited by John S. Earle, Roman Frydman, and Andrzej Rapaczynski. New York: St. Martin's Press, 1993.

Michie, R. C. *The London and New York Stock Exchanges: 1850–1914*. Boston: Allen & Unwin, 1987.

Mirza, Khalid A. "Pakistan." In *The World's Emerging Stock Markets: Structure, Developments, Regulations and Opportunities*, edited by Keith Park and Antoine Van Agtmael, 197–222. Chicago: Probus Publishing, 1993.

Modigliani, Franco, and Merton Miller. "The Cost of Capital, Corporation Finance, and the Theory of Investment." *American Economic Review* 48 (June 1958): 261–297.

Morgan, Edward Victor, and W. A. Thomas. *The Stock Exchange: Its History and Functions*. London: Elek Books, 1969.

Munting, Roger. "Industrial Revolution in Russia." In *The Industrial Revolution in National Context: Europe and the USA*, edited by Mikulas Teich and Roy Porter, 329–349. Cambridge: Cambridge University Press, 1996.

Myers, Stewart. "The Capital Structure Puzzle." *Journal of Finance* 39 (1984): 575–592.

Nagaishi, Makoto. "Stock Market Development and Economic Growth: Dubious Relationship." *Economic and Political Weekly* 34 (July 17, 1999): 2004–2012.

Niepold, John R. "Indonesia." In *The World's Emerging Stock Markets: Structure, Developments, Regulations and Opportunities*, edited by Keith Park and Antoine Van Agtmael, 161–180. Chicago: Probus Publishing, 1993.

North, Douglass C. "Institutions and Economic Growth: An Historical Introduction." *World Development* 17 (1989): 1319–1332.

Palda, Kristian. "Czech Privatization and Corporate Governance." *Communist and Post-Communist Studies* 30 (1997): 83–93.

Park, Keith K. H. "Growing Pains of the Korean Equity Market." In *The World's Emerging Stock Markets: Structure, Developments, Regulations and Opportunities*, edited by Keith K. H. Park and Antoine Van Agtmael, 483–497. Chicago: Probus Publishing, 1993.

Parker, William. *The Paris Bourse and French Finance*. New York: AMS Press, 1967.

Partnoy, Frank. *F.I.A.S.C.O. Blood in the Water on Wall Street*. New York: Norton, 1997.

Pauly, Louis W., and Simon Reich. "National Structures and Multinational Corporate Behavior: Enduring Differences in the Age of Globalization." *International Organization* 51 (Winter 1997): 1–30.

Pearson, Margaret M. *Joint Ventures in the People's Republic of China: The Control of Foreign Direct Investment Under Socialism*. Princeton, NJ: Princeton University Press, 1991.

Perez, Sophia. "Systemic Explanations, Divergent Outcomes: The Politics of Financial Liberalization in France and Spain," *International Studies Quarterly* 42 (December 1998): 755–784.

Perotti, Enrico C., and Serhat E. Guney. "The Structure of Privatization Plans." *Financial Management* 22 (Spring 1993): 84–98.

———. "The Structure of Privatization Plans." Graduate School of Management and Department of Economics, Boston University, December 1992. Photocopy.

Phongpaichit, Pasuk, and Chris Baker. *Thailand: Economy and Politics*. New York: Oxford University Press, 1995.

Pitiyasak, Saravuth. "Corporate Governance in Family Controlled Companies: A Comparative Study between Hong Kong and Thailand." *Thailand Law Forum*, http://members.tripod.com/asialaw/articles/governance.html (accessed March 19, 2003).

Platt, D.C.M. *Finance, Trade and Politics in British Foreign Policy*. Oxford: Clarendon Press, 1968.

Polanyi, Karl. *The Great Transformation*, 6th printing. Boston: Beacon Press, 1965.

Porter, Tony. "The Budapest Stock Exchange and the Global Political Economy." Paper presented at the annual meeting of the International Studies Association, New Orleans, LA, March 2002.

Poser, Norman S. *International Securities Regulation: London's "Big Bang" and the European Securities Markets.* Boston: Little, Brown, 1991.

Postan, M. M. *Medieval Trade and Finance.* New York: Cambridge University Press, 1973.

Putnam, Robert D. "Diplomacy and Domestic Politics: The Logic of Two-Level Games." *International Organization* 42 (Summer 1988): 427–460.

Quiroz, Alfonso. *Domestic and Foreign Finance in Modern Peru, 1850–1950: Financing Visions of Development.* Pittsburgh, PA: University of Pittsburgh Press, 1993.

Rabb, Theodore K. *Enterprise and Empire.* Cambridge, MA: Harvard University Press, 1967.

Rabelo, Flavio M., and Flavio C. Vasconcelos. "Corporate Governance in Brazil." *Journal of Business Ethics* 37 (2002): 321–335.

Raghavan, Chakravarth. *Recolonization, GATT, the Uruguay Round and the Third World.* Atlantic Highlands, NJ: Zed Books, 1990.

Rajan, Raghuram G., and Luigi Zingales. "The Great Reversals: The Politics of Financial Development in the Twentieth Century." *Journal of Financial Economics* 69 (2003): 5–50.

Randall, Linda M. *Reluctant Capitalists: Russia's Journey Through Market Transition.* New York: Routledge, 2000.

Reed, Ananya Mukherjee. "Corporate Governance Reforms in India." *Journal of Business Ethics* 37 (2002): 249–268.

Reed, Darryl. "Corporate Governance Reforms in Developing Countries." *Journal of Business Ethics* 37 (2002): 223–247.

Reinsch, Paul S. *Colonial Administration.* New York: MacMillan, 1905.

Roe, M. J. *Strong Managers, Weak Owners: The Political Roots of American Corporate Finance.* Princeton, NJ: Princeton University Press, 1994.

Rosenthal, Eric. *On Change Through the Years: A History of Share Dealing in South Africa.* Cape Town: Flesch Financial Publications, 1968.

Rossouw, G. J., A. van der Watt, and D. P. Malan. "Corporate Governance in South Africa." *Journal of Business Ethics* 37 (2002): 289–302.

Rothschild, Joseph. *East Central Europe Between the Two World Wars.* Seattle: University of Washington Press, 1974.

Rudolph, Lloyd I., and Susanne Hoeber Rudolph. *In Pursuit of Lakshmi: The Political Economy of the Indian State.* Chicago: University of Chicago Press, 1987.

Rudolph, Matthew C. J. "The Diversity of Convergence: Global Finance, Capital Control, and the Politics of Securitization in China." Paper presented to the annual meeting of the International Studies Association, New Orleans, LA, March 2002.

Rudolph, Richard L. *Banking and Industrialization in Austria-Hungary.* New York: Cambridge University Press, 1976.

Ruggie, John Gerard. "International Regimes, Transactions, and Change: Embedded Liberalism in the Postwar Economic Order." In *International Regimes,* edited by Stephen Krasner, 204–214. Ithaca, NY: Cornell University Press, 1983.

———. "Multilateralism: The Anatomy of an Institution." In *Multilateralism Matters: The Theory and Praxis of an Institutional Form,* edited by John Gerard Ruggie, 3–47. New York: Columbia University Press, 1993.

Rungta, Radhe Shyam. *The Rise of Business Corporations in India, 1851–1900.* London: Cambridge University Press, 1970.

Saez, Raul E. "Financial Aspects of Privatization in Chile." In *Privatisation in Asia, Europe and Latin America.* Paris: OECD, 1996.

Sassen, Saskia. "Global Financial Centers." *Foreign Affairs* 78 (January/February 1999): 75–87.

Sauvant, Karl P. *G-77: Evolution, Structure, Organization.* New York: Oceana, 1981.

Schumpeter, Joseph. *Capitalism, Socialism, and Democracy.* New York: Harper Torchbooks, 1950.

————. "The Sociology of Imperialism." in *Imperialism and Social Classes.* Cleveland: World Publishing, 1955.

Schwartz, Herman M. *States Versus Markets: History, Geography, and the Development of the International Political Economy.* New York: St. Martin's Press, 1994.

Scott, Kenneth E. "Corporate Governance and East Asia: Korea, Indonesia, Malaysia, and Thailand." In *Financial Markets and Development: The Crisis in Emerging Markets,* edited by Alison Harwood, Robert E. Litan, and Michael Pomerleano, 335–365. Washington, DC: Brookings Institution Press, 1999.

Scott, William Robert. *The Constitution and Finance of English, Scottish and Irish Joint-Stock Companies to 1720.* Cambridge: Cambridge University Press, 1912.

Seaward, Nick. "Malaysia." In *The World's Emerging Stock Markets: Structure, Developments, Regulations and Opportunities,* edited by Keith Park and Antoine Van Agtmael, 143–159. Chicago: Probus Publishing, 1993.

Sheth, Atsi Tarun. *Emerging Market, Emerging Contradictions: The Politics of Economic Liberalization in India.* Ph.D. dissertation, Northwestern University, 1997.

Shiller, Robert J. *Irrational Exuberance.* Princeton, NJ: Princeton University Press, 2000.

Sidaway, James D., and John R. Bryson. "Constructing Knowledges of 'Emerging Markets': UK-based Investment Managers and Their Overseas Connections." *Environment and Planning A* 34 (March 2002): 401–416.

Sidaway, James Derrick, and Michael Pryke. "The Strange Geographies of 'Emerging Markets.' " *Transactions* 25 (2000): 187–201.

Silva, Eduardo. "Business Elites and the State in Chile." In *Business and the State in Developing Countries,* edited by Sylvia Maxfield and Ben Ross Schneider, 152–188. Ithaca, NY: Cornell University Press, 1997.

Singh, Ajit. *Corporate Financial Patterns in Industrializing Economies.* Washington, DC: World Bank, 1995.

————. "The Stock-Market and Economic Development: Should Developing Countries Encourage Stock-Markets?" *UNCTAD Review* 4 (1993): 1–28.

Smith, Roy C., and Ingo Walter. *Global Banking.* New York: Oxford University Press, 1997.

Southall, Roger J. "South Africa." In *The Political Economy of African Foreign Policy,* edited by Timothy M. Shaw and Olajide Aluko, 221–262. New York: St. Martin's Press, 1984.

Stark, David. "Path Dependence and Privatization Strategies in East-Central Europe." In *Changing Political Economies: Privatization in Post-Communist and Reforming Communist States,* edited by Vedat Milor, 115–146. Boulder, CO: Lynne Rienner, 1994.

Steensgaard, Niels. "The Dutch East India Company as an Institutional Innovation." In *Dutch Capitalism and World Capitalism,* edited by Maurice Aymard, 235–257. New York: Cambridge University Press, 1982.

Stone, Irving. *The Composition and Distribution of British Investment in Latin America, 1865 to 1913.* New York: Garland Publishing, 1987.

Stopford, John, and Susan Strange, with John S. Henley. *Rival States, Rival Firms: Competition for World Market Shares.* Cambridge: Cambridge University Press, 1991.

Sudweeks, Brian Lorin. *Equity Market Development in Developing Countries.* New York: Praeger, 1989.

Sutton, Michael H. "International Harmonization of Accounting Standards: Perspectives from the Securities and Exchange Commission." Remarks to the International Accounting Association, August 17, 1997, http://www.sec.gov/news/speeches/spch174.txt.

Szomburg, Jan. "The Decision-Making Structure of Polish Privatization." In *Privatization in the Transition to a Market Economy*, edited by John S. Earle, Roman Frydman, and Andrzej Rapaczynski. New York: St. Martin's Press, 1993.

Tam, On Kit. "Ethical Issues in the Evolution of Corporate Governance in China." *Journal of Business Ethics* 37 (2002): 303–320.

Tapia, Eduardo. "Argentina." In *The World's Emerging Stock Markets: Structure, Developments, Regulations and Opportunities*, edited by Keith Park and Antoine Van Agtmael, 321–343. Chicago: Probus Publishing, 1993.

Thomas, W. A. *Western Capitalism in China*. Burlington, VT: Ashgate, 2001.

Tignor, Robert L. *State, Private Enterprise and Economic Change in Egypt, 1918–1952*. Princeton, NJ: Princeton University Press, 1984.

Tiberghien, Yves. "State Mediation of Global Financial Forces: Different Paths of Structural Reforms in Japan and South Korea." *Journal of East Asian Studies* 2 (Summer 2002): 103–141.

Turrell, Robert Vicat. "Review Article: 'Finance . . . The Governor of the Imperial Entine': Hobson and the Case of Rothschild and Rhodes." *Journal of Southern African Studies* 13 (April 1987): 417–432.

———. *Capital and Labour on the Kimberley Diamond Fields, 1871–1890*. New York: Cambridge University Press, 1987.

Turrell, Robert Vicat, with Jean-Jacques Van Helten. "The Rothschilds, the Exploration Company and Mining Finance." *Business History* 23 (April 1986): 181–205.

Tyler, Christian. "Third World Tunes into Capitalism," *Foreign Times*, June 11, 1987.

Van Zandt, David E. "The Regulatory and Institutional Conditions for an International Securities Market." *Virginia Journal of International Law* 32 (1991): 46–81.

Vernon, Raymond. *Sovereignty at Bay*. New York: Basic Books, 1971.

Vignau, Cristian Larroulet. "Privatization in Chile." In *Privatization: A Global Perspective*, edited by V. V. Ramanadham, 233–253. New York: Routledge, 1993.

Visentini, G. "Compatibility and Competition Between European and American Corporate Governance: Which Model of Capitalism?" *Brooklyn Journal of International Law* 23 (1998): 833–851.

Vitols, Sigurt. "Varieties of Corporate Governance: Comparing Germany and the UK." In *Varieties of Capitalism: The Institutional Foundations of Comparative Advantage*, edited by Peter A. Hall and David Soskice, 337–360. New York: Oxford University Press, 2001.

Vudthitornetiraks, Manimai. "The Privatisation Experience in Thailand." In *Privatisation in Asia, Europe and Latin America*. Paris: OECD, 1996.

Wade, Robert. "Globalization and Its Limits: Reports of the Death of the National Economy are Greatly Exaggerated." In *National Diversity and Global Capitalism*, edited by Suzanne Berger and Ronald Dore, 60–88. Ithaca, NY: Cornell University Press, 1996.

Walder, Andrew G. "Corporate Organization and Local Government Property Rights in China." In *Changing Political Economies: Privatization in Post-Communist and Reforming Communist States*, edited by Vedat Milor, 53–66. Boulder, CO: Lynne Rienner, 1994.

Walker, Gordon, and Mark Fox. "Corporate Governance Reform in East Asia." *Corporate Governance* 2 (2002): 4–8.

Wallerstein, Immanuel. *The Modern World-System II: Mercantilism and the Consolidation of the European World-Economy, 1600–1750*. New York: Academic Press, 1980.

Weimer, Jeroen, and Joost C. Pape. "A Taxonomy of Systems of Corporate Governance." *Corporate Governance* 7 (April 1999): 152–166.

White, Jerry, Steve Foerster, and Andrew Karolyi. "Huaneng Power International Inc. Raising Capital in Global Markets." Richard Ivey School of Business, University of Western Ontario, 9A98N001 (1998).

Williams, Mark Eric. "Market Reforms, Technocrats, and Institutional Innovation." *World Development* 30 (2002): 395–412.

Woo, Jung-eun (now Meredith Woo-Cumings). *Race to the Swift*. New York: Columbia University Press, 1991.

Yao, Chengxi. *Stock Market and Futures Market in the People's Republic of China*. New York: Oxford University Press, 1998.

Yebi, Hu. *China's Capital Market*. Hong Kong: Chinese University Press, 1993.

Young, Crawford. "The African Colonial State and its Political Legacy." In *The Precarious Balance: State and Society in Africa*, edited by Donald Rothchild and Naomi Chazan, 25–66. Boulder, CO: Westview Press, 1988.

Zysman, John. *Governments, Markets and Growth*. Ithaca, NY: Cornell University Press, 1983.

# Index

Abidjan bourse. *See Bourse Regionale des Valeurs Mobilieres* (BRVM)
Accra stock exchange, 74, 78, 164, 166, 181–183, 186
Air Senegal, 180
Alexandria Shipyard, 176
Alexandria stock exchange, 14, 27, 40, 166–167
American Depository Receipt (ADR), 11–12, 224nn.32 and 34
  and Brazil, 96, 98–99
  and Chile, 106
  and China, 133
  and India, 119
  and Thailand, 137
American Stock Exchange, 11
Amsterdam bourse, 32, 196
Anglo-American corporate governance model, xv, xix, 193
  and Africa, 171, 176
  and Asia, 115, 121, 127
  and Eastern Europe, 142–143, 153, 155, 158, 162
  and Latin America, 99–100
Anglo-American PLC, 166, 169–170, 185–186
arbitrage, 34, 38, 167, 195
Argentina, xviii, 93, 106, 111, 194–195. *See also* Buenos Aires stock exchange
  British investment in, 27, 99–100
  country reviewed, 99–103
  debt crisis in, 99
  family ownership of firms, 102
  MERVAL, 103
  monetary crisis, 103
  New York listings, 71
  stock market and financial institutional structure in, 102–103

Argentina Fund, 66
Ashanti Goldfields, 77–78, 181, 185–186

Babaev, Igor, 155–156, 162
Bangkok Bank Public Company, 137
Bangkok Land Company, 137
Bangkok stock exchange. *See* Stock Exchange Thailand
Bank for International Settlements (BIS), 233n.39
Bank of England, 32, 47
Barings, 34, 47
Basle Committee, 69, 233n.39
Berlin Congo Conference, 36, 164
Bharatiya Janata Party (BJP), 119
"Big Bang," 58
Bolsa de Comercio de Santiago, 40, 104–105
Bolsa de Valores do Rio de Janeiro, 40, 95
Bolsa Mexicana de Valores, 40, 107–108
Bombay stock exchange, 27, 122, 134, 167
  history of, 41, 113, 115–119
Bond Corporation International (BCI), 105–106
bonds, 9, 14, 224–225n.37, 228n.27
  defined, 7, 222–223n.12, 230n.23
  Chinese bond market, 130–131
  Dutch bond market, 32
  rating of, 223–224n.28
  Russian bonds, 3
  trading in Hungarian transition, 145
*Bourse Regionale des Valeurs Mobilieres* (BRVM), 74, 78, 166, 176–180, 186
Brazil, xviii, 55, 106, 111, 194–195. *See also* Bolsa de Valores do Rio de Janeiro, Sao Paulo Bolsa de Valores

Brazil (*continued*)
BOVESPA, 99
British investment in, 93, 94–95
country reviewed, 94–99
debt crisis in, 61, 96
family business groups in, 95–96, 99
New York listings, 71
stock market and financial institutional
structure in, 98–99
Brazil Fund, 65–66
Bretton Woods system, 21, 46, 48–49. *See also*
International Finance Corporation (IFC),
International Monetary Fund (IMF), World
Bank
British corporate governance model, xiv, 5
British financial revolution, 31–32
British industrial revolution, 32–34
British informal empire, 18, 28, 36, 93–94, 226n.58
British Petroleum, 97
Brussels bourse, 36
Budapest stock exchange, 144–148, 158
Buenos Aires bolsa. *See* Buenos Aires stock
exchange
Buenos Aires stock exchange, 27, 41, 100, 102

Cairo stock exchange, xix, 15, 40, 166–168
Calcutta stock exchange, 42, 116–117
Canadian International Development Agency
(CIDA), 74
Capital structure of the firm, 14, 109, 225n.42
Caracas stock exchange, 41
Casablanca stock exchange, 56, 180
CFA franc zone, 177–178, 180
*chaebol*, xix, 124–127
Cherkizovsky Group, 153, 155–157, 162
Chile, 93, 111, 171, 194. *See also* Bolsa de
Comercio de Santiago
ADRs in, 105–106
"Chicago boys," 103
CORFO, 104–105
country reviewed, 103–106
New York listings, 71
stock market and financial institutional
structure in, 106
China, xviii, 114. *See also* Communist revolution,
Hong Kong stock exchange, Shanghai
Sharebroker's Association, Shanghai stock
exchange, Shenzhen stock market
classes of shares in, 131–134, 241n.79
Communist revolution in, 114, 128–129, 133
country reviewed, 128–134
stock market and financial institutional
structure in, 133–134
civil law tradition, 192
codetermination. *See* German-Japanese
corporate governance model

Colombo stock exchange, 37, 42, 113
colonialism. *See* imperialism
common law tradition, 192
Communist revolution, xv, 17, 46, 54. *See also*
China, Czech Republic, Hungary, Poland,
Russia
Compania de Telephonos de Chile (CTC), 105–
107, 111
Coopers & Lybrand, 74, 182
corporate governance, xvii, 91, 192–193. *See also*
Anglo-American corporate governance
model, British corporate governance model,
German-Japanese corporate governance
model, golden share, price mechanism,
stock, Wall Street Rule
concentrated ownership of stock and, 86, 147,
160
contradictions in, 5
controlling minority structures and, xx, 9, 86–
87, 111, 123, 139, 169, 195
Czech republic, 160
dual classes of shares and, 86, 99
family controlled, 99, 102, 86, 176
and Ghana, 184
and South Africa, 166
and stakeholder model, 143
stock pyramids and, 86, 99, 139, 153,
173, 176
U.S. type of, 17, 87
cross-border transaction, 10–11, 38, 69
cross-exchange transaction, 11–12, 106
cross-holding, 82, 87
Egypt, 165
Hungary, 162–163
Korea, 124, 139
South Africa, 169–170
Thailand, 135
cross-listed securities, 16, 71–73, 94, 110, 137
and Ashanti Goldfields, 181, 183
and colonial metropole, 166
and Hungarian listing, 162
and political goals, 85
cross-ownership, 86–86, 123–124, 162, 185
custody arrangements, xiv–xv, 60
Czech Republic, 142–144, 162–163 192
country reviewed, 157–161
National Property Fund, 157–158, 160
pre-Communist stock exchange, 157
stock market and financial institutional
structure in, 159–161
transition from communism in, 157–158
vouchers in, xix, 17, 84, 158–160

Daewoo, 127–128
DeBeers, 169–170, 186

debt crisis of 1980s, xvi, 22, 58, 60, 61, 71. *See also by country*
    African dimension, 67–68, 165
    International Finance Corporation, 63, 69
    International Monetary Fund and World Bank, 74
demutualization, 195–196
disclosure requirements, xiv, 21, 91, 140, 189

East India Company (Dutch), 30–31, 189, 227n.11
East India Company (English/British), 29, 34, 116
Economic Commission for Latin America (ECLA), 94, 110, 114
Egypt, 165–166, 185–186. *See also* Alexandria stock exchange, Cairo stock exchange
    country reviewed, 172–176
    European investment in, 172–173
    stock market and financial institutional structure in, 176
Egyptian Bottling Company, 174
emerging markets. *See by individual country and stock exchange*
Emerging Markets Data Base (EMDB), 63–64
Emerging Markets Growth Fund (EMGF), 66–67
Enron, 196
ENTel, 99–102, 106–108, 111
equity capital, 53–54, 56–57, 118, 125, 137. *See also* stock
European Economic Community. *See* European Union
European Union, 150, 156, 196

financial institutional structure, xv, 7, 75. *See also by country*
    problems with Western models, 8–9
Financial Times Stock Exchange (FTSE), 170, 224n.31
First Boston, 51, 125, 233n.25
Ford Motor Company, 195
foreign direct investment, xvii, 8, 45–46, 51–54, 66
    and Brazil, 95, 98
    defined, 230n.23
    and distribution of power, 190
    and Hungary, 146
    and India, 139
    measured, 226n.3
    and Poland, 161
    and Russia, 153, 156
    and South Korea, 123
    and Thailand, 136
France Telecom, 109, 180, 185–186, 234n.16
French bourse, xvii, 35–36, 162

funds, 21, 224n.34. *See also* Brazil Fund, Japan Fund, Korea Fund
    Chinese country funds, 133
    Czech privatization, 157–161
    industry develops, 64–67
    open/closed types, 12, 224n.35, 233n.30
    Thai country funds, 136–137

Garside Miller, 74, 145
Gdansk shipyard, 151
Gdynia shipyard, 151–152
General Agreement on Tariffs and Trade (GATT), 45, 49, 107–108
Generally Accepted Accounting Principles (GAAP), 79, 133
German-Japanese corporate governance model, xv, 5, 17, 148, 161
    Samsung compared, 127
    Szczecin shipyard imitates, 152
Germany, 3. *See also* German-Japanese corporate governance model
    exporter of capital, 27
    industrial revolution in, 8, 44, 143, 152
    Nazi threat in Latin America, 48
    Samsung expands to, 126
    and Szczecin, 150, 152
    Volkswagen of Germany, 196
Ghana, xix, 166, 185–186. *See also* Accra stock exchange
    British investment in, 181–184
    country reviewed, 181–184
    economic crisis in, 181–182
    stock market and financial institutional structure in, 184
Ghana stock exchange. *See* Accra stock exchange
Glass-Steagall Act, 47, 51
global depository receipt (GDR). *See* American Depository Receipt (ADR)
globalization literature, xx, 4, 76, 196–198
gold standard, 32
golden share, 4, 10, 22, 193, 195–196
    and Ashanti Goldfields, 184, 186
    and Russia, 157
Goldsmith, Raymond, 62–63
Godrej Conglomerate, 118, 123
great depression of the 1930s, 46, 48, 54, 94
Grunderzeit, 143
Grupo Carso, 109

Habsburg empire, 143
Harvard Capital, 157–159, 162
Hatton Garden share market, 246n.8
Hindustan Lever. *See* Unilever
Hong Kong stock exchange, 42, 128–130, 132–133

Huaneng Electric, 128, 132–133, 140
Hungary, 142–144, 156–158, 162. *See also*
    Budapest stock exchange
    country reviewed, 144–148
    pre-Communist stock exchange, 144
    stock market and financial institutional
        structure in, 147–148
    transition from communism in, 144–146

Ibusz, 146–147, 162
Ideal Company, 175–176, 185–186
imperialism, xvii, 27–28, 45, 51, 57. *See also by
    individual country colonized*, British
    informal empire
    British, 18, 36–44
    and colonial markets, 189–190
    Dutch, 18
    and Egypt, 172–173
    French, 39–44, 48, 56, 166, 177
    and investment in Africa, 164–165
    Japanese, 57, 113–114, 189
    Spanish, 42, 93, 100, 103
    U.S. multinational investment compared, 53–
        54
India, xviii, 16, 17, 93, 114, 167. *See also* Bombay
    stock exchange, Calcutta stock exchange,
    National Stock Exchange (of India)
    British investment in, 27, 36, 115–117
    business houses in, 117–118
    country reviewed, 115–123
    economic crisis in, 118
    independence of, 45, 49, 117
    stock market and financial institutional
        structure in, 121–123
Indian Petrochemicals Corporation (IPCL), 122–
    123
industrial revolution. *See by individual country*
initial public offering (IPO), 14, 80, 137
    favoring domestic purchasers, 178
    IPO-Plus, 81
    privatizations by IPO, 77, 81–82, 85, 110, 146
Inter-American Association of Securities
    Commision (IOSCO), 69–70
International Depository Receipt (IDR). *See*
    American Depository Receipt (ADR)
International Finance Corporation (IFC), 22, 46,
    60, 233n.25
    capital markets department, 62–64, 69–70
    and classification of South Africa, 164
    established, 49–50
    and funds industry, 64–67, 74
    future role of, 193–194
    investible index, 68
    involvement in financial sector and
        privatization projects, 199–219
    and Korea, 124–125

and role in privatization, 232n.19
and Russia, 155
and Thailand, 136
and Zambia, 68–69
and Zimbabwe, 68
international financial architecture, 193
international financial organizations, xvi, 45–46,
    61–64, 75. *See also* General Agreement on
    Tariffs and Trade (GATT), International
    Finance Corporation (IFC), International
    Monetary Fund (IMF), World Bank
    contribution to emerging market growth, 21–
        23, 71–74, 161, 166
International Monetary Fund (IMF), xvi, 5,
    231n.4
    and African stabilization programs, 185–186
    and Asian cases examined, 140
    and creation following World War II, 45, 49
    and debt crises, 22, 60, 61, 74
    and Egypt, 173–174
    future role of, 193–194
    and Ghana, 182–183
    and India, 118
    and privatization, 76
    and Senegal, 179
    and Thailand, 136, 138
Israel, 38

Jakarta stock exchange, 16, 42, 54–55, 113
Jamaica, 16
Japan, xiii, 3, 5, 52, 126. *See also* German-
    Japanese corporate governance model
    and colonialism, 57, 189
    and corporations, 125
    and cross-border stock transactions, 11
    industrial revolution in, 8, 17
Japan Fund, 64–65
Johannesburg stock exchange, xix, 15, 27, 40, 186
    history of, 164, 167–172
    integration with world markets, 37, 197
joint stock company, xvii, 39
    and Brazil, 95
    created 27
    and Egypt, 173
    European history of, 28–36, 44, 143
    and Hong Kong, 128–129
    and Hungary, 145
    and India, 115–116
    and Poland, 149
    and Russia, 154, 156
    and South Africa, 166–167, 169

Kampala stock exchange, 28
Karachi stock exchange, 55
Kenya, 28, 39, 56
Kimberley stock exchange, 167–168

King Report, 171
Korea, 114–115. *See also* Korea stock exchange
    colonialism in, 57, 123
    country reviewed, 123–128
    financial crisis in, 126, 127
    New York listings, 71
    stock market and financial institutional
        structure in, 127–128
Korea Fund, 65–67, 125, 233n.23
Korea stock exchange, xix, 42, 57, 65, 134
    history of, 114–115, 123–127
Kozeny, Viktor, 159, 162
Kuala Lumpur stock exchange, 37, 56, 127

Lagos stock exchange, 56–57
Lahore stock exchange, 55
level I and level II considerations, xvii–xviii, 22,
    59–60, 70–71, 75, 89–90, 191. *See also* two-
    level game metaphor
    defined, 17–18
    and Africa, 185, 186
    and Asia, 114, 140
    and Eastern Europe, 144, 161, 162
    and Latin America, 111
Lima stock exchange, 41
London stock exchange, xix, 7, 32, 186, 197,
    246n.8. *See also* Stock Exchange
    Automated Quotation (SEAQ)
    "Big Bang," 58
    and India, 115
    and Ghana, 181
    Latin American firms and, 94
    listing requirements of, 71
    of nineteenth century, 8, 33–34, 37, 46, 47
    South African firms' listing on, 71, 166, 168,
        171, 224n.31
Lonmin, 183–185
Lusaka stock exchange, 69

Malaysia, 37–38, 55–56, 127
McNamara, Robert, 50, 62
merchant banks, 224–225n.37, 228n.27
    Bangkok presence of, 137
    British history, 32, 34–35, 47
    and Viktor Kozeny, 159
    and South Africa, 168
Mexican stock exchange. *See* Bolsa Mexicana
    de Valores
Mexico, xviii, 93, 111, 194. *See also* Bolsa
    Mexicana de Valores
    country reviewed, 106–109
    debt crisis in, xvi, 22, 60
    group structure in, 107, 109
    New York listings, 71
    stock market and stock market and financial
        institutional structure in, 109

Mexico Fund, 65
Milan bourse, 196
Modern Food, 121, 140–141
Morgan Stanley, 51, 64, 156
Morocco, 56
multinational corporation. *See* foreign direct
    investment

Nairobi stock exchange, 28, 56
Nasser, Gamel Abdul, 54, 165, 173, 186
National Association of Securities Dealers
    Automated Quotation (NASDAQ), 11, 57–
    58, 127, 133
National Stock Exchange of India (NSE),
    119
Nestle, 195
New Deal, 45, 47
New York Stock Exchange (NYSE), 7, 66, 104,
    111
    Argentine firms, 100
    and Ashanti Goldfields, 183
    Chinese firms, 133
    listing requirements of, 11, 18, 71
    "Mayday," 57
Nigeria, 56–57, 77, 87
North American Free Trade Agreement
    (NAFTA), 107–108, 111

Olympic Group, 175–176, 185–186
Oppenheimer family, 169, 186
ownership structure of firm, xv–xvi, xx. *See also*
    cross-ownership
    coexisting within a state, 94, 99, 102, 112
    and decisions in large firms, 5, 8, 61, 74
    and families, 169–170, 172, 175–176
    and firms in the United States, 87
    and former Communist states, 143–144, 147,
        154–155, 159–160
    and market for managerial control, 109–110,
        127, 139, 176
    and privatization, 88, 90
    and Unilever, 121

Pakistan, 55. *See also* Karachi stock exchange,
    Lahore stock exchange
Paris bourse. *See* French bourse
Pax Americana, 45
Pax Britannica, 45
Pearson Commission, 62
pecking order theory of capital structure, 14
Perez Companc, 194
Petrobras, 94, 96–98, 194–195
    compared with other cases, 101, 105, 107, 110–
    112
Philippines, 38
Piotrowsky, Krzysztof, 151, 162

Poland, 142–144, 156–158, 161–163. *See also*
    Warsaw stock exchange
  commercialization of enterprise, 149–150, 151
  country reviewed, 148–153
  pre-Communist stock exchange in, 148
  stock market and financial institutional
    structure in, 152–153
  transition from communism in, 148–150
portfolio investment, 16, 82
  defined, 224n.34, 230n.23
  and Hungary, 146
  and IFC, 64, 66, 69,
  and Korea funds, 124–125, 127
  and nineteenth century, 28
  and South Africa, 169
  and Thailand, 136
Prague stock exchange, 157–158, 160, 191
preferred shares, 222–223n.12
price mechanism, xiv–xvi, xx, 197
  in advanced, industrial economies, 5, 7, 57, 191
  in emerging market economies, 9–10, 91, 112,
    114
  and international purchases of stock, 12
  role in corporate governance, 16–17, 22–23, 84,
    86
privatization, 61, 69, 93, 103, 176. *See also by
    individual country and company*
  buyout or management-employee buyout, 83–
    84
  case-by-case, 81, 94
  IPO, 77, 80–82, 85
  and political considerations, xviii–xix, 5, 9–10,
    22
  share auctions, 96
  as source of shares, 75–88
  spontaneous, 82, 154
  stable core or *noyeau dur*, 82
  and two-level game metaphor, 17–18, 22
  union opposition to, 88, 89, 110–111, 151, 184
  voucher-based, 81, 83–84

qualified institutional buyer (QIBs), 11, 241n.86

Rawlings, Jerry, 182–183
Reagan administration, 61, 66, 76
regulated company, 29
Rio de Janeiro. *See* Bolsa de Valores do Rio de
    Janeiro
Rockefeller, Nelson, 48, 49
Romania, 74, 83
Rothschilds, 34, 168, 246n.14
Rule 144A, 11, 137, 241n.86
Russia, 87, 142–144, 162, 165, 190. *See also* St.
    Petersburg bourse, Russian Trading System
    (RTS)

Communist revolution in, 44, 46, 143–144, 153
  country reviewed, 153–157
  equities market in, 153, 157
  industrial revolution in, 35–36
  privatizations in, 85
  stock market and financial institutional
    structure in, 156–157
  transition from communism in, 153–155
Russia Company, 30
Russian Trading System, 153

St. Petersburg bourse, 35–36, 143
Samsung, 123, 125, 126–127, 140–141
Santiago stock exchange. *See* Bolsa de
    Comercio de Santiago
Sao Paulo Bolsa de Valores, 41, 95
Scudder, Stevens, and Clark, 66, 126
Securities and Exchange Commission (SEC),
    50
Senegal, 166, 185–186. *See also Bourse Regionale
    des Valeurs Mobilieres* (BRVM)
  country reviewed, 176–181
  French investment in, 43, 177
  stock market and financial institutional
    structure in, 180–181
Senelec, 180
Seoul Stock Exchange. *See* Korea stock
    exchange
Sepoy Mutiny, 36, 115
Shanghai Sharebrokers Association, 37, 42, 113,
    128–129
Shanghai stock exchange, 42, 54, 130–131
  shareholder patterns, 21, 27
Shenzhen stock market, 130–131
Singapore, 37, 55–56, 136–137
Slim, Carlos, 108–109, 111, 194
Societe des Bourses Francaises, 74, 149
*Societe Interprofessionnelle de Compensation de
    Valeurs Mobilieres* (SICOVAM), 149
Sonatel, xix, 78, 176, 178–181, 185–186
Sophonpanich family, 137
South Africa, 164–166, 185–186, 197. *See also*
    Johannesburg stock exchange, Kimberley
    stock exchange, London stock exchange
  British investment in, 166–169
  cross-holdings in, 169–170
  country reviewed, 166–172
  stock market and financial institutional
    structure in, 170–172, 193
South Sea Company, 32
Southwestern Bell, 109
Soviet Union. *See* Russia
Sri Lanka, 40. *See also* Colombo stock
    exchange.
stock. *See also* stock exchange, stock markets

characteristics of, 4, 6, 10, 16
defined, 4, 6
political logic of, 3, 5, 89
role in monitoring firm, 3, 163, 192–193
and territory, 4, 113–114
and unions, 5
stock exchange, 3, 222n.3. *See also by individual
exchange*, stock markets, stock
benefits of, 15, 192, 194–196
and concentrated trading, 93, 107
and control of the firm, 59, 84
as a functional requirement for equity trades,
14–15
as a political product, xiv, 4, 189
and tax structure, 13
volatility, 64
Stock Exchange Automated Quotation (SEAQ),
11, 18, 58
Stock Exchange Mumbai. *See* Bombay stock
exchange
Stock Exchange Thailand, 135–138
stock markets. *See also* stock, stock exchange
connections to states, 27
costs in developing countries, 13
distribution of political benefits, 15–16
growth measurement, 78–81, 90
problems associated with, 15–16
role in financial institutional structure, 7, 13,
23, 29, 84–85
Stockholm stock exchange, 195–196
structural adjustment lending, 60–62, 165–166
and international financial organizations, 61,
179, 183, 186
and two-level game metaphor, 18, 60, 70
Suez Canal, 39, 172, 247n.33
Szczecin shipyard, 148, 150–152, 162–163

Taiwan, 16
Tanzania, 15
Tata Group, 122–123
Telephonos de Mexico (Telmex), 107–109, 110–
112
Telfonica of Spain, 101, 106, 111
Thai Airways, 138, 140–141
Thailand, 115. *See also* Stock Exchange
Thailand
country reviewed, 134–139
history of, 134–136
financial crisis in, 136–137
stock market and financial institutional
structure in, 138–139
Thai-Chinese families, 135, 137–139
Thatcher, Margaret, 61
privatizations of, 5, 75, 76
transparency, xv, 70, 226n.61

and international financial organizations, 194
and Korea, 127
and Prague exchange, 160
Tunis stock exchange, 56
Tunisia, 56
two-level game metaphor, xvii, 17–18, 59–60. *See
also* level I and level II considerations

U.S. Agency for International Development
(USAID), 174
Uganda, 28, 39
Unilever, 181, 184
Hindustan Lever, 119–121, 123, 140
United Nations (UN), 45, 49, 114
Uruguay Round, 108, 111

Van Agtmael, Antoine, 64
varieties of capitalism approach, 9
Venezuela, 42
venture capital, 49–50, 62, 65, 67
Vienna stock exchange, 143, 146, 162
Volkswagen Germany, 196

Wall Street Rule, 8, 86, 112, 196
Wall Street Walk. *See* Wall Street Rule
Warsaw stock exchange, 148–151, 158
West African Central Bank, 177–178
West African Monetary Union, 176, 178
West India Company (Dutch), 30, 227n.11
World Bank, xvi, 5, 22, 76, 165, 231n.4. *See also*
debt crisis of 1980s, structural adjustment
lending
and Africa, 165, 174, 178, 182–183, 186
future role of, 193–194
history of, 45–46, 49–52, 60–64, 66, 68, 74
and India, 118, 140–141
and South Korea, 114, 124
and Thailand, 135, 138
WorldCom, 196
World War I, 21, 45–47
and Egypt, 172
eve of, 35–36, 44
prewar era, 27–28, 38
and South Africa, 168
World War II, xiv, 21, 43, 76, 190
and Asia, 113–114, 117, 120, 123, 129
and international financial organizations, 45,
49, 51, 62
and Latin America, 48, 94–95, 99, 104
and Egypt, 172–173

Zambia, 68–69, 170
Zimbabwe, 15, 68